Praise for *No Ri*

Winner of the P

"The streets of Black Boston come alive in *No Right to an Honest Living*, a sensitive, immersive, and exhaustive study of African American workers, their dreams, and their disappointments in the diasporic port city on the bay. A gifted practitioner of labor history and urban history, Jacqueline Jones pulls back the curtain of everyday life in this book, revealing the complexities of Black class positionality, the financial costs of abolitionist activism, the contours of the underground economy, the hidden contributions of Black women's labor inside their own homes, the dramatic effects of Irish immigration and economic recession on Black job prospects, and the fight of Black Civil War soldiers to gain fair pay for their service. In Jones's careful rendering, Boston is sometimes a safe haven and always a place of marginalization for the Black migrants and laborers who changed the city even as they made it home."

—Tiya Miles, National Book Award–winning author of *All That She Carried*

"Jones has done a superb job of capturing the complexity and hard edges of a turbulent era in US history. Her compelling book demonstrates that neither Boston's powerful current of abolitionism nor a great war that destroyed the institution of slavery could remove the race-based social and economic constraints that bedeviled the city's Black residents."

—Gary W. Gallagher, author of *The Enduring Civil War*

"In *No Right to an Honest Living*, Jones provides a deeply researched, provocatively rendered, and engagingly written analysis of the conflict between Boston's egalitarian rhetoric and its racially segregated and economically exploitative reality. Black Bostonians were free, fiercely political, and comparatively successful in their fight against legal segregation and the rendition of fugitive slaves by an antebellum Federal system dedicated to the 'peculiar institution.' Yet, even as they launched a radical abolition movement alongside white antislavery allies, Black Bostonians faced employment discrimination and workplace exclusion that belied the city's self-righteous professions of racial exceptionalism. Through attentive descriptions of individual Black Bostonians—the attorney Robert Morris; the Reverend Leonard Grimes and his wife, Octavia C. Grimes; Union Army surgeon Dr. John V. DeGrasse—and the segregated economy in which they lived, Jones provides a prescient analysis of race and labor that resonates in our current political moment. A triumph of historical research, this book will be a foundational text in nineteenth century labor history."

—Kerri Greenidge, author of *Black Radical*

"Jones is one of our greatest historians of race in American society. In this elegantly crafted, deeply researched book, she reconstructs the troubled history of Black labor in nineteenth-century Boston through compelling biographical vignettes of workers and reformers alike. Her book is a profound reflection on the enduring tensions between America's high-minded rhetoric of liberty and equality and the persistence of racial injustice."

—Thomas J. Sugrue, author of *Sweet Land of Liberty*

"Jones's *No Right to an Honest Living* demonstrates the deadly convergence of the racial and capitalist orders in Civil War–era Boston, where there was no pathway to freedom but through work—and Black people were excluded from work. A singular contribution to the history of racial capitalism in the Deep North."

—Walter Johnson, author of *The Broken Heart of America*

"An essential labor history and an incredible history of the Civil War era. By focusing on Boston as a site of abolitionist activism and racist work policies, Jones offers expansive insights into the stakes of ending the institution of slavery and ushering in a period of freedom. With graceful writing and sharp analysis, Jones brings us a fuller story of the transition from Emancipation to Reconstruction to Jim Crow."

—Marcia Chatelain, Pulitzer Prize–winning author of *Franchise*

NO RIGHT TO AN HONEST LIVING

ALSO BY JACQUELINE JONES

Goddess of Anarchy: The Life and Times of Lucy Parsons, American Radical

A Dreadful Deceit: The Myth of Race from the Colonial Era to Obama's America

Saving Savannah: The City and the Civil War

Creek Walking: Growing Up in Delaware in the 1950s

A Social History of the Laboring Classes: From Colonial Times to the Present

American Work: Four Centuries of Black and White Labor

The Dispossessed: America's Underclasses from the Civil War to the Present

Labor of Love, Labor of Sorrow: Black Women, Work, and the Family, from Slavery to the Present

Soldiers of Light and Love: Northern Teachers and Georgia Blacks, 1865–1873

NO RIGHT TO AN HONEST LIVING

THE STRUGGLES OF BOSTON'S BLACK WORKERS IN THE CIVIL WAR ERA

Jacqueline Jones

BASIC BOOKS
New York

Basic Books
Hachette Book Group
1290 Avenue of the Americas, New York, NY 10104
www.basicbooks.com

Printed in the United States of America

First Edition: January 2023
First Trade Paperback Edition: January 2025

Published by Basic Books, an imprint of Hachette Book Group, Inc.
The Basic Books name and logo is a registered trademark of the Hachette Book Group.

Print book interior design by Jeff Williams.

The Library of Congress has cataloged the hardcover edition as follows:

Names: Jones, Jacqueline, 1948- author.
Title: No right to an honest living : the struggles of Boston's black workers in the Civil War era / Jacqueline Jones.
Other titles: Struggles of Boston's black workers in the Civil War era
Description: First edition. | New York : Basic Books, [2023] | Includes bibliographical references and index.
Identifiers: LCCN 2022031966 | ISBN 9781541619791 (hardcover) | ISBN 9781541619807 (epub)
Subjects: LCSH: Boston (Mass.)—History—Civil War, 1861-1865—Social aspects. | African Americans—Employment—Massachusetts—Boston—History. | Free black people—Massachusetts—Boston—Social conditions—19th century. | Fugitive slaves—Massachusetts—Boston—Social conditions—19th century. | Working class African Americans—Massachusetts—Boston—Social conditions—19th century. | Labor—Massachusetts—Boston—History—19th century.
Classification: LCC F73.44 .J66 2023 | DDC 974.4/6100496073--dc23/eng/20220706
LC record available at https://lccn.loc.gov/2022031966

ISBNs: 9781541619791 (hardcover), 9781541619807 (ebook), 9781541607026 (paperback)

LSC-C

Printing 1, 2024

To Anna and Erica

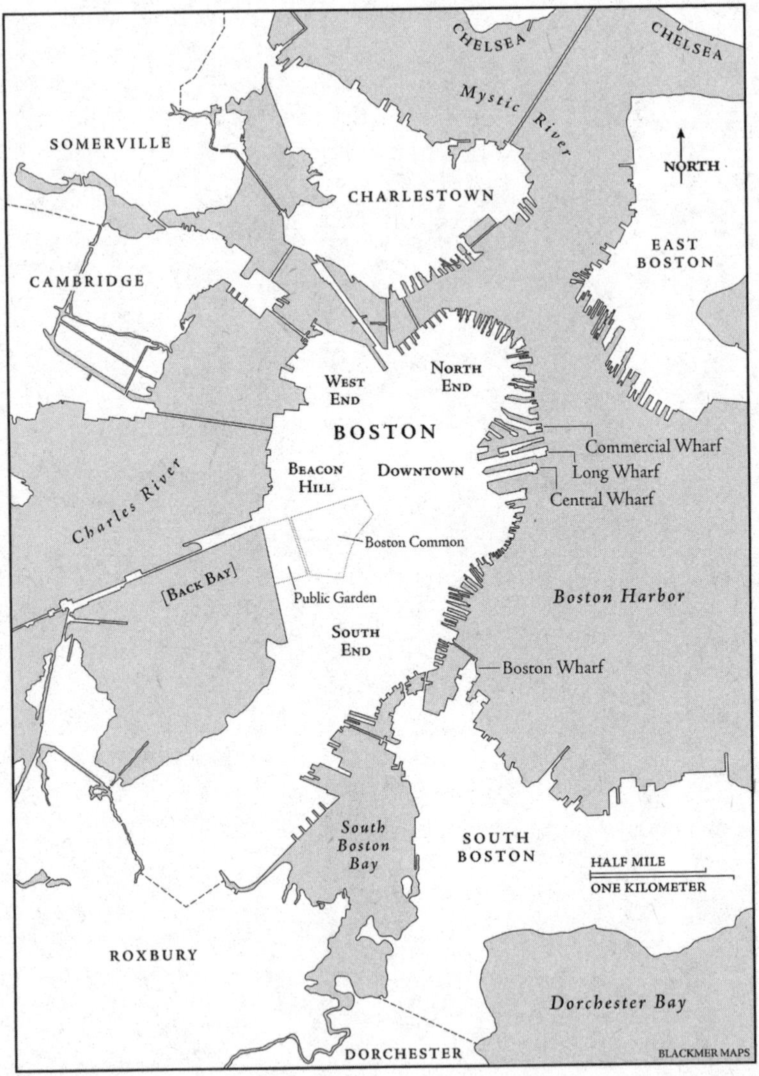

Boston and Its Environs, ca. 1860. (Kate Blackmer, from H. McIntyre, cartographer, *Map of the City of Boston and Immediate Neighborhood: From Original Surveys*, 1852, 142 × 192 cm, Boston Public Library, Norman B. Leventhal Map Center; J. H. Colton & Co., *Map of Boston and Adjacent Cities*, 41 × 33 cm (New York: J. H. Colton & Co., 1856).

Contents

Introduction

"Words Are Easy"

On the evening of Monday, March 5, 1860, a group of Bostonians gathered to mark the ninetieth anniversary of the death of Crispus Attucks. A man of African and Indigenous descent, Attucks was one of the first casualties of the American Revolution, killed by British troops in the Boston Massacre. For Boston's Black community, Attucks remained a powerful symbol of their forebears' fight for the Patriots' cause—for "liberty." That evening, the featured speaker, the erudite physician Dr. John S. Rock, warned his audience that he intended to dispense with the usual platitudes praising Attucks *qua* martyr: "If, under the circumstances, I should give you a little plain talk, differing somewhat from that which you have been accustomed to hear, on occasions like this, you need not be surprised. The times require us to speak out." Rock took as his theme a quotation attributed to Shakespeare: "Words are easy, like the wind; / Faithful friends are hard to find" ("The Passionate Pilgrim").[1]

Rock then launched into an angry denunciation of Boston's white abolitionists, men and women who professed sympathy for enslaved men and women of the South yet cared little about the struggles of their Black neighbors at home. Here in the heart of the nation's militant antislavery movement, young Black men could not find apprenticeships, even in the shipbuilding and construction trades their fathers and grandfathers had followed. Shop owners and manufacturers refused to hire Black workers out of deference to the prejudices of their white employees. Of the four dozen or so wharves jutting out into Boston Harbor, only one employed Black stevedores. Black job-seekers faced competition from desperate, destitute men and women recently arrived from Ireland, some joining their well-established kinfolk in their new home. The surplus of willing workers depressed wages for all the city's laboring classes, and most Blacks had to cobble together a living, hunting for day jobs subject to the vagaries of the weather and the needs of individual employers.[2]

Rock lambasted white abolitionists for ignoring the hardships Black laborers had endured as their job opportunities had deteriorated over the past few decades. "It will not do to judge men by what they say," he advised, urging people of color to demand deeds, not words, from their so-called white friends. Even as these whites denounced the plight of enslaved Black southerners, they failed to challenge Boston's segregated workplaces, and in their own counting-houses and dry-goods stores they hired only white men as clerks. Since coming to Boston in the mid-1840s, Rock had attended far too many antislavery meetings dominated by white people who spoke movingly about the sufferings of bondmen and women but showed a studied indifference to the impoverished Black community in their midst. Addressing white Bostonians in general, Rock charged, "That is the idea—colored men have no right to earn an honest living—they must be starved out." He implied that by denying Blacks a decent livelihood, whites hoped to spur a mass exodus of them out of the city. Now he declared,

Like many Black Bostonians of distinction, John S. Rock pursued a series of jobs in a relentless effort to earn a decent living. In his native New Jersey he worked as a schoolteacher, dentist, and physician, and then, after his move to Boston in 1853, as a public speaker, newspaper correspondent, attorney, and army recruiter. In 1865 he became the first Black man admitted to practice before the US Supreme Court. *(Library of Congress)*

"I believe in insurrections—and especially those of the sword and the pen."[3]

Rock was aware that, despite the well-founded grievances of the state's Black workers, egalitarian-minded people heralded Massachusetts as a vanguard in the fight for equal citizenship rights for Black people. In 1860 when he gave his commemorative oration about Attucks, Black men in the Bay State enjoyed rights denied to their counterparts in other parts of the North. Those who met a property qualification could vote, and white officials were just beginning to open the jury box to them. The commonwealth imposed no legal restrictions on what jobs Black men and women could hold. State law legalized intermarriage, and Black children attended integrated schools. Unlike their counterparts in the Midwest, people of color in Massachusetts could enter, leave, or move around freely within their state. Black activists throughout the North mounted strenuous campaigns on behalf of their own rights, and the Boston Black community was particularly well organized in this respect.[4]

Still, Rock remained unconvinced that Massachusetts deserved the credit accorded it as a haven for him and his people. Political realities and social conditions rendered Blacks vulnerable to the prejudices of landlords, employers, and working-class whites. Rock and other Black leaders lacked political influence in their hometown and home state. Blacks remained a tiny percentage of Boston's overall population—in 1860, 1.5 percent of the total of 177,840, compared to 3 percent thirty years earlier (out of 61,392). The small number of Black voters had virtually no influence within the city's partisan political system. More generally, abolitionists remained a distinct minority; their loud voices on street corners and in public venues, their insistent petitions and multiple publications, all suggested considerably more power—and numerical strength—than they possessed.

Rock knew from hard-won firsthand experience that, as a group, abolitionists regardless of skin color had shown extraordinary courage in their daunting fight against slavery. Through the 1850s, the full weight of the federal machinery—the Supreme Court, the Congress, and the office of the chief executive—had preserved and supported the institution of bondage, and most white Americans cared little about the injustices embedded in slavery and other systems of racial prejudice affecting all Black people, regardless of legal status. Abolitionists, in contrast, had forged, through eloquent speeches and writings, a discourse of democracy that challenged those systems, and their reasoned and outraged words mattered, to other Americans then and since. Compared to the general population, white antislavery activists, together with their Black comrades-in-arms, represented the moral heart and soul of the nation, and they labored at great personal financial sacrifice and the risk of bodily harm to themselves.

Nevertheless, in his speech, Rock was appealing to a group of white Bostonians not only as abolitionists but also as potential employers and advocates of Black workers. He was aware that, like the fight against slavery, the fight for integrated workplaces faced overwhelming odds. Black men and women had no right to make an honest living, but it was also true that the US Constitution stipulated no such right for any person. At the same time, in a slaveholding country such as the United States, wage earning was a key signifier of citizenship, North and South. Boston's Black workers' chronic wage insecurity prevented them from enjoying full citizenship rights and also highlighted the hypocrisy of so-called white friends who refused to address the city's discriminatory division of labor.[5]

Blacks in antebellum Boston toiled under immense liabilities that the often-used term "second-class citizenship" hardly captures. The piecemeal, ill-defined nature of citizenship rights forced the city's Black activists into never-ending battles for discrete advances—for example, elimination of the label "colored" from the names on tax and voting lists; legal penalties for commercial-venue owners who segregated their meeting and entertainment spaces; and the ability of Black men not only to serve in the US Army but also to earn commissions as officers and receive pay equal to that of their white counterparts. White supremacy assumed public, performative aspects, rendered in protean spectacles in the streets and parks. The state legislature repeatedly rebuffed Black men's attempts to join the Massachusetts militia or create one of their own. Newspapers and popular writings caricatured Black people as ignorant buffoons. Self-identified "fashionable" churches enforced discriminatory seating policies; West Congregational required that all Black worshippers, including the frail and the elderly, ascend a steep set of steps to what was derisively called "the pigeon house" above the main sanctuary. Fraternal orders such as the (white) Freemasons and the Sons of Temperance barred Black men from membership. Minstrel shows ridiculed Black hucksters, horse groomers, and stevedores doing their jobs. Even foreign visitors to Boston could discern the distinction between legal equality and true equality. In 1852 a tourist noted of Boston, "The laws of Massachusetts give perfect equality to the coloured people. They are here full citizens; nevertheless socially, even here they cannot become equals of the whites."[6]

In 1860 John Rock's Boston was transforming itself from a small colonial seaport laced with sinuous cow paths into a modern city, growing in both acreage and population. Bounded by Boston Harbor and the Charles and Mystic Rivers, the Puritans' early settlement consisted of a small peninsula, just 800 acres in area—1.25 square miles—connected to the mainland by a narrow isthmus; over the ensuing centuries, landfill projects would expand the landmass to 46 square miles. Critical to its growth were straight, paved streets facilitating the efficient circulation of people and goods. Massive infrastructure projects, such as filling in the Back Bay with sand and gravel and razing poor neighborhoods, required thousands of hours of labor. Beginning in the mid-1840s, the work of constructing sewers, widening and grading streets, and building new wharves proved affordable because of the supply of cheap labor, mainly Irish immigrants. The Irish began to displace not only Black laborers, but also Black barbers and wharf workers. In a process that played out in Philadelphia and New York as well as Boston, "Black" jobs quickly became "white" jobs when Black workers were excluded from them.[7]

Antebellum Boston was more complicated than Black and white. It was a place of people and goods coming and going: Farmers and their daughters fled the hardscrabble life of rural New England and the Canadian Maritime provinces. The Irish arrived each year by the thousands. Native-born men headed west, while freedom-seekers, fugitives from slavery, made their way to the city and then either stayed or moved on. Mariners briefly alighted in boardinghouses, and professional con men and women fleeced their prey and got out of town before the police could track them down.

In the 1850s, Boston was becoming an ever more fractious society, riven by simmering class, ethnic, religious, gendered, and political tensions punctuated by sporadic violence among groups.

In 1860 the photographer James Wallace Black took this aerial photo, titled "Boston, as the Eagle and the Wild Goose See It," at 2,000 feet from a hot-air balloon. Long Wharf is in the upper left-hand corner, and Washington Street runs as a diagonal in the lower half of the picture. The city's residential density proved unhealthy for impoverished residents. Its congested thoroughfares made life difficult for Black job-seekers, laundresses, peddlers, and porters. *(Metropolitan Museum of Art)*

The merchant princes, adherents to the establishment Whig Party, sorted themselves out into either "Conscience" (i.e., antislavery) or "Cotton" (pro-southern) factions. Before too long, though, it would become clear that even those with a conscience believed that all southern Blacks, whether enslaved or free, should continue to grow cotton for the benefit of New England textile-mill owners.

With an overabundance of labor, master craftsmen squeezed the wages of younger journeymen, prompting angry recriminations on both sides. Native-born Protestants warned that immigrant Roman Catholics would spell the end of the American republic. However, the Irish were quick to accommodate themselves to American racial ideologies, gradually overcoming their intragroup animosities based on religious, clan, and county loyalties and embracing antagonism toward Blacks as part of their identity. Meanwhile, fully half the adult population lacked any formal representation in the body politic: married women, regardless of class or ethnicity, remained vulnerable in a society that deprived them of the right to vote and hold property.

Social tensions emerged within the antislavery movement itself. Even whites sympathetic to abolitionism sought to keep Black activists in their place, reminding them that they should be supremely grateful to their white benefactors. In 1845 the poet James Russell Lowell observed that "the colored people of the so-called free states" faced obstacles that were "more terrible than the cannon and bayonet—the force of a depraved and unchristian public opinion. We shut them rigidly out from every path of emulation or ambition." White abolitionists, he noted tartly, might best further their "holy cause" by "seeking to elevate the condition of the colored race in the free states, and to break down every barrier of invidious distinction between them and their privileged brothers."[8]

THIS BOOK EXAMINES how the casual cruelty endemic to the Boston job market contrasted with the soaring rhetoric of egalitarian-minded white men and women during the turbulent era of the Civil War. Many white radicals expressed sympathy in general for "labor" at home and abroad and condemned the concentration of capital in the North and the South; but in Boston these whites failed to extend their critique of an exploitative economic system to segregated worksites. Part of this apparent blind spot stemmed from some whites' overt racial prejudice toward Black people in general (even while advocating for the destruction of slavery); another part from some whites' fears that pressing for the cause of free Black workers would prove a liability in raising money from wealthy individuals; and still another part from a hard-nosed calculation that the white laboring classes were too potent a political force to aggravate with calls for Black economic opportunity.[9]

The city gained national and international renown for its outspoken abolitionists before the war and for the reformers it sent south to work among the freedpeople during and after the war. Yet that tale must be juxtaposed to the life stories of a spectrum of Boston's Black workers—some famous, most obscure, a few infamous—who tried to make a living in a city enshrined in myth. For many Black men and women, finding and keeping a job amounted to a near-daily challenge. Individual job-seekers followed often circuitous, challenging paths in a time and place when white support for Black rights too often stopped at the factory gate and the workshop door. Although Black workers faced profound structural barriers to economic equality, many persevered, demonstrating resilience and resourcefulness in carving a livelihood out of unjust conditions.

White abolitionists were not the only potential allies who turned their backs on northern Black workers before, during, and after the war. Despite upheavals in the American party system during the 1840s and 1850s, white politicians of all stripes, in Boston and around the country, failed to advocate for northern Black workers. In national political debates, the contentious subject of slavery hardly touched upon the plight of wage-earning free people of color. The Irish immigrants who came to Boston in such great numbers became loyal members of the Democratic Party, hostile to Blacks as potential rivals in the workplace. The founding of the antislavery Liberty Party in 1840 and the Free Soil Party eight years later signaled a breakdown in the old Democratic-Whig party system; but together with the new

Republican Party (1854), these partisans focused on opposing slavery, and, more particularly, on keeping slavery out of the western territories. In Massachusetts, the anti-immigrant American Party—the Know Nothings—enjoyed a brief ascendency in the early 1850s, capturing many state offices in 1854; but two years later the party was defunct, and abolitionists of all stripes, as well as Whiggish merchants and manufacturers in favor of a strong central government, joined the Republicans.[10]

Beginning in the late 1850s, white Republicans rewarded a few loyal Black supporters with civil-service jobs or nominations to elected office, but they refrained from calling for integrated workplaces for fear of losing their own white constituencies. City officials who might have hired Blacks, in recognition that some were taxpayers, instead reserved street-paving, clerking, and teaching for whites exclusively. Textile-mill owners employed only whites as factory operatives, though the whole cotton manufacturing industry owed its existence and profits to enslaved laborers in the South. White military officers enforced a discriminatory division of labor in army encampments and on naval vessels. After the war, despite the heroic sacrifices made by Black soldiers and sailors on behalf of the Union, few white veterans pressed for the rights of Black job-seekers. White workers in a variety of occupations attempted to organize, all the while fearful of Black competitors, real or imagined, coming from nearby areas or from the South; these whites refused to admit Blacks into their unions or fraternal organizations, a move that would have diminished the threat of Black strikebreakers. For the most part, Boston's social division of labor remained intact in 1865 despite the cataclysm of the Civil War and the loss of 750,000 lives.

It was one of the great failures of the United States that, after the war, governmental and elected political officials did little to address the health, well-being, and citizenship rights of 4 million Black southerners. Whites avoided articulating a self-evident truth: that the forced labor of Black Americans had enriched the nation, from the cotton belt of Mississippi to the cotton mills of Massachusetts. In any case, few nineteenth-century white Americans considered the federal government to be an appropriate vehicle for large-scale social-welfare efforts. Immediately after the war, a new federal agency, the United States Bureau of Refugees, Freedmen, and Abandoned Lands, made a brief four-year foray into the areas of immediate relief and common schooling for the formerly enslaved; but overall, both Republicans and Democrats believed that even though people just freed from slavery possessed little, if anything, in the way of dwellings, land, or money, they should fend for themselves. This selective hands-off approach applied to the Blacks in the North as well as in the South in an era when subsidies and tax breaks for railroads and other profit-making businesses garnered widespread political support. No public entity at the local, state, or federal level took responsibility for paying a debt to the formerly enslaved, a debt of immense proportions. The vast majority of freedpeople continued to till the soil under exploitative conditions, and the vast majority of northern Black wage earners remained mired in low-paid, menial jobs.

The prevalence of all-white workplaces in Civil War–era Massachusetts calls into question contemporary (and current) claims that the state was uniquely enlightened in terms of granting full citizenship rights to its male residents. Workplaces represent more than sites of production: they are sites of fellow-feeling or rivalry among and between coworkers, and sites of either accommodation or resistance to high-handed bosses, poor pay, and hazardous conditions. Specific jobs (and the legal statuses that define them) are social signifiers of great political import. As the formidable fugitive-activist Frederick Douglass noted in 1853, "Men are not valued in this country, or in any country, for what they *are*; they are valued for what they can do."[11]

In many ways Boston's Black-white labor relations in the era of the Civil War resembled a caste-like system, for no amount of education or evidence of courtly bearing would allow a Black person to escape the stigma of skin color or reputation of "Blackness." At the same time, employment segregation was not absolute, as Black and white domestic servants laboring in a single household could attest. However, even these workers, and the Black and white stevedores who worked in proximity to each other in the rain or snow or searing heat, rarely identified their interests as identical, so divergent were their life experiences and possibilities in after-work hours. Shared economic interests among Black and white workers did not translate into a shared fellow-feeling or class identity.[12]

Unlike a true caste system, however, social relations in nineteenth-century Boston, either between Blacks and whites or among Blacks themselves, were not entirely rigid. The color line was no barrier to intermarriage. People who toiled in the city's underground economy often slept and drank with each other regardless of the color of their skin. The Black community itself drew distinctions between the educated and the uneducated, the light-skinned and the dark-skinned, and the well-to-do and the impoverished. Too, patterns of upward and downward mobility suggest some fluidity in status and intergenerational stability.

Indeed, class relationships were extraordinarily complex among Black Bostonians. Conventional indicators of status, including formal educational attainment, occupational categories, and financial well-being, do not always pertain here. There were a handful of professionals (doctors, lawyers, preachers); some entrepreneurs (barbers, clothing dealers, seamstresses); and many servants and laborers (cooks, laundresses, custodians, and porters). Still, these categories do not always reveal either the wider influence or the material well-being of the worker. Many Black leaders were autodidacts who had a difficult time supporting their families in spite of their social influence. A porter or teamster who established a patronage relationship with a dry-goods merchant could earn more money than a preacher. A barber with white customers might enjoy a more secure living than a physician with only Black patients. A prosperous entrepreneur might leave his widow a pile of debt rather than a comfortable cushion for her old age. A well-to-do businessman might have to contend with the consequences of a daughter arrested for prostitution. The label "laborer" might obscure the true nature of a person's work, especially when that person owned luxury items such as silver and china and lent hundreds of dollars to a neighbor. Many men and women embraced different kinds of work over their lifetimes, making it difficult, if not impossible, to peg them to a single occupation.[13]

With their entrée into a whole host of jobs thwarted, some Black men and women turned to selling alcohol or engaging in sex work, gambling, pickpocketing, or scamming. If, as Rock maintained, Black Bostonians had "no right to earn an honest living," then some would go underground, where cunning and physical courage could reap impressive if ill-gotten gains. Men and women who lied and claimed they were fugitives from slavery could tap into the sympathies of whites as well as other members of the Black community. Brothel owners and dance-hall operators were themselves employers, and some demonstrated remarkable longevity despite the violence that characterized places where alcohol flowed freely. Of all the worksites and entertainment venues in Boston, those associated with illicit activities were the most integrated, for they responded to the demands of the seaport's sailors and transients as well as well-to-do men of all kinds. A successful Black dance-hall operator might gain respect among both Blacks and whites, and even grudging admiration among police on the beat and whites in the jury box.

Patterns of Black influence and leadership reflected a complex matrix of factors. Well-known professionals and activists possessed of extraordinary speaking and writing gifts often reside atop a community's occupational structure. Yet in Boston, full-time antislavery agitation paid very little. If agitators such as Frederick Douglass and Charles Lenox Remond, a Salem-based Black abolitionist, are considered as waged workers, their life stories take on a different cast compared to the traditional emphasis on them as writers and orators. At times Black abolitionists had to devise creative ways to earn a decent livelihood, prompting whites to cast a suspicious eye on money-making efforts that supposedly sullied the purity of the cause.

In fact, of course, much political work—like the work of community mobilization and family nurture—paid nothing, a particularly heavy burden for Black wage earners and small shop owners who made so little money to begin with. Some secondhand clothing dealers devoted nearly all their time and resources to feeding and housing men and women fleeing from slavery, receiving no financial compensation in return. Women provided essential services to churches, benevolent societies, and antislavery groups in their roles as fund-raisers, and to the well-being of fugitives when they cooked and laundered for them. Wives, mothers, daughters, and sisters maintained households and cared for children, thus freeing their menfolk from the chores of everyday home life. Nevertheless, women's unwaged work often failed to win for them public expressions of either praise or gratitude, in contrast to men's activism, heralded as the labor of manly freedom fighters.

While many white Bostonians remained ignorant of or indifferent to the challenges Black men and women faced, these whites often did express a profound interest in the future of southern enslaved workers: Would freedpeople migrate en masse to the North, in the process depressing wages and displacing white artisans and construction workers? Textile-mill owners worried about a diminished cotton crop. Employers eyed a workforce of potential strikebreakers, and white laborers feared the same. Thus the agricultural labor patterns that emerged during the reconstruction of the postwar South had more than theoretical significance to Massachusetts generally and Boston particularly.

The postwar years in fact saw a Boston-bound mass migration of Black southerners, many of them refugees from Virginia, highlighting the continued cynical exploitation of Black workers on the part of white powerbrokers, politicians, and employers. Transporting and placing these migrants amounted to a business itself, one that provoked fierce rivalry among Black and white men and women eager to profit from Boston's enduring demand for Black domestic servants. The migrant community remained ambivalent about these newcomers, who were fellow southerners and coreligionists, but also rivals for a finite number of "Black" jobs.

SLAVERY CAST A menacing shadow over mid-nineteenth-century Boston, a shadow emanating not only from the South but from the city's own history. In 1630, Massachusetts Bay Colony governor John Winthrop intended that Boston would become a "city upon a hill," a model of Christian charity for the world to emulate; but he needed workers to build and provision it. The first Africans arrived in the colony in 1638, and three years later its Puritan lawmakers legalized slavery, the first colony in New England to do so. Winthrop's West Indies kinfolk traded in slaves; like their famous relative, they were men of empire as well as men of strong religious convictions. Of course, Massachusetts was not alone in utilizing bound labor to advance the interests of the British Crown, and in Boston, as in other Atlantic seaport cities, the institution of slavery became integral to the wider world of commerce and mass migration. The enslaved served multiple functions, as producers, objects of trade, and potent symbols of God-ordained systems of social inequality. Bondage was inhumane whether carried out in the rice fields of South Carolina or the workshops of Boston: owners sold workers and bequeathed them to their heirs, separating families at will, and used sadistic forms of "discipline" on men, women, and children. Forced to justify this brutal system, owners overlaid it with a veneer of charity, claiming that Africans' contact with or conversion to Christianity justified their enslavement. This rationalization came easily to the hierarchical-minded Puritans.[14]

By the middle of the eighteenth century, the system of bondage had become thoroughly implanted in Boston's political economy. The city included a Black population of 1,541 (10 percent of the total), about two-thirds of whom were enslaved. Many prominent whites, including lawyers, members of the clergy, merchants, and physicians, owned human beings. Shippers pursued the transatlantic slave trade, a source of income for wealthy families with names like Faneuil and Emerson.[15]

On the eve of the American Revolution, visitors to Boston might arrive on a vessel constructed by Black carpenters and sailmakers, one operated with a noticeable presence of Black crew members, some enslaved and some free. These visitors might pay a free man of color to transport their luggage to a nearby tavern, where they would enjoy a fine meal served by an enslaved waiter, and then perhaps complain to an enslaved chambermaid that their room was not to their liking. Or they might stay with a wealthy friend in the city, someone who owned a Black coachman, outfitted in full, ostentatious livery. On the streets and down by the docks they would see Black faces among the men loading and unloading casks, barrels, and boxes onto and from ships. After a week or two of sightseeing, the weary visitors might take their boots for resoling to a shoemaker or their coat for repairing to a tailor and watch Black apprentices at work in both shops. At the same time, visitors would *not* expect to see a Black person sitting next to them in a church pew, at a table in a coffeehouse, in a chair at a barbershop, or in a carriage or streetcar, or walking anywhere on Boston Common after dark.[16]

In the 1770s, as the colony's resentment against the highhandedness of the British Parliament intensified, so, too, did the glaring contradiction between slavery, on the one hand, and the ideals professed by those who rocked the "Cradle of Liberty," on the other. The American Revolution eroded the rhetorical, if not the actual, justification for degrees of bound labor. In 1774 a group of enslaved men petitioned Thomas Gage, the royal governor of Massachusetts, pointing out that they could not fulfill their Christian duties as husbands or fathers as long as they were subject to the demands of their owners: "Thus we are deprived of every thing that hath a tendency to make life even tolerable, the endearing ties of husband and wife we are strangers to for we are no longer man and wife than our masters or mistresses thinkes proper marred [married] or onmarred [unmarried]. Our children are also taken from us by force and sent maney miles from us wear we seldom or ever see them again there to be made slaves of for Life." Whether out of principle or in a bid for personal freedom, about eight thousand Black men fought for the Patriot cause, bequeathing a powerful legacy to their descendants. Jeremiah Asher, grandson of an enslaved African-born soldier who fought in the American Revolution, remembered, "My first ideas of the right of the colored man to life, liberty and the pursuit of happiness, were received from those old veterans and champions for liberty." (A Baptist minister, Asher himself volunteered for service as a chaplain during the Civil War; while ministering to Black soldiers he contracted and died from typhoid fever.)[17]

In Massachusetts, chattel slavery was well on its way to extinction before the institution was essentially abolished by a decree of the Supreme Judicial Court in 1783. Many households had begun to rid themselves of their enslaved workers in the years immediately before as well as during the early years of the Revolution. To some extent, shifts in "publick opinion" reflected the compelling nature of freedom suits brought by individual Black people. Yet, in 1795, Patriot leader John Adams gave an additional reason why attitudes toward slavery had so dramatically changed among the general population: "The real cause was the multiplication of labouring White People, who would no longer suffer the Rich to employ these Sable Rivals, so much to their injury. . . . The common People would not Suffer, the Labour by which alone they could obtain a subsistance, to be done by Slaves." Anticipating the rise of the Republican Party, white laborers argued that slavery was harmful to their own economic interests, an argument based on hostility toward Black people in general.[18]

Massachusetts's highest court ruled that the institution of bondage was incompatible with the state's Constitution of 1780. That document made no distinction between Black and white in extending the franchise to all adult men who could meet a property qualification. Still, the vote did not bring equality in the workplace or in the public square. Faced with persistent discrimination, Boston's emancipated slaves and their descendants banded together to press their own interests and worship their own way. Around this time, Prince Hall, a Boston leatherworker, founded Black Freemasonry's first African Lodge, recognized by the British but not the white American group. The lodge promoted responsibility and upright leadership among men, as Freemasonry in general did, but also stressed its unique connection to Africa based on the heritage and culture of its members. Hall came to see public insults as a burden to be borne, an additional form of toil: in 1797 he declared, "My brethren, let us not be cast down under these and many other abuses we at present labour under; for the darkest is before the break of day."[19]

After slavery, many Blacks found themselves alternating between menial labor and enforced idleness, a characteristic of post-emancipation societies in general. These men and women joined a subset of other chronically poor people, but with the stigma of slavery attached to their darker skin color. The free sons of enslaved skilled laborers lacked white patrons and faced stiff competition from whites; over the generations the craftwork that had identified individual Black families disappeared. Gone were the Black blacksmiths and carpenters, replaced by men scrounging for day work as bootblacks and window washers. Black women retained their positions as laundresses and domestic servants, earning starvation wages, and in some cases no wages at all, just room and board with a white family. Like other destitute households, those of Blacks often needed multiple wage earners—whether grown children or boarders—to pay the rent and feed and clothe their members.

Northern whites regarded free Blacks as a potential drain on the community's resources, paupers seeking to stake a claim to public assistance from town authorities. Deprived of the chance to make a living wage, Black men and women occupied a seemingly permanent subordinate position, which in turn fueled whites' belief in the "natural" inferiority of Black people. Despite many obvious exemplars to the contrary—hardworking Black householders engaged in church and community life—the stereotype of the lazy, promiscuous, and thieving Black person persisted into and through the antebellum period.[20]

In Boston, a rising chorus of Black voices exposed not only the horror of slavery, but also the injustice of job discrimination in the North. In their writings and speeches, these activists paired a hatred of southern slavery with a pointed critique of northern Blacks' pinched economic circumstances. Indeed, in 1860 John Rock was echoing the angry protests of his intellectual forebears. Black activists in the Mid-Atlantic region had long protested legal discrimination against their fellow workers and entrepreneurs. In 1829, Samuel Cornish, preacher *cum* journalist, urged revisions to the New York City Charter that would guarantee that "the pursuit of an honest living will be secured to all our citizens"; he objected to the standard practice of denying city licenses to Black cartmen and porters. Among the most prominent advocate of access to equal employment was Boston's David Walker, born free in Wilmington, North Carolina, in 1796. As a young adult Walker lived in Charleston, South Carolina, before moving to the Bay State city around 1825. There he married Eliza Butler, a native of the city, and opened a secondhand clothing shop.[21]

David Walker was committed to increasing Black organizational strength in the United States and around the world; his internationalism reflected the social dimensions of Atlantic Coast seaports, where Black mariners from diverse backgrounds, enslaved and free, settled and comingled. Soon after arriving in Boston, he helped found the Massachusetts General Colored Association, a Black advocacy group. His angry manifesto of 1829, *Walker's Appeal . . . to the Coloured Citizens of the World*, urging that people of African descent resist their subordination, caused a sensation at home and abroad. In it he pronounced Black Americans the "most wretched, degraded and abject set of beings that ever lived since the world began," and cited Boston's all-white workplaces as proof of that degradation. Walker's rage radiates across the page. He denounced the idea of "race" as a pernicious fiction concocted by whites determined to exploit the labor of Blacks, North and South, enslaved and free. He urged whites to acknowledge what they refused to admit—that the destruction of slavery in Massachusetts did not bring real freedom for Black workers. He pointed to the dwindling number of Black artisans in the North, compared to the South, where enslaved men worked at skilled jobs, especially in the construction trades. The hard reality: learn a skill and take pride in one's craft as a slave or work at a demeaning job and endure chronic unemployment as a free man.[22]

Walker also excoriated Boston's service workers for doing for white people what white people should do for themselves, cooking their meals and blacking their boots. "My objections are, to our *glorying* and being *happy* in such low employments; for if we are men, we ought to be thankful to the Lord for the past, and for the future. Be looking forward with thankful hearts to higher attainments than *wielding the razor* and *cleaning boots and shoes*." Still, Walker was mistaken in assuming that barbers, bootblacks, and porters were necessarily servile. In Boston, these jobs afforded a few Black men a relatively stable livelihood, which in turn allowed them to devote their energies and money to the abolitionist cause and to the rescue of fugitives from the South.[23]

In 1830, Walker died, probably of tuberculosis, an illness that claimed many lives in Boston's crowded, poorly ventilated houses and tenements. Soon after his death, a friend and admirer of his,

Maria W. Stewart, took up his standard. Born free in 1803 in Hartford, Connecticut, Maria W. Miller was twenty-three when she married James Stewart, a Boston mariner and agent who placed Black seamen with ship captains. James died in 1829, and soon after, at the behest of a group of scheming white businessmen, the executors of his estate denied his widow her rightful inheritance. (David Walker claimed that in Boston such fraudulent practices and legal machinations routinely deprived lawful Black heirs of their property.) Maria embarked on a speaking career protesting the liabilities of Black womanhood, becoming the first woman of color to address "promiscuous" (mixed) audiences of Black and white women and men on issues related to politics. Like Walker, she was an abolitionist activist, and she decried the division of labor that consigned northern Black men and women to menial pursuits, their ambitions for "headwork" denied, their virtue mocked. Stewart described in vivid detail the emotional price paid by "a servant of servants, or hewers of wood and drawers of water!" Here in the white woman's kitchen were the "fair daughters of Africa . . . compelled to bury their minds and talents beneath a load of iron pots and kettles." Here on the streets were the "aged sires, whose heads are whitened with the front of seventy winters, with their old wood-saws on their backs." How could Black workers possibly advance "by spending their lives as house-domestics, washing windows, shaking carpets, brushing boots, or tending upon gentlemen's tables"? Men and women condemned forever to hard labor understandably suffered from irritability and sour dispositions, "worn out with toil and fatigue." Young men, constantly reminded of the fact that "they can be nothing but the humblest laborers, on account of their dark complexion," lost their ambition and sank into hopelessness. With the mass of Blacks relegated to lives of drudgery and ignorance, "the world thinks we know nothing," therefore the world granted them nothing.[24]

Stewart singled out for special opprobrium those white women entrepreneurs who refused to hire Black women in any but menial pursuits; these business owners offered the familiar excuse that "it was not the custom," and "were they to take them [young Black women] into their employ, they would be in danger of losing the public patronage." The result was workers condemned to a kind of labor that "deadens the energies of the soul, and benumbs the faculties of the mind." In bringing to the fore the backbreaking labor of Black washerwomen and domestics, Stewart highlighted the way that women's waged work—always in demand by whites—served as the economic mainstay of Black households, even as it crushed the bodies and spirits of those who did it.[25]

In her speeches Stewart eschewed the gendered rhetorical strategies common among nineteenth-century men, white and Black. David Walker and virtually all the other male radicals and reformers invoked "manliness" to define personal integrity and physical courage; but Stewart claimed that, as a woman touched by the spirit of God, she, too, had the obligation to call whites to account and Blacks to action. In the fall of 1833, she felt forced to abandon Boston for New York City. In a farewell address she alluded to insurmountable opposition, not only from whites, but also from Black leaders, especially the preachers. When these men admonished her in private, she went public with her lament.[26]

Most white abolitionists remained unmoved by Black activists such as David Walker and Maria Stewart, preferring to fix their gaze on the South and call for justice to be done there. Black abolitionist Charles Lenox Remond criticized whites for failing to recognize that "the free colored and slave population of our country are identified together, and that identity makes our interests one and the same." Nevertheless, the career of one of Boston's most famous white abolitionists suggests that antislavery strategists had financial incentives to ignore the plight of the Black workers they saw every day in the streets and on the wharves.[27]

In 1831, William Lloyd Garrison, a Massachusetts-born twenty-seven-year-old printer, began publishing an abolitionist

Charles Lenox Remond was born in Salem, Massachusetts, in 1810 to parents who were hairdressers. A fierce advocate for justice, he spent much of his working life on the road, speaking out on behalf of the enslaved and free Black workers in the North. Appearing before a committee of the Massachusetts House of Representatives in 1842, he protested, "[Skin] Color is made to obscure the brightest endowments, to degrade the fairest character, and to check the highest and most praiseworthy aspirations." *(Collection of the Massachusetts Historical Society)*

newspaper, *The Liberator*, and two years later he founded the American Anti-Slavery Society. Garrison considered the US Constitution a proslavery document, and he believed that partisan political activity amounted to complicity in a corrupt, nationwide system; people of conscience should "come out" from or eschew identification with established institutions, whether religious denominations or political parties. His brand of abolitionism depended on the conscience of the white northerner and the moral regeneration of the southern slaveholder. Initially he stressed the need for economic opportunity for Boston's Black men and women. An early issue of *The Liberator* included a survey of the Black workers listed in the 1830 Boston city directory. Just eight job categories—hairdressers and barbers, mariners, clothing dealers, waiters, laundresses, bootblacks, boardinghouse keepers, and laborers—accounted for 130 out of the total 175 people listed.

None held skilled-trades jobs. The author concluded, "From most employments, they are almost entirely excluded."[28]

In May 1831, *The Liberator* gave a favorable view of *Walker's Appeal.* The editor early hired a Black apprentice, the talented Boston-born William Cooper Nell, who would become a distinguished writer and historian. It was around this time that Garrison also joined with others to propose "a seminary on the labor system for the manual education of colored youth of both sexes," with the men instructed in "useful employments in agriculture and the mechanic arts" and the women in "domestic concerns." This plan aimed to win Black approval for Garrison's new antislavery society and to gain a reliable Black subscription base for the paper—this at a time when whites were greeting the emerging abolitionist movement with "suspicion or apathy," in his words. Yet before too long *The Liberator*'s subscription list grew, and Garrison came to recognize the danger of offending potential white supporters in general, and wealthy employers in particular, by pressing for integrated worksites. The manual-labor school proposal came with a $50,000 price tag, money that Garrison felt would be better spent on the Anti-Slavery Society. The association proceeded to narrow its interests to the cause of abolition, although *The Liberator* did carry news related to the Boston Black community, primarily Black antislavery activity. In his religious fervor, Garrison could express concern for the overworked, underpaid laboring masses without calling for expanded or equal job opportunities for Black people.[29]

Throughout the years, despite his silence on the conditions of Black workers in Boston or the North, Garrison showed an ardent dedication to abolitionism, demonstrating physical courage amid violent opposition. It was no wonder that most Black leaders were reluctant to criticize him over the jobs issue, and only well-established figures dared to do so. John Rock was one, and Frederick Douglass another. Indeed, an eventual, bitter break between Garrison and Douglass centered not only on their divergent views of the Constitution and partisan politics, but also on the plight of Black labor in the free states.

Not all whites who called for northern Blacks' rights were abolitionists or supporters of the struggles of Black workers. Bostonians decried laws passed by several southern states (beginning with South Carolina, in 1822) that required Black seamen to be incarcerated while their ships were in southern ports. After the publication of *Walker's Appeal*, enforcement of these laws became more urgent, as crew members circulated the inflammatory tract calling for violent resistance to slaveholders. Whites came to fear Black seamen as agents of subversion and unrest. In response, Boston merchants and sea captains argued that free Black sailors were US citizens, and thus beyond the reach of southern sheriffs. And yet the Black seamen's laws represented a clear threat to northerners' commercial interests as much as to their constitutional principles. For captains, retrieving Black crew members from port-city jails delayed sailings and wreaked havoc with shipping schedules. In some cases, those incarcerated had to be left behind, leading to a frantic scramble to find white men to fill their places. Some states required captains to post bonds, or pay fees, or pay fines for noncompliance with the law. All in all, the loss of time and money was the central concern of maritime interests, not the rights of Black people per se, no matter how many times white lawyers invoked the Constitution's rights and immunities clause. In fact, one could oppose these discriminatory laws and at the same time show no interest in opposing slavery or advocating for the economic interests of northern Blacks.[30]

For the historian no less than the nineteenth-century white abolitionist, a pervasive focus on legislation and legal rights pushes the inequities associated with wage labor out of sight and into the background. In Boston, Black citizenship was a process, with right added incrementally upon right over the years, but never yielding the workplace opportunities that would serve as pathways to homeownership, financial security, and the health and well-being of one's family. Gradually, grudgingly, white residents of Massachusetts came to accept a full panoply of legal rights for Black citizens; but those same whites continued to resist Black people's proximate equality in the form of integrated worksites.

Civil rights form the bedrock of any democratic project, and righteous rhetoric is integral to that project. Words matter. Yet the history of the United States indicates that many individuals and groups indulged in self-congratulation based on their often-stated principles of equality without taking tangible steps to extend those principles to the workplace. In that regard Boston was—and is—the nation writ small: a place where words were—and are—easy, and where the material manifestations of a just society were—and are—stubbornly elusive.

Prelude

The Edloe Sixty-Six

On September 15, 1847, the schooner *Thomas H. Thompson* approached Boston from the south, rounding the tip of Cape Cod and sailing northwest, toward the city about fifty miles away. The ship's passengers anxiously scanned the horizon, and before long they could see off in the distance gently rolling hills of early autumn; but Boston Harbor, sheltered by two peninsulas and dotted with many islands of various sizes, presented a mirage of sorts—plenty of land, but no mainland, to be seen. Captain Gideon Wixon made this packet run between Boston and Richmond on a regular basis, taking boots and shoes made in New England to points south and bringing lumber back to the Bay State. This Wednesday morning, he once again maneuvered the *Thompson* through a circuitous, well-worn sea-lane, past the Boston Light and past George's Island, site of the imposing Fort Warren, its walls made of Quincy granite twelve feet thick.

The Boston Harbor islands were sites of notorious, deadly concentration camps for Indigenous prisoners of war, places of buried treasure and double-crossing buccaneers, shipwrecks, and Revolutionary War battles. Historically, the different islands housed Boston's "undesirables," windswept sites where the dangerous and contagious might be isolated and exiled—in the mid-nineteenth century, on a farm and trades school for indigent boys, in an almshouse, a workhouse, and a prison. Deer Island was the site of a quarantine barracks that held passengers from vessels infected with smallpox and yellow fever, with the surrounding fields full of hundreds of unmarked graves.[1]

The *Thomas H. Thompson* arrived in Boston with a human cargo of sixty-six Black men, women, and children from Prince George County, Virginia. Recently freed from slavery, they regarded the future with a mixture of triumph and trepidation. In Boston, they became objects of fascination among white abolitionists, who wondered aloud whether these freedpeople could support themselves without private or government aid. Over the next half century, the collective biography of the Edloe Sixty-Six would reveal the everyday struggles of Boston's Black workers—struggles that encompassed family life and military service no less than the pinched opportunities that hobbled job-seekers.

The harbor that day in September presented a magnificent sight, crowded with brigs, schooners, and barques just arrived not only from the East Coast ports of Portland, Philadelphia, and Annapolis, but also from scattered places around the globe. Stashed away in the ships' holds and soon to be stacked on the city's wharves were mackerel and salmon from Halifax; coal from Nova Scotia; ginger, raw silk, and indigo from Calcutta; sugar from the Caribbean; goatskins and ivory tusks from Cape Town; and pig iron, paper, and tin plates from Liverpool. The docks were piled high with hundreds of bales of cotton, fodder imported for the immense brick textile mills located in Boston's hinterland. Those factories in turn churned out fabric bound for southern plantations, rough "Negro" cloth to be sewn into pants and dresses by and for enslaved workers.[2]

The voyage out of Richmond had not been a smooth one. Five days in, on Saturday the 11th, the *Thompson* faced stormy "thick weather" and strong headwinds. Wixon decided to put in near a settlement of his kin in Harwich, on the Cape, until the skies cleared. There, two members of the local Baptist church, alarmed at the sight of the shivering passengers in their thin, threadbare garments, took up a collection that netted some used clothing and $20 in cash. This apparent outpouring of New England generosity was not unalloyed, however, for, in the sarcastic words of one abolitionist, some of the other townspeople began to make "a hue-and-cry about [Wixon's] bringing the emancipated slaves away from their prison-house, to breathe, if possible, a little free air in Massachusetts." As in the rest of the commonwealth, opinions were bitterly divided on the Cape, where, throughout the early eighteenth century, many a seafaring captain had made his fortune off the slave trade. Now, in 1847, Boston's grandeur was bound even more tightly to the slaveholding South—its abundant supply of cotton, but also its growing demand for northern textiles, footwear, and fish. The North's economic dependence on traffickers in human flesh was enriching but also humiliating for Boston, the once proudly independent city, conceived as a model for God-fearing people everywhere.[3]

When the *Thompson* finally docked at Long Wharf, several well-dressed white men boarded the vessel to welcome the weary passengers. Alerted to the arrival of the ship, Samuel May Jr., a thirty-seven-year-old Unitarian minister and assistant to William Lloyd Garrison, had run down from offices of the abolitionist newspaper *The Liberator*, on Cornhill Street, to inspect the newcomers as much as to greet them. Also present among the welcoming party were the well-known lawyer-abolitionists Wendell Phillips and John A. Andrew. The Virginians disembarked to face a large crowd of curiosity-seekers, with a smattering of enthusiastic well-wishers. Recalled Peter Randolph, one of the newcomers, "We left the vessel and the wharf, and found ourselves promenading up the free streets of Boston."[4]

The newcomers hailed from "Mount Pleasant," an 1,800-acre plantation on the James River about 70 miles southeast of Richmond. They had spent their lives in the countryside growing wheat and foodstuffs, and so nothing prepared them for the sights and sounds of Boston, with a population of 135,000, five times as large as Richmond. As they processed through the streets, some white people hollered out to them in an Irish brogue, giving voice to more than 18,000 recent immigrants who now called Boston home. The relative absence of Black faces (about 2,000 in the whole city) must have struck the migrants as odd, if not alarming. The streets, crisscrossed by omnibus and railroad lines, were crowded with fine carriages driven by footmen and heavy drays loaded with barrels and lumber. Black and white boys, truants from school that weekday morning, hawked goods of dubious provenance. Wending their way up State Street into the commercial and financial heart of the city, onto Court Street and past the courthouse, the group turned right on Cornhill, marveling at the imposing brick facades, the offices of printers and publishers. In the office at number 21, for the first time in their lives Randolph and the other passengers shook hands with white men.[5]

The sixty-six former slaves included several interlocking kin networks—in all, twenty-five men, fifteen women, and twenty-six children. Together they had been freed by the will of their master, Carter H. Edloe, who had died in 1844 at age forty-six. At least fifty-two of them came in families consisting of parents and children, and only two men had no identifiable kin. The emigrants' ages ranged from one to eighty. Seven-year-old Thomas Selden traveled with an extended family that spanned three generations and included his parents, Carter and Louisa, and four siblings, ranging in age from four to twenty-five. His grandmother, Lucy Fountain, seventy-six, was the oldest woman on the *Thompson*. The rest of the passengers accorded her great respect and took care to see that she was comfortable while sitting on deck. Louisa Selden also traveled with two cousins, Charles and William Fountain. Called "Blacksmith Peter" by the others, Peter Randolph, twenty-seven, arrived with his eighteen-year-old wife, Mary Amelia, and daughter, Sylvie, who was three years old; three brothers (James, ten; Richard, twenty-two; and Anthony, twenty-four); and his aunt, Fanny Bailey, thirty. The last names of individuals suggest the group's deep roots among networks of extended kin in Tidewater Virginia—Randolph, Lee, Carter, Taylor, Ruffin. Not one had taken the last name of Edloe.[6]

As financial assets, producers, and reproductive laborers, the enslaved had made Carter's plantation a profitable place and its owner a rich man. Ranging in value from $25 for Ben Selden, age twenty-five and possibly disabled, to $600 for Carter Selden, and $550 for Peter Randolph, the Edloe workforce had a total 1847 value of just under $20,000 ($700,000 in 2022 dollars). The estate included $32,000 in cash. It was no wonder that Edloe's heirs and estate executors were reluctant to part with these workers.[7]

Most slave owners proclaimed the institution of bondage a positive good, so Carter Edloe was unusual. He refused to attend church, holding that it was impossible to be both a slaveholder and a Christian. In his will, he freed all his bound workers, and not just a favored few. He had several children by an enslaved woman named Harriet Barber (sometimes Barbour) and bequeathed her the munificent sum of $8,000 (the equivalent of nearly a quarter of a million dollars in today's money). According to Samuel May, "This Harriet—sister Harriet all the slaves call her—was the only wife he [Edloe] had, and she of course not legally such, and with her he lived on perfectly good & pleasant terms." Edloe's will made clear he intended to give his enslaved workers the choice of leaving Virginia immediately upon his death, penniless, or continuing to work, bound, until they had each earned $50 (about $1,700 in today's money). By state law they would not be allowed to remain in Virginia after they became free. However, in violation of Edloe's wishes, the executors of the estate forced all of them to remain hard at work for another three years. The group might have been deprived of their freedom indefinitely were it not for their growing, vocal resentment, which whites feared might infect other enslaved workers on nearby holdings.[8]

Informed in the early spring of 1847 that they would soon be manumitted, the group "appeared to be perfectly satisfied and went to work more cheerfully than usual," in the words of an official overseeing Edloe's affairs. By the beginning of May, however, the official continued, "they became very careless and negligent and when spoken to would reply that they were distressed and had no heart to work or do anything else having heard what their situation was." It was necessary, then, that officials seek to send off members of the group as soon as possible: "They have become discontent and will not be of any service to the estate or themselves hereafter, but on the contrary will be a great disadvantage not only to the estate but to all the slaveholding in this part of the country." Another official offered a disingenuous good riddance, writing that "only a small part of the negroes were efficient laborers; . . . [T]he land they cultivated was poor and the crops [they grew] indifferent."[9]

White clergy and lawyers in and around Richmond had urged the Edloe workers either to stay enslaved forever or to move to Liberia under the auspices of the American Colonization Society, a group founded in 1817 that was intent on getting freed Blacks out of the United States. Of the estate's total of eighty-one enslaved people, some went to other states, including Barber, who with her children and a teenaged nursemaid named Sarah eventually made it to Philadelphia, and a family of six that went to Ohio. Some chose to stay behind, still enslaved and now owned by Edloe's heiresses, his nieces the sisters Mary and Elizabeth Organ. Peter Randolph later claimed that whites told him and the others that if they removed to Boston, "we should be killed, or put in prison, where we should have to work underground or be obliged to drag carts all round the streets; but we were determined to try it, live or die."[10]

The Edloe workers probably chose Boston because of the large number of fugitives who had fled there over the generations. The James River was a well-worn, watery route on the Underground Railroad (the term given to established patterns of assistance offered to those men and women seeking freedom and refuge in the North); flowing three hundred miles from the Appalachian Mountains to the mouth of the Chesapeake Bay, it was a conduit for runaways from Richmond, Petersburg, Newport News, Norfolk, and Hampton. William Still, a conductor on the Railroad, believed that "no one Southern city furnished a larger number of brave, wide-awake and likely-looking Underground Rail Road passengers than the city of Richmond." Its lively proto-industrial economy of ironworks, mechanized flour mills, and tobacco processing plants—combined with a robust shipping business—depended on enslaved workers, many of whom were hired out to employers and earned modest sums of cash. One white man complained that these slaves "had too much liberty," and squandered their meager wages on whiskey; but the greatest threat to Virginia society was that these laborers "got a habit of roaming about and *taking care of themselves*."[11]

The Edloe Sixty-Six were not fugitives, but like those who hid on ships, emerging from the forecastle stiff-limbed and disoriented in Boston Harbor, they carried little in the way of material belongings. Each person on board was in possession of $14.96, the sum due them, according to the estate's lawyers, after they had worked all their lives, including three years and thirty-five days since their owner's death. The stipulated $50 had been whittled down after deductions for clothing, provisions, a physician's services, and passage on the *Thomas H. Thompson*. One lawyer perversely justified these deductions and others—for the "purchase of utensils, necessary current repairs of buildings, &c"—by classifying them as "all the expenses of the slaves and of the plantation while cultivated for their benefit"—in other words, all the funds expended on the upkeep and maintenance of the plantation while the workers were toiling on and "benefiting" from it. The executors also charged the Edloe group a "commission" for marketing the farm produce they grew. Legal services to settle the estate cost from $5 to $60 to $150, depending on who was providing the account. Abolitionists divined in this story of the abrogated will a warning to conscience-stricken whites: "Let every slaveholder, who mediates an act of justice to his slaves, see to the execution of it himself instead of leaving it to his heirs."[12]

Within a few years of his arrival in Boston, Peter Randolph would write a graphic account of life under slavery. Just as in death Carter Edloe had deferred to what he thought would be the wise men disposing his estate, so in life he had deferred to overseers managing his workforce. In *Sketches of Slave Life, or, Illustrations of the "Peculiar Institution"* (1855), Randolph told of overseers administering five hundred lashes while swigging from a bottle of whiskey, tearing children from their mothers to be sold on the auction block, and raping women and girls. Wrote Randolph, "Slaveholders carry the price of blood upon their backs and in their pockets; the very bread they eat is the price of blood; the houses they live in are bought with blood; all the education they have is paid for by the blood and sorrows of the poor slaves." Left unsaid was another question: Did the same indictment apply to those smug Bostonians who also carried the price of blood in their pockets, stuffed with cotton and cash?[13]

The twenty-two-year-old Randolph was a likely leader of the group; literate since the age of seventeen, he had taken the extraordinary step of seeking out legal assistance for his coworkers soon after Edloe's death, when it became clear that the local court was violating the spirit and letter of the will. At the same time, Randolph must have felt some greater obligation to these families. His father, Anthony, had worked as a driver on a nearby plantation, his very existence dependent on the brutal discipline he meted out to men, women, and children. As a blacksmith Peter had forged the shackles and hooks used to restrain and torture his fellow slaves. Peter's brother Benjamin was an incorrigible runaway, the story of his resistance imprinted on his scarred back. At one point, after Benjamin had been caught trying to flee aboard a ship anchored in the James River, he had been sold to a nearby plantation and then finally sent to an uncertain fate farther south. Randolph's mother, like the other elderly people who were presumably too frail to make the trip to Boston, had stayed behind. Peter learned that she died (after being attacked by dogs, he believed) soon after they sailed. Eight years after their arrival in Boston, Randolph would track down all the surviving original emigrants and sue to reclaim the $35.04 he believed was owed to each of them.[14]

From the moment they boarded the *Thomas H. Thompson*, the passengers faced scrutiny from a series of northern white men. Captain Wixon later reported that they had conducted themselves well on board. He noted "their great love for each other,"

Self-taught, Peter Randolph arrived in Boston from Virginia at the age of twenty-two. In the early 1850s he sought a permanent position as a Baptist preacher, visiting towns throughout New England and upstate New York. Between 1846 and 1866, he and his wife, Amelia, had eight children, but seven of them (between the ages of one day and sixteen years) had died by 1866. *(National Park Service)*

citing their respect for the elderly Lucy Fountain—"an old grandmother," as he described her, "who had almost worn herself out in the service of slavery." She "had the most comfortable seat on the deck of the vessel, where like all other grandmothers, she was ready to point out her children and grandchildren, and tell of their good qualities." *The Emancipator*, the first abolitionist newspaper in the United States, now published in Boston, informed its readers that during the voyage the group had been "quiet . . . cleanly and obliging, and he [Wixon] believes them trust-worthy." One of the men who had met the ship at Long Wharf watched the newcomers carefully as they packed their meager belongings onto a wagon; in an odd formulation of the task at hand, this observer noted that "they evinced a good deal of tact and skill," a promising sign, he thought.[15]

Over the next several years Samuel May, Garrison's assistant, "observed the course of these emancipated slaves with attention and some curiosity." He explained why: "I regarded the experiment they were making as an exceedingly interesting one; such an one as, if successful, ought to convince even the most skeptical, of the ability of the colored man, even when reared in ignorance and partial dependence which the condition of slavery imposes, to 'take care of himself.'" May sought to distinguish the Edloe folk from the many fugitives who had made their way to Boston, men and women who had demonstrated extraordinary cunning and physical courage. He probably had in mind Harriet Jacobs of North Carolina, who hid in her grandmother's attic off and on for seven years before finding her way north; and Ellen and William Craft, who had made a successful escape from Georgia when the light-skinned wife dressed as a white gentleman and her husband posed as "his" manservant. The most famous fugitive of the time, Frederick Douglass, had donned mariner's garb and forged papers to make the treacherous trip out of Baltimore and into freedom. Surely these well-known fugitives were not typical of the millions of enslaved workers in the South.[16]

In contrast, May believed the Edloe group he met in September 1847 to be "the ordinary working force of one plantation,—of all ages and capacities, and in various states of health; and might be presumed to be a fair representation of the average condition of at least Virginia slaves." Their arrival provided the ingredients of an "experiment" that bore close watching—field hands plucked from a wheat farm in the Virginia Tidewater and settled in the city of Boston, to make their own way, or not. By focusing on the issue of work and the migrants' capacity for self-sufficiency, May pointedly ignored the prejudgments of less sympathetic whites—that the group had no chance of success, either because of their inferior "race" or because of slavery's permanent, baleful effects on their work ethic and temperament.[17]

In fact, many abolitionists feared their cause would founder if Black people released from bondage proved forever dependent on private charity or the dole. After half a century, New England's own emancipation project had yielded not the hoped-for class of sturdy Black yeoman farmers, but, apparently, a group chronically underemployed and impoverished. And then there were concerns about the constant and growing drain on the public coffers: between 1845 and 1855, Boston's cost of caring for its poor grew fourfold, from $15,000 to $60,000 a year, reflecting the large number of penniless Irish immigrants arriving in the city (in 1847 alone, the deadliest year of the great potato famine, more than 13,000). In the five-year period after 1846, the police force beefed up its foot-patrol force from twelve to sixty-six men. Meanwhile, Black men waited restlessly outside dry-goods stores, hotels, and commission merchants' offices hoping for day work; they were a ubiquitous presence on Boston's streets and sidewalks. The inability of so many to find a steady job boded ill for the Edloe "experiment."[18]

Like most well-to-do whites, May believed that personal industry was ultimately a matter of choice, a moral imperative that one consciously embraced or rejected. He seemed oblivious to both the trauma suffered by the migrants and the constraints of the labor force, as well as to how those factors might affect their life prospects in Boston. Perhaps Peter Randolph wrote his book *Sketches* to instruct May and other abolitionists on the plantation's brutality, which would continue to haunt him and his fellow passengers into their new lives. In the book Randolph told of how an overseer "shot one of Edloe's men, because he would not submit to the lash." The man, Wyatt Lee, survived the shooting and came to Boston with his wife, Betsy, and their children, Eliza and Albert. Lee's memories of the ordeal, like the scars from the bullet, were impossible to leave behind. May, however, remained focused on the migrants' need for gainful employment, now. While admitting that some immediate assistance was warranted because of "their destitution and the strangeness of a new home," in 1855 he held up as a positive exemplar Levi Scott, the oldest passenger on the *Thompson*, who, though an "aged and nearly worn-out man," had persisted in working; Scott "maintained himself by his daily labor, and only ceased to attempt it longer, when told he must desist by reason of infirmity of age, at upwards of four score years."[19]

In the fall of 1847, *The Liberator* published a handful of articles about the Virginians, probably all of them penned by May; but Garrison himself evinced little interest in the fate of the group and their collective or individual success. For one thing, they held far less claim on his energies than the suffering enslaved masses of the South. Also, he understood that finding jobs for the men especially presented enormous political difficulties. Individual employers might be sympathetic in theory to fugitives, but they knew that their white employees would probably strike or quit if a Black person showed up for work one day. The experienced ship caulker Frederick Douglass found himself barred from his trade when he arrived in New Bedford and had to support himself and his wife by picking up odd jobs here and there.[20]

However, Garrison was not there to welcome the *Thompson* because he was indifferent toward its passengers, but because he was out of town, ill, and preoccupied with a growing rift between himself and Douglass. In April 1847, Douglass had returned to the United States from a successful nineteen-month tour of England and Ireland, free (bought from his owner by a group of British supporters) and full of confidence in his own intellectual abilities. His time abroad had led him to think more broadly and deeply about the meaning of his own truncated US citizenship. He was now much less inclined than before to take orders or accept ideas uncritically from white men such as Garrison, who reacted strongly to the Black man's suggestion that he might start his own paper, a presumed rival to *The Liberator*. In late July Garrison and Douglass embarked on a speaking tour; for the last time they traveled together, now to Pennsylvania and Ohio, and, as they had so many times before, faced epithets, rocks, and eggs hurled their way by proslavery crowds. In early September the exhausted Garrison became ill and retreated to Cleveland to rest and recover, leaving Douglass to journey on to New York State alone. Within a month of the landing of the Edloe Sixty-Six, Douglass would launch *The North Star*, later called *Frederick Douglass' Paper*, from Rochester.[21]

For their part, local Boston editors did little more than mention the Edloe group in passing soon after their arrival. On September 24 the *Christian Watchman* warned that these "unsophisticated strangers" would be tempted by two different kinds of "influences," both "very injurious to them." They might find themselves drawn to "unprincipled" Blacks in the city—presumably those who frequented dram shops and dance halls—or they might find themselves beseeched by the "ultra-abolitionists, who will no doubt attempt to make them suppose that at least nine-tenths of this community are their enemies, and they alone are the only true friends of the colored race." The first path led to moral degradation and ruin, the second to cynicism and disillusionment. Salvation ran through hard work, avoiding both hard drink and blind allegiance to loud-mouthed idealists. This was the view of most members of the established clergy, regardless of denomination, especially the most powerful ministers in the city, the Congregationalists.[22]

Throughout September and October, Richmond authorities and Boston abolitionists offered competing accounts of the Edloe migrants' three-year odyssey out of bondage. In effect, these white men were reprising the historical rivalry between Virginia and Massachusetts, two commonwealths that presumed to speak for the nation. *The Emancipator* considered Captain Gideon Wixon "a generous hearted son of Cape Cod" deserving of "the thanks of the benevolent for his kindness" to his forlorn human cargo. A native of Dennis, Wixon was, according to *The Liberator*, "a fine specimen of an honest, generous Cape Cod Yankee," a brave soul who had transported the Edloe people "at some considerable inconvenience to himself."[23]

On September 28, the *Richmond Enquirer* slammed what it called the "Boston fanatics" and their "libelous imputations," claiming that the voyage had netted Wixon the tidy sum of $400 in passengers' fees. He had hardly provided his services for free out of the goodness of his Yankee heart, and besides, he carried a full load of goods in his vessel, which meant that the money paid by the Edloe group was a supplement, not a substitute, for his regular compensation. More generally, according to the *Enquirer*, the various parties involved in the execution of the Edloe will—court officials, estate commissioners, attorneys—all "treated the negroes with due care and kindness and were especially watchful of their future happiness and interests." This narrative held that only a few of the enslaved workers were actually "efficient laborers"; most were children or elderly, hardly worth holding in bondage. The executor of the estate had urged the group to wait until their wheat was sold that fall, but they ignored his advice and insisted on departing in early September, forfeiting whatever proceeds were due them from the harvest. Virginia officials acknowledged that they had impressed upon Randolph and the others the "impropriety of their choice" of destination—a big city with a cold climate and false friends, abolitionists eager to exploit them for their own selfish, propagandistic ends.[24]

In the South, planters measured the value of their laborers by how well they worked, affixing prices to their bodies accordingly. In the North, white "friends of the slave" used a different standard of measurement, judging people of color according to their willingness to work hard regardless of the paucity of the pay or the meanness of the job. Yet in both cases productive labor was the pivot upon which political and economic relations turned, for white southerners and northerners alike shared a preoccupation with a kind of "freedom" defined in terms of work: in the South, the freedom of whites to own other people; in the North, the freedom of whites to work alongside whomever they chose. Peter Randolph recognized that he and his fellow migrants were the human variables in a closely watched experiment: "Now, we had to prove to the world, whether or not, the oft-repeated assertion was true, 'That the slave, if emancipated, could not take care of himself.'"[25]

WHERE THE EDLOE group initially found shelter remains unknown. Apparently, some for a while at least huddled in makeshift shacks and under primitive lean-tos in back alleys, ramshackle places home to increasing numbers of Boston's impoverished residents. Some of the Virginians probably used their small stash of cash to secure refuge in one of the many hundreds of basements that had been converted to damp, dank apartments for whole families and kin groups. But most of the Edloe group probably stayed at least temporarily with sympathetic conductors on the Underground Railroad, Black and white men and women who had the necessary space and resources. Abolitionists were reluctant to publicize the names of those daring souls willing to board newcomers, even temporarily. Possible hosts included a tight-knit group on Southac Street in the West End, north of Boston Common. Of one household, a fugitive from Norfolk recalled, "So many of my acquaintances" took refuge there "that I almost imagine my self to bee in the old country."[26]

Regardless of their living situations, the Edloe migrants were largely on their own. According to Randolph, "thus distributed, we had to work out our own destiny with all the disabilities that the peculiar institution had entailed upon us." However, many of the "disabilities" that confronted them entailed factors other than their history of enslavement. In Boston, the liabilities of Black job-seekers would not have been readily apparent to visitors impressed by the city's crowded docks, lively streets, and impressive brick and granite buildings. Cosmopolitan elites prided themselves on creating a compact commonwealth, where even the lowliest worker might share in the prosperity and profits enjoyed by the merchant, factory owner, or banker; but in fact the city possessed a large number of the working poor. Distanced from the textile mills of Lowell and Lawrence, the city had a manufacturing base that relied primarily on men skilled in assembling locomotives, ships, pianos, and watches and in producing glass and ironworks. Artisan shops amounted to fraternal orders in miniature, off-limits to Blacks, Catholics, foreigners, and women. Machines and cheap immigrant labor gradually doomed these worksites.[27]

An oversupply of workers existed for even the most unappealing jobs—scraping the streets of horse waste, emptying night soil from tenements, cleaning out the overflowing vaults and privies. Most Black men were casual laborers, working by the day, finding piecemeal tasks here and there. One common job category, "tender," a catchall term, included a wide range of activities, from cleaning to running errands and transporting goods. Many men and women, desperate for work, created their own jobs and crafted their own working conditions; they operated on the premise, or the hope, that pickpocketing, thieving, counterfeiting, and conning the gullible could offer a living wage.

The insecurities of the workplace were replicated outside it. In contrast to the South, where the protocols of "racial" etiquette were well known and rigidly enforced, in Boston those protocols remained fluid and inconsistent. The omnibus driver who one day accepted the fare from a Black rider might the next day be replaced by a driver who did not. The hotel that paid Black men to remove fireplace ashes might decide to hire white men in their stead. This uncertainty afflicted all people of color regardless of their status, formal education, or personal comportment. A study of Massachusetts published the year before the Edloe group arrived in Boston noted, of Black job-seekers, "They cannot obtain employment on equal terms with the whites, and wherever they go a sneer is passed upon them, as if this sportive inhumanity were an act of merit." They remained impoverished, a liability that "impairs the duration of life itself."[28]

In October, a visitor to a cluster of the Edloe migrants found that "they looked needy, anxious, and sad," crowded into a "poor shelter" and trying to "pick up a little work in the city." Although "the abolitionists have been invited to come forward and give them homes and employment," thus far that invitation had gone largely unanswered. Where, then, were those men of privilege who had "enough talent to direct the labours and supervise the welfare of all"?[29]

In fact, like Garrison, the most prominent white abolitionists offered little to these formerly enslaved people. Randolph would eventually describe the future governor John A. Andrew as a warm personal friend. Yet initially Andrew had an unfavorable impression of the Edloe newcomers. Early on he thought "most of them looked to be a very crooked sort of old men. And those who didn't claim to be more than 50, had a way of lifting up their feet in the morning and putting them down in the afternoon; and every one was crooked in the back except Peter." By using the word "crooked," Andrew may have been attempting to compare these men unfavorably with their respectable white counterparts, who in the parlance of the day were often described in terms of their upright manliness. Or perhaps he meant it literally, and these men were disabled from years of toil in the wheat fields.[30]

The Edloe group would by and large make their own way, depending on each other and on other Virginia migrants for housing and job contacts. In the process they had to adjust to a city that was crowded, dirty, and sickly, and becoming more so. In the fall of 1847, a dysentery epidemic swept through that was "very prevalent and fatal," according to Samuel May, and within a few months the scourge would be cholera. Proud of its municipal sewer and gas lighting systems (the country's first, in 1824), the city nonetheless suffered from epidemics of contagious diseases imported by seafaring vessels, including respiratory diseases (especially tuberculosis) that spread quickly in close quarters. An omnipresent stench emanated from piles of animal waste befouling the street, and human waste puddling under tenements and in backyards. The practice of dumping sewage into the Charles River or the harbor was self-defeating, for what the tide took out it also brought back in. Hundreds of rum shops, where the liquor could be bought and consumed on the spot, contributed to mayhem—shootings, stabbings, robberies, and quarrels over and between lovers. The West End, on the north side of Beacon Hill, home to many people of color, was also a district of brothels and dram shops, where deadly weekend fights were routine.[31]

Besides its unhealthiness, Boston afforded Blacks a much narrower range of possibilities compared to southern plantations in terms of how they might use their skills. When he came north, "Blacksmith Peter" carried with him no tools of his trade, as those were now the property of Carter Edloe's heirs. In 1847 Boston was home to a handful of Black blacksmiths, but most of them were migrants from the South, and whether they actually worked at their trade (as opposed to identifying themselves that way to a census-taker) is unknown. In any case, few of them could afford to hire an employee or a journeyman, or house and feed an apprentice. Some whites had predicted (wrongly) that the Edloe migrants would "soon get situations as carpenters, blacksmiths, farmers, &c." May noted that they were mainly farmers "and would like immediately to go to work as such," but that was not always possible. Meanwhile, for women, familiar tasks such as washing clothes, cooking, and caring for children could yield small sums essential to maintaining their families.[32]

GARRISON DID NOT return to Boston until late October. May complained to a correspondent that, in the absence of any concerted effort among Bostonians to help the Edloe group find jobs, it had "fallen very much" to him "to find places for them, ie., for those who wished to go out in the country." In part he was successful. As he reported, "Upon favors I have secured good places for quite a number of them." He later estimated that half of the adults stayed in Boston and the other half fanned out to the suburbs of Cambridge, Brighton, Brookline, and Chelsea, or went to other parts of Massachusetts or rural New England. Most of the Edloe men eventually worked as waiters, laborers, or tenders.[33]

One of the migrants, Davy Jones, forty, found at least temporary work in Jonathan Walker's household on the South Shore of Boston. By this time Walker had become a national celebrity in abolitionist circles by virtue of the letters "SS" (for "slave stealer") burned into his right hand. Born in Harwich, Massachusetts, in 1799, Walker was a sea captain and, after 1831, a fervent supporter of Garrison. In 1845, a Pensacola, Florida, court convicted Walker of attempting to transport seven enslaved men to freedom—or, according to authorities, trying to "abduct" or "steal" them. Walker endured two trials, imprisonment, an hour-long stint in a pillory, a fine, and a branded hand before his release in July 1845.

He immediately returned to Massachusetts to find his large family in dire straits. Hoping to support them by capitalizing on his new-found fame, for two years he toured the antislavery circuit, fearless in his denunciation of the conservative clerical establishment. He once charged, for example, that "the man who wields the blood-clotted cow-skin during the week fills the pulpit on Sunday and claims to be a minister of the meek and lowly Jesus."[34]

Like so many others before and after him, Walker found public speaking a difficult way to make a living. He lacked Douglass's eloquence—that voice that one Boston paper described as "strong, musical, and pliant; his utterance measured and prompt; his language choice, pointed and beautiful." Walker's one feature that drew audiences—his branded hand—lacked staying power as a novelty that would impel listeners to part with a few coins. Yet for all his tribulations, he was able to report to *The Liberator*, on September 26, that he had one of the Edloe group with him in his household. Of the new arrival, Walker wrote that he was "to all appearances . . . well behaved, industrious, and of excellent disposition."[35]

Walker's brief stint on the antislavery lecture circuit yielded a cautionary tale for others who hoped to earn a livelihood while promoting the slave's cause. In November he set out on a speaking tour for several months in the company of John S. Jacobs, the fugitive brother of North Carolina's famous Harriet Jacobs. In the mid-1840s, John Jacobs had served as corresponding secretary of the New England Freedom Association, formed to help runaway slaves. Now he and Walker trudged around upstate New York, trying to sell a book that Walker had written about his Florida trials; but the two made precious little money and often worried about where their next meal was coming from. Reported Walker, "On several occasions, a little rowdyism was manifested," no doubt an understatement of the hostility they encountered. (Speaking in Bridgewater, Massachusetts, in 1848, the abolitionist Lucy Stone was hit with dried apples, smoked herring, beans, and plugs of chewed tobacco; but it was the large prayer book aimed her way that severely wounded her.) Both Walker and Jacobs joined a long line of antislavery agitators disappointed to find public speaking insufficient to sustain a family.[36]

PETER RANDOLPH LATER summed up his first three years in Boston this way: "My chief difficulty was not in getting much work, but in getting much pay—I had much work but little pay." In fact, the growing city spawned many discrete tasks for wage earners, but taken together in any one day, those tasks hardly yielded a decent wage. Randolph earned a paltry $1.50 (about $50 in today's money) a week plus board, presumably with one of his employers. (It is uncertain whether his wife and daughter were permitted to live with him under this arrangement.) In certain key respects his first years in Boston were emblematic of the hardships other Black workers faced. Yet he was unusual in that he quickly made connections with successful white men in the city, several of whom would serve as his patrons; Randolph described his years as a "tender" not by recounting the many different establishments he worked for, but rather by expressing gratitude to the individuals who employed him. Some of them he met at the annual antislavery bazaar in December 1847, where he found temporary employment hauling boxes and moving tables and gained the attention of some prominent merchants and activists.[37]

Boston's Fourteenth Annual Anti-Slavery Bazaar, held in historic Faneuil Hall, opened on December 21 and stretched over five days, attracting hundreds of Christmas shoppers and raising thousands of dollars for the abolitionist cause. The affair highlighted the extensive unwaged labor performed by Black and white women in their roles as producers of goods and organizers of the event. When Frederick Douglass's family was living in Lynn, Massachusetts, about fourteen miles north of Boston, his wife, Anna, looked forward to coming to the city for a week to prepare for the annual fair; she worked side by side with white women and enjoyed the sense of collective purpose. Recalled her daughter Rosetta, "The New England women were all workers and there was no shirking of responsibility—all worked."[38]

By this time the bazaar had become a major attraction for well-to-do, liberal-minded white Bostonians. There they could indulge their expensive tastes for luxury items from around the world and purchase products not found in any Boston shop. Patrons browsed among displays of goods donated from England, Scotland, Ireland, France, and China as well as from other parts of the United States: tartan and plaid shawls and scarves, rich silk table covers and sofa cushions, rare editions of literary works in French and English, Parisian "gentlemen's dressing gowns," women's satin cloaks. The event took months to plan. In addition to Anna Douglass, the organizers included Mary May, Helen E. Garrison, and Ann T. Greene Phillips (the wives of Samuel, William, and Wendell, respectively). Estimates of the proceeds ran as high as $10,000 (in today's currency, about $350,000).[39]

The connections Randolph made at the bazaar led to a series of short-term jobs. As a tender, he ran errands, dusted and stocked store shelves, moved furniture, stoked fires, and hauled goods through the street. By 1850 he had worked briefly for a printer and publisher; a carpet company; a shoe manufacturer; a series of wholesale dealers specializing in dry goods, teas, groceries, and clothing; a supplier to footwear makers (leather, hides, buttons, lastings, threads); a banker; a watchmaker; and a yarn manufacturer. Most of these establishments were clustered on Pearl Street near the docks. Randolph believed he gained the trust of one white merchant because both were Freemasons, though he and other Black men belonged to the segregated Prince Hall Grand Lodge.

Randolph worked hard to carry out the tasks assigned him, no matter how new and confusing. Describing himself as "green as a cucumber," he set off one day to a bank to make a deposit for one employer. When he got there he realized that he had no idea what he should do with the slip of paper in his hand, prompting ridicule from the white clerks. James Brown of the decade-old publishing firm Little, Brown arranged a janitorship at Harvard College for him—no doubt a plum position for any Black man. But Randolph, writing later, noted, "I refused, because I did not feel myself competent to assume such a place and responsibility." Thus it was with faux modesty that Randolph expressed his distress at the limited jobs available for a literate, intelligent man of color. When state representative Charles Francis Adams asked Randolph to wash his office floor, the Black man suggested pay of $3 a day; Adams exclaimed that that was more than he was making as a legislator, prompting Randolph to say he "was worth more per day scrubbing floors, than he [Adams] was in making laws for the state of Massachusetts." (Adams no doubt mistook this brazen critique of the prevailing social division of labor as an impertinent joke.) Before long, Randolph would launch a speaking career and begin lecturing on "The Misery and Folly of Idleness," a topic that pleased his white patrons. Frank Merrett of the commercial firm Merrett & Mullen heard that talk, and, according to Randolph, "afterward, whenever in his store he saw a place where the feather-duster did not reach, or a stray cobweb about, he would remind me of that lecture, intimating that I should practice what I preached."[40]

Randolph's first years in Boston in some respects paralleled Douglass's years in New Bedford, from 1838 to 1841. Both skilled men worked as tenders for three years before finding vocations that answered to their talents and ambitions. Excluded from his trade because of "the strength of prejudice against color, among the white caulkers," Douglass, too, reported that he found "a plenty of work"—sawing wood, shoveling and carrying coal, and sweeping floors. He described stowing a ship with a load of oil this way: "It was new, dirty, and hard work for me; but I went at it with a glad heart and a willing hand. I was now my own master.

It was a happy moment, the rapture of which can be understood only by those who have been slaves."[41]

Nevertheless, in 1848, with his New Bedford days now several years in the past, Douglass offered a less sanguine view of menial wage work. In a speech in Cleveland in early September, he charged that ill-paid northern Blacks were "slaves of the community," oppressed by contemptuous employers and hostile white employees. He called for solidarity among all Black people, north and south: "As one rises, all must rise, and as one falls all must fall." Only when Black men learned skilled trades would they become truly independent of the white taskmaster. Should the cities not afford opportunities in the construction and other skilled trades, Black families must move to the countryside, where the tilling of the soil was a respectable profession and black people might "reap the reward of honest labor."[42]

Douglass was becoming increasingly radicalized. In 1848, he broke from Garrison and hailed the founding of the antislavery Free Soil Party, a splinter group from the abolitionist wings of the Whigs and Democrats. In an odd twist, the Whigs nominated General Zachary Taylor for president. Taylor was a prominent military officer in the Mexican-American War (1846–1848), which many in their party had opposed. By this time whites were divided over the meaning of the conflict, which, together with the annexation of the Republic of Texas in 1845, expanded the country's slave territory by nine hundred thousand square miles. Congress, the Supreme Court, and the executive branch all seemed in thrall to southern planters and their hunger for more land. Boston industrialists and merchants together fueled that hunger in their demand for slave-grown cotton. Douglass and others supported the Free Soil Party in spite of the Garrisonian injunction to avoid politics on the theory that such activity only reified a corrupt slave system, one that was national, and not just regional, in its reach. To participate in partisan politics would necessitate tacit complicity in the evils spawned by the slave owners' Constitution.

The Edloe Sixty-Six adjusted to their first years in Boston while mourning the deaths of several of their members and welcoming the births of children. Thomas Selden and his siblings lost their mother, Louisa, within just a few months of their arrival. Their father, Carter, remarried soon after—his second wife, Sarah, was twenty years younger than he and a native of Massachusetts. The couple had a daughter, Mary, in 1848, and several other Edloe migrants, including Peter and Amelia Randolph, had babies between 1847 and 1850.

Thomas Selden, who had been seven years old when the Edloe group came to Boston, would begin his lifelong career of paid employment a decade later, at the age of seventeen. He married and endured a series of family tragedies. Working as a waiter and a porter, he had an otherwise unremarkable career save for the fact that at the age of twenty-three he joined the army and became part of one of the first US regiments of Black soldiers.

Yet, inscribed within the very ordinariness of his life were the grand themes of history—the nation's no less than Boston's. Making a living was a central, lived experience for Selden and the other Edloe migrants, and the hardships they faced spoke to national preoccupations with questions of rights and work. They arrived in Boston when the great social and political movements of the day focused on a series of momentous questions—who would labor for whom, under what conditions, and for what kind of compensation (if any). The fight against slavery and the fight for rights on behalf of the laboring classes converged in the struggles of northern Black workers, yet this convergence went unnoticed among many white reformers. Thomas Selden was part of Samuel May's "experiment," but then so, too, was Boston part of America's grand democratic experiment, one that was still very much in its formative stages during the 1850s.

PART I

1850-1860

1

The Fugitive Economy

Antebellum Boston consisted of a large, churning colony of fugitives from slavery—in 1850, as many as one-quarter of the Black population of 2,000 (out of a total of 136,000 people). Indeed, the Boston Black community functioned as a restless maroon colony (a hidden settlement of freedom-seekers), northern-style, where physical barriers—in this case, subterranean rooms and narrow alleyways—served to thwart kidnappers and federal authorities. The city offered only an imperfect refuge, but the newcomers transformed life there in dramatic ways, material and political.[1]

Boston provided a waystation for some and a permanent home for others; regardless, a fugitive economy based on waged and unwaged labor shaped the entire Black community and, by extension, the abolitionist agenda. Though dominated by US-born persons of African descent, this economy was ultimately cosmopolitan and multiethnic. In the 1850s, substantial numbers of Boston's Black residents were born abroad, in places that charted the trade routes of outgoing and incoming vessels—the Canadian Maritimes (New Brunswick and Nova Scotia); Africa; the "West Indies" (Cuba, the Bahamas, Bermuda) and Suriname; Western Europe, including England, Ireland, Spain, Portugal, and the

Netherlands; and India. A large proportion of these immigrants were mariners, and some hailed from slave societies; fugitives arrived in Boston from the East as well as from the South. Many of these foreigners, together with seamen from the Deep South, had abandoned or literally jumped ship in Boston Harbor. Seafaring newcomers infused Boston's Black community with ideological sensibilities forged in the crucible of the Atlantic world shaped by mass migrations, cultural clashes, and the rise of industrial capitalism.

The fugitive economy was a moral one that enlisted the energies of people with antislavery impulses. It was also political, pitting southern Black runaways and their supporters against the laws of the United States, which reflected the interests and national influence of southern slaveholders. Another component of the fugitive economy relied on the exchange of money for goods and services—services that included, for example, transporting, housing, and defending runaways—and yet another component, on the unwaged labor of activists. Community leaders made strenuous efforts to assist fugitives, expending time, energy, and resources that many could ill afford to spare, and the newcomers also helped to determine the contours of abolitionist agitation and fund-raising. In February 1850, an antislavery meeting featured an appearance by a fifteen-year-old named Elizabeth Blakeley, a fugitive recently arrived from North Carolina. One member of the audience described her as "a most interesting looking creature," a curiosity, and presumably an inducement for audience members to open their wallets. The mass meeting with a recent runaway on the platform—whether a man, a woman, or a child who looked nearly white—became a staple of abolitionist activism.[2]

This maroon-like colony intersected with the Boston job market. Fugitives who intended to stay in Boston sought out waged labor. For the most part they constituted an underemployed workforce of domestic servants, waiters, and menial laborers; exceptional were those few enterprising men and women who made a livelihood out of speaking and writing about and otherwise documenting their own harrowing life stories. Most fugitives had to piece together a living with the help of the Black community, since local antislavery societies earmarked aid for the escape and temporary lodging of fugitives, but not for their permanent resettlement in the Bay State city. George Teamoh, who fled Virginia and arrived in Massachusetts in the winter of 1853–1854, noted, "Once there you were 'free indeed,' and then thrown on your own resources after a few weeks of indulgence" by local abolitionists. Ultimately, the fugitive economy was an unstable one, made even more so by the high mortality rates suffered by the many Black Bostonians living in cramped quarters.[3]

Unpredictability was the hallmark of virtually every fugitive's existence. In 1844, the runaway Harriet Jacobs was living in New York City and working for the family of Nathaniel Parker Willis, a successful magazine writer. Fearing that her North Carolina master was pursuing her, Jacobs made her way to Boston, where she found employment as a seamstress; there she eventually rejoiced at a long-awaited reunion with her brother John and her two children, eleven-year-old Louisa and fourteen-year-old Joseph. Jacobs believed her family was finally "beyond the reach of the bloodhounds." Still, not all fugitives residing in Boston shared her sense of relief, for slave-catchers remained on the prowl in the city, especially down by the docks. Moreover, the possibility that not only runaways but also free-born men, women, and children could be snatched off the streets of Boston and sold south meant that the whole Black population existed in a state of perpetual alert.[4]

In 1850, an intense new fear gripped the community as Congress debated the Fugitive Slave Act, a proposal that would require ordinary northern citizens—not just local officials or federal commissioners—to capture, or assist in capturing, runaway slaves, and return them to their southern owners. It was no wonder that some Black Bostonians told the federal census-taker that summer that they did not know where they were born, or that they only knew they were born in "America."

The Fugitive Slave Act, which took effect on September 18, was part of a series of congressional measures, known as the Compromise of 1850, intended to allay the anxieties of white northerners and southerners over the future of slavery. Under these new laws, California was admitted as a free state, the two new territories of Utah and New Mexico were formed out of the land the United States had seized from Mexico in the Mexican-American War, and the slave trade (though not slavery) was abolished in the District of Columbia. The stringent legislation related to fugitives provided for a process of rendition that denied the accused runaway all semblance of due process. Suddenly, all northerners, regardless of their politics, found themselves in the middle of the controversy over slavery, forced to act, in effect, as slave-catchers themselves. Even Boston's proslavery whites resented the intrusion of federal marshals, the havoc that ensued from enforcement of the law, and the high cost affixed to each rendition, which could run into thousands of dollars. The so-called compromise ignited the outrage of abolitionists and inflamed northern public opinion in general.[5]

On the evening of Friday, October 4, an overflow crowd met in the African Meeting House on Smith Court to protest the new law, galvanizing the Black community as never before. The meeting featured a report by William Cooper Nell, the Boston-born secretary of the gathering. He declared that the odious bill, though just recently passed "in hot haste," had "commenced its bloody crusade o'er the land, and the liability of ourselves and families becoming its victims, at the caprice of Southern men-stealers, imperatively demands an expression whether we will tamely submit to chains and slavery, or whether we will at all and every hazard, *Live* and *Die* freemen." Organizers titled the proceedings "Declaration of Sentiments of the Colored Citizens of Boston on the Fugitive

Slave Bill," a nod to the "Declaration of Rights and Sentiments" approved by delegates to the Seneca Falls Convention of 1848 in favor of the rights of women—which was itself an homage to the 1776 Declaration of Independence.[6]

According to an account in *The Liberator*, in attendance that night were "a vast concourse, including fugitives and their friends." Presumably so many people of color would protect each other from slaveholders' menacing minions, whether private agents or federal marshals. Robert Johnson, a fugitive from Richmond (and a Boston resident since 1829), warned his listeners "that they should be on the constant look-out for the Southern slave-catcher and the Northern mercenary, [and] as they valued their liberty, be prepared for any emergency." Johnson noted that "the meeting was largely composed of ACTORS, and not speakers merely; they were men of over-alls—men of the wharf—those who could do heavy work in the hour of difficulty." He also "administered a timely caution to the women," who, in pursuit of washing and other work in hotels and boardinghouses, should look out for kidnappers and agents of planters. The caterer Joshua B. Smith rose to speak and advised the men to arm themselves with revolvers.[7]

Most of the men who spoke that night were representatives of Boston's Black entrepreneurial and professional class (about 5 percent of all Black adults), and several besides Johnson had escaped from slavery. Also at the meeting were free-born people who had moved to Boston from other parts of the country. Smith, originally from Pennsylvania, had begun his career in Boston as a waiter but soon started his own business, gaining the title "Prince of Caterers." John T. Hilton, a barber and sometime clothing dealer, was also a native of the Keystone State. Nell had recently returned to Boston from Rochester, where he had helped to edit Frederick Douglass's new newspaper, *The North Star*. At the time of the meeting, Nell and Lewis Hayden, another attendee, were running as candidates for the Massachusetts Legislature on the antislavery Free Soil ticket.[8]

From Prince Hall, the founder of a Freemason movement that took his name, to David Walker and beyond, Boston boasted a luminous leadership class of Black people who believed that their strength lay in unity of purpose. Founded in 1845 to assist fugitives, the New England Freedom Association (NEFA) was notable by virtue of its being an all-Black organization, with two women (Judith Smith and Mary L. Armstead) on its board of directors. Its stated mission was "to extend a helping hand to all who may bid adieu to whips and chains, and by the welcome light of the North Star, reach a haven where they can be protected from the grasp of the man-stealer." Such was "the appropriate work of those at the North"—not, as some would suggest, to raise a penny toward ransoming the fugitive and paying the aggrieved slave owner. Five years later whites formed the Boston Vigilance Committee (BVC), which superseded but continued the work of the NEFA and grew to consist of two hundred members, all men. The BVC admitted only a small, select group of Blacks, including Hayden, Hilton, Nell, Smith, and the attorney Robert Morris. Also prominent in Boston's hub of abolitionist activity were Charles Lenox Remond, from Salem, who carried out a full schedule on the antislavery lecture circuit; George T. Downing, a prosperous caterer from Providence, Rhode Island; and Frederick Douglass, the editor-agitator from Rochester.[9]

Boston's leading Black families lived near each other on or around Southac Street in the West End. They lent each other money and their children intermarried. They did not always fit into the neat categories defined by particular jobs. John P. Coburn was a clothing dealer and a tailor, offering "clothing cut and made in the neatest and most fashionable style." He sold fine fabrics such as cashmeres, doeskins, and tweeds, and took "gentlemen's cast-off garments" on consignment for resale. He and his brother-in-law, Ira Gray, ran a gambling establishment. Hilton, the barber and clothing dealer, also sold furniture and operated an employment agency. Hayden, frequently referred to as a "second-hand clothing dealer," sold umbrellas, trunks, valises, watches, and jewelry, as well as "custom garments made to order."[10]

Hayden exemplified the courage of practical-minded fugitive assistants. The formerly enslaved Kentuckian; his wife, Harriet; and their son, Joseph, arrived in Boston in 1846. Over the years, the Haydens were responsible for concealing, feeding, employing, and otherwise aiding hundreds of southern escapees, taking in as many as thirteen people at a time. The men found work as whitewashers, tailors, tenders, hairdressers, waiters, and workers in the Haydens' clothing store.[11]

For the most part, men of this leadership class controlled their own workplaces, owned their own tools, and pocketed the profits, meager though they might be, when they sold their wares and services. They raised their voices at frequent "indignation (i.e., protest) meetings," of which the October 4 gathering was a typical, if a particularly large and fervent, example. They founded debating and literary societies and patronized each other's lectures as well as those of visiting dignitaries. They organized petitions to present to the Boston City Council, the State of Massachusetts, and the federal government. Their names—perhaps forty or so in total—were ubiquitous on lists of fugitive assistants. Self-conscious in their roles as leaders, many of these men joined Black fraternal orders. Some of these orders paralleled a white group that purposely excluded Blacks; examples included the Prince Hall Masons (founded in Boston in 1775) and the Bay State chapter of the Grand United Order of Odd Fellows (Boston, 1846).[12]

In contrast to these associations, which admitted only men, some independent orders, such as the Independent Order of Samaritans and the Daughters of Samaria (Boston, 1847), included women. In addition to joining groups such as these, Boston's Black women founded their own: the Afric-American Female Intelligence Society in 1832, Daughters of Zion in 1845, the Female Benevolent Forum in 1850, and a plethora of church missionary societies. They also played a critical role in the abolitionist cause, raising money, organizing petitions, speaking, and serving as fugitive assistants via the Boston Female Anti-Slavery Society (1833–1840) and the gender-integrated American Anti-Slavery Society.[13]

Some outspoken Black Bostonians also used their workplace to make an explicit political statement about the Fugitive Slave Act. Henry Weeden owned a tailor shop on Franklin Avenue. He served as president of the NEFA and helped to organize opposition against segregated schools and the annexation of Texas. One day in December 1850, a customer, Watson Freeman, entered Weeden's shop carrying an overcoat that needed to be repaired. Freeman was one of six US marshals in Boston appointed by President Franklin Pierce to enforce the new law. Weeden sent Freeman a letter explaining why he refused to mend the coat: "Principle first. Money afterwards." Outraged by a comment Freeman had made about his own eagerness to abide by the letter of the new law, Weeden wrote, "Though a poor man I crave the patronage of no Being that would volunteer his services to arrest a Fugitive Slave or that 'would hang 100 Niggers for 25 cents each.'"[14]

Other Black Bostonians used their professional skills to aid individuals and groups fleeing slavery. The prominent attorney Robert Morris (the grandson of a man captured and enslaved in Africa) did legal work for some recent arrivals forced to sort out thorny family relations in the North but unable to afford a white lawyer. During the 1850s his clients included a woman who sued a man she claimed was her husband for support; he defended himself by arguing that she was a fugitive, and as an enslaved woman could make no demands upon him. Morris also represented Lewis Howard, a fugitive carpenter from Richmond, and his wife, Nancy, in the sensational Ellen Starr case of the late 1850s; the couple sought to adopt the formerly enslaved girl against the wishes of a man claiming to be her grandfather. Morris found his clients' legal difficulties to be a source of personal

Born in Salem, Massachusetts, in 1823, Robert Morris was admitted to the Massachusetts bar in 1847, becoming one of the first Black attorneys in the country. He combined routine tasks related to wills, real estate, mortgages, and evictions with work on behalf of fugitives from bondage and advocates of public-school integration. He built a highly successful private practice as a criminal defense lawyer as well; his clients included Irish immigrants as well as native-born Blacks and whites. *(Boston Athenaeum)*

income, though his pay for such services at times came in the form of their gratitude, not cash.[15]

All sorts of workplaces proved to be sites of resistance to the Fugitive Slave Act. By cooking and washing clothes for the freedom-seekers, wives and daughters played a prominent if largely unheralded role. Indeed, it is notable, but not surprising, that women were absent from the podium on October 4, though they were in the audience, applauding and cheering on the speakers. The paeans to manly resistance and the rights of free men made the meeting, like other formal protests in Faneuil Hall or Tremont Temple, a decidedly masculine enterprise.

Within weeks of the protest meeting, federal officials were on the hunt for the famous fugitive married couple William and Ellen Craft (now hidden away by members of the BVC) and others.

Attendance at local churches, including, most notably, Twelfth Baptist (which included many escaped enslaved workers among its congregants), fell precipitously, as some members stayed away from public spaces and others headed to Canada. Fifteen families migrated from Boston to the small town of Biddulph Township in southwestern Ontario. As hundreds in hiding found themselves no longer beyond the reach of the bloodhounds, Black Bostonians embraced the roles of picket and scout, posting notices of slave owners' agents newly arrived in town, and urging the use of guns and knives as weapons of individual and collective self-defense.[16]

One day in mid-March, 1856, an enslaved woman named Rebecca Robinson Jones and her three daughters, ages six to nine, stepped off a Norfolk, Virginia, dock and onto the deck of a schooner captained by Alfred Fountain. Unlike many other fugitives, the twenty-eight-year-old mother wore no disguise, and she boldly ushered the children onto the boat with her. Later, William Still, an Underground Railroad conductor in Philadelphia, remembered that she "firmly resolved to be the slave of no master, nor to allow her three interesting children to grow up in slavery."[17]

Jones's decision to rely on Captain Fountain carried its own risks; he was well known to Norfolk authorities as a committed abolitionist who had transported many runaways to freedom in the North. The November before, he had bluffed his way out of a tough spot with the Norfolk mayor, who, together with a "posse of officers," had boarded Fountain's vessel in search of stowaways. In a show of bravado, the captain seized an axe and vigorously began to chop a hole in his own deck, a ploy to convince the startled onlookers that no one was secreted below. Satisfied, the mayor and his entourage departed the ship, and Fountain sailed off, with twenty-one men and women hidden underneath a cargo of wheat stowed in the hold.[18]

William Still considered Jones an uncommonly courageous woman—"a true-born heroine"—and, tellingly, once in Boston she kept her name and found a job right away. Back in Norfolk, her owner offered a $150 reward for her and her daughters. Yet it took a great deal more than raw courage to escape by water from the Virginia Peninsula; it took money. The quest for freedom was a serious business, with cash changing hands several times over. Jones had used the services of Norfolk's mysterious Dr. Harry Lundy, sometimes identified as a doctor and sometimes as a dentist. An illiterate free person of color, Lundy employed a scribe who took care of his correspondence and forged papers. The routine charge per clandestine passenger was $25 (about $800 in today's money); most of those who availed themselves of Lundy's services were men who had hired themselves out or otherwise earned enough to afford passage. Lundy kept some of the fee and paid his helper, and Captain Fountain received a share as well. On board, members of the crew might demand an additional fee (a bribe), pushing the price of liberty even higher. Still, Lundy was a miracle-worker for those determined to journey to Boston and for those Bostonians who wanted to bring loved ones north.[19]

The week before Rebecca Jones made her dangerous voyage, her brother Isaiah Robinson had escaped to Boston. The many refugees from Virginia living there encouraged and enabled others to follow. In October Rebecca wrote to Still from the Parker House in Boston, a new hotel catering to a wealthy clientele; she was probably living there while working as a domestic. In a few years she would marry William Riley, two years her junior, who worked alternately in the city as a laborer, a jobber, a barber, and a porter. Riley's father was part of a cohort of Brattle Street clothing dealers who lived and worked near each other, and his family sheltered fugitive slaves, as did their next-door neighbors, the Haydens.[20]

Once safely in the Bay State, both Rebecca and her brother had probably relied on help from Mark DeMortie, a shoemaker and one of Lundy's former employees, who had settled in Boston four years before the siblings' arrival. Born in Norfolk in 1829 to Haitian Francophone parents (it is unclear whether he was born enslaved or free), DeMortie had worked for Lundy for several years, probably beginning in 1848, and took credit for helping twenty-two people reach freedom. He traveled to Boston and back with some regularity, consulting with fugitive assistants about the financing of upcoming rescues. Sometime in 1851 or 1852, the young man wrote a letter on behalf of an enslaved woman who was hoping to join her brother in Boston; but, as he later recalled, the letter was "intercepted by her so called master, and I had to resort to the same means to make my own escape as I had sent the poor slaves." DeMortie's precocious sister Louisa married another Norfolk man, John Oliver, and all three moved to Boston in 1852, soon to be joined by the siblings' mother, Frances. The Virginia diaspora in Boston—at least the permanent element of it—functioned as a bulwark of freedom, accommodating many newcomers.[21]

Virginia-born Peter Randolph was also able to supplement his income by boarding runaways, though it is uncertain whether he and Amelia lost or made money or broke even in the process. In January 1854 the BVC paid Randolph $51 to hide three men, who eventually made their way to Canada. In fact, the business of assisting fugitives proved to be a lively and varied enterprise. Lewis Hayden got paid for distributing handbills warning of slave-catchers and for boarding fugitives, and he was reimbursed for covering funerals of children who died, as well as for the carriage fare he paid for fugitives to go on to points north and west. Other assistants were paid for clothing, food, and fuel they provided for people on the run. Antislavery ship captains received compensation as well: Austin Bearse, for example, for monitoring incoming ships in Boston Harbor, and Alfred Fountain for transporting enslaved people from the South to New York City or Boston (up to $100 per passenger). Fugitive assistance was both a moral calling and a business, though a business that provided very few with a full-time livelihood.[22]

Samuel May Jr. and other white abolitionists scrutinized fugitives and recent southern migrants and assessed their willingness to work in Boston; yet these whites rarely factored into their "experiment" the trauma suffered by men and women who fled from slavery and made their way north. To expect the refugees to find a job immediately upon arriving in Boston was to ignore the tremendous emotional and physical residues of slavery and flight itself. Indeed, these individuals constituted a peculiar subset of Boston workers—native southerners bringing with them vivid memories of loved ones left behind and of the perilous journey north. Unlike newcomers from foreign countries, these freedom-seekers lived and labored under the constant threat of deportation (i.e., rendition back south).

Many fugitives made the decision to escape after they had endured some sort of horrific physical or emotional abuse or the threat of it. In recounting their last days in slavery, they described vicious beatings, floggings, and shootings, the fear that they or family members were about to be sold, or the reality of such separations. A goodly number started out on a surreptitious journey only to be caught and dragged back to their owners, slaveholders who had no compunction about maiming, selling, or even killing those captured that they might serve as examples to others.[23]

Even for successful runaways, the journey north, by sea or land, held its own terrors. Once aboard ship, most fugitives had to remain hidden. Squeezed into the hold during what could turn out to be a weeks-long voyage, sweltering or freezing, depending on the weather; concealed somewhere in or among the ship's cargo, whether on top of a pile of logs or in a hole cut in a bale of cotton; immobilized next to a steamer's boiler, where the heat and coal dust were almost unbearable, many runaways arrived at the Boston docks wounded, physically ill, and shaken to the core. One woman stowaway who kept her child in her arms for seven straight days, relying on the ship's cook to feed them both, disembarked nearly paralyzed. For seventy-five days Clarissa Davis hid in a "miserable coop" in Portsmouth, Virginia, hoping for a rainstorm that would reduce visibility and also the number of people on the docks, which might give her a chance to sneak aboard a steamship in the harbor. She reached Massachusetts safely after traveling in a wooden box on board the packet *City of Richmond*. Those who traveled by foot suffered from hunger, frostbitten feet, and exhaustion, not to mention the constant fear they would be discovered. Some dared to earn money along the way, working for a farmer in his fields or for a ship's engineer in the fire room, always looking over their shoulder. In his flight from rural Maryland, Frederick Douglass disguised himself as a seaman and traveled by foot, train, ferry, steamboat, and stagecoach—seven legs in all, before reaching New Bedford. The passage between slavery and freedom was an ordeal from which many might never fully recover.[24]

Responding to the demands for payment from brokers, dockworkers, crew members, and captains—not all of them imbued with lofty abolitionist principles—some fugitives had to pay up to $100 for a safe escape, leaving them penniless when they finally arrived on free soil. A few managed to abscond with cash or a gold watch or some other kind of pocketable valuable that they could sell in Boston for a few nights' worth of lodgings. (In these cases, sheriffs added "thief" to the crime of running away.) Some wore their assets in the form of fine clothes purloined from a master's or mistress's wardrobe, hoping to fetch a good price for them in a secondhand clothing shop. Leonard Black left Virginia for a place called Boston—"though I knew not whether Boston was a State or a city"—and at one point along the way abandoned the bundle of clothes and $3.75 he had with him when he saw a menacing white man. Most left as unobtrusively as possible, bearing little of material value to begin their new lives.[25]

Together with Norfolk's Fountain, Boston's Austin Bearse was one of only a handful of ship captains determined to transport enslaved people from the South to the North. He ran a packet between Boston and Virginia from the summer through the fall, and then some years went coasting to South Carolina and Georgia during the winter months. He worked with the BVC, which at times enlisted a Black woman to sell pies and fruit to the crew of a vessel anchored in Boston Harbor; she would report back about whether stowaways were on board, and, if so, under the cover of darkness, committee members rowed out to ships and spirited men and women off sloops, barques, and steamers. Those rescued first needed a change of clothing—the men perhaps a "fishing suit" to replace the "slave dress of tow cloth." Some heeded advice and found a position on a fishing vessel, or went "a whaling," a voyage that might last several years.[26]

Unremitting toil was the hallmark of enslavement, and fugitives and migrants generally understood that wage earning represented the next and necessary step on the way to safety and independence in the North. Baltimore's William Howard noted, "I expected to work for a living, go where I would. I could not be stopped from working." Many men and women who departed from a southern port and had the cash to pay or bribe their way north also had some experience working in a city. In certain respects, then, the transition from dock work in Richmond to dock work in Boston was not a difficult one. The same could be said for the jobs of gardeners and porters. However, fugitives skilled in plantation work—blacksmiths, coopers, carpenters—rarely found the same jobs in Boston. Nor did formerly enslaved hostlers, carriage drivers, or teamsters always secure employment working with horses. Upon his arrival in Boston, Peter Randolph, who had been a blacksmith, became a janitor and a tender.[27]

An unknown number of fugitives filled the ranks of dockworkers and waiters in Boston. Harvey Parker, proprietor of his eponymous restaurant in a cellar on Court Square, offered his downtown clientele "breakfasts, dinners and suppers at all hours of the day and evening." Two waiters targeted by federal marshals soon after the passage of the Fugitive Slave Act were serving customers at Parker's. Formerly enslaved house servants might work at the elaborate banquets sponsored by fraternal groups and city authorities. The largest hotel dining rooms seated up to two hundred guests at a time and catered to tourists, who expected Black men to serve them their gin slings and mint juleps as well as their food.[28]

The siblings Harriet and John S. Jacobs had to make a living while keeping an eye out for their owner or his agent. Abandoning the lecture circuit after canvassing upstate New York in the late 1840s, John moved to Rochester, where he worked on *The North Star* and opened his own oyster restaurant. When that venture failed, he and his sister went back to New York City, but before long he was on his way to the West Coast. Meanwhile, Harriet spent her days anxiously scanning the newspapers to see which white southerners had taken up residence in local hotels. In June 1851 John was working in California, prospecting for gold but, according to Harriet, by October he "came out poorer than when he went in," despite moving from the mines to the "dry diggings," riverbeds of gravel. The end of 1852 found him once again in dire financial straits. He took off for Australia, where gold had been discovered the year before. William Cooper Nell wrote that he "hope[d] John will be lucky in Australia—how richly he deserves success."[29]

Harriet had her own struggles as a servant wholly reliant on the well-to-do Nathaniel Parker Willis and his wife, Cornelia. In the 1840s Jacobs had worked in Boston as a seamstress. Now, as the nanny for the Willises' children, she accompanied the family as they moved back and forth between New York City and New

Bedford, Cornelia's childhood home. Jacobs missed her own son and daughter, who were in the care of others, as she could not keep them at the Willises'. She resented that Cornelia showed no interest in either of them—their current whereabouts or even their scandalous origins. (They were the children of a white man.) When her daughter, Louisa, turned seventeen and began to make her own way in the world, Harriet noted that the life of a servant was hard and demeaning: "Louisa would not be happy to live that way. She wants to seek her own livlihood [*sic*] where she thinks she can be most useful."[30]

The runaway Mary Walker was similarly distressed that her white employers failed to appreciate the heartache she felt at leaving her children behind. In 1850, with the help of acquaintances, the thirty-two-year-old Walker had managed to escape from Philadelphia, where her owner had traveled with her from North Carolina. She eventually found refuge with a white clergyman, Peter Lesley, and his wife, Susan, in Milton, Massachusetts. A Philadelphia relative of the Lesleys assured them, of Walker, "All she asks is work, and this she is willing to perform cheerfully." Though she was a skilled seamstress, specializing in shirts, Mary Walker took on a peripatetic life as a housekeeper. Wracked with guilt about her own enslaved offspring, she balked at situations that required her to care for children. She explained to Susan Lesley, "Mrs. L., it is not the life I am fit for. I don't want to be with children. It is always reminding me of my own, & what shall I do?" Mary's refusal to serve as a nanny or a governess made her difficult to place in a white family, despite the concern of sympathetic benefactors.[31]

It was the women who often faced challenges in adapting to new ways of work. Bethany Veney's sense of dislocation was not unusual among southern women recently arrived in the North. She had been purchased by an antislavery man in Virginia, who had sent her and her son to live in Providence, Rhode Island, beyond the reach of the overseer, the jailer, and the auctioneer.

Still, she wrote later, "I had left behind me every one I had ever known." She was, she thought, "a stranger in a strange land; and it was no wonder, perhaps, that a dreadful loneliness and homesickness came over me." Adding to her misery was the kitchen of her new employer, for it contained "all sorts of Yankee inventions and improvements to make work easy and pleasant. There were dishes and pans of every description, clean and distinct cloths for all purposes, brushes and brooms for different uses." While she yearned for her "own people" back in Virginia, she wrote, "never could I forget to be grateful for my escape from a system under which I had suffered so much."[32]

THOUGH BLACK PEOPLE were shut out of many different kinds of jobs, one potentially lucrative means of making a living was available to them and to them alone—pretending to be an escaped slave. These were the small number of fugitive impostors seeking funds to free their fictional families in the South. Given the ease of a quick name change and the absence of any standard kind of identification, impostors of all kinds were ubiquitous, their true identities often revealed only after they had fled town for fresh fields of labor. Although mainly men, the pretenders—as "unprincipled persons," in the words of *The Liberator*—were not limited to one gender. One Mary Adams—tall, slender, stooped, with a "yellow complexion" and curly hair—managed to dupe the noted abolitionist Abby Kelley Foster.[33]

These clever tricksters, some of them consummate performers, represented a subset of people who presented themselves to the public as agents raising money for churches, orphanages, missionary societies, or schools. One Black man made the rounds in eastern Massachusetts posing as a Methodist minister, soliciting funds for a church in the West. He also claimed to be an agent for his brother, a jewelry store owner in La Salle, Illinois. The *Boston Herald* reported that he was "dressed up splendidly in black broadcloth and wore a white neck-tie of unusual dimensions." Carrying a letter of introduction from a John Tappan of Poughkeepsie, he also told the clerk for Palmer and Bachelder on Washington Street that he had a reference from a respected reverend—surely a golden ticket for any thief trying to prove his respectability.[34]

The key to a successful career as a fugitive impostor was a knack for narrative. An evening lecture at Tremont Temple that featured a woman presented as a runaway and perched (or displayed) on the dais could net over $200, a sum too large for many a talented storyteller to resist. Especially effective was a convincing tale of immediate family members still languishing in the South. William Smith knocked on doors in East Cambridge "narrating a pitiful story about a wife and large numbers of children, for whom he wanted relief." The major abolitionist groups denounced him as an impostor. If they were to root out this scourge of fraud, though, they would need contacts in the South, or paid informants, to track down the origins of everyone who applied for aid. The proliferation of con artists encouraged skepticism among fugitive assistants and prompted dismay among members of the Black community.[35]

Some cases were straightforward—when the impostor admitted the deception, or when a source revealed that the individual in question was actually a free person of color with a bogus story to sell. However, many other cases were murky, and at times the benefactor had to make an educated guess based on the supplicant's demeanor. John W. Browne, an agent for the Boston Vigilance Committee, kept a detailed log of the persons who presented themselves to that group in 1846 and 1847. His rendering of their life histories, along with a commentary on each, suggests the standard by which the fugitives' stories were judged as either genuine or fake. For example, fugitive assistants saw impure motives in a Black person's failure either to express sufficient gratitude or to use donations in the stipulated manner. Boston's John

R. Taylor, who lodged several runaways, expressed his doubts about one Thomas Miller—"thinks him an imposter"—because Miller wanted to take his family to Canada, but refused the proffered tickets and supplies and asked for cash instead. In another case, Browne made no mention of the inconsistent details of the supplicant's story, but instead drew on Taylor's observations of the fugitive. Taylor reported seeing the fellow "in a house of ill fame in Ann St. with his companion, on the forenoon of the 27th of March, his head in a white woman's lap, his arm around her waist." (What the well-to-do Taylor was doing in the North End vice district was left unsaid.)[36]

A similar case in which untoward behavior was considered a tip-off concerned William Cockerell, who did not help the antislavery cause by canvassing Boston "for the purpose, as he stated, of purchasing the freedom of his eldest son, who is held in slavery." He stole two pairs of pants and a coat from his host, whose "liberality was but ill repaid." The pilfering of clothing did not necessarily unmask an impostor, but fugitive assistants expected truly worthy objects of their benevolence to demonstrate upright behavior. With the right story, the impostor could make a living, but only if he or she moved from one place to another; this job entailed a life on the run.[37]

Impostors knew what many fugitives learned: that stories of bondage sold. Frederick Douglass proved that Boston presented an attractive market for slave narratives well told, whether in literary or visual form. Still, some autobiographies, such as Peter Randolph's, ultimately failed to find a large audience. Henry Watson, who had managed to talk his way onto a brig leaving for Boston from a Mississippi river port, wrote a *Narrative* of his life in 1848. He traveled around New England selling copies for 12½ cents each in order to provide for, as he put it, "a family of small children dependant upon me." Turning to other media, some fugitives hoped to make a living by exhibiting panoramas: large, circular panels of paintings on a theme related to their own experiences.

In April 1850, the famous fugitive Henry "Box" Brown obtained a license from the Boston City Council to show *Mirror of Slavery*, depicting scenes from the "peculiar institution." (The year before, he had mailed himself in a large crate to Philadelphia abolitionists.) Still menaced by slave-catchers a year after arriving in the North, Brown took the exhibit to England, where it competed with a panorama developed by another runaway slave, William Wells Brown (who also published his life story). Panoramas, like other kinds of exhibits, earned some enterprising fugitives a livelihood.[38]

For abolitionist activists who could secure financial backing, mounting this kind of show seemed preferable to hawking an autobiography or lecturing on the evils of slavery. Indeed, by the mid-1850s, speakers were venturing farther into the northern hinterland in search of fresh, untapped audiences, with mixed success. Many whites found the whole subject of slavery unpleasant; in the words of one white man, "it was too hard for their wives and families to be obliged to sit and hear me tell of the brutality of slaveholders and their abettors." Under these conditions, fugitives and white abolitionists who lacked the name recognition of a Douglass had no choice but to explore alternative ways to make money for themselves, their families, and the cause.[39]

PETER RANDOLPH AND his fellow passengers from the *Thomas H. Thompson* arrived in Boston as free people, but they lived, worked, and worshipped among fugitives from slavery. Most Black men in Boston were moving things—ashes, coal, furniture, consumer goods, supplies for stores, and, with a few exceptions, in the summer of 1850 all the Edloe men were working as laborers or "jobbers." Carter Selden quickly found a job as porter, a stable position that earned him a listing in the 1849 city directory; he had secured a patron, or a number of them, who furnished him steady work over the next decades. The daily toil of wives, sisters, and daughters remained hidden from official census-takers, who paid no mind to the labor, waged or unwaged, of many Black seamstresses, boardinghouse keepers, cooks, and domestic servants if they were laboring under the roof of their own families and not that of a white employer. Spouses living together, mothers keeping house, and children attending school—all were welcome changes from family life under slavery.

Yet death took a heavy toll on the migrants. Several, including Carter Selden's wife Louisa, died before they could celebrate the third anniversary of their promenade up "the free streets of Boston." Selden then married Sarah Hazard of Kingston, Rhode Island, and together they had two daughters in short order—Agnes, born in 1848, and Mary, in 1849; a third daughter, Elizabeth, born in 1850, lived only five weeks. Carter also lost his former mother-in-law, and his children their grandmother, when Lucy Fountain, Louisa's mother and the oldest woman of the Edloe Sixty-Six, died of smallpox in June 1850.[40]

Peter and Amelia Randolph had endured several tragedies since their decision to travel north—the deaths of baby Harriet and of Peter's brothers, twenty-two-year-old Richard and ten-year-old James. Sustaining the Randolphs during this early period was their connection to the Twelfth Baptist Church, which included many migrants from Virginia, some born free and others enslaved. On Sundays they sang Baptist hymns and heard the cadences of the Reverend Leonard Grimes, his sermons echoes of their worship services in the brush arbors of the Mount Pleasant plantation. The pastor also officiated at the weddings of several Edloe migrants. Marriages, new babies, and baptisms, no less than the deaths of several of the original migrants, marked the intermingled joy and sorrow of those first few years in Boston.[41]

Grimes himself proved to be one of Boston's most resourceful fugitive assistants. Born in 1815 in Leesburg, Virginia, to a free woman of color, he had developed his own drayage business. In 1839 he was arrested, convicted, and jailed in Richmond for trying to help an enslaved family escape to the North. Released in 1840, he became an ordained Baptist minister, and six years later he moved his family to New Bedford. In 1848 he answered a call to preach from a small splinter group that had separated from Boston's Independent African Church. His wife, Octavia, born free in Washington, DC, in 1820, became his lifelong partner in sustaining Twelfth Baptist. Ignoring the dictates of the NEFA, which opposed rewarding slaveholders with a purchase price for their human property, Twelfth Baptist sponsored fund-raisers to buy fugitives from their owners as well as fugitives' families still in the South. For his part, Leonard Grimes had no compunction about descending from the pulpit and injecting himself into two spectacular 1851 rendition cases.[42]

The first case centered on Shadrach Minkins, thirty-seven, who was still wearing his waiter's apron when he was arrested at Harvey Parker's Court Square restaurant on February 15. In what was now a familiar scenario, Minkins had saved enough money from working in Norfolk to make his way north aboard a Boston-bound vessel. The flagrant lawbreaking by the Boston Vigilance Committee members who had masterminded the Crafts' successful escape to England in 1850 had infuriated federal and local authorities alike. One of Boston's six federal commissioners, George Ticknor Curtis, was now hoping to make a national example of Minkins deep in the heart of radical abolitionist territory.[43]

As soon as Minkins was taken into custody, the BVC distributed handbills announcing the arrest and urging local businesses not to serve the professional slave-catcher who had pursued him. The afternoon of his arrest, he was marched across the square from the restaurant and into the courthouse, where the Reverend Grimes took his place next to him, providing moral support for one of his own congregants. Then, about twenty men rushed into the courtroom, and before the astonished officials could act or react, the rescuers had hustled Minkins down the steps of the building and thrust him into a waiting carriage. With the aid of supporters he eventually made his way to Montreal. Robert Morris, Lewis Hayden, and John P. Coburn facilitated the escape. Boston Mayor John P. Bigelow, together with merchants of the slave provisioning trade, howled, convinced that Boston's loss of export business to southern planters would be New York City's gain. The *Savannah Republican* joined in the chorus of outrage: "*The City of Boston is a black speck on the map—disgraced! by the lowest—the meanest*, THE BLACKEST kind of NULLIFICATION!!!"[44]

The conservative Boston city establishment resented the way renditions disrupted the social order and hoped both the protests and the arrests would soon end. The sea captain Austin Bearse ridiculed the mayor, the board of aldermen, and the common council: "[They] plump themselves down on their knees," he said, the better to prostrate themselves before the federal authorities and southern stealers of flesh, and "hold up their cheeks, both sides at once, to be smitten and spit upon. With a cowardly humility they exclaim, 'We are more ready than ever to do any dirty work you can find for our hands to do!'" At its meetings the September before, the city council had made no mention of the new Fugitive Slave Act or its ramifications, only expressing concern that an upcoming protest on the Common would lead to an unfortunate uptick of carriage traffic in the surrounding streets.[45]

Minkins had just barely made it to Canada when a new Boston case renewed tensions. On February 21 in Savannah, a skilled bricklayer named Thomas Sims stowed away on the *M. & J. C. Gilmore*, a brig bound for Boston the next day. Thin, with delicate features, and looking younger than his twenty-three years, Sims had probably heard of the Minkins episode the week before. His master, a rice planter named James Potter, allowed Sims considerable latitude in living on his own and making money, a portion of which he owed to his owner each month. Sims most certainly had the means to bribe a crew member, or two or three. He survived a two-week journey on the ship and promptly found a place to live in a large seamen's boardinghouse on Ann Street in the North End, where no one asked for papers or checked last names. Potter had dispatched two agents to Boston, and it was a tip from them that alerted the police, who found Sims walking on Endicott Street the night of April 3. As the officers moved to arrest him, he whipped out a knife and stabbed one of his captors in the thigh, yelling for help from passers-by, "I am in the hands of the kidnappers!"[46]

Beginning the next day, the US marshal Charles Devens and his deputies, the US Circuit Court commissioner George Ticknor Curtis, the justices of the Massachusetts Supreme Judicial Court, and a battery of attorneys prepared to do legal battle over the Fugitive Slave Act. For the next few days, crowds gathered outside the courthouse where Sims was being held. On Friday, April 11, Leonard Grimes planned to position a mattress outside his third-story cell and urge him to take a literal leap of faith, a scheme that collapsed when workmen outfitted the cell windows with iron bars. Whether someone had alerted them to Grimes's plan is unknown.[47]

Denied the right to defend himself, Sims had little recourse but to remain silent during the proceedings. The court wasted little time ruling that he must be returned to Potter. Wary of a reprise of the Shadrach Minkins debacle, on Saturday morning Boston authorities enlisted 150 men—members of the city watch armed with clubs and hooks, and police armed with swords—to escort Sims from the courthouse to the brig *Acorn*. No doubt hoping to absolve himself of responsibility for the whole affair, the captain of the *Gilmore* paid the expenses for Sims's five-day trip back to Savannah. The *Acorn* sailed out of Boston Harbor with two newly mounted cannon to ward off abolitionist pirates. The estimated cost of Sims's capture and return to Potter amounted to between $10,000 and $20,000 (today's equivalent of $370,000 to $740,000), most of it borne by the city. Even proslavery cotton merchants considered the process too exhausting and expensive to bear.[48]

The rescue of Minkins and the rendition of Sims intensified the ongoing process of radicalization among Boston's Black community. Now leaders spoke openly about armed self-defense. In 1852 attorney Robert Morris and Charles Lenox Remond of Salem began petitioning the Massachusetts Legislature for a charter for an all-Black militia, to be called the Massasoit Guards. Appealing to the rising nativist sentiment in Massachusetts, Morris claimed, "Some of the petitioners whom I have the honor to represent, can trace back their ancestry to a time long before an Englishman or any white foreigner stood upon American ground." Lawmakers denied the men's request; soldiering was a form of labor fit only for (white) men of honor.[49]

Ironically, the decidedly militant turn among Black leaders manifested itself in a heightened interest in partisan politics. The rise of the short-lived Free Soil Party (active between 1848 and 1854) foreshadowed the end of the national two-party system of Whigs and Democrats, a system premised on the need to avoid the issue of slavery altogether. Most Blacks revered William Lloyd Garrison, and they knew that wealthy whites looked down on him because of his modest origins. At the same time, an increasing number of activists began to renounce both his apolitical stance and his call for Christian love and forgiveness in the fight against slavery.

Still, the path to Black political influence was almost insurmountable, so relatively few were enfranchised. In 1850 the city's 136,000 residents included 88,000 who were born in the United States and 48,000 born in another country; 2,000 of the total were Black. Only property owners who had paid their taxes could vote, though renters might qualify with taxable personal property; an estimated 50 percent of eligible Black men actually paid the $1.50 poll tax, in the 1850s yielding a bloc of perhaps 200–250 registrants. Overall, the Black community remained highly engaged in partisan activities, and in late 1852 public meetings under the auspices of the Colored Citizens of the Free Soil Party urged political action. At one of their meetings the group endorsed a way forward that would leave the traditional two parties behind: "That as the Whig and so-called Democracies of this country are endeavoring to crush, debase, and dehumanize us as a people, any man among us voting for their respective candidates, virtually recognizes the righteousness of their principles and shall be held up to a public reprobation as a . . . pest and a nuisance."[50]

Impatient with Garrison's strategy of moral suasion, Frederick Douglass ramped up a public feud with his former mentor. On August 2, speaking at Twelfth Baptist, Douglass railed for more than an hour against the "spirit of caste" that infected the city of Boston, an ugly spirit that manifested itself in white men's refusal to hire Black men for decent jobs. According to Douglass, employers were hostage to their white employees—"the working men—the democratic part of the community—who hate the colored man." "Even abolitionists do not reduce their theory to practice," he said. "*They* will not take us into *their* stores, their counting houses, as clerks, bookkeepers, &c 'because,' say they, 'It will hurt our business.' They will not take our children into their workshops for their hands [i.e., employees] will not allow it. Everything is seemingly against us. We must do something for ourselves."[51]

Around this time Douglass was imploring white antislavery employers to cease talking and act: "We appeal to the abolitionists," he wrote in his paper. "What boss anti-slavery mechanic will take a black boy into his wheelwright shop, his blacksmith's shop, his joiner's shop, his cabinet shop? Here is something practical; where are the whites and where are the blacks who will respond to it?" In his speeches and writings, Douglass focused on the lack of Black clerks and skilled craftsmen, while the paucity of Black lawyers and physicians scarcely warranted mention. In charting their own course, at least some Black leaders were breaking with Garrison over his "come-outerism"—from established churches, from political parties of any kind—in an effort to work with and within established institutions for the abolitionist cause; but they now also began to take him to task over his indifference toward Black job-seekers all over the North.[52]

Not long after Douglass's speech, at a meeting held at Twelfth Baptist, a group of Massachusetts Colored Convention leaders, including Hayden, Morris, Grimes, and Nell, sought to repudiate Douglass's harsh words toward Garrison and other whites. Meeting as a state council, they acknowledged that the Black man found economic success difficult to achieve, but "let him work the harder, urge his way through the various avenues of commercial, mechanical, and social advancement, and eventually the summit of success will be attained." This optimistic assessment had little basis in reality, and it is unclear whether these men actually believed it. But it echoed the uplift ideology of which white abolitionists were so fond, the notion that gainful employment was a matter of personal responsibility on the part of the job-seeker.[53]

Boston's fugitive economy touched the lives of virtually all the city's Black workers, many of whom were vulnerable to slave-catchers whether they had fled from bondage or not. Transporting and assisting desperate freedom-seekers from the South involved financial transactions as well as gestures of goodwill and self-sacrifice. Newcomers to the city sought to find wage work and carve out their own communities in boardinghouses, churches, and workplaces. Various groups and individuals exploited the public's fascination with men, women, and children who had successfully escaped slavery; fugitives marketed their stories, impostors earned a tenuous livelihood, and antislavery societies enhanced their coffers. Ultimately, the entire Black population mobilized itself against federal marshals and bounty-hunting slave-catchers; going about one's everyday work necessitated a heightened vigilance. On the surface, the crooked streets and brick canyons of Boston seemed to bear little resemblance to the isolated, swampy maroon colonies of runaways in the South; but both places existed as precarious refuges where freedom-seekers hoped to live life on their own terms, far from slave drivers and overseers.

The fugitive economy intersected with an underground economy that depended on the illicit provision of goods and services. The celebrated Thomas Sims had been hiding out in the North End's red-light district, where Black and white men and women worked side by side every day and night and stood side by side together in Police Court. In fact, gambling dens, dance halls, and brothels claimed the energies of those who created their own jobs in defiance of respectable society. These men and women accepted the threat of heavy-handed law enforcement and physical danger as a routine part of their jobs.

2

Underground Commons

Late one night a Boston police officer stopped an elderly Black man named Jum, who was walking on Salem Street in the North End, carrying a large sack on his back. Startled by the officer, Jum dropped the bag on the ground, but took care to keep its opening closed. Inside were two and a half dozen angry, squirming rats. Jum was delivering them to a smoke-filled basement where men would drink cheap New York whiskey and, with much hollering and carrying on, bet on how many of the rodents a dog could tear to pieces. Jum had caught his rats in the dark of night at a nearby stable, using a lantern to illuminate the stalls and a pair of curling tongs to pluck his prey off the floor. Stable hands appreciated his labors; it meant more hay for the horses and less for the rats. Meanwhile, Jum's haul this evening was bound to fetch him five dollars from the local rat pit owner. "Rats scarce now," said Jum, noting with satisfaction that he had collected "big ones, too," in his bag. The officer had to admit that it was "a pretty good evening's work," and let Jum go on his way. Such was the nature of a peculiar kind of entrepreneurship: recognizing the demand for rats and supplying it.[1]

For Black Bostonians, personal ambition and physical prowess could yield jobs not listed in the city directory. Indeed, a whole host of laborers carried on their work away from the scrutiny of newspaper reporters, police officers, and city officials—until, in some instances, they landed in the columns of the daily court report. Rat catchers, youthful errand-runners for professional gamblers, dance-hall musicians, and scammers toiled under risky conditions, thwarted in their ambitions by discrimination in conventional workplaces, but enterprising enough to embark on activities that promised financial gain.

Boston was first and foremost a port city. Many of its Black mariners, now mingling with men and women from the Upper South, the Mid-Atlantic, the Boston hinterland, and rural New England, hailed originally from far-flung places. The fortunes (such as they were) of dockworkers and haulers depended on the weather and on the annual rhythm of the seasons, with late fall and early spring the busiest times for shipments of cotton from the South. These men, together with casual workers of both genders, sought release from their strenuous labors at night, contributing to a vibrant, often violent, underground economy, an underground commons apart from "respectable society," where men and women pursued money, illicit pleasure, visceral thrills, or some combination of these—a place of shared danger. Grog shops, dance halls, brothels, and large seamen's boardinghouses defined the area around Ann and Richmond Streets near the wharves, an area variously called the "Black Sea" or the "Murder District" of Boston. Sex workers, professional gamblers, con men, musicians, and liquor dealers made money, but only if they could dodge the local police and survive the occasional knife fight.

Residential segregation was becoming ever more pronounced in mid-century Boston. However, certain aspects of city life defied the rigid lines drawn between Blacks and whites in the public schools and in the minds of many white people. At times on the streets or in a park people from all walks of life came together to glimpse the latest technological wonder on display. In the winter, "coasting on the Commons" attracted rich and poor,

Black and white boys whose various types of sleds were a study in "aristocracy and democracy," according to one amused reporter. In 1850, the census indicated that at least fifty-one couples had intermarried, Black and white; that figure was probably an undercount, given that some Indigenous husbands and wives might have been counted as either. Some white immigrants boarded in Black households, and some white servants worked for well-to-do Black employers. Some wealthy households included Black and white servants working together, and a few Black householders took in white boarders. The Massachusetts Peace Society, the Massachusetts Anti-Slavery Society, and a millennial sect called the Second Advent welcomed "promiscuous" audiences of Black and white women and men. Seamen of all hues gambled shoulder to shoulder with each other. In the infamous Ann Street district, white men slept with Black women, and Black men slept with white women—indeed, Police Court proceedings brought to light every possible permutation of entwined male and female bodies, some involving commercial transactions, others not. In the basement "halls" and at fancy balls a range of skin colors was on display, as they were when witnesses took the stand in trials of accused assailants, murderers, pickpockets, and pickpocketresses. Men from all walks of life bet on their favorites in the bloody rat pits. One foreign visitor described these places, which came to life after 9:00 p.m., as drawing "a line between those who can afford to turn night into day, and those who cannot."[2]

For whites, Black neighborhoods were synonymous with illegal activities, primarily because those neighborhoods were composed largely (though not entirely) of impoverished people. In the early 1800s, the West End, on the north side of Beacon Hill and in a low-lying area near the Charles River, had gained a reputation for late-night carousing; but in this case the stigma of disorderliness attached firmly to people of color. By 1850 the households of respectable Black barbers, dressmakers, laundresses, bootblacks, whitewashers, and clothing dealers were intermingled with dwellings occupied by more transient day laborers. Peter and Amelia Randolph were property owners that year, with $1,400 in real estate, probably because he had secured a loan through the goodwill of a patron. They chafed at the association of their community with vice, and with the nighttime revels of drinkers and gamblers; whites referred to the area just west of the State House as "Mount Whoredom." In March 1850, a wealthy white broker named Madison Beal petitioned the city council "to have a nuisance abated, occasioned by coloured and other persons congregating in and about West Centre Street, in the night time, creating riots and noises." The Committee on Licenses threatened to shut down the offending enterprises, whose owners promised that in the future "there shall be no cause of complaint." Yet these enduring "congregations" often included young and old, male and female, Black and white.[3]

MEN AND WOMEN from all backgrounds pursued time-honored criminal and underhanded opportunities. The so-called *bagging fraternity* was not necessarily a fraternity at all, but mostly women, those skilled in concealing large bags under their dresses, the better to shoplift. Pickpockets at times worked in pairs, one blowing cigar smoke in the eyes of the unsuspecting pedestrian while the other lifted his wallet. This line of work appealed to "almost every age, sex, and color," according to one of the city's former police chiefs, Edward H. Savage. Most of the thieves relied on fencers to get rid of the goods, with a haul of fine clothing worth $1,200 earning the wayward seamstress a net of $100 (a reason why the city council demanded that every secondhand clothing dealer be licensed).[4]

In 1856 a Black cook, Francis Wiseman, was found guilty of stealing "considerable quantities of butter, flour, sugar, lard, and other groceries" from the household of his employer, B. F. Wilson. In pilfering the supplies, Wiseman had run a risk: if caught, he must either pay $20 in court costs or spend two months in the House of Correction; whatever the sentence, he would also forfeit Wilson's patronage. During the 1850s, the Boston police gradually slowed their arrests for crimes against morality such as drunkenness and fornication in favor of catching more thieves. Some chronic offenders circled in and out of the House of Correction so many times that their stealing seemed more a matter of compulsion than making a living.[5]

For some, the thrill of a lie well told or a heist well executed was worth the possible punishment. In the summer of 1853, a Black man named John Rogers tried to pull off two scams over just a few days. At one point he pretended to be the servant of a fictitious North Carolina visitor to Boston—a "Col. Prindle" staying at the Adams Hotel—and used that identity to gain access to the rooms of other guests and steal their belongings. Shortly after that he presented himself at a jewelry store, introducing himself as a successful gold miner recently returned from Mexico and California; he selected some watches and took them away, with the promise of returning with "the [gold] dust to pay the bill." Although most of Boston's thieves operated without a fake identity, some—Black or white—showed ingenuity in how they presented themselves, relieving stores and individuals of clothing, jewelry, and cash in the process. Others took wraps off of coatracks and laundry off of clotheslines.[6]

Kentucky's Leo L. Lloyd was the opposite of a fugitive impostor; he was a fugitive (from Kentucky) who pretended to have been born free. A man of great performative power, he hoped that his impressive talents as a storyteller would provide a livelihood more satisfying and lucrative than his job as a barber. He curried favor with the Boston scientific and reform establishment, presenting himself as an African ("Nubian") prince yearning to return to his native land and redeem it from its benighted condition by spreading the Christian gospel. Henry David Thoreau met him in Worcester in January 1855—Lloyd "introduced himself as a native of Africa and lectures on 'Young Africa'!! I never heard of anything but old Africa before." That year Lloyd joined luminaries John Rock, Leonard Grimes, Charles Lenox Remond, and William Cooper Nell in representing the Bay State at a national convention of Black men in Philadelphia.[7]

The Liberator began warning its readers about Lloyd, whom they called this "Prince of Humbug," in early 1856, claiming (correctly) that he was a runaway journeyman barber from Brattle Street by the (real) name of Baker. Over the next three years the editors continued to fulminate against him: "Still Deceiving the Public," warned one headline; perhaps his lack of a foreign accent was a tip-off. In 1859 Lloyd was distributing handbills announcing an upcoming concert he would be giving with two young Black women—the three performers together "the most highly cultivated and intelligent persons that have ever appeared in any public capacity in the United States." A review from the *Philadelphia Bulletin* commended him to audiences of discernment: "They are no roving Company of Squealers, but musicians of rare talent and culture."[8]

Lloyd managed to raise money because he had won the favor of prominent white Boston cultural and academic figures, politicians, and clergy. Bayard Taylor, a noted composer and author of Middle Eastern travelogues, was quoted as saying that Lloyd was "a cross between one of the Desert Tribes on the Western Frontier of Nubia (perhaps Kababbish), with one of the Central African Blacks of the Negro Race." Lloyd received endorsements from the legal scholar Rufus Choate and the Harvard biologist and geologist Louis Agassiz, a proponent of scientific racism. These men continued to believe Lloyd's origin story and to vouch for him, while Garrison continued to try to discredit him. In exposing Lloyd, *The Liberator* inadvertently praised his talents as a showman, describing him as "a small black man, of neat figure, short hair, bright eyes, and has a somewhat wirey walk, and has done much in the way of committing other persons' speeches and poetry, all of which he gets off with much ease." Only time would reveal his true motivations. Until then, he made money giving concerts and appealing to the curious.[9]

In the North End, seamen spent their days ashore and squandered their pay before shipping out again. Their desire for release, for the thrill of gambling, and for female companionship, no matter how fleeting, fueled various business enterprises. The career of one Black man, Joseph F. Clash, illuminates that part of Boston where all sorts of people came together either to have a good time, or to take advantage of those looking to have a good time. Clash himself pursued several ventures, as barber, dance-hall operator, pimp, and con man, ever ready to become the bare-knuckled aggressor when he felt circumstances demanded it. His money-making activities showcased the qualities of any successful businessman—financial investment in a physical plant, newspaper advertising, shrewd management of employees of various talents and temperaments, a good product for the money, and the cultivation of local police on the beat. Ultimately, Clash inhabited a world where elements of commercialized leisure—dancing, eating, gambling, prostitution—were enhanced by the consumption of copious amounts of alcohol. In a rum-soaked haze, entertainment, entrepreneurship, and mayhem all came together.

Clash was born in 1808 in Salem, Massachusetts. His father, Anthony (born in Maryland around 1771), was a ship's cook. At age nineteen, Joseph was sentenced to four years in the state penitentiary for larceny, though he did not serve the whole term. As early as the fall of 1840, the thirty-two-year-old was operating a barbershop on Boston's Hanover Street and selling tickets to vocal and instrumental concerts in Abiel Smith School. In the summer of 1842, together with several male and female associates, he was running a brothel and selling liquor on Sundays. A subsequent six-month stint in jail failed to dampen Clash's ambitions. Soon

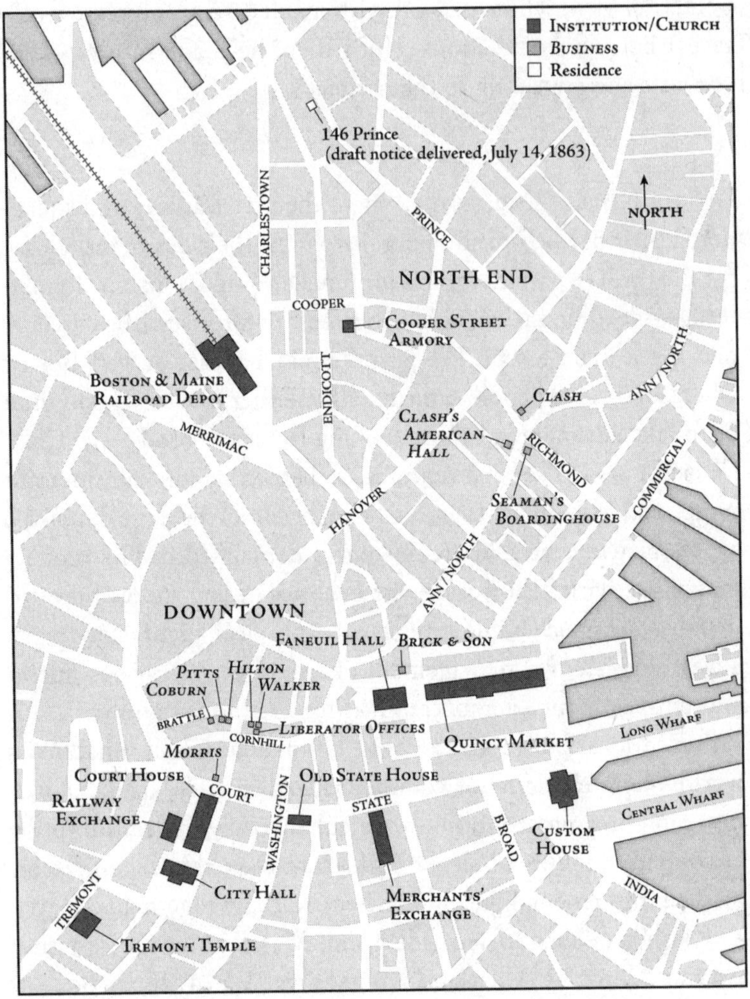

Downtown Boston and the North End, ca. 1860 *(Kate Blackmer)*

after he got out, he married a Black woman, Elizabeth Brown, twenty-six, in Boston.[10]

Clash figured in several high-profile murder cases in Boston. In the summer of 1844, the newspapers offered up salacious details—a victim bleeding to death from stab wounds administered with a Spanish dirk knife, several young Black and white prostitutes hovering near the scene on the sidewalk. The prelude to the late-night deadly encounter was a dance in Clash's basement "hall," where seamen played cards, enjoyed a fiddler's music, and paid to socialize with young women who would, for a fee, accompany them back to their lodgings. A few witnesses were sitting in their apartment windows on the night in question, smoking and enjoying the moonlit street scene. As usual, tempers were short from too much to drink. James Gilmore, the fiddler for the evening and a presumed witness, testified that one of the white men had asked him, "Where are you going, nigger?," and he replied, "I am going home sir." The defense lawyers in the case, Richard Henry Dana and Wendell Phillips, argued that the alleged assailant, their client, a white man named Peter York, had committed manslaughter, not premeditated murder, an argument that won the day and spared York the hangman's noose.[11]

In 1846, Clash testified in the trial of Albert Jackson Tirrell, a white man who had allegedly killed one Maria Bickford, a prostitute. Clash said that Bickford had once lived with him in his house on Ann Street. The case garnered national headlines when Tirrell's defense team argued that their client, a married man and father, had been sleepwalking when he had slit Bickford's throat, and this novel defense strategy had led to the defendant's acquittal. In a third case three years later, Clash served as a witness in the sensational Washington Goode case. Goode, a Black sailor, was charged with killing a romantic rival, Thomas Harding. Testifying for the prosecution, Clash admitted he knew the principals of the case, patrons of Ann Street's dram shops ("cellars"), and the one his friend Jeptha Harris owned, in particular. The woman in the middle of this triangle, Mary Ann Williams, was apparently a prostitute but made extra money by doing her clients' laundry. Clash spoke at some length relaying what he knew of her, but the defense challenged Clash's testimony on the grounds of his "competency," given the fact that he had served time in jail for keeping a brothel and selling liquor without a license. The district attorney then surprised the court by claiming that the governor, Edward Everett, had pardoned Clash, thus expunging his conviction. Clash's attorney, Robert Morris, presented the judge with a signed document to that effect. Goode was hanged after a public outcry that the trial had been unfair.[12]

Like other seaports, Boston had its share of brothels ("disorderly houses"). One perverse Boston booster, a correspondent for *Frederick Douglass' Paper*, claimed that "in no city in the Union are houses of ill-fame conducted so publicly and so shamelessly as in this city." For decades young Black and white women had been coming into Boston from the surrounding area in search of work only to be disappointed with their limited options. In the second decade of the nineteenth century, Nancy Prince, a Black woman, had moved from the North Shore to Boston "to get a higher price for my labor." Her older sister Sylvia also went to Boston, intending to work as a "nursery girl," but, in Nancy's words, she was "deluded away" and became a prostitute. Nancy found Sylvia in a brothel, held by force and intimidation by "the mother of harlots," surrounded by her "girls" and their customers.[13]

Some young women themselves were entrepreneurial. One night in November 1853, Jeremiah White, a white teamster from the small town of Stoughton, arrived in Ann Street with $20 in his pocket and an eagerness to sample the pleasures of big-city life. White paid 25 cents each to dance with a succession of Black women in one of the "halls," women whom he treated "liberally." Late that night he fell asleep—whether it was from fatigue, from too much to drink, or from the effects of something slipped into his drink was not reported—and when he awoke the next morning, he found that all his money was gone. The "sable" dancers knew a mark when they saw one, and one teamster's hard-earned wages paid for at least one Black woman's take that night.[14]

Faced with constant calls from the public for the police to address the noise, knife fights, and gun battles in the Ann Street district, city authorities acted periodically to quell the uproar. These efforts were often random and always ineffectual. Police Court on August 6, 1850, featured repeat offenders described as "a batch of colored night walkers, from the dark haunts of Ann Street [who] were complained of by watchman Ross, for going about in the dark hours of the night, soliciting weak men to do naughty family honors." A similar raid took place later in the month on Southac Street, netting two other young Black women; they were fined $30 and costs for their "bad behavior" and promptly went back to soliciting on the street.[15]

In the spring of 1851, the city marshal, Francis Tukey, decided that if he could not win a war against sin he could at least wage a public battle against it. He sent plainclothesmen to survey the dance halls and take note of the owners, customers, and servers. At 9:00 p.m. on April 23, fifty police officers and fifty members of the local watch launched an operation arresting sixty-one men and ninety-two women. According to one of the local papers, around 10:00 p.m. police officers and watchmen had "made a grand descent upon the low haunts of vice and crime in Ann Street and vicinity, including the *purlieus* yclept the 'Black Sea,' the 'Murder district' and other appropriately expressive names." Those arrested were caught "in the midst of their usual disreputable orgies" and escorted to a local jail, to the howls of jeering bystanders. Notably, many of the women arrested were very young, having just recently come to "the street." Most were immigrants, "with a sprinkling of those of mulatto hue." (Another reporter described those arrested as "of all colors, ages, sexes, sorts, and condition, exhibiting much the appearance of Jacob's sheep—black, white, grey, ring-streaked, speckled and spotted.") Those with prior arrest records faced sentences in the House of Correction, while novices had to pay $3 and court costs. The men were charged with keeping brothels and violating the licensing and Sunday laws. Caught up in the dragnet were vagrants, gamblers and cardplayers, drunks, and fifteen pipers and fiddlers who entertained dance-hall patrons.[16]

Their arraignment in court turned into a public spectacle when "whites and blacks mingled together in the crowd, almost as freely as they did in some cellars of Ann Street," according to the *Boston Herald*. The women arrived in a police wagon called "Black Maria," and the assembled throng enthusiastically greeted those who were well known, including Fanny White, an "old comer." Of the nearly one hundred female "denizens of the 'Black Sea,'" half could not pay the fine and went to the House of Correction. One of them, Emeline Thacker, however, found herself sent off to jail for six months "at the request of her father," Henry L.W. Thacker, a prosperous homeowner living on Southac Street. A bootblack turned waiter turned caterer, he had helped Joshua B. Smith launch his own catering business. Thacker no doubt hoped that jail time would teach his sixteen-year-old daughter Emeline a hard lesson. She died that July of typhoid fever, presumably while serving her sentence.[17]

Looking back on the 1851 "Descent on Ann Street," Edward H. Savage, the former police chief, acknowledged that community members were of three minds when it came to addressing this human "*cesspool*." Some believed that it was better to limit the moral contamination to a specific district; such a quarantine would preserve the health and safety of the rest of the community, especially since there was no way to eradicate the "orgies" completely. Others thought it incumbent that as citizens they periodically take matters into their own hands and send a firm signal to the reprobates that their behavior would not be tolerated. The police had apparently decided that a massive if temporary cleanup of the area would remind criminals that the larger community disapproved of what went on there. Nevertheless, the descent had unwelcome, unanticipated consequences, according to Savage. He reported that upon their release, many of the women arrested for prostitution feared returning to their old haunts, but they also feared going home to disapproving neighbors and family members. Instead, he wrote, "they were scattered as domestics in the families of respectable citizens throughout the city and its suburbs." "They were not reformed," he added, and suggested that reports of burglaries had spiked because many of the workers displaced from dance halls and brothels turned to stealing.[18]

The local press made no mention of Joseph Clash in its account of the descent, though certainly he would seem to have been a prime target. Somehow he routinely avoided prosecution and other measures that would have curtailed his businesses. Some police were in the habit of patronizing his hall, and he probably developed a scheme of payoffs to keep them from interfering in an enterprise that enriched both him and them. The exploits of Clash and his partners in crime sold newspapers to voyeuristic readers. The *Herald* called Clash "a very distinguished barber, fiddler, and sporting character in the North End," a description that conveyed a degree of admiration for his many talents and his loyal clientele. Periodically he did face charges of assault, however, including, at one point, for knocking down "a boy in a dancing school." Still, even after one of his frequent fights, the *Herald* could describe him as "somewhat celebrated at the North End," his reputation unsullied by serial appearances in Police Court. Perhaps his good fortune was due to his talented defense lawyer, Robert Morris.[19]

In the midst of periodic "descents," Ann Street continued to offer employment to Black and white women, who circulated through Police Court on a regular basis during this period. They plied their trade on Boston Common, on the streets, in their own dwellings, in dance houses in the North End, or in brothels. In publicizing the problem of prostitution, the local papers and the police offered dual narratives based on the woman's skin color: young white women came to Boston from the countryside or a neighboring state seeking work, only to fall victim to the seducer—"Fallen,—deserted,—and betrayed"—while Black women accused of the same crime seemed unmoored from family and devoid of any tragic history that would make them objects of the public's sympathy. Ignored was how the relentless downward pressure on women's wages pushed some into sex work. Boston's servants labored within a wider regional economy where the wives of even well-to-do farmers did piecework—sewing wallets, hat linings, collars, and shirts, or making shoe bindings, for extra money. Some reformers indicted these rural women, charging they spent their modest wages on fine dresses and jewelry and refused to do housework themselves. Presumably these pieceworkers provided a poor example to young women, who saw domestic service as inherently degrading. Despite this misplaced blame on both rich and poor women for an exploitative wage structure, it is true that rural outworkers depressed wages for city workers, and neither seamstresses nor servants made a living wage.[20]

Prostitution was not only the object of reformers' wrath, but also an integral component of Boston's underground economy. Although men owned most of the brothels, Black women could be employers as well as sex workers in the trade. One of them, Boston-born Sarah Cotton, kept her own "house of ill repute." On August 20, 1852, police raided her living quarters on Southac Street and found her in bed with a Mr. Hall, a Black cooper. The couple explained to the judge that they planned to wed, and so he called in a justice of the peace, who married them on the spot. Yet Sarah continued to keep a "disorderly" house (under the name Cotton), impervious to stints in the House of Correction. She died there of unknown causes in December 1856 at the age of thirty. Purveyors of vice served as the economic mainstay of the undercommons, yet they faced constant threats from disgruntled customers and the brutal conditions of Boston's prisons.[21]

Clash's ability to trick the gullible apparently extended beyond the realm of his dance-hall patrons to include a second wife, Louisa Williams, whom he married in the summer of 1852. He told her and the presiding justice of the peace that this was his first marriage.

By this time Clash had perfected the art of separating the naïve and unsuspecting from their cash. A Black man named Henry Plummer was one such victim. On June 30, 1853, Clash struck up a conversation with Plummer on Richmond Street. Plummer was a North Carolina–born self-described physician living alone not far from where the two met. Clash escorted his new friend to his barber shop, where Clash's accomplice, a cardsharp named Edward J. Gray, took advantage of Plummer and won a considerable amount of money from him in a game of "Seven Up." As consolation, Clash offered Plummer "some very good wine," which induced a deep sleep. It was at this point that Clash lifted a tidy sum from Plummer's pocket. Sued by Plummer, Gray and Clash together mounted a spirited defense. At a grand jury hearing, their attorney, Morris, called Plummer's account of the night into question, arguing that he was responsible for his own foolish choices. On July 9, the two defendants were discharged, "the Grand Jury not finding bills against them."[22]

Joseph Clash exhibited a kind of ruthlessness that allowed him not only to survive, but to thrive—with some outside help, including the legal counsel of Robert Morris, the implicit tolerance of the local law-enforcement establishment, and the growing demands of his grateful customers. He ran several integrated operations, some legitimate, others havoc-wreaking. He operated a barbershop separate from the hall, and in the latter he employed cooks, musicians, "dance girls," and professional gamblers. This mix brought in customers. Some of his Black workers had made a conscious decision to try to avoid working in white women's kitchens and shining white men's boots. Others were driven by desperation and the threat of starvation. Regardless of what brought them to Ann Street, those caught up in Clash's orbit suffered from occupational hazards. The women faced the prospect of venereal disease, unwanted pregnancy, beatings from their johns, and periodic confinement in the House of Correction. Rivalries over potential marks could turn deadly; the sisterhood of sex workers and con artists was a fragile one, if it existed at all. Brothel keepers such as John Harris used a whip on the women they employed. The young "mulatto girl" Lydia Redding, caught up in the "descent" on Southac Street in August 1850, was back at work soon after, now in a different location in the city. A year later she died in what a local paper called "one of those noisome [Ann Street] cellars . . . from a combination of diseases incident to the course of life which has been pursued." The men, too, took their lives in their hands, with knives, pistols, and fists the tools of their violent trade.[23]

Meanwhile, Clash was prospering, building a new venue and honing his remarkable talent for self-promotion. In the spring of 1854, he was advertising in the *Herald*, announcing one Friday night affair—"a grand levee and dancing assembly"—that would feature "the friends of Joseph Clash, Esq. . . . present[ing] him with a silver cup as a token of their respect and esteem." He continued to appear in court to answer the charge that he kept a "noisy place," and he periodically served as a witness in murder cases and as a defendant in assault cases, though he was invariably released because "the charge could not be sustained."[24]

By early 1857 Clash had established a new hall, this one on the corner of North and Ferry Streets. With a flourish he named it Clash's American Hall. He was partnering with a Black New Jersey–born musician, Harry F. Williams. Special events drew in patrons—in January of that year a "Bloomer and Prize Ball," with cash awards bestowed on the "four best dressed bloomer ladies" (attired in the new, scandalous billowy pants) and a "beautiful card case" to "the lady who dances the best Fancy Dance in costume." The night also featured a serenade—"the beautiful duet of Araby's daughter" by Clash himself. As usual, men paid a fee of 25 cents, and women were admitted free. Other novelty evenings included a "Military and Civic Ball" in February and another "Grand Fancy Dress, Bloomer, and Prize Ball" in April, then a "Grand May Day Festival" the month after.[25]

The "Great Union Ball" on May 24 attracted the usual patrons but also three noteworthy guests—a reporter for the *Herald* and two police officers, A. C. Whitcomb and Joseph B. Emerson. With his North End beat, Whitcomb was a fixture in Police Court, testifying about his own exploits breaking up fights, going after gambling rings, and tracking down unfaithful wives. Emerson was newer to the force, and it is unknown whether his wife was aware of this particular nighttime assignment. The *Herald* story highlighted "The Mixed Races on the Light Fantastic Too," and provided an elaborate description of Clash's "gorgeous establishment." In keeping with the hall's grandiose aspirations, the furnishings included a US flag and an American eagle. Patrons enjoyed beer and mineral water along with hard-boiled eggs, doughnuts, cake, mince pie, baked beans, cold chicken, lobster salad, and sausage. A small orchestra, with Clash playing the bass viola, entertained the boisterous crowd.[26]

Praising their host's "mingled suavity and energy," the reporter noted that "no class, color, or condition [was] excluded" from the hall and that Clash had extended a standing invitation to members of the city government, who could attend for free. The assemblage included "a miscellaneous crowd" consisting of "sailors, shippers of vessels, mates, butchers, negroes, drovers, respectable store keepers, city officials, policemen, [and] thieves and garroters," making it a true Boston "institution." The reporter made fun of the women present—their elaborate hairdos bedecked with ribbons, their fox-skinned furs and hoop skirts—these "dark complexioned females sporting flashy silks." The ill-fitting dresses suggested that the current wearers were not their original owners. Readers could ascertain the skin color of quarreling antagonists by the fact that Blacks invariably spoke in dialect. One of the women recognized Whitcomb and alerted the others to his presence—"Bishop Whitcomb in de hall," she called out in a jolly way. The reporter concluded that Clash was a remarkably "self-possessed individual with an eye like a peeled onion for the main chance." And more main chances were yet to come, for the simple reason that the demand for his services—salacious or otherwise—was infinite, and appreciation of a good fiddler near universal.[27]

Clash's dance hall testified to both the business savvy of its owner and the thoroughly integrated nature of the underground commons at night, under the flickering light of indoor candles and outdoor gas lamps. His employees routinely risked their livelihoods and their lives. Ultimately, however, it was on the streets, in the arteries pumping the lifeblood of commerce through Boston, where many men of modest means found jobs. There, then, yet another great drama over the meaning of work unfolded.

3

The World of the Streets

In January 1855, Boston's mayor, Jerome V.C. Smith, used the occasion of his annual address to highlight elements of the city's natural and built landscape that posed barriers to the city's unfettered growth and prosperity. The low-lying areas, he declared, were "thousands upon thousands of feet, barren, sunken, gloomy reservoirs for the accumulation of offensive nuisances"; but, he predicted, "stately edifices" would soon "rise in beauty and grandeur" in these formerly noxious places. Moreover, the city's "extensive commercial relations" depended upon its streets, and "crooked, narrow thoroughfares" were "a misfortune to Boston, entailed upon it altogether by accident." These byways must be extended, widened, and paved. Always searching for the perfect road surface, the city had experimented with iron-block streets in 1853, finding them superior to wood planks and granite, and "an exceedingly handsome pavement to drive on," but too expensive to be practical. Smith also called for the construction of sewers and drainpipes: taller buildings meant more cellar cisterns and apartments flooded with raw sewage, leading to recurring cholera and typhoid epidemics. Backed by the anti-immigrant Know Nothings, Smith took care in his address to laud "the benevolence, foresight and free spirit of our ancestors" that had made the city great. Now the city council must confront the natural landscape and improve the primitive infrastructure that was the legacy of colonial settlement.[1]

The stern policy pronouncements of city authorities hardly conveyed the carnivalesque world of the Boston streets, with brightly colored signboards set against red brick and white stone buildings with green trim and silvery doorknobs. Colorful flags and pennants adorned various structures and the top of Telegraph Hill. On a normal weekday, wharf workers sang as they unloaded cargo, and hawkers shouted out the delectability of their wares. Pedestrians as well as conveyances of various sizes and levels of mechanical sophistication rushed to their destinations. The streets formed a stage, and upon it a continuous enactment of white supremacism, with Black workers visible emblems of their own diminished opportunities.[2]

In the 1850s, Boston was a city on the move—literally. Workers demolished small buildings to make way for big ones; dragged wooden houses down the street or across the river to make way for brick ones; flattened and enlarged the "Neck" (a thin sliver of land linking the city to its western suburbs) by removing immense amounts of mud and sludge from swampy areas; cut down hills and transported the dirt to low-lying areas to increase the city's landmass; extended the wharves farther into the harbor; laid pipes for the city's water supply; built bridges connecting the city to its northern suburbs across the Charles River; and constructed seawalls, sidewalks, sewers, and new streets. When Back Bay was filled in, the city grew by 450 acres. The city also created imposing institutions emblematic of a commonwealth—public schools, hospitals, jails, a juvenile reformatory, an almshouse, and a public library. Taxpayers paid dearly for all these public improvements and for the upkeep of the Common, the Public Garden, and other city parks. These new construction projects and routine maintenance tasks were affordable because of an oversupply of men willing and able to labor outdoors, some regularly, others on a sporadic basis. The vagaries of New England weather, however, meant that few could work more than twenty days a month at a stretch, even in the best of times.[3]

During the 1850s, Boston's population increased by 40,000 people (from 136,881 to 177,840) as Irish immigrants, migrants from the distressed countryside, Canadians from the Maritime provinces, and displaced New England textile-mill workers streamed into the city in search of work. Boston beckoned as a manufacturing center, with iron and brass foundries; a sugar refinery; shops that made a variety of goods, from locomotives and machines to pianos and organs; and alcohol distilleries. East Boston shipyards produced the famous fast clipper ships. And on the busy docks and in the huge warehouses and distribution centers, imports came in and exports went out.

Added to the workforce in these years were the inmates of the House of Correction, who toiled on the public works, receiving nothing in return except a mean subsistence and a roof over their heads. They spent their days carting off dead horses; sweeping the streets of dirt, animal waste, and ashes; and removing ice and snow. However, most of the men working on public infrastructure projects were employed by individual contractors who billed the city. These contractors enjoyed great leeway in whom they chose to hire for any one project, and indeed, the city government did not even require a reckoning of the workers' hours and pay or a list of their names. Shaped by the proclivities of individual contractors, this system favored white laborers and left Black men scrambling for work and waiting on street corners for a chance at a job that would last for a few days or an hour or two. Because the population of Black men was so small, city councilmen had no incentive to provide them with public-works employment and secure their votes in return.

The Transcendentalist writer-philosopher Ralph Waldo Emerson linked the transformation in Boston's layout to the exploitation of Irish immigrant labor. He could remember when the narrow peninsula was dotted with pastures, gardens, and wastelands, but now all those places of natural beauty had been built upon and paved over: "Acre after acre has been since won from the sea, and in a short time the antiquary will find it difficult to trace the peninsular topography," he wrote. He deplored the city's treatment of the "poor Irishmen," men paid very little "to work from dark to dark for sixty or even fifty cents a day . . . pitiful wages for a married man." Gouged by both grocer and landlord, Irish families lived on the edge of starvation, and besides, according to Emerson, the work itself was hard, "excessive, and the sight of it reminds one of negro-driving."[4]

Black men also labored out of doors, but not on construction or street-improvement projects. Carter Selden, formerly a highly valued enslaved worker on Carter Edloe's plantation, found relatively steady work as a porter throughout his life, making him better off than many other laborers. Since his arrival in 1847, Selden had come to know the city's districts well, and he understood that the streets were more than just a means of circulation and distribution for people and goods. They were also sites of danger, disorder, and conflict, as well as stages for performances both ritualistic and spontaneous. For Selden and other laborers, the streets had their own peculiar choreography.

Many workers spent most of their days outside. Truckmen daily hauled off piles of shells from oyster bars and the "house offal" from hotels and private residences, their carts reeking with the stench of decaying animal matter and hundreds of slop jars. Drivers operated carts and carriages carrying passengers, barrels, baskets, casks, and boxes; the conveyances included everything from horse-drawn omnibuses and wagons, to hackney coaches and stagecoaches, to elegant barouches and landaus. By the mid-1850s, twelve different railroad lines converged on the city, all of them in need of engineers, conductors, and workers assigned to their regular maintenance and repair. A three-day "Railroad Jubilee" in September 1851 featured a parade that stretched for more than three miles, culminating in a banquet for 3,600 guests in a pavilion on the Common—all to celebrate "the mercantile interests of Boston."[5]

In regulating the railroads and policing the streets, the city aimed to promote business and protect the inhabitants from fire and disease, priorities that were highly visible on a daily basis. Police patrolled the streets and alleyways, their numbers bolstered during public celebrations or instances of disorder with temporary deputies, so-called special police. Lamplighters and extinguishers tended to their tasks at dusk and dawn, and watchmen took night duty. The town crier, a holdover from colonial days, called out the news in a way that was quaintly inefficient in the growing city. When a fire did start, firemen drove their state-of-the-art steam-powered fire engines through the streets, bells clanging, pedestrians scattering.

City authorities sought to regulate virtually everyone who sold goods, victuals, or alcohol; owned a theater or other business serving as a gathering place; kept a coach or hackney stand; or sponsored an exhibit or performance. Vendors plied their wares on street corners, setting up small, portable stands or selling out of boxes or bags that could be easily packed up should the police arrive and demand to see a license. Many failed to get the requisite permission to sell oysters, lobsters, fruits, vegetables, and other "agricultural products"; live animals; brooms or farm implements; fuel; or books, pamphlets, tracts, and newspapers. Youngsters hawking purloined goods were a perpetual preoccupation of the city council. In February 1856, its members stipulated that anyone under the age of twenty-one must secure the sponsorship of a parent or guardian, attend school at least three months of the year, and wear a leather badge on his cap with the word "Licensed" on it "in polished letters, fastened thereon." Fake credentials, either written or sartorial, often thwarted the council's intentions.[6]

The 1856 peddler statute further stipulated that licensees must abide by certain hours of work and not "congregate together, make any loud noise or in any other way disturb or annoy people as they pass." Boys, alone and together on the streets, proved a perpetual source of disorder. Truants gathered on street corners and in alleys, to the annoyance of those wishing to exit their homes or places of business without pushing through a group of foul-mouthed youths. Vagrants, drunkards, and Ann Street grifters as well as "idle and dissolute boys" blocked sidewalks and assaulted passers-by.[7]

Mayor Smith's successor, Alexander Rice, who was elected on the "Citizens" ticket in 1856, was more favorable than Smith to the foreign immigrants of the city, who had faced considerable prejudice from the Know-Nothing politicians. Some of the boys granted licenses to sell goods in early 1856 had surnames such as Mahoney, Murphy, Leary, Kerrigan, and Hogan. Many Black peddlers could not afford a license, but that did not prevent them from offering up goods of questionable origins—the *Herald* decried their large numbers on State Street, referring to them sarcastically as "the colored merchant princes." Some southern migrants accustomed to selling eggs or baked pies considered the transition to Boston a challenge—it was difficult to keep chickens or grow food in a northern city—but not an insurmountable one.[8]

In their attempt to make a living or go about their business on the streets, workers found themselves menaced by hostile passers-by and endangered by an assortment of life-threatening conditions. A Black woman named Sarah B. Thompson paused one day from her work on a sidewalk washing windows to smack a white boy with a broomstick she had on hand. He had called her "nigger," and she wanted to teach him a lesson; her fury cost her a fine of $5. In 1850, Joseph F. Clash was engaged in the same task, standing on a barrel outside his barbershop, when a drunken man came along and kicked the barrel out from under him; Clash broke one of his legs in the fall. Construction workers lost their limbs to blasting rocks and their lives to rickety scaffolds. Porters such as Carter Selden had to navigate narrow streets clogged with piles of bricks, the remnants of collapsed chimneys and walls suddenly dislodged by hoisting machinery. Piles of animal excrement turned streets into avenues of a stinking mess. Pedestrians and workers alike suffered grievous bodily harm from falling into open cellar doors, stumbling on uneven sidewalks, and finding themselves under an awning, store sign, loose gutter, or chunk of ice just as it crashed to the ground. Horse-drawn omnibuses and steam-powered trains ran into and over people. Rabid dogs and runaway horses endangered human lives, as did young swells racing their steeds in the summer and their sleighs in the winter, careening down congested thoroughfares.[9]

One man's nighttime joyride was a city watchman's nightmare. Joseph H. Elisha, a Black youth, found it difficult to resist appropriating a horse or even a team of horses for an evening's gallop through Boston. The son of a laborer, Elisha proved incorrigible

This 1857 drawing of the corner of Winter, Washington, and Summer Streets conveys the energy characteristic of Boston's downtown. A fast-moving carriage forces pedestrians to scatter, while an organ grinder and his monkey attract a crowd. The well-to-do show off their finery, as cartmen and streetcar drivers go about their business. *(Boston Public Library)*

when it came to taking other people's horses, especially those left unattended in the street after dark; such escapades no doubt offered a welcome diversion from his job as a shoemaker, which he began at an early age. In October 1853, he and a friend, George Sawtelle, stole a carriage belonging to the caterer Joshua B. Smith, and together that night they went "driving the same over 'all creation.'" An amused reporter covering Police Court reported that the two had not intended to steal the carriage, just borrow it.[10]

Group identity displayed on the streets could take the form of pitched battles (as when Protestant and Catholic Irish immigrants fought each other in Dorchester in 1852) or orderly processions of fraternal orders, their members resplendent in colorful uniforms. Boston boasted an impressive number of volunteer militias, including the National Lancers, the Washington Light Infantry, the Mechanic Infantry, the Boston Light Artillery, and the Ancient and Honorable Artillery Company. Composed exclusively of white men, these groups often paraded through the streets en route to drill on the Common, attracting large numbers of spectators along the way. Some of these militias employed Black men or boys to carry their equipment for them.[11]

Together with uniformed police, watchmen, and firefighters, the white fraternal orders and militias proclaimed the whiteness of the city's administrative and law-enforcement units. No wonder, then, that the Prince Hall Grand Lodge of Freemasons chafed at their exclusion from the white parent group; at the same time, they turned that insult into the basis of Black solidarity and pride. Nevertheless, barred from the militias sanctioned by the city and the state, Black men felt keenly the lack of a voluntary military group that would signal their full citizenship as well as their need for self-defense. Despite the absence of official approval after many futile years of petitioning, in August 1855 Robert Morris and John P. Coburn organized the Massasoit Guards, the first African American militia in Boston's history. Morris noted that it was "not founded on *caste*," but open to all young men of good character. Sixty strong, the group never received a state charter, though Morris renewed the call for formal authorization periodically thereafter.[12]

The Massasoit Guards disbanded in early 1857 without ever getting underway, but a new group, the Liberty Guard, took shape that August. It did not receive certification from the state, either, but it did make a striking public appearance on Monday, November 16, when its members processed through the streets accompanied by a cornet band. William Cooper Nell, notebook in hand, chronicled every movement of the thirty-five men during this public display. Dressed all in black, they marched from their armory on Joy Street to the State House a few blocks away under police escort. At one point they had to push their way through the throng of spectators, proud people of color but also surly whites. The six top officers included Lewis Gaul, a coachman, along with three laborers, a printer, and a keeper of a billiard saloon on Joy Street—a decidedly less well-off group compared to the Massasoit Guards.[13]

Earlier that day Gaul had instructed the men "to keep eyes constantly ahead, to disregard every insult that might be thrown at them by jealous and rowdy white folk, and above all things, not to leave the ranks in any emergency without orders." On their return to the armory the marchers faced not only whites' "howls and curses," but also a hail of brickbats, stones, and small paper bags filled with flour (this last missile no doubt intended to highlight the men's dark skin when its contents spilled on them). According to Nell, these provocations were "too much for Negro-manity to endure," and several of the Black men seized the clubs of their tormenters or "charged bayonets on the rowdies, who fled like cowards before a desperate foe." That night the Guard celebrated with coffee, pies, apples, and ice cream, the repast catered by Joshua B. Smith, at Faneuil Hall. The day proved that a singular event such

This studio portrait of a man in a stovepipe hat was taken in 1859. Identified only as "Old Patterson," he is possibly a hawker selling wares from his basket. Many Black workers toiled well into advanced age. *(Courtesy of Historic New England)*

as this could bring together elements of ritual, violent conflict, the performance of white hegemony, and productive labor (in the form of Nell's reporting for *The Liberator*).[14]

Black workers were targeted by authorities aiming to quell untoward behavior on the streets such as smoking and loitering, and by white pedestrians aiming to humiliate them. In December 1853, a Black man protested his arrest for smoking a cigar while in his cab, claiming that "the officer complained of him on account of personal feeling against him." The driver was nevertheless fined $2 and court costs. Streets were places where white men, women, and children taunted Black workers, where Black pedestrians had to yield the sidewalk to their white counterparts, and where police officers could arrest a Black peddler and let a white one continue on his or her way.[15]

The many meanings of street life and work found expression in the curious history of Deacon Cyrus Foster, whom white observers described as "one of the venerable institutions of this city," and "one of the most faithful men of our city, and an honor to his race." (The title "Deacon" was apparently an ironic honorific, similar to the way southern whites called elderly enslaved men "Uncle.") Foster was an alchemist of sorts, turning whites' prejudice against Blacks in general and their ridicule of him in particular into cash. Born in 1785 in Chelmsford, northwest of Boston, he was a veteran of the War of 1812; for years after, he "turned out most bravely" when a militia active in that conflict, the Ancient and Honorable Artillery Company, marched through the city. Foster worked as a coachman, but he also specialized in waiting on well-to-do whites, including guests at the Whig Ball of November 1848. When President Millard Fillmore visited Boston in September 1851, Foster served as his private attendant, a position fit (only) for a Black man.[16]

Foster's eccentricities were legendary, and he had a talent for monetizing them. Beginning in the late 1840s, he sponsored an annual concert, a benefit for himself. He would rent an impressive venue, such as the Boston Music Hall or Tremont Temple, and contract with a local band or choral group, such as the Weymouth Brass Band or the German Musical Society. Occasionally he featured a novelty act like "the celebrated whistler, Dr. Juniper." Foster's bombastic style was a source of entertainment for whites, who paid to hear him declaim in a faux-serious, grandiose way on religion, politics, and the "state of the country." The papers rendered his comments in dialect, as when he condemned "de Irish boys and everything else . . . allowed to go on der Common on de Lord's day." The highlight of the evening was always his lecture—"His peculiar style of remarks is unrivalled," said one account—for he was "both an orator and a gentleman of close observation." A brief stay in the Boston Lunatic Hospital (in the summer of 1852) hardly slowed him down.[17]

As an entrepreneur, Foster operated on the notion that any mention of his name in the papers would burnish his celebrity status and therefore grow his livelihood. The day before his annual concert, he appeared in downtown Boston on horseback and "in full regimentals" as a way of advertising the event. His horse would prance sideways "in the most approved military style," delighting the crowd. He periodically commanded a "brigade" of Black workers—servants, waiters, and "clothes brushers"—and would march them single file ("Indian file") up State Street, putting them through maneuvers in front of the Boston Exchange. Just as he hoped and planned, the local papers covered the scene and alerted readers to the upcoming concert, where they would have the privilege of listening to "Deacon Cyrus Foster, so well known in military and militant, as well as financial, musical and political circles."[18]

Foster was mocked in a popular song—words by "Timothy Coalbin, Esq.," and music by "Anthracite Carbon"—titled "Deacon Foster and the Coal Dealer." The song joined the deacon's skin color to the blackness of the coal. Yet if he embraced the ridicule heaped upon him, not everyone was amused. The day after his March 1, 1854, concert, an unnamed Black assailant attacked him on Exchange Street, demanding to know, according to Foster, "What I was talkin' about sir." A reporter referred to the offender as "an envious colored individual, who has no feelings of reverence in his soul." On another occasion, when a group of white newsboys taunted Foster, he seized two of them and kissed them on the face, leading the others to "hoot 'em down de street, for bein' kissed by a nigger." The streets served as a venue for Foster's self-publicity, but also as a site of his vulnerability.[19]

In 1860, Foster was living alone in Ward 6 and reporting that he was worth $2,000 (equivalent to $70,000 in today's money). He was probably exaggerating, but he no doubt believed that his peculiar way of making a living—the annual concerts interspersed with work as a coachman, porter, servant, and waiter—was well worth the trouble. And who was the fool—Foster, or the well-heeled whites who bought tickets to his shows?

STREET DRAMAS WERE a hallmark of fugitive slave renditions, and so it was that the case of Anthony Burns in May 1854 echoed those of Sims and Minkins three years before. On Wednesday, May 24, Burns closed up the Brattle Street clothing shop of Coffin Pitts and headed toward Court Street. A twenty-year-old runaway from Virginia, Burns had been hiding out, living with and working for Pitts. Suddenly three US marshals approached him, grabbed him, and dragged him off to the courthouse. There he was confronted by his owner, Charles F. Suttle of Virginia.[20]

The Boston Vigilance Committee had been busy over the past few years. They rescued fugitives from ships in Boston Harbor, paid for their food and lodging in the city, and in some cases spirited them to Canada—all efficiently and quietly. The fight over Burns offered a reprise of previous incidents—the fugitive caught by surprise, the owner and his agents tenacious in court, Black people and their white allies outraged, the distinguished Black and white lawyer-abolitionists eloquent in their defense of their client. At the same time, Burns's story, beginning in Virginia and continuing in Massachusetts, then back to Virginia and eventually to the Bay State again, sheds light on the necessarily peripatetic work histories of Black men: many either waited on the streets for work or took to the streets to inquire about a job. Boston thoroughfares were worksites, but they were also well-trod paths for the job-seeker.

Anthony Burns had toiled for whites since he was nine years old. Born in 1834 in Stafford County, Virginia, on the western shore of the Potomac River, he was the youngest of thirteen children, the son of a plantation cook and a stone quarry worker. His family had been enslaved by two generations of the Suttle family. In 1843 Anthony was minding his sister's baby while she labored in the fields. The following year, Charles Suttle began to hire the youth out to a series of employers in the surrounding countryside and nearby towns—the owners of a grocery store, a sawmill (where the machinery mangled one of his hands), a tavern, and an apothecary, along with a wholesale merchant. One of his employers, William Brent, became Suttle's agent, overseeing the contracts that bound Burns to a new employer each year. At the age of nineteen Burns had gained Suttle's and Brent's confidence, and in January 1853 he hired himself out to a flour mill. His employer in 1854, a Richmond druggist named Charles Millsbaugh, struck a deal with him: Burns could find work for himself as long as he paid off the druggist's $125 leasing fee. After that, he and Millsbaugh would split whatever money he could make.

By this time, Burns, like so many other enslaved men and women who ultimately fled the South, was a "decidedly unhappy piece of property in the city of Richmond," as Underground Railroad conductor William Still put it. An imposing figure, strong and six feet tall, Burns had no trouble finding work on the city docks. He soon made the acquaintance of a northern sailor and decided to use his hard-earned wages to pay for passage to Boston. In early 1854 Burns was reporting only infrequently to Millsbaugh. Brent had lost track of the Black man, and Suttle cared only that Millsbaugh had already paid him the leasing fee of $125. This lax supervision helps to account for the argument at the heart of Burns's later legal defense, for it was clear that none of these three white men had the slightest idea where Burns was at the end of February. Brent would later say that he saw the enslaved man on March 19 in Richmond, when in fact Burns had left that city three weeks earlier.[21]

Following the river route of the Edloe Sixty-Six and many other Black migrants to Boston, Burns was counting on a trip of a week and a half or so, but because of bad weather it stretched out to two weeks, and then three. Although the exact date is uncertain, Sunday, February 19, was probably the day that he emerged from the vessel, the worse for wear after a long, cold voyage. His arrival in Boston coincided with heightened agitation among Black leaders now that Congress was debating a piece of legislation called the Kansas-Nebraska Act. This bill kept the number of free states and slave states equal, with the admission of Maine as one of the former and Missouri one of the latter. The Missouri Compromise of 1850 had outlawed slavery north of the 36°30' parallel, but the new law made a way for slavery to be introduced above that line, in the territories of Kansas and Nebraska. It was becoming abundantly clear that the moralism of the Garrisonians was insufficient to halt the proslavery juggernaut. Boston's Black leaders also expressed alarm at other disturbing developments closer to home: various forms of out-migration were draining their community—men and women chasing riches in California and Australia, as well as emigrants seduced by colonization efforts in Sierra Leone and Haiti. Harriet Beecher Stowe, author of the best-selling novel *Uncle Tom's Cabin*, had apparently reneged on an offer to solicit donations of $15,000 in England to fund a manual training school for Black youth. Once again, white allies had fallen short of their promises. Boston's Black leaders proposed a Massachusetts State Protective Union "under the control of the colored people" to advance their own interests.[22]

While Black leaders were denouncing deteriorating national and local conditions, Burns was working as a cook on a mud scow in the harbor; but of all the varied tasks he had had in Virginia, none had involved food preparation, and within a couple of days the captain fired him. After that, the fugitive's whereabouts for the first three weeks in March were chronicled (at trial) by William Jones, a Black laborer living in South Boston. Whether or not Jones's narrative was accurate in its details, he provided a credible account of a casual laborer seeking work in Boston.

According to Jones, on March 1 Burns had walked up to him while he was on Washington Street and asked if he knew of any storekeeper who needed help. In response to Jones's question about what he could do, Burns had said he "could do most anything." Jones was a day laborer, familiar with white employers looking to hire Black men on an irregular basis—for a few weeks, a few days, a few hours. Jones later told the court that he professed little curiosity about Burns at the time, saying he called him John or Jack—"or any short name that came handy"—not bothering to inquire about his true identity. Burns's Virginia drawl would not have caught Jones's attention, since so many newcomers came from that state.[23]

Jones suggested that Burns go with him to see a friend, a bootblack named Russell, who kept a small notebook of accounts for him (Jones was illiterate). On Jones's instruction, Russell recorded an arrangement by which Jones would pay Burns 8 cents for every window the fugitive (as his assistant) washed at South Boston's Mattapan Iron Works. Then Burns and Jones walked to John Favor's carpentry shop on Lincoln Street. Jones asked Favor where "he could find employment for the colored man with him," a query that led them to their next stop, an apothecary shop in the basement of the United States Hotel; but the two found there was no work to be had there either.[24]

Luckless thus far, the pair proceeded to the shop of Stephen Maddox on Essex Street. A longtime resident of Southac, Maddox was a leader in the Black community and a well-known fugitive assistant. He had owned his own business since at least 1843, when he posted in a local paper that he "respectfully informs his friends and family and the public at large, that he has taken an office on Court Avenue, where he is ready to wait on all who may favor with a call in his line of business, such as waiting on dinner and supper parties, and also windows, paint, and carpets cleaned." A culinary broker of sorts, he offered to supply cooks and waiters to establishments of any size: "Tavern keepers in the city or vicinity would do well to give him a call." He also advertised for "a colored young man" to work for him: "None need apply unless he can bring good references for honesty and good behavior." (As it would turn out, Maddox would one day look for the same qualities in a son-in-law.) He also made some money by washing "towels &c" for the Boston Water Works. He and his wife, Betsy, belonged to the Methodist Bethel Society, a church for seamen, where Stephen was an officer.[25]

Maddox testified at trial that around March 1, Jones approached him in his shop and introduced him to Burns, saying, "Here is a man that wants some work." Maddox told him that he had nothing to offer at the present, but that his busy season would begin in about two months, and that the two men should check back with him around the beginning of May. Suttle's lawyers tried to impugn this testimony, charging that Maddox himself was a runaway slave (he was born in Maryland) and could not be trusted to give an accurate timeline of Burns's movements. For his testimony and time and trouble, the Vigilance Committee paid Maddox a "witness fee" (on June 20, 1854).[26]

According to Jones, he and Burns ended their long, discouraging first day of job hunting at the studio of a Mr. Bell, a dancing master, who was not there. They then went to Jones's South Boston home, where Burns spent the night. By this time it must have dawned on Burns that he would be able to find only piecemeal work on an hourly or daily basis, in contrast to the annual contracts that had bound him as a hired-out slave in Virginia.

The next morning, Jones recalled, he left Burns behind and "went to get employment for myself." He inquired at the Mattapan Iron Works and returned that afternoon to begin washing windows, with Burns as his helper. Jones had worked at the ironworks before, and he would find jobs there off and on for the next few months, until May. In March Anthony Burns worked with him for five days washing windows in the blacksmith shop, from 7:30 in the morning until 6:00 at night. Cold weather made the job difficult and unpleasant.[27]

Burns's lawyers maintained that he could not be Suttle's slave if Brent had seen that person in mid-March in Richmond. The defense relied on several white men to show that Burns had been working in Boston earlier that month. Among those providing an alibi were white ironworks employees, including a teamster, a machinist, and a carpenter. This last witness was especially crucial, since at the time of the trial he was working as a police officer. All three of these men remembered seeing "Jones and his companion" washing windows. In testimony, Jones said that the shop's bookkeeper, George H. Drew, asked Jones if Burns was his brother, to which Jones had replied, "All men are my brothers." Drew paid Jones, but at some point Burns wanted to know the amount ($1.50) and objected that Jones "hadn't settled up with him right."[28]

After the stint at the ironworks, Jones and Burns went on to Boston City Hall on March 10 and again on the 16th and 17th, and worked in the Probate Court Building, washing floors, cleaning up, and performing other custodial tasks. Soon after, the two dissolved their informal partnership. Jones claimed that he had last seen Burns around March 18. In April or May, Burns connected with Coffin Pitts, who hid Burns in his home and hired him to work in his clothing store. By that time Burns had joined Twelfth Baptist Church.

Burns's rendition trial took place against the backdrop of the passage of the Kansas-Nebraska Act in the US Congress on May 22, a provocation to abolitionists. The ten days following Burns's capture were punctuated by several incidents of high drama centered around the fugitive. In a Friday night mass meeting at Faneuil Hall led by the Reverend Leonard Grimes and the attorney Robert Morris, an overflow crowd roared its approval at several defiant resolutions, including, "That which is not just is not law, and that which is not law ought not to be obeyed." Those leading a Saturday evening meeting raised subscriptions, aiming for $1,200 to buy Burns. The prominent abolitionist and Unitarian clergyman Theodore Parker responded to a merchant's pledge of $400 with the words, "I have nothing to subscribe but brains and bullets." On Monday, there was an attack on the courthouse, and an angry crowd used a battering ram on the door. The court swiftly rejected Burns's defense, however, and on Thursday, June

1, ordered him returned to Virginia and Suttle, with the transfer to take place on the following day. To prepare, the authorities mounted a show of force that included thousands of armed federal officers, local police, deputized civilians, and volunteer militias, including US Marines deployed from the Charlestown Navy Yard. On Friday morning, a crowd of as many as ten thousand gathered along the streets to watch as Burns was marched to Long Wharf. The procession—some likened it to a funeral cortege—wended its way down State Street, the same path that Sims and Minkins had been forced to follow three years before.[29]

Lewis Hayden had hoped to rescue Burns by force; later he speculated that a plan to do so had faltered because of the exodus out of the city of so many fugitives, presumably those men and women who felt they had nothing to lose by violently resisting the law. Within a few months, however, Rev. Grimes had the last word, as it were, for by his arduous labors he had managed to net the $1,300 that Burns's new owner (in North Carolina) demanded, a sum delivered in February 1855. (Like other owners of enslaved workers caught in the North, Suttle had sought to rid himself of this person who was likely to continue to cause trouble.) A year after his rendition, Burns returned to Boston, now a free man.[30]

William Lloyd Garrison had his say about the Burns saga, highlighting the fugitive's admirable history of scrounging for work. In February 1855, in a speech to the Massachusetts Legislature, Garrison declared of Burns, "By hard work he earns his daily bread and with patient assiduity. . . . He has finished his day's work, and under the free stars, wearied, but full of joyful hope that words could never express, he seeks his home"—and then he is captured, an honest wage earner just trying to make a living. *The Liberator* printed a letter from a Lynn, Massachusetts, abolitionist who used a similar standard to stress the nobility of William Jones, a plain workingman who might provide a fitting example "to some of the noisiest and loudest praying professors of the religion of Christ in Boston." Jones "was poor, out of employment, awaiting for days a job by which to earn a little money." He had every reason to ignore Burns, but instead took him home and "went with him from place to place to obtain work, and when found, shared that employment with him."[31]

Two literary icons were among those weighing in as well, though to them Burns the man seemed less significant than the cause he represented. Frederick Douglass, in the June 2 issue of his paper, asked, "Is it Right and Wise to Kill a Kidnapper?" He answered the question by declaring that "every slave-hunter who meets a bloody death in his infernal business, is an argument for the manhood of our race. Resistance is, therefore, wise as well as just." The poet Walt Whitman was appalled by the Burns rendition. He began his 1854 poem "A Boston Ballad" with the words, "To get betimes in Boston town I rose this morning early, / Here's a good place at the corner, I must stand and see the show." The spectator watches as Revolutionary War heroes emerge from their graves to behold the return of tyranny ("the crown is come to its own"), King George's issue in the form of federal marshals invading the city of Boston. The rebels of old have been replaced by smug merchants, men tolerant of a monarchical-like government as long as they can line their pockets. Whitman's poem did not mention Burns.[32]

When Burns returned to Boston in March 1855, the *Courier* saw fit to criticize him for not capitalizing on his newfound fame. The paper reported that impresario P. T. Barnum had made him an offer: "It is a pity that Burns,—since he has suffered himself to be lionized at all,—did not accept Mr. Barnum's offer of $100 a week for five weeks. That sum would have put him in possession of funds to enable him to commence business which would give him an honest and comfortable livelihood." Burns had declined Barnum's audacious offer because, as he exclaimed to friends, "He wants to show me like a monkey!" However, he did agree to a lecture tour, which featured a panorama titled "The Great Moving Mirror of Slavery," and approved sales of a new biography of himself by a Worcester businessman. That summer, Burns enrolled in Oberlin College on a scholarship from an anonymous donor, aiming to put a life of menial labor behind him.[33]

THE DRAMATIC CAPTURE and rendition of fugitives offered spectacles that took place on the streets as well as in the courtroom. More generally, with so many people, animals, and vehicles circulating, Boston's streets and sidewalks played an outsized role in the city's public culture, serving not just as conduits of commerce, but also as workplaces and as byways for workers. For Black laundresses hurrying to pick up a load of washing, or for tenders carrying goods and messages from one store to another, life outside was as necessary to their livelihood as it was threatening to their well-being and safety.

As Black workers passed through the Boston streets, they could not help but be struck by the myriad ways that this northern city offered new opportunities for work and socializing compared to the slave quarters back home. Black Bostonians welcomed the recent newcomers, eager and exhausted, into the fold of the community, which by this time had become highly inflected with the religious and cultural practices of Virginia. The South loomed large in the lives of recent migrants: some of them even tried to settle the score with their former oppressors. At times, then, the crooked streets of Boston seemed not so far from the docks of Richmond or the expansive wheat fields on the Mount Pleasant plantation.

4

Boston in the Shadow of Slavery

Like many migrants from Virginia to Boston, "Blacksmith Peter" Randolph knew he could never free himself entirely from his slave heritage; as it turned out, Boston whites would not allow him to do so in any case, for ideologies of "racial" difference pervaded this city celebrated for its abolitionist activists. Indeed, in notable ways, certain aspects of Boston's Black life and labor patterns replicated conditions south of the Mason Dixon line, reminding people of color that they remained subordinate to whites by custom and whim. A near-constant infusion of fugitives into Boston kept alive the folkways, religious practices, and kin and family feeling of the enslaved, further blurring the distinctions between North and South. Enterprising free people of color from the Mid-Atlantic and the South made their way to the Bay State and joined the fight against slavery; together, members of these groups enriched the Boston leadership class and highlighted the struggles of Black people to find work that matched their considerable talents. Nevertheless, echoing their southern counterparts, many white Bostonians insisted on seeing all Black people through a lens of inherent "racial" inferiority.

Referring to the arrival of the Edloe Sixty-Six in Boston, Randolph wrote, "Truly we were in a new world," one he and his fellow migrants had entered "empty-handed and ignorant of their environments." Those new "environments" were the brick canyons of downtown Boston; the congested streets, sunless alleyways, and bustling waterfront area; and the hilly neighborhood of the West End—all of these a dramatic departure from the river bottoms of Virginia's Prince George County. In those lowlands, the woods, rivers, and swamps had shaped enslaved people's patterns of worship and rituals of mourning, connecting them to ancestors buried there. Families could count on supplementing their meager rations of bacon and cornmeal with the small animals they trapped, the fish they caught, and the roots and berries they gathered. In Boston, new foods would take the place of ash cakes, possum, and pokeweed salad. Now it would not be possible for the migrants to line coffins with wheat straw, or to collect their own firewood to stay warm in the winter. The rhythms of the planting season were replaced by the rhythms of commerce. And in the colder climate there would be the endless challenge of finding sturdy coats, cloaks, and shoes and keeping them in repair. In the city, virtually all necessities came at a price—a cash price.[1]

In 1851, a Massachusetts supporter of the American Colonization Society predicted that Black southerners would not be able to survive north of the Hudson "under the combined influence of our severe winters and a degraded position." Boston's Black community proved otherwise. Nevertheless, the social and natural configuration of the city presented a challenge for those who were used to relying on traditional healing practitioners when they got sick, as well as for those seeking to practice as or consult with counselors, root doctors, dream interpreters, conjurers, and fortune tellers. The cherry blossoms and roots from the Adam and Eve, May apple, and Sweet William plants—all ingredients in medicinal concoctions—were nowhere to be found in the city (though rat veins were). On some Virginia plantations, a hawk signaled an imminent death in the community; Boston was lacking in such a sign, as well as the rabbit feet, frog tongues, and feathers that some healers depended upon. Some root doctors were accustomed to planting a bottle in the dirt in front of a cabin, intending to render a victim weak and ill; now, brick and stone sidewalks fronted many dwellings. The adage that it was bad luck to meet a woman walking very early in the morning had to be abandoned or revised amid crowded city streets. In the end, what a newcomer might lose in this "new world" was his or her reputation; the fugitive William Wells Brown said that the appeal of his fortune-teller uncle lay not in whether he was right or wrong in his predictions, but rather in his "*name* . . . about half of what one needs in this gullible age."[2]

INFORMAL PATTERNS OF influence within the Edloe cohort remain hidden, but outwardly, at least, it appears that they soon settled into their new lives. Virtually every nuclear family was able to live independently while at the same time near kin, their fellow migrants, and other Black Virginians (most of whom were no doubt fugitives). Some way or another, the southerners had learned to navigate Boston's steep, icy streets in the wintertime, to haggle for food at the stalls at Quincy marketplace, and to contend with the many other difficult tasks imposed by this novel, noisy, congested cityscape. The Charles, bounded on both sides by thick settlements, was no James River coursing through a countryside of farms. The migrants relied on networks of neighbors and fellow congregants for support. And the heart of those networks was Ward 6, where six out of ten Black Bostonians lived in 1850. Still, out of every one hundred residents there, sixty-five were native-born whites; twenty-one were foreign-born; and fourteen were Black. Fewer than half of the ward's Black residents had been born in Massachusetts.

Residential clusters of Virginia-born Bostonians spoke to larger issues related to the process of assimilation into city life. In August 1850, Carter Selden was living in Ward 6 with his new wife, Sarah; their baby, Meg; and his five Virginia-born children by his late wife, Louisa. The Seldens lived on Southac Street, an overwhelmingly Black neighborhood that included many Virginians. Keeping families and kin groups intact, the Edloe men and women had managed to avoid the fate of one out of ten Boston Blacks, those who were either living and working in a white household or living in one of the city's institutions of confinement and punishment—the House of Correction (for convicted criminals), the Boston Lunatic Hospital, the Boston Almshouse (for paupers), or the Boston City Hospital. In the Black community, households of a single person were unusual; most had a mother and father together with their children, and perhaps boarders or extended kin members. Married and unmarried adult children often remained with their parents for various reasons—because they were unable to afford to rent a place of their own, or because they felt obligated to help support their mother and father, for example. The Black servants living in white families were few, and their numbers were dwarfed by Irish immigrants in those jobs.[3]

In the end it was remarkable how many of the Edloe families—probably at least four-fifths or so—remained in Boston or its suburbs. Though most had spent their whole lives on a plantation, they presumably chose the alleys and narrow streets of the city over the family homesteads of rural New England. Or perhaps they had no choice, given the apparent lack of job offers emanating from the countryside. More likely, these families wanted to continue to live near each other and to partake of the advantages, relative though they were, that urban life could offer.

A city dweller could stop by a friend's house for tea in the afternoon, or gossip with a neighbor in a tenement hallway, or linger outside a church sanctuary after Sunday services. One need not have money to enjoy the flowers in the Public Garden on a day in May, or practice with the Attucks Glee Club on a winter's evening. Black Boston also prized civic engagement, with mass gatherings at the African Meeting House (also known as the Belknap Street Church or the First Independent Baptist Church), or in Tremont Temple, or on the Common. Parades of proud Black men wending their way through the city, including an annual August "excursion on horseback" to celebrate British West Indian emancipation, offered thrilling spectacles previously unknown and unimaginable to enslaved workers in the South. The children could attend the Abiel Smith School on Joy Street, an imposing brick structure segregated and inferior to white schools, but a welcome gateway to literacy for the formerly enslaved. The churches offered a range of denominational choices, Sunday schools, and women's groups. In some cases, the migrants brought with them the small, ephemeral mutual aid associations they had started in the South—informal credit, medical insurance, and burial societies.[4]

The sociability of city life came at a price, and renters faced tight quarters and high living costs. By the late 1840s, labor competition had led to declining wages for the half of all Boston workers who were either unskilled or semiskilled, sending some Black families to the periphery of the city. Gradually, Boston manufactories were consolidating their operations, mechanizing, and forming larger firms, in the process pushing smaller shops out of the central core or out of business altogether.[5]

Still, Boston's liveliness helped draw rural folk from all over New England and kept a hold on people already living there. The famous impresario P. T. Barnum organized novelty shows and concerts. Prices for tickets to hear the international singing sensation Jenny Lind, the "Swedish Nightingale," were probably out of reach for ordinary people. However, for a modest sum, people of all ages could enjoy a circus in the Public Garden, or marvel at demonstrations of novel devices in the open air or in a local theater—there were panoramas, sparring and fencing contests, ventriloquists, exotic animals (and people—in one case, two children from Central America put on display), wax figures, a variety of exhibits featuring equestrians, and even a telescope by which to view the heavens.

In early 1855, Peter Randolph was living in Charlestown, a Boston suburb just across the Charles River, and finishing two major projects. By now he had a mortgage to pay as well as a family to feed. He had become an ordained Baptist preacher, but with the pulpit of Twelfth Baptist filled, he had decided to take to the road. His mission was, in his words, "working for, and laboring with, other churches and telling the story of my bond-brethren in the South." In 1852 he was in St. John, New Brunswick, where he visited the Lake Loma colony of Black people living under hardscrabble conditions, with no schools and little wage work. Finding the prospects of starting his own church there discouraging, he returned to Boston, where he accepted preaching invitations from whites as well as Blacks. One day he was addressing a mixed audience in Somerville when a white teamster, offended, got up and walked out of the hall, only to return a short while later, willing to listen. Wrote Randolph, "This man, full of prejudice, could not tell how far a toad could hop, by looking at his size."[6]

In the fall of 1854, Randolph had decided to avenge the injustices inflicted upon the Edloe Sixty-Six. He began preparing a suit against Edloe's heirs, the two Orgain nieces, seeking to recover the money promised the freed slaves in their master's will but never paid to them. With the help of abolitionist attorney John A. Andrew, Randolph secured legal representation in Petersburg, Virginia. The suit argued that the group had left Virginia before the proceeds of the wheat harvest had been distributed; each formerly enslaved person was due $35. Levi Cooper, age thirty-five, a white member of the crew of the *Thomas H. Thompson*, supplied an affidavit. The New York–born Cooper, now working as "a waiter, etc." in Boston, testified that he had helped the group board the vessel in Richmond and had witnessed the scene where they were presented with their freedom papers. Since then, he had "known and frequently seen and talked with a considerable number of their company." Cooper affirmed that "Peter Randolph has always maintained the reputation of good moral character, since I have known him, and I consider him a truthful and upright citizen and good man." Randolph officially filed the papers for his claim on January 22, 1855.[7]

Randolph expended considerable time and expense tracking down survivors of the original group—they were, he reported, "scattered around in the neighboring towns." They gave him their permission to move ahead with the suit: "All has been done with their consent." In the intervening seven years, sixteen of the original sixty-six had died—not just the elderly, but also children, young adults, and middle-aged men and women. However, most of the original migrants and their children were still clustered either in Ward 6 (six households) or Roxbury (four households), with three families in Charlestown and two in Plymouth. The nuclear families remained intact. Except for Randolph, now a preacher; Carter Selden, a porter; and Andrew Clark, a mariner, the adult men were working as laborers. Randolph managed to account for all the original migrants, living or dead.

In May, Randolph and the others learned (no doubt to their great surprise) that they had won their suit. A Virginia court awarded the group a total of $660—that is, $463.84 for their share of the crop, and $196.16 in interest. For each deceased member, families would get one-half a share, with a full share amounting to $10.64. Peter Randolph received compensation for himself, his wife and daughter, and his two deceased brothers for a total of $58.55.

The largest sum, $74.51, went to Carter Selden for his children and for his kin who had died—a baby named Charlotte; his first wife, Louisa; and his former mother-in-law, Lucy Fountain. The family now lived next door to Charles Fountain, Louisa's cousin, and several other laborers who had been born in Virginia. By this time, Carter's son Thomas, finished with his schooling and working as a laborer, had made friends who would remain loyal to him his whole life, notably Aaron Joseph, the son of an English-born ship steward and his New York–born wife. Within three years or so Thomas would become a husband and father himself, though perhaps not in that order. His brother Benjamin had found work as a waiter, and his brother Edward had moved to New York City and married a woman from Halifax. For all of them, Peter Randolph's assiduous efforts had yielded a welcome and totally unexpected windfall.

Neither Randolph's legal efforts to reclaim the funds due the Edloe Sixty-Six nor his itinerant preaching offered much in the way of a steady income, however, so he began to write his autobiography. The first edition of *Sketches of Slave Life: Or, Illustrations of the "Peculiar Institution,"* which came out in May 1855, provided a vivid description of the Edloe migrants' suffering under slavery. In endorsing the book, *The Liberator* described it as "a neat little pamphlet." The paper printed a quotation from the author, who said that the Edloe migrants were "proving to the world, by their conduct, that slaves when liberated, can take care of themselves, and need no master or overseer to drive them to their toil." This statement presumably helped sell the volume: a second edition was published later in the year, suggesting that it met with some favor among abolitionists.[8]

Many enslaved people continued to walk, ride, and sail into Boston without attracting attention and causing an uproar, perhaps at least partly thanks to Massachusetts's new 1855 "personal liberty" law, the Act to Protect the Rights and Liberties of the People of the Commonwealth of Massachusetts. It stipulated that no state authorities could participate in a fugitive rendition, nor could any attorneys in the state represent slaveholders in those legal proceedings. In July of the following year, the barque

Growler arrived from Mobile. A man named Johnson, the fugitive on board, was "in a nearly starving condition," according to one observer, but managed to jump overboard into the harbor, only to be picked up by crew members on orders from the captain. At a hearing, the man was represented by John Andrew, and the judge said, simply, "Let Johnson be discharged," and he was.[9]

Once on dry land in Boston, freedom-seekers had to hunt for wage work immediately. As a reform movement, the Massachusetts branch of Garrison's American Anti-Slavery Society was a money-making machine, but little went to the fugitives themselves. The annual Boston bazaar was enjoying considerable success; now held in Faneuil Hall, it attracted more visitors and registered a greater profit each year—$5,000 by the mid-1850s—as wealthy Bostonians sought out imported jewelry, art, clothing, and furnishings donated by antislavery supporters in foreign lands. In 1855, one of the chief organizers, Maria Weston Chapman, declined an invitation to cosponsor the fair with its New York counterpart; she wanted the Boston society to keep all the money, and she also refused to work with women focused on the plight of fugitives; such an arrangement, she believed, would not be "honourable to the cause."[10]

In the summer of 1855, a state census-taker was able to identify about 200 southern-born Black men living in Ward 6. (Many fugitive respondents no doubt hid their origins.) By far the largest number, 84, were born in Virginia; the next highest numbers were from Maryland (50) and Delaware and Washington, DC (20 each). A few hailed from South Carolina, Alabama, and Florida or the interior states of Kentucky and Tennessee. Other countries were also represented, including India, Suriname, Portugal, Spain, Cuba, and Bermuda (mostly mariners). Among the Virginia migrants were laborers, waiters, barbers, and seamen (in that order), with a handful of shoemakers, blacksmiths, porters, carpenters, peddlers, and boardinghouse operators. Together, the laborers, porters, servants, waiters, and mariners amounted to three-quarters of all male wage earners, with lecturers, doctors, and clergymen comprising 3 percent of the total. Around this time, whites who had been born in Massachusetts were working at 660 different occupations, immigrants from Ireland at 362, and Blacks at only 46.[11]

THROUGHOUT THE 1850S, many remarkable Black newcomers to Boston infused the city with their entrepreneurial energy, protesting the southern-like conditions they encountered in their new home. Several notable free people of color from Norfolk, Virginia, moved to Boston around this time. John Oliver, a carpenter, had settled in Boston by the summer of 1850. He boarded with a Black couple (a hairdresser and his wife) in Ward 5, and, after setting up shop on Friend Street, began to advertise his services. The thirty-year-old was no ordinary craftsman, but someone who could build, repair, and renovate structures of any kind: he promised to, "by prompt attention to all orders, endeavour to give entire satisfaction to his patrons." In June 1852, he briefly returned to Norfolk to marry Louise DeMortie, who, together with her brother Mark, moved to Boston soon after. Louise eventually embarked on a career of public speaking and gained renown for her recitations of famous poems and literary passages. Mark opened a boot and shoe store with a partner.[12]

The marriage between Louise and John Oliver was not a happy one. Two years after their wedding, their son Wendell Phillips Oliver died at the age of sixteen months. Within a month, John was in San Francisco, alone, advertising his services, work "done with promptness and dispatch, also on the most reasonable terms." A year later he was back in Boston and living with his wife, brother-in-law, and mother-in-law, Frances, who had moved to Boston from Virginia. Within the next two years Oliver would leave Boston once again, this time to attend the preparatory class at Oberlin College for a year. He was seeking a new livelihood, and his marriage was failing.[13]

George W. and Nancy Ruffin, also free people of color, came from Richmond, where he was a successful barber and hairdresser and owner of his own shop. The Ruffins were able to afford a Latin and English-literature tutor for their four sons and two daughters. They moved to Boston in 1853, stung by a recent Virginia state law that would deprive even free children of an education. For several years George W. traveled back and forth between his new home and his old one, continuing to make money to support his family in Boston.[14]

George W. and his sons, James D. and George Lewis, became well-known leaders in the community. However, once the family arrived in Boston, much of the day-to-day business of managing the household fell to Nancy. She had been a property owner before her marriage, and she now had to borrow money from friends and neighbors and negotiate with an unforgiving landlady while waiting for her husband to send cash. She found asking for credit to be a most disagreeable task. She was also annoyed that her husband bought expensive clothing and bedsteads and rented a house too large to keep up and heat: "This house has so many dets [*sic*] hanging on it makes me so low spirited I don't know what to do," she wrote to George W. At one point, in November 1858, Nancy told him that she would rather take the children and enter the poorhouse than have to rely on loans. But by the end of the decade, she was working with her son George L., importing foodstuffs from Richmond to sell in Boston.[15]

John S. Rock arrived in Boston the same year as the Ruffins. As a young man he had established a dentistry practice in Philadelphia, where he joined the Freemasons and became an outspoken anti-colonizationist. By 1852 he had completed a course of study at the American Medical College and was offering night classes for Black students. In November of that year, a fire swept through a dwelling that housed his practice, and not long afterward, he moved to Boston with his wife, Catharine, twenty-two. Before long they had a baby, Toussaint, probably while they were boarding with the Haydens.

Rock provided medical care for some fugitives, but he found it difficult to make a living as either a doctor or a dentist. Instead, he established himself as a lyceum speaker, and a uniquely distinguished one. Among his early lecture topics were "The Unity of Human Races" and "The Popular Objections to the Masonic Institution." A review of his appearance in Worcester in early 1855 described him as "a handsome speaker, and his lecture evinced a fine education, superior scholarship, and much careful research, especially with reference to the unity of the race." The following year a Philadelphia observer offered the ultimate testimonial, saying, of Rock's oratorical ability, "If he was not a black, our newspapers would fail to find a language rich enough to praise it." Rock also served as a perceptive, perpetually indignant correspondent for *Frederick Douglass' Paper*, which had taken on a decidedly Know-Nothing (anti-immigrant) tone as a result of the support of the Roman Catholic establishment for the Fugitive Slave Act of 1850. Rock quickly formed an opinion of his new home state. In 1855 he admitted that Massachusetts Blacks "enjoy more civil liberty and are more respected than in any other state south of her." At the same time, anti-Black bias pervaded the Bay State in public and private relations: "Unfortunately for us, wherever the white Yankee plants his foot, there he fixes his prejudice."[16]

The Rhode Island–born Christiana Babcock Carteaux had also moved to Boston by the mid-1850s, when she was in her twenties. Of African and Narragansett Indian descent, she soon opened her own hairdressing business (under the name "Madame Carteaux"), divorced her husband, a clothing dealer, and married Edward Mitchell Bannister. A native of New Brunswick, Bannister had lived in Boston since 1848, working as a mariner and barber. It was probably his wife's commercial success that allowed him finally to

Christiana Babcock Carteaux Bannister sat for this formal portrait painted by her husband, the artist Edward Mitchell Bannister. He was the first Black man to win a national award for painting (at the Philadelphia Centennial Exposition in 1876). Born in Rhode Island in 1819 of Indigenous Narragansett descent, "Madame Carteaux" advertised regularly in *The Liberator* and other Boston newspapers, touting her "Root and Herb Restorative Cures" for hair.

(Courtesy of the Rhode Island School of Design Museum, Providence, Rhode Island)

pursue a career as an artist, a painter. For two years this couple also boarded with the Haydens.[17]

Another newcomer, the lawyer Aaron Alpeoria Bradley, showed little interest in joining the rarefied Boston Black elite that welcomed the Ruffins, John Oliver, and the DeMorties. In any case, Bradley's brash personality and questionable legal ethics made him a foil to Robert Morris. Born to an enslaved mother in South Carolina around 1815, Bradley was working as a shoemaker in Augusta, Georgia, when he managed to escape (perhaps as early as the mid-1830s) and make his way to New York City, where he was practicing law by 1848. Three years later he spent two years in prison for "the crime of seduction" (presumably for having sex with a woman he promised to marry). Released in 1853, he moved to Massachusetts and became the third Black man to be admitted to the state's bar. Over the next few years he would fall out of favor with judges and fellow attorneys; some of his clients charged that he had withheld money from them. In 1856 he was expelled from the Suffolk bar "on charges of malpractice and fraud in certain specified instances," but that temporary setback did not slow him down. In December he was back in the courtroom representing an Irish immigrant woman. He had no intention of withdrawing from his troubled legal practice.[18]

LIKE FREE PEOPLE of color in the urban South, Boston's Blacks had to contend with whites who persisted in promoting discriminatory racial ideologies despite the presence in their midst of ambitious, and even in some cases prosperous and accomplished, nonwhite men and women. Though based on the fiction of a "racial" hierarchy, these ideas of social difference materially affected the well-being of Black people and manifested themselves in multiple ways—within Boston's school system, at entertainment venues, and throughout society generally. Ultimately, white northerners' notions of race remained inconsistent and contradictory as they parsed elements of culture, skin color, and biological lineage in an effort to categorize Blacks as a "race" apart and inferior.

The meeting at Twelfth Baptist on September 6, 1855, was joyful but subdued. Parents had gathered to mark the beginning of the school year and the closing of the segregated Abiel Smith School. A correspondent for *Frederick Douglass' Paper* reported that "their appearance was unusually cheerful, neat and intelligent." Together, the attendees issued a public statement: "We the colored parents of Boston, do hereby pledge ourselves to have our children punctually at school, and neat in their dress and in all other ways will aid their instructors in the task which has been assigned to them." Douglass exulted, "We have no longer a Caste School among us."[19]

The integration of Boston's public schools stood as a milestone in the Black community's fight for equality under the law. For longtime advocates, this battle had been maddening. Parents had initiated one petition after another from the mid-1840s onward. In 1848, Benjamin F. Roberts sued the city on behalf of his daughter Sarah, who walked past five public primary schools on her way to Abiel Smith, which was half a mile from her house. Roberts was a Boston-born activist and printer (named after Benjamin Franklin) with English, African, and Native forebears. Hearkening back to the American Revolution and its ideals of universal equality, he deplored the insidious obsession with skin color that infected virtually every element of life in Boston. The state Supreme Judicial Court had rejected his argument, claiming that Black children were inferior to white children, and that the Smith school provided equal accommodations for its students in any case. An increasingly bureaucratized public school system—reflected in the classroom's straight rows of desks and standardized instruction—aimed to prepare the state's white children for factory work and the rigors of US citizenship; neither goal pertained to people of color. After the decision, Roberts's attorneys, Robert Morris and Charles Sumner, who in the near future would be elected to the US Senate (1851), switched tactics and took the issue to the state legislature. As a result, in April 1855, Massachusetts banned segregated public schools from the commonwealth.[20]

Satisfaction over this hard-won victory was not unalloyed, or even universal. A small but vocal number of Black people feared that the new integrated system would deprive them of a handful of precious teaching positions for their own community. One of them, a used clothing dealer named Thomas Paul Smith, suffered vicious verbal and physical attacks from integrationist-minded leaders. Regardless of their views on the Smith School, however, most Black people understood that its shuttering was not going to herald a new day of equality. White prejudice would persist regardless of legal interventions. Observers of the event stressed the respectable demeanor of the attendees, who aimed to distance themselves from the Black nightwalkers and thieves who made routine appearances in Police Court. These parents and others believed that an outward show of respectability on the part of Black Bostonians would hasten the demise of racism.[21]

Nevertheless, whites' contempt reflected a nation-based ideology of social difference. The city's school board members had described Black schoolchildren in terms of their "race," suggesting that their inferiority was genetic and unalterable; in contrast, William Cooper Nell echoed Benjamin Roberts and denounced what he called "colorphobia," an irrational aversion to a superficial physical characteristic. Local newspapers continued to routinely ridicule Black men and women, making snide comments about phenotype ("as if they had just come from Moore's dye house"), describing their comportment in sarcastic ways, and rendering their speech in dialect. Owners of confectionary shops summarily ejected girls who attempted to order refreshments, even in cases where, in the words of *The Liberator*, the girls were nearly white, their "characters and manners . . . irreproachable." Sarah Parker Remond, from the well-to-do family of Salem activists, protested when she was relegated to the gallery of the Howard Athenaeum, and an usher pushed her down the stairs, injuring her. She sued the owner of the venue and won $500 from him, but this did not eliminate the practice of seating Blacks separately from whites at some venues. Even Robert Morris was subjected to numerous indignities, and the famous Frederick Douglass was turned away from a restaurant and an exhibit on the Common and ejected from an omnibus.[22]

Such offensive treatment inspired some individuals to make a pointed protest in their workplaces. A barber, Julian B. McCrea, decided to turn the tables on a Mr. Fleming, owner of one of the offending theaters that enforced segregated seating. When Fleming arrived for a shave, McCrea ushered him into a small storeroom at the back of his shop. In response to the puzzled look on Fleming's face, McCrea declared, "You set apart a place in your theatre for men of my color. I do not measure men by

Sarah Parker Remond became a full-time abolitionist lecturer in 1856 at the age of thirty, speaking to audiences in the United States and, from 1859 to 1862, in England, Ireland, and Scotland. As agents of the American Anti-Slavery Society, she and her brother Charles Lenox Remond contended with meager, irregular pay; poor accommodations and other difficulties involved in traveling as Black people; and at times skeptical if not downright hostile audiences. *(Collection of the Massachusetts Historical Society)*

their color, but anyone who will proscribe a man on account of his color, deserves to be proscribed. Walk in, sir." Fleming left the shop in a huff.[23]

To some extent, Boston's whites, regardless of class, remained flummoxed by the whole notion of "race." On the one hand, they stigmatized people of color (including those of Indigenous descent) with the legacy of slavery; on the other hand, people with a Black ancestor but white skin seemed impossible to categorize. This curiosity factor extended to "Black" children who looked "white." On March 29, 1855, Sumner appeared at Tremont Temple, where a ticketed event drew a standing-room-only crowd. Appearing on the stage with the senator were Anthony Burns, who had recently returned to the city of his trial, and a little girl named Mary Mildred Williams. Organizers of the event billed the seven-year-old as a "white slave," and indeed, she had been born to an enslaved mother named Elizabeth in Prince William County, Virginia.[24]

That night in Tremont Temple, Mary Williams proved a fitting representative of Sumner's claim that slavery constituted a "deadly injury to morals, in substituting concubinage for marriage and changing the whole land of slavery into a by-word of shame." She continued to appear at subsequent antislavery meetings, drawing crowds and spawning a new fund-raising and propaganda device—a daguerreotype of her that was marketed to supporters of abolition. The picture showed her in a plaid dress with white sleeves, her brown hair parted in the middle with gentle curls framing her face. This portrait of a serious-looking little girl would have otherwise held no interest; however, as Nell pointed out, the fact that she was formerly enslaved produced "intense excitement" over her appearance at the State House.[25]

In September, another exhibit in Boston, this one featuring many Black children, attracted another large white audience willing to pay. Horatio Bateman's Colored Baby Show (at Chapman Hall) took place at the same time P. T. Barnum was holding his own show of white children at Music Hall. For both events (ongoing simultaneously, for five days), mothers entered a contest to win cash prizes, sitting with their babies on their laps for hours at a time over several days. More than twenty thousand visitors attended the Bateman affair, and it was estimated that he took in $5,000 in ticket sales. According to a disapproving John Rock, writing in Douglass's paper, those mothers whose babies failed to win a prize were paid one or two dollars "for their trouble of sitting there a week dandling their babies and answering all kinds of questions that an inquiring visitor or an insulting loafer, [*sic*] chose to propound to them." Several "white mothers with colored children," evidence of the lack of anti-miscegenation laws in Massachusetts, proved a source of irritation for at least one judge, who suggested that these children should be ineligible to compete. Rock noted, "The exhibition was by no means popular among the colored people, though many very respectable colored persons visited it, and many took part in the exhibition, who would not be likely to take part in another. The whole affair was farce played at the expense of the colored people." Among the categories were "fattest child" and "blackest child."[26]

Baby contests in general shattered the supposedly bright line between family feeling and crass commercialism. The first shows took place at agricultural fairs and livestock exhibitions, suggesting that babies, vegetables, and pigs could all be bred to produce a superior strain of their respective life-forms. One New York woman denounced Barnum's "monstrous exhibitions" and added that no true American woman would tolerate this "rude gaze of a prying curiosity," which evoked the slave markets of the South. However, Barnum knew what would appeal to an audience, whether elephants, snake charmers, or the Feejee Mermaid (the upper half of a stuffed monkey sewn to the lower half of a large stuffed fish). He also knew to take advantage of controversy and keep his name in the papers—in news stories, ads for upcoming shows, and high-minded letters to the editor. Defending himself in the *Herald*, he claimed that after twenty-five years in the business of "public amusement" he knew best what the masses wanted, and he resented the characterization of the baby show as a kind of "cattle show."[27]

The paper reported that these children perked up when they heard the strains of a pianoforte, "but as this is a well-known characteristic of the colored race, it is not to be wondered at." If, as the paper claimed, "the public have pronounced it *the* show of the week," even more popular than Barnum's, it was perhaps because Bateman promoted it as an "opportunity to determine whether or not color has any effect on the intellectual organization of mankind." In their convoluted attempts to define Black people's "race," white Bostonians resembled their southern counterparts and attempted, fitfully, to reconcile skin color with inborn "racial" characteristics.[28]

In addition to contending with persistent forms of discrimination, Black leaders lurched from one political crisis to another. In June 1856, a crowd gathered at Twelfth Baptist to decry the recent horrific beating of Charles Sumner on the floor of the Senate by Preston Brooks, a US representative from South Carolina. The attendees designated Rock and George W. Ruffin as officers of the meeting, and Rock condemned the "brutal, murderous, and cowardly assault" on their senator. Within a few months, in early fall, Rock was part of a group that submitted a petition to the city council "praying that the word 'colored' which now stands against their names on the voting lists and tax bills, may be removed, and that they may stand as fair on the record as their fellow white citizens." The lawmakers voted to table the issue, stating that the "col" signifier was necessary because so many men had the same names. The petitioners remained convinced that the city's true aim was to exclude Blacks from the jury box.[29]

Still, even Rock had to admit that, for all its failings, the Bay State allowed the robust participation of Black men in politics—not only for those who owned taxable property of some kind, as voters, but for all members of the community as participants in mass protest meetings. In 1854, he and other Black leaders had thrown their support behind the bigoted Know Nothings of the American Party, more as a matter of principle than nativism; they saw the party as a vehicle to express their disgust at the Roman Catholic clergy, the diocese's paper *The Pilot*, and the Irish-immigrant rank and file, a formidable collective force opposed to abolitionism. These Black leaders objected to the rights and privileges granted to those men newly arrived in the country but denied to other men, some of whom could trace their US lineage back to the early seventeenth century.[30]

The year 1854 marked the founding of the Republican Party, a new, regional political party dedicated to the elimination of slavery in the territories. It gained the enthusiastic support of many of Boston's Black leaders, who welcomed the downfall of a two-party system based on a fragile national "compromise" that upheld the practice of human bondage. That fall, the Republican candidate for president, John C. Fremont, lost the election, but Republicans carried the Massachusetts state legislature, dislodging the Know Nothings. The new party consisted of a coalition of Whig, Know-Nothing, temperance, and antislavery factions coexisting uneasily with one another.

Robert Morris and Lewis Hayden became stalwart Republican ward heelers. Yet skeptics abounded. Charles Lenox Remond, for one, was wary of a party that promised to preserve slavery in the South. And it remained unclear what the Republicans had to offer Black people in Boston. In July 1856, an anonymous correspondent ("H. B. B." from Cambridge) wrote a lengthy piece for a local Democratic newspaper. The writer assumed that the Republicans were the party of Boston's abolitionists, a group quick to condemn southern slaveholders but silent when it came to the plight of their Black neighbors. White abolitionists, according to the writer, cared less about rooting out prejudice at home than they did about improving various strains of apples and oranges. The author charged that, for all their raising of funds, passing of resolutions, and editing of newspapers and tracts, whites had not materially improved the condition of Black Bostonians, or even shown much interest in doing so. Most Black residents lived in basements, stables, attics, and back lanes, in "dirty, unhealthy and ill-ventilated holes," and not one in five hundred owned any real estate, "even if they live[d] in respectable neighborhoods." As for employment, "Who will hire or work with a nigger?"[31]

The author also condemned whites who insulted Black people—even those "cleverly dressed"—on the streets and in the public parks. White men and boys would greet Black passers-by "by *sneezing*, contemptuous jests, and low, vagabond slurs and remarks." Boston compared unfavorably to the slave-owning

South when it came to the loud and vocal denigration of Black women: "Everywhere, in all our streets and public places, the colored female is insulted!" And not just women of poor means, but the wives and daughters of the enterprising clothing dealers on Brattle Street as well. The author concluded, "Female slaves are not treated as licentiously in the Southern streets as many respectable, well dressed colored females are treated every day in the streets of Boston by abolitionists and others." In the South, the institution of bondage established strict parameters for Black behavior, while in the North, individual whites assumed that task themselves. It was not clear to this writer how the Republicans' opposition to slavery in the territories would materially affect the caste-like system in Boston.[32]

That system, which included the skill-dilution of Black workers over the generations, was not unique to the Bay State city. In 1855 an annual Colored National Convention met in Philadelphia. John S. Rock, Leonard Grimes, Charles Lenox Remond, and William Cooper Nell represented Massachusetts. The delegates acknowledged the difficulty of young Black men in securing apprenticeships and the fact that skilled migrants moving north—either openly, by steamship or train, or clandestinely via back roads and forests—had "ceased to follow their trades for want of encouragement." To make their point, convention organizers included a list of all the northern states, with their Black workers divided into two categories—"Working at their Trades and Professions" and "Not Working at their Trades and Professions." For Massachusetts, the latter list included blacksmiths, tailors, masons, shoemakers, printers, and musicians—men who could not find employment commensurate with their skills.[33]

The convention, a mostly all-male affair, urged Blacks around the country to consider the creation of a "Mechanical Bureau" to promote "Mechanic Arts amongst colored men." In an unexpected turn, it was resolved that "private residences" were "the most suitable places to conduct these conversations as thereby we should get better access to the minds of our females." However, this concession reflected not an acknowledgment of women qua workers, but women qua unpaid caretakers: wives and mothers should have their say about these pressing issues because it was they who would "shape the future for part of the great duties which they are to perform in moulding the future character of our youth for improvement." As a resolution from a convention protesting the northern social division of labor, this injunction missed the mark, limiting women to their roles as mothers and nurturers. Unlike their menfolk, Black women performed many of the same jobs in the North as free workers as they had in the South as enslaved workers, and, unlike their menfolk, they found an unlimited demand for their services, waged or unwaged.[34]

5

Women in Service

For a preacher's wife, Octavia Janet Coleston Grimes cared a great deal about money—where to get it and how to come by more of it; but then, she had little choice in the matter. In 1848, her husband, Leonard, had responded to a call from a small breakaway congregation in Boston. He assumed the pulpit at what would become Twelfth Baptist Church at a starting annual salary of $100—less than what a menial laborer could earn. The Grimeses helped to plot rescues and raise money to free fugitives; estimates pegged their 1850s payoffs to slave owners at $4,000. Meanwhile, the church was constructing a new two-story house of worship at a cost of $13,000. Despite the couple's skill at extracting donations from white men and women, Twelfth Baptist remained mired in debt for years; in 1858, with the building completed, the mortgage was still a hefty $5,000.[1]

Octavia Grimes was her husband's helpmate, or, more accurately, his partner. It was up to her to figure out how to feed and clothe their growing family on his meager salary. She entertained a constant round of guests, from runaways to visiting dignitaries. She kept the household going when her husband was out of town negotiating with slaveholders in Richmond and attending annual denominational and political meetings. She served as superintendent of the Twelfth Baptist Sunday School and provided refreshments for weeknight gatherings held at the church. And she and other women took it upon themselves to retire the congregation's outstanding debt by sponsoring fairs and appealing to white women of means.[2]

Twelfth Baptist, a renowned site of antislavery activism, occupied an iconic place in Boston's Black community. Octavia Grimes was integral to the many purposes of the church, but her work brought her no pay and few public accolades. Black men judged their womenfolk by a standard defined as "refinement." Women who met the standard tended to homemaking and remained aloof from the presumably cruel world of money-making inhabited by their husbands and sons. A preacher's wife bore an extra burden; she was supposed to be a model of delicacy and propriety. Yet it was difficult for Octavia to fulfill all her many duties and remain delicate at the same time.

Octavia J. Coleston was born in 1818 in Washington, DC, to free parents. She and Leonard were married there in 1833. Soon after, he was sent to prison for two years for helping groups of enslaved workers escape in a wagon he owned. In the words of an admiring, contemporary biographer, Leonard was punished for "piloting into the land of freedom, those whom slavery has marked as her children,—or rather, her 'goods.'" Upon his release from prison, Leonard found that authorities had confiscated all his property, and in 1845 the couple decided to move to New Bedford. He opened a small grocery store and worked on and off as a painter. When the couple arrived in Boston with their four children—Emma (fourteen), Julia (twelve), John (eleven), and Leonard (four)—Twelfth Baptist consisted of twenty-three members who met in a small room on the third floor of a building on Belknap Street. As Leonard's stature in the Black community grew, so did the size of the congregation—from a couple of dozen people in 1848 to 278 twelve years later; by 1860 the Sunday school had 14 teachers and 124 pupils. Together with several of their congregants,

The Reverend Leonard Grimes and his wife Octavia C. Grimes were the mainstays of several overlapping communities in antebellum Boston—abolitionists, civil rights activists, fugitive assistants, and Black Baptists. After the Civil War, their church, Twelfth Baptist, became a favored meeting place of Black Republicans. *(Boston Athenaeum)*

the Grimeses hid fugitives and either found them work in Boston or arranged their safe passage to the north or west. At the same time, their family suffered a series of heartbreaks—daughter Julia died in 1850, and son Leonard died the following year.[3]

The new structure on Southac Street, 40 feet by 60 feet, accommodated 600 people. This church, together with Tremont Temple and First Independent Baptist (the African Meeting House on Smith Court), were favored, accessible gathering places for the Black community. In contrast, use of the larger Faneuil Hall required not only a fee, but also a petition submitted to the city council signed by 100 voter-taxpayers. In addition to the Haydens, Twelfth Baptist members included Shadrach Minkins, Anthony Burns, and a considerable number of other

Virginia-born fugitives. However, fund-raising was slowed by the church's precipitous drop in membership after the passage of the Fugitive Slave Act; the law "struck the church like a thunderbolt, and scattered the flock." In 1853, members of the church were still worshipping in the vestry, lacking a sanctuary and needing to pay off the costly debt.[4]

Led by Octavia, the ladies of the Church Society called upon "the benevolent citizens of Boston" without regard to color or creed to patronize a fair to be held on November 21 of that year, no doubt hoping to appeal to the same open-minded whites who planned to attend the Anti-Slavery Society bazaar the following month. By 1854, more than half of the original loan had been paid off, yet four years later the church was still hosting a series of guest speakers, charging admission to raise money. This vigorous outreach effort enlisted white allies, who in turn urged the larger Boston community to honor the Reverend Grimes, described by George S. Hillard (a white abolitionist and fugitive assistant) as "a truly pious and excellent man."[5]

A biographer of Grimes later described the family's straitened circumstances: "His salary barely paid his rent, but by working with his hands, as Paul did, and through the frugal industry of his wife, he was enabled to get along." It is possible Leonard continued to work as a painter, now part time; many Black clergy had to supplement their salary with outside work. Octavia had some help at home; in 1850, twenty-year-old Maria Watson was living with the family. A native of South Carolina, Watson was probably a fugitive from slavery.[6]

In running the Sunday school and presiding over the Ladies' Society, Octavia Grimes was doing the work expected of a preacher's wife; but just as Twelfth Baptist was no ordinary church, Octavia shouldered duties that were more expansive than was typical for a woman in her position. By 1857, when the sanctuary was finished, the church was hosting not only the Boston Vigilance Committee, abolitionist speakers, and indignation meetings, but also many other kinds of events—testimonials to local leaders, anniversaries of historic events (the end of slavery in the British Empire, August 1), plays, debates ("Whether the condition of the Colored People has been advanced or retarded during the last twenty-five years"), and concerts by such groups as the Northern Vocalists ("pieces both sentimental and humorous"). The American Baptist Missionary Convention held its annual meeting at Twelfth Baptist when it met in Boston. Literary enrichment was provided by the dramatic Histrionic Club (at times featuring an original poem by George Lewis Ruffin). Georgianna O. Smith, the Nova Scotia–born wife of the successful barber John J. Smith, presided over a short-lived group called the Ladies Benevolent Firm that met in the church. The Reverend Peter Randolph periodically addressed the congregation on weeknights. These events drew in all elements of the overlapping Black and abolitionist communities, intensifying Octavia's responsibilities. She served as building custodian as well as church diplomat, welcoming multiple constituencies both spiritual and secular.[7]

By this time, Boston had six established Black churches, and folk preachers and itinerant ministers were also vying for the souls and dollars of the faithful. Some congregations appealed to recent migrants by offering southern-style worship services, one of which was described in condescending terms by a reporter as a "strange scene," with churchgoers' "mingled voices . . . raised in a loud wild chorus of petitions, ejaculations and exultations." Still, denominational loyalties could dissolve on the banks of the Charles River, as African Methodist Episcopal (AME), African Methodist Episcopal Zion (AME Zion), and Black Baptist churches came together for old-style baptisms on a springtime Sunday afternoon—no matter how chilly and stormy—with Rev. Grimes playing a leading role. These ceremonies could draw hundreds of observers.[8]

Even after Twelfth Baptist completed its sanctuary, it did not necessarily offer a refuge from controversy or a disordered world.

Rev. Grimes kept his distance from William Lloyd Garrison, whose "come-outerism" philosophy, critical of proslavery ministers, could veer into anti-clericalism. And a church composed of many fugitives posed its own problems. Grimes reacted with consternation upon learning that the groom of a couple he had recently married already had a wife in the South. The minister also unwittingly officiated at the wedding of what the *Herald* called "A Colored Blue Beard"—a man named Isaac Holland, a South Boston barber, who, as it turned out, was engaged in "Trigamy"—still married to two other wives, a Black woman in Philadelphia and an Irish immigrant in Boston.[9]

Octavia Grimes demonstrated impressive event-planning and logistical skills. She organized the annual Sunday school exhibition and the church picnic, the latter an elaborate affair in the suburb of Hyde Park that involved shepherding adults and children onto a train and making certain they brought their own food and paid for their tickets. There were weddings to witness, receptions to host, and meals to prepare for special occasions. In August 1859 a series of public meetings attended by Black leaders culminated in the organizing committee offering "a vote of thanks to the ladies of Boston and vicinity for their very successful arrangements in promoting the objects of the Convention, their hospitality to strangers, &c." Behind this bland expression of gratitude were the multiple tasks necessary to feed, house, and accommodate many out-of-town guests.[10]

Among Octavia's routine domestic tasks were stretching the household's budget and mothering children in a city full of temptation. A "Donation Visit" to the Grimes residence at 28 Southac on March 4, 1856, was an opportunity for all church members to show their "social and benevolent regard for [the pastor] and his family," an invitation to charity, perhaps. The BVC paid Leonard Grimes for services rendered to fugitives who boarded with the family; this modest compensation was a welcome supplement to the household income, for a church full of fugitives could afford to pay its pastor very little. Meanwhile, Octavia worked hard to ensure that her own children stayed on the path of righteousness, avoiding the many diversions of 1850s Boston—the new bowling alleys and billiard saloons, the pull of some crowd-pleasing exhibit on the Common. In November 1856 she was able to list her daughter Emma as one of the "ladies" sponsoring the annual Church Society fair to pay off the debt on their new house of worship. She must have been proud, too, when, in March 1858, her son John took his place on the stage of Faneuil Hall to sing "Freedom's Battle," an original song composed for the occasion, the eighty-eighth anniversary of the death of Crispus Attucks.[11]

Octavia oversaw the day-to-day management of the household, but at least Leonard was not absent from home nearly as often as some of the other famous abolitionists of the day. The challenges faced by the wives of prominent reformers became the stuff of legends. Fueled by a dedication to the cause leavened with varying degrees of male ego, some antislavery lecturers felt little compassion for the womenfolk and children they left behind for weeks, months, and even years at a stretch. Frederick Douglass toured overseas and throughout the United States for long periods of time, leaving his wife, Anna, to care for their five children (all born within a span of ten years). Later, their daughter Rosetta remembered that, during their years in Lynn, her mother worked as a shoe binder and "struggled to maintain the family amid much that would dampen the courage of many a young woman of today." When Frederick moved the household to Rochester, New York, Anna mourned the loss of her Massachusetts friends, as she was largely homebound. Still, she entertained a steady round of visitors and took great pride in her famous husband; according to Rosetta, "in every possible way that she was capable [Anna] aided him by relieving him of all the management of the home as it increased in size and in its appointments." Frederick's return was always an occasion "worthy of extra notice, and caused renewed activity. Every thing was done that could be to add to his comfort." Anna was a strict disciplinarian, especially when it came to keeping her two sons from the temptation of alcohol. She was relieved when Frederick introduced them to the printer's craft; they had few other prospects because of what Rosetta called the "hostile feelings" in Rochester "against the colored boys." She remembered her parents' relationship this way: "Father was mother's honored guest."[12]

Yet Frederick Douglass could be remarkably impatient with his wife. In 1857 he confided to a correspondent that she was complaining about ill health, but he refrained from listing all her maladies, for, "if I should write down all her complaints there would be no room to put my name at the bottom, although the world would have it that I am actually at the bottom of it all." And perhaps alluding to her lack of formal education, he remarked, "She still seems able to use with great ease and fluency her powers of speech, and by the time I am home a week or two longer, I shall have pretty fully learned in how many points there is need of improvement in my temper and disposition as a husband and father, the head of the family!" If Frederick was Anna's "honored guest," at times her demeanor toward him was less than hospitable, and his toward her less than gracious.[13]

In recounting her own childhood, Rosetta failed to mention the immense emotional and financial burdens borne by her mother, who took in boarders to make ends meet. Frederick's paper was an expensive enterprise, and he had to embark on lecture tours to help support it. Too, he had close relationships with two white women who cohabited with the couple and their children over the years. An Englishwoman, Julia Griffiths, moved in and assumed responsibility for chasing delinquent subscribers to the paper. She held the mortgage on the family homestead, and her sister Eliza lent Douglass the substantial sum of $1,000. Julia moved out in 1852, but four years later Frederick met another admirer of his, Ottile Assing, a German woman; the two struck up a friendship based on their shared political and intellectual interests and traveled to meetings and conventions together. Assing, too, at times lived with the family. Understandably resentful of her husband's relationships with these two women, Anna also had to endure the gossip of Garrison and others who questioned the morality of the arrangement, and had to endure as well the contempt of her husband's two confidantes. Assing considered the illiterate Anna nothing more than a drudge and referred to her as that "stupid old hag."[14]

Anna Douglass, Octavia Grimes, Harriet Hayden, Georgianna O. Smith, and Amelia Randolph rarely, if ever, received mention in the ubiquitous, glowing accounts of their well-known husbands within the abolitionist firmament. Yet these women boarded fugitives, raised money for churches, and oversaw family life for their busy spouses. The attorney Robert Morris betrayed his own dismissive attitude when he remarked at one meeting, to great laughter, that women could serve as fugitive assistants by hiding the runaways in the folds of their enormous skirts. His wife, Catharine, a member of the Roman Catholic Church, played no role in the expansive social circles of Protestant Black women.[15]

Dutiful preachers' wives and daughters were no doubt aware of their sisters of color who tried to make a living by proselytizing and agitating. For Black women hoping to bypass the denominational establishment and proclaim the gospel, conditions had not improved since the days of Maria Stewart—or Anne Hutchinson, accused of heresy and banished from Boston in 1638, for that matter. Julia A.J. Foote, born to formerly enslaved parents in Schenectady, New York, began her working life at age ten as a domestic servant. She underwent a religious conversion in 1838, when she was fifteen years old, and three years later married George Foote. Together they moved to Boston. She joined the African Methodist Episcopal Zion Church; but, she recalled, when she told its minister, Jehiel Beman, that she intended to preach, he said, "No, not in this place; I am stationed all over Boston." She began to hold prayer meetings in the homes of her friends, but Beman was

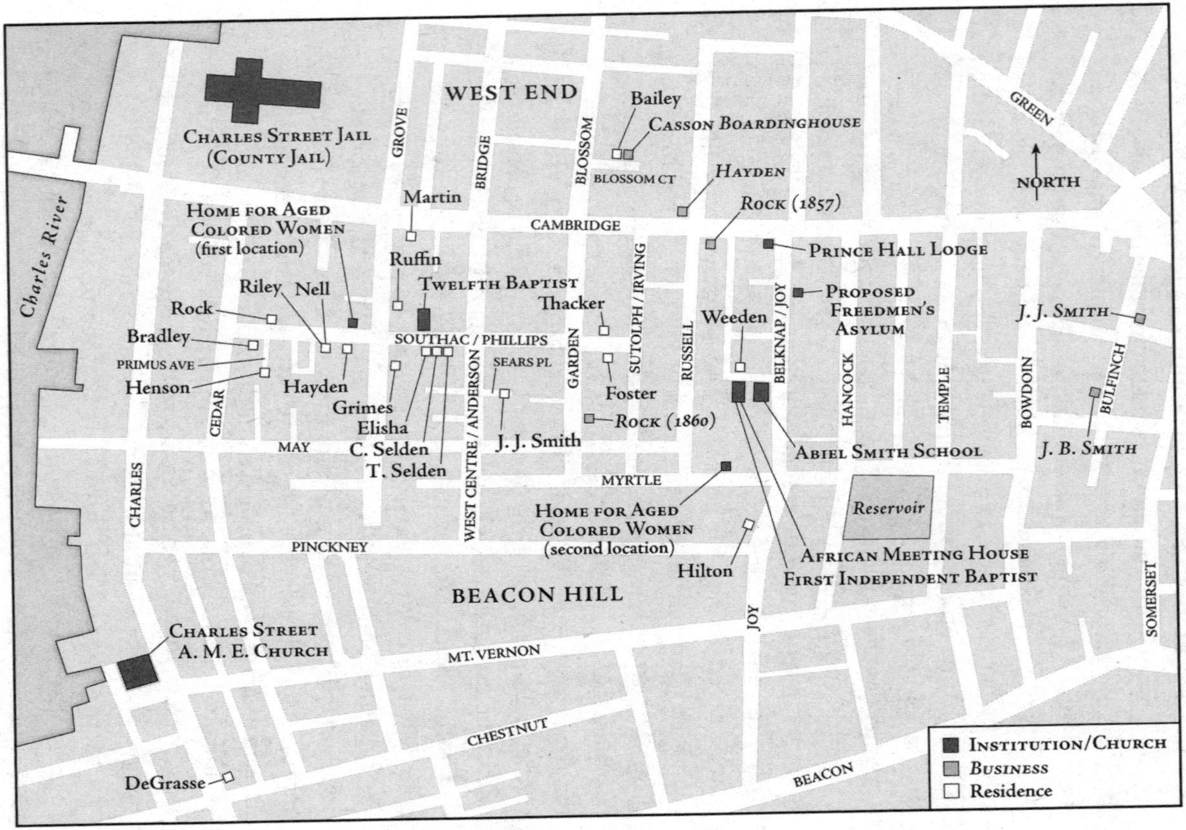

Boston's Beacon Hill and West End neighborhoods, ca. 1860. *(Kate Blackmer)*

unrelenting in his disapproval; Foote later wrote that he talked to her in a "sneering, indifferent way": "He looked very coldly upon me, and said most plainly: 'You don't know anything.'" Eventually Beman organized the community against her—"She can't preach her holiness stuff here"—and managed to have her excommunicated from the church. By the mid-1840s and into the 1850s she was traveling around New England and the Mid-Atlantic states, eventually settling in Cincinnati. Throughout her itinerant career, she considered herself a "thresher," harvesting souls in fields inhospitable to her: "I went forth laboring for God, and he owned and blessed my labors."[16]

Sarah Parker Remond was among a handful of Black women who worked as full-time antislavery lecturers. The sister of activist Charles Lenox Remond, she was not the only Black woman activist to tour, but she was unique in that she achieved a measure of fame and respect. She knew firsthand the humiliations visited upon people of color in the North—authorities had barred her from the Salem High School for Girls because of the color of her skin, and in 1853, an usher had pushed her down the stairs of Boston's Howard Athenaeum when she attempted to take her seat in the white section. In 1856, she began speaking as an agent of the American Anti-Slavery Society, at times accompanied by her brother. Reporting on an event in September 1858, *The Liberator* noted that her "eloquent and stirring words and faithful testimonies were listened to with the deepest attention, and produced a powerful impression upon the minds of those present." The following year she traveled with Samuel May Jr. to England, where she lectured to large audiences "in the most touching manner upon the social degradation of her sisters in slavery."[17]

Together with the Quaker sisters Angelina and Sarah Grimké, the daughters of a wealthy Charleston, South Carolina, slaveholder, Parker Remond addressed the white Christian women of the South, claiming that wives and mothers had a special responsibility to speak out against slavery. That argument propelled and built upon an emerging women's movement in the North. By this time, however, Frederick Douglass was becoming less sympathetic to women's rights, especially the rights of white women, though he had conspicuously supported the resolutions passed at Seneca Falls in 1848. Now, a decade later, he was distressed at what he considered too many extraneous reforms attaching to antislavery: "The battle of Woman's rights should be fought on its own ground; as it is, the slave's cause, already too heavy laden, had to bear up under this new addition." He failed to understand that this "new addition" spoke to the needs of Black as well as white women, North and South.[18]

Many jobs available to white women were not open to Black women. The integration of the public schools meant that white teachers would instruct Black children. Native-born and immigrant white men, women, and children labored as machine operatives in the textile mills outside of Boston. Some department stores in the city employed white female seamstresses and clerks. Charitable and city-sponsored residential facilities hired white women exclusively; they earned wages as matrons, nurses, "watchers," domestics, cooks, ironers, scrubbers, and seamstresses at the House of Industry and its hospital, at the Lunatic Hospital, and at the House of Correction. On the other hand, both Black and white women worked as servants, seamstresses, and boardinghouse operators, although the task of laundress seems to have been reserved exclusively for women of color. Among the most successful Black women workers in New England was the energetic entrepreneur and real-estate investor Elleanor Eldridge of Providence, who combined domestic service with a catch-all list of jobs, including wallpaper hanger, soap boiler, laundress, whitewasher, painter, nurse, spinner, weaver, cattle drover, and egg gatherer.[19]

Servants worked in hotels and boardinghouses as well as private homes, a few living on the premises of their employers, toiling alongside white coworkers. Echoing colonial practices, Black women, appropriately attired, could serve as status symbols of sorts for their employers, as did the two women employed by a Mrs. Thompson. Called to testify about a recent burglary of her home, she swept into court one day accompanied by her two servants, all three of the women "dressed in the latest style, and all wearing thick veils." (One was described as a "colored porteress.") The sight of the three women in their finery created a sensation in the courtroom.[20]

Some Black domestics in Boston labored under slave-like conditions. Beginning in 1852 when she was fifty-seven, Charity Green lived with and worked for Lavinia and John Williston on Kendall Street. Mrs. Williston was the daughter and granddaughter of Green's former owners (in Virginia), and Green continued to work for the Williston family in Boston without pay. In 1860 Green was attending to the Williston household, which included the couple and their seven children, ranging in ages from nine to twenty. And some domestic servants were actual slaves—those brought north by their owners during visits. The city's abolitionists expressed bewilderment whenever these women and men refused to seize their freedom in Boston. In the summer of 1853, Hayden, Morris, and others learned that an enslaved woman named Ann had accompanied her owner, a Mrs. McClenathan visiting Boston from New Orleans. The Black men initiated court proceedings to liberate Ann, but the judge interviewing her decided that she was not being held against her will—if true, probably because she wanted to return south to her family.[21]

During the second half of the 1850s, Harriet Jacobs and Mary Walker continued to toil as domestics, their careers emblematic of the liabilities of Black servants regardless of region. Jacobs, in New York City working for the Willis family, dealt with chronic fatigue, no doubt a result of her distaste for the job combined with the aftereffects of her seven long years in hiding before her escape from slavery. At times Jacobs asked her daughter Louisa to work for the Willises temporarily in her stead, but then fretted about it, writing, "Louisa tried to fill my place and with the extra care of me she got entirely run down." Harriet would periodically visit friends in Cambridge to rest. In December 1854, at the Willises', she worried about her brother John and her son Joseph, who had been seeking in vain for their fortune in the Australian gold mines. She yearned to go to Boston to work at the annual Anti-Slavery Society bazaar, "with busy hands doing much good."[22]

Harriet had begun to write her autobiography, an effort she hoped would earn her some money and relieve her and Louisa from the hardships of service forever. Distracted from the manuscript while caring for Mrs. Willis's infant and four other children, the forty-four-year-old Jacobs lamented, "Housekeeping and looking after the Children—occupy every moment of my time." Meanwhile, Louisa had taken a new position, this one as a governess for the writers James Parton and Fanny Fern. She visited her mother in Cambridge in the summer of 1857, and Harriet found her "not well but looking miserably thin." The next year the aspiring autobiographer traveled to England seeking a publisher for her book. The trip ended in disappointment; she had to accompany a white family as their servant, only to find that many British abolitionists disapproved of a story that featured an enslaved woman who had had sex with a white man to escape the advances of her own lascivious master.[23]

Mary Walker was living in Cambridge when Harriet Jacobs came to the city for her brief visits, and the two met each other sometime in the 1850s. As fugitives from North Carolina, mothers of half-white children, and weary domestic servants, the two had much in common. Walker had accepted the position of companion and housekeeper to the mother of her former employer, Susan Lesley. The widowed Anne Jean Lyman was slowly slipping into dementia and complained that her daughter had foisted

Walker on her—that she had "drop'd her down upon me"—now that the young Black woman was in a weakened state after a serious illness. Despairing over her children still enslaved in Raleigh, Walker, with the Lesleys' help, hired a rescuer to recover her children. When that effort failed, she sought guidance from Lewis Hayden and other fugitives, although speaking with them made her even more miserable, hearing "so many of them talking of friends restored by so many different methods" while she was "doing nothing." Meanwhile, because of her poor health and the hard work of keeping house in a dwelling with no running water, Mary gave up sewing, though that work had provided a crucial part of her income. In the fall of 1856 Susan Lesley suggested to her mother that Mary be paid $1.50 a week, indicating that she had been getting less than that all along.[24]

Some Black servants worked in boardinghouses, the range of their duties varying according to the size of the place and the age, occupation, and inclinations of its residents. The women who worked for Henry Foreman, a Black man who mandated alcohol-free living among his boarders on Ann Street—"Genteel Boarding for Respectable Colored Seaman"—probably had an easier time of it compared to those laboring in a conventional seaman's boardinghouse. However, a few Black women were operators themselves, utilizing their domestic and cooking skills on their own terms and offering a service to the community in the process. Few Black men or women, whether single or married, could afford to rent a room or apartment on their own, and boardinghouses provided a kind of communal living for southern migrants. Contending with boarders' finicky dietary preferences and their high turnover rates, and with the endless rounds of meal preparation and the infinite mounds of laundry, made this type of work exhausting.[25]

Women's time-honored roles as healers and midwives took several forms, both credentialed and informal, in mid-nineteenth-century Boston. In 1848, Samuel Gregory founded the Boston

Female Medical College (later the New England Female Medical College; in 1874 it merged with Boston University). Despite its name, which would seem to encompass more, Gregory limited the school's training to obstetrics. He had acted out of what he considered a moral imperative, believing that only women should deliver babies, and that "man-midwifery" was "an outrage on decency, and grossly immoral and licentious in its tendency." Midwives throughout New England and beyond sought out the new school. A Black migrant from Delaware, twenty-one-year-old Rebecca Davis, arrived in Boston in 1852. Soon after, she married the widower Wyatt Lee, one of the original Edloe Sixty-Six now working as a porter. Rebecca spent the next eight years in the employ of several different white doctors in Charlestown. Within a few years she would become the first Black graduate of Gregory's Female Medical College and strike out on her own as a physician.[26]

Hidden from public view were those informal patterns of influence and power that southern migrants brought north with them. Tucked away in alleyways were the residences of "conjurer doctors" feared and respected by their neighbors. These healers proved to be reluctant subjects for reporters who tried to interview them, curious about the use of certain bones, snakeskins, roots, liquids, and incantations for medicinal—and also at times allegedly nefarious—purposes. The city's large number of Virginia-born Blacks, worshipping in the style traditional to their forebears, relied on Black "grannies"—elderly women who combined the roles of midwife, healer, conjurer, and diviner of spirits. The existence of curated natural and unusual objects buried in sites in the vicinity of Southac Street—for example, the lower canines of a raccoon, and cowrie shells—suggest that some healers used protective charms and amulets characteristic of West African customs, or at least West Africa via the American South. These folk doctors, like their patients, saw no distinction between the individual and their community, or between the material and the spiritual worlds. Whether in the North these women were rewarded for their labors with cash, in-kind gifts, or just the gratitude of the ill, the lovelorn, or the new mother is unknown; but surely those communal bonds provided ample opportunities for at least some Black women to exercise their ambition in ways distinct from conventional wage earning.[27]

At the same time, caring for neighbors or extended kin might or might not involve money. Thomas Cole paid his neighbor Elizabeth Riley (Rebecca Jones's mother-in-law) for the nursing services she provided him; just as significantly, in his will he left her his featherbed and his best china tea set, no doubt additional expressions of his appreciation for her ministrations. When he died, John Robinson owed Harriet Hayden $426 "for Services &c," perhaps related to housekeeping or caretaking. Thus within the confines of informal networks some women might make money for services that others provided for free, or for non-cash compensation. In these ways the lines between waged and unwaged blurred according to the circumstances and the inclinations of the worker and her patient-customer.[28]

Not all Black women lived a life of service to their families, their community, their church, or their white employers or customers; freed from waged and unwaged work, a few wives lived well, supported by their successful husbands. Rarely did the worlds of church ladies and streetwalkers collide in a single household, but that was the case when Joseph Clash married for the third time. In April 1858, Louisa, his second wife, died of burns from a fire when an oil lamp ignited. Two years later Clash married a thirty-one-year-old divorcee, Mary Ann Thacker. Mary Ann was the daughter of Henry L.W. Thacker and the sister of the wayward Emeline. Though a respected member of the community, in 1851 Henry Thacker had received some unfavorable attention in the press when he had assaulted his then son-in-law William

Robinson. Mary Ann had married Robinson when she was just fifteen (in 1844), and the couple had two children. Within a few years, though, claiming that her husband was abusive, she left him and took the children to Philadelphia. When she returned to Boston in the fall of 1851, William came after her, and a fight ensued between him and Henry Thacker. The scandal unfolded in public view, in court. A reporter described Mary Ann as "very agreeable and amiable looking, and conduct[ing] herself throughout the trial with much propriety."[29]

The gala Washington's Birthday Ball that Mary Ann Thacker attended in 1852 offered a mighty contrast to Clash's nightly frolics in American Hall. Local papers provided breathless accounts of the holiday celebration, which brought out the "Upper Ten" of Black Boston. Richly dressed couples descended from their "carriages of the most exquisite workmanship, drawn by caparisoned steeds," at the steps of Washingtonian Hall. There the revelers danced the Schottische and the Polka Redowa and partook of a bounty of refreshments. In attendance that night and receiving gushing coverage from the *Herald* was the "*petite* and elegant" Mary Ann Thacker Robinson, now separated from her husband William for several years. She wore a becoming white gown. The reporter praised "her visage, in which Ethiopian hue is crossed by Anglo-Saxon traces." She certainly earned her "claim to be considered one of the magnates of the most polished society of Boston"—with "polished" perhaps a play on "bootblack" and an allusion to Henry Thacker's modest origins.[30]

How the lovely Mary Ann and the swaggering Joseph Clash first met remains a mystery. One local Police Court reporter noted in passing that her father was "well known in this city and elsewhere as the distinguished polisher, and favorite of the ladies everywhere; and particularly when a social party was to come off"—perhaps a reference to his frequenting the American Hall or patronizing some of Clash's women employees. And then, his own daughter Emeline had been caught in an Ann Street vice raid in 1851.[31]

Joseph Clash made a worthy suitor for Mary Ann Thacker, given his remarkable resilience as a successful entrepreneur. He saw his business weather another "descent" in the fall of 1858, a dragnet that ensnared fifty-four women. Still, the proprietor of American Hall continued to advertise, promising, for example, as he put it, "a tip-top time" at a Grand Calico Dress Ball: "Good order will be preserved. Good music will be in attendance."[32]

Mary Ann Clash inhabited a rarefied realm, married life with a husband who could free her from the drudgery of waged labor that was the lot of many Black women in Boston. His vice-ridden empire set him apart from other high-profile, well-to-do Black men, yet he managed to join the Thacker extended family and bask in the glow of their social respectability. Still, Clash was exceptional. Most Black men and women who started their own businesses did so against great odds, and their risk-taking could carry them to the pinnacle of the Black elite, or land them in jail, with few managing to survive for any great length of time in between.

6

Making a Living in Unsettled Times

Two cataclysmic events in 1857—a Supreme Court decision and an economic downturn—reverberated through Boston's Black community, already reeling from the effects of the Fugitive Slave Act and ongoing job displacement. Even for many enterprising men and women, the way to self-sufficiency and a stable income remained beyond reach. Moreover, as abolitionists intruded ever more loudly and insistently into the public square, and as some brazen souls dared to take up arms against slavery (in Virginia), influential whites' indifference toward Blacks morphed into outright, unapologetic hostility. In late 1860, a presidential election shook the country's foundations to its very core. In response, leading members of the powerful Boston political, mercantile, and religious establishment cast antislavery activists generally, and Blacks particularly, as agents of national disunion and disorder, troublemakers unentitled even to physical protection. Together, these sweeping developments reminded all people of color that their calls for justice were yielding little or no tangible progress in material terms.

On March 6, 1857, the Supreme Court handed down the infamous Dred Scott decision, which decreed that Black people "had no rights which the white man was bound to respect." The *Dred Scott v. Sandford* decision also called into question the ability of Congress to regulate the existence of slavery anywhere in the nation, thereby nullifying not only the tortuous congressional "compromises" of the past thirty-seven years but also "personal liberty" laws such as the one enacted in Massachusetts. At an indignation meeting, John Rock expressed his disgust with the Scott decision and angrily denounced abolitionists' endless, fruitless protests: "We can come here and make brilliant speeches, but our field of duty is elsewhere," he said. "Let us go to work—each man in his place, determined to do what he can for himself and his race." Rock argued that whites were inconstant and ultimately irrelevant allies: "How very few colored men are encouraged in their trades or business! Our young men see this, and become disheartened. In this country, where money is the great sympathetic nerve which ramifies society, and has a ganglia in every man's pocket, a man is respected in proportion to his success in business." Rock reminded his listeners that the fate of northern Black workers was inextricably tied to the liberation of the slaves.[1]

William Cooper Nell took a different tack and cited *Scott* in appealing to Boston's white laboring classes. If before this decision some whites had worried that the destruction of slavery would result in freed Blacks streaming northward to compete for jobs, now all whites should know that, someday soon, enslaved workers would replace them on the docks and in the streets, even in Boston. Nell argued that whites' outrage at that prospect should yield a more open-minded approach toward potential Black coworkers: "Northern white mechanics opposed to the Dred Scott decision can here show their faith by their works in opening their shops to these colored Americans and boys." Decent pay and working conditions for Black employees would be the best hedge against threats to white men's jobs. Still, Nell's lone voice calling for unity among the laboring classes moved neither the mass of whites nor their leaders. Most men in well-organized trades—especially such men, in fact—sought to uphold the social exclusivity of their own workplaces in a bid to preserve their "integrity."[2]

And then, in the early fall, the Panic of 1857 plunged the United States into a depression, the result of financial uncertainty stemming from a bubble in railroad stocks and a slowdown in the mining of gold in California, among other factors. The downturn led to a contraction in commercial credit as businesses closed, workers lost their jobs, and consumers lost their purchasing power. The effects rippled across the Boston economy, affecting wage earners in every sector, from seamstresses and female department store clerks to shipyard workers, porters, and tenders. Meanwhile, labor-saving machinery thrust some white men who had previously made a precarious living into the ranks of casual laborers and into competition with Blacks. As the Black community struggled, many of its entrepreneurs fell on harder times. In Rock's words, "Colored men in business in Massachusetts receive more respect, and less patronage, than in any place I know of."[3]

The forces of deskilling and business consolidation affected a range of workers. Craftsmen regardless of skin color lost their jobs to huge businesses employing a thousand men or more; such economic behemoths began to dominate the market for steam engines, pianos and organs, furniture, and other items. Some craftsmen, pushed out by larger establishments, simply sold their tools, while others went bankrupt. A distraught few committed suicide.

Machines transformed menial jobs as well as skilled ones. The massive public works project of filling in the Back Bay achieved its dual purpose in spectacular fashion—it expanded the landmass of the city and provided a fashionable new address for well-to-do whites. City authorities hoped to stem an exodus of the affluent: by May 1858, when they started the landfill project, a Boston merchant could live five miles outside the city and commute via train to downtown every day; it was hoped that the spacious townhouses to be constructed on the new site would provide an appealing alternative to living in the suburbs. Within its first year the project cost city taxpayers $150,000, the price of hauling 300,000 cubic yards of landfill into the site on the south bank of the Charles River. Not all that money went into the pockets of laboring men, however. Instead, engineers used a new machine, a steam shovel, to dig gravel out of a pit in the western suburb of Needham and transport it into Boston by rail. Eighty engineers and brakemen worked around the clock to fill 145 "dirt cars," a car every ten minutes, with each train making sixteen trips in the daytime and ten at night, arriving at Back Bay every forty-five minutes. This frenetic pace produced the equivalent of two house lots (previously necessitating hundreds of shovelers) every day. A story in a popular pictorial included a drawing by the artist Winslow Homer of "Back Bay scavengers," men, women, and children who sorted through the onsite trash—the oyster shells and old hoopskirts mixed in with the Needham gravel. The impoverished pickers offered a fitting counterpoint to the wealthy residents expected to purchase the townhouses in the future.[4]

Some Black men and women did their best to avoid working for whites; but these were not good times to start or manage a business. In September 1856 the *Daily Atlas* ran a notice announcing an upcoming hearing in the case of Lewis Hayden, an "insolvent debtor." Competition from clothing stores, combined with the considerable ongoing expenses of boarding fugitives at the Hayden household, had led to the failure of his business. Still, Hayden was fortunate: in 1858, Republican friends in high places secured him a position as messenger to the Massachusetts secretary of state, a job that entailed running errands, and one that would provide him with welcome long-term security.[5]

The challenges that Black entrepreneurs faced reflected not only the downturn of 1857 but also the difficulties of operating any small business in Boston during this period. In working with his mother, Nancy, George Lewis Ruffin showed a keen business

This 1859 drawing by Winslow Homer depicts scavengers sifting through newly deposited landfill in the Back Bay along the Charles River. In the far distance, a train brings dirt and gravel from the western suburb of Needham. *Ballou's Pictorial* identifies these "pickers-up of unconsidered trifles"—men and women using hoes and their hands to reclaim detritus of any use or value—as illustrative of "the lower strata of life" in the city. *(Cleveland Museum of Art)*

sense, accurately gauging the Boston market for any number of goods that could be profitably imported from Richmond. He calculated the potential profits for dried and fresh fruit—sliced apples would bring 8 or 9 cents a pound; cut in quarters, 7 or 8 cents a pound—and he imported barrels of merchandise as well as bacon, ham, and fruitcakes to sell. With his father still living in Richmond and acting as middleman there, they could save a considerable amount of money: "By increasing and feeling our way cautiously," wrote the son, "we might lay the foundations of a Business that would make us independent." When his father moved to Boston permanently, though, their dream of "a trade that would pay largely" came to an end; paying a Richmond-based broker would be too costly.[6]

Occasionally, *The Liberator* featured Boston's Black business owners, mechanics, and professionals, hoping to win for a select group the recognition and the customers they deserved—for example, an installer of lighting fixtures; a cleaner and repairer of silver and plated ware and jewelry; and an expert in the art of electro-gilding, fine gilding, and silver plating. Nell took Douglass's 1853 plea to heart by featuring Black men looking for work, not only as porters and laborers, but also as bookkeepers, plowmakers and ironworkers, carpenters, sign painters, piano tuners, and "experts in the Daguerrotypian and Ambrotypian arts" (the latter perhaps Rev. Leonard Grimes's son John). Nell wrote, "These young men have devoted themselves assiduously to their respective occupations, and it is hoped that an opening may soon gladden their prospects." It is unknown if readers of *The Liberator* answered the call.[7]

The paper also singled out Robert Morris, "Madame" Christiana Carteaux (who "elicited encomiums from the ladies of Boston, for her preparations for improving the hair and complexion, and also her skill in applying the same"), Lewis Hayden, and John S. Rock. Here, too, were profiles of a physician, Dr. John V. DeGrasse ("laboring under the obstacles that beset all young physicians"), and the "Prince of Caterers," Joshua B. Smith. A recent event for a white fraternal order catered by Smith won plaudits for "the abundance and variety of the well-prepared viands; the prompt attention of the well-disciplined waiters; the elegant bouquets, and the other adornments of the tables [which] conspired to render the entertainment one of the best public dinners ever provided in the city of Boston." Smith also oversaw a July 4, 1858, banquet for the mayor, the members of the city council, and other honored guests, a magnificent repast that was held in Faneuil Hall. By any measure, though, Smith was exceptional by virtue of his white patrons and large-scale catering enterprise.[8]

The fate of Black barbers and waiters told a larger, more representative story about gradual job loss among Black wage earners and small business owners. For generations, shaving (at times called hairdressing) provided a niche occupation for Black men.

However, the 1850s saw more immigrants entering the ranks of barbers in Boston, from one-fifth of all men in that occupation in 1850 to one-third ten years later. By that time Blacks accounted for just a third of all barbers, a job they had long monopolized. Irish immigrants also worked as waiters and domestics, though at least one English visitor thought that most immigrants considered these positions only temporary: "The Irish man is seldom long in America before he, too, begins to assert the supremacy of his white blood, and to come out of what he considers the degrading ranks of servants."[9]

Black seamen, too, lost their hold on a kind of work they had counted on for generations. Historically, seafaring had offered plenty of difficult, dangerous jobs for men seeking to escape the confines of a white household or the uncertainties of the street; they became part of multinational, multiethnic crews that challenged tyranny on the land and water. Yet by the 1850s men of color were serving less often as mates and more often as cooks and stewards. Boston Police Court proceedings revealed the hazards of these jobs—featuring Black seamen beaten by white crew members, cheated out of wages by a ship's owner, or scammed out of wages by a local shopkeeper. "Crimps" associated with various seamen's boardinghouses set wage rates; these middlemen felt no loyalty to the men they dealt with, in contrast to the sea-captain patrons who had hired their own crews. The standard pay was $18 a month on all voyages east of the Cape of Good Hope and $15 for those west of Cape Horn, though the fact that Black seamen lived in segregated boardinghouses casts doubt that they received equal pay for equal work.[10]

By the end of the 1850s, depressed wages and degradation in status had considerably diminished the appeal of voyages for Black men, especially when trips led to long absences from home. Meanwhile, several southern states followed South Carolina's 1822 lead and required that Black seamen be incarcerated or remain on board their ships when in port, to prevent abolitionist heresies from reaching the ears of enslaved workers. The United States considered Black mariners to be citizens when they were impressed by the captain of a foreign vessel, but these men had no rights when they stepped foot on a Charleston dock.[11]

The most successful and stable householders tended to be those men who could count on a white clientele. This was true not only for attorneys and caterers, but also for those working within the realm of physical culture, a movement that stressed the need to exercise the body as well as the mind. In this era of indoor machine work and (in the eyes of some) frivolous popular amusements, several Black men became integral to Boston's reputation as a center of boxing, gymnastics, and riflery. A Boston native, Richard Seavers—his admirers called him "the renowned Big Dick"—offered boxing instruction in Boston as early as the 1820s. From 1847 to 1849, another sparring master, Alexander Dorsey, owned and operated an establishment called the Boston Gym. After Dorsey's death, another man, Peyton Stewart Jr., elevated the gym to a prosperous business. Housed in a large, well-appointed building, it charged fees from $10 to $14 a year and limited its clientele to whites (with separate times for white women). Stewart spared no expense in advertising and provided patrons with amenities such as slippers and after-exercise showers, gaining endorsements from prominent whites. By the middle of the decade, he had more than six hundred students performing at his annual exhibitions.[12]

Beginning in 1853, Stewart faced a formidable competitor, John B. Bailey. Born in 1819 in Maryland, Bailey established himself as a pugilist and boxing master in Baltimore, later giving exhibitions and sparring lessons in that city as well as in Saratoga Springs, Boston, New York, and Washington, DC. From 1851 to 1853, he lived in California, where he taught rifle and pistol shooting. (He was reputed to have fired five bullets that hit a one-half-inch bull's-eye.) Returning to Boston in 1853, he bought an old gym on Franklin Street, and then three years later opened a boxing school and a pistol gallery on Brattle Street. In 1859 he became an instructor of sparring at the Boston fencing school. He gained a reputation as "one of the most popular sparring teachers in the country." Though he was a "boxing master," he also worked as a hairdresser and exhibited a "Panoramic Tour of America" in Boston's Melodeon Theatre (in the fall of 1856).[13]

The prominence of Black men in Boston's antebellum physical-culture scene testified not only to their technical skills and entrepreneurial savvy, but also to the slavery-era stereotype of the Black body as strong and resilient. By limiting their clientele to white middle-class men (and women), gym owners assured themselves of a stable, relatively well-off customer base. For many entrepreneurs in the service industry, the ruthless contest to provide luxurious facilities could prove their downfall—that contest led Stewart, for example, to overextend himself financially. Still, Bailey did well for himself and became a prominent member of the Boston area's Black community.

Some full-time antislavery activist-lecturers relied on a modest stipend from a sponsoring society, but others were solo operators, seeking out ever larger popular audiences for their speeches and books in order to make a decent living. In this regard Douglass set an impossibly high standard. In 1855 he published an enhanced version of his autobiography, this one called *My Bondage and My Freedom*. Within a couple of years there were 18,000 copies in print, and, with a price tag of $1.25 each, the Douglass family would seem poised to enjoy financial security at long last. However, he plowed much of the profits from book sales into the debt-ridden *Frederick Douglass' Paper*. Other writers also aimed to make a living: in the late 1850s Harriet Jacobs was counting on sales from her autobiography, *Incidents in the Life of a Slave Girl*, to relieve her and Louisa from domestic service. Nell had published *The Colored Patriots of the Revolution* in 1855, but lost money on the venture.[14]

All abolitionists faced antislavery fatigue among northern audiences, as well as lively competition from a variety of singing groups, acting troupes, and traveling circuses. These new realms of public entertainment forced full-time activists to become ever more resourceful. William Wells Brown took up residence in the West End's Smith Court after his return from England, and, bursting with creativity, gave lectures ("Mahamet and Confucious," "Notable People of France and England") and concerts, delivered scripted dramatic performances ("Experience; or, How to give a Northern Man a Backbone"), took part in debates, and wrote poetry and song lyrics. Winning for himself a high level of public name recognition, he developed a sophisticated marketing network based on tickets sold by shopkeepers and ads in local papers. In "The Escape," his one-man show chronicling his own life as a slave and then a fugitive, he played all the characters himself. Nevertheless, Samuel May Jr. expressed disapproval of Brown's reach, complaining that "Brown likes to make popular and taking [i.e., money-making] speeches, and keeps a careful eye upon his own benefit." Perversely, May expected fugitives to support themselves through honest work, but criticized Brown for his high-profile efforts to do just that.[15]

John S. Rock sought to capitalize on the fact that northerners with any discretionary income were more likely to attend plays and concerts than want to hear about the horrors of slavery. In the fall of 1857, he was offering popular lyceum lectures on literature, history, geography, and "race"—on Madame de Staël, "Lights and Shadows of the African Character," "The Ancient and Modern Tribes and Nations in Africa," and "The Popular Objections to the Masonic Institution." For ten months beginning in the early summer of 1858, he sought treatment for a chronic illness in Paris, and on his return to Boston he used his travels as a basis for another lecture topic—"The Voyage of an American Outlaw." Rock, like Wells, cultivated his rhetorical gifts at a time when dramatic readings and poetry recitations could attract appreciative audiences.

Unlike their white counterparts, however, these learned Black lecturers could also hope to dispel the prejudices of their listeners, to disabuse them of the notion that Black men were only fit to be field hands and drudges. A Philadelphia newspaper gave Rock this endorsement, which he distributed widely: "Dr. Rock displays great mental power, a habit of close reasoning, and a carefully cultivated and positively superior style of oratory."[16]

In the late 1850s, ill winds were blowing across the United States, and Boston was an epicenter of the storm. In 1858, US senator Jefferson Davis of Mississippi, a former army officer and secretary of state, spent the summer in Maine, stopping in Boston on his way back south that fall. The city's Democrats welcomed "the distinguished soldier and statesman" and invited him to address the party regulars at Faneuil Hall. On October 12 an overflow crowd cheered as he made passing reference to the brave sons of the Bay State, Samuel Adams and John Hancock, before turning to "that ever-intrusive question, the right of property in black men." Morality had nothing to do with it, Davis declared; rather, at stake was the constitutional right to own property. Davis predicted that "States Rights Democracy" would always overcome "the Black Republicans," and that the ballot box would prevent "fire"—a violent conflagration between North and South.[17]

The Democratic Party enjoyed the full support of the Catholic clergy and many of their parishioners, immigrants who recoiled at the Republicans' anti-immigrant, anti-Catholic prejudices and policies. Some former conservative Whigs also went over to the Democrats to protest the Republican Party's strident, no-slavery-in-the-territories rhetoric. Most abolitionists embraced the new party, and even Garrison departed from his customary apolitical stance and showed a surprising degree of respect for it. In contrast, some Black people agreed with Douglass, who hated the Republicans' timid, halfway measures: "Free Soilism is lame, halt, and blind, while it battles against the spread of slavery, and admits its right to exist anywhere [i.e., in the South]."[18]

As a center of militant antislavery agitation, Boston continued to attract Black men and women who sought out abolitionists' money as much as their inspiring rhetoric. The indefatigable rescuer of slaves Harriet Tubman visited the city off and on in 1859, staying in the spring at the Cambridge Street home of Burrill Smith, a porter and fugitive assistant, and in the fall with acquaintances on Southac Street. Tubman had come to Boston with a specific aim: to earn enough money to pay off the mortgage of a new home she had purchased, a debt that obligated her to make payments of $10 four times a year. She followed a familiar path to successful fund-raising, giving lectures on her remarkable exploits bringing dozens of enslaved people safely to the North.[19]

That spring Tubman met with John Brown, who was also in Boston to raise money. Brown was a fierce abolitionist warrior—some would say domestic terrorist—who had no scruples against murdering unarmed proslavery men in cold blood, as he had done in Pottawatomie, Kansas, in May 1856. Now he was canvassing Boston and its environs for financial support for his next venture against the slavocracy. Wealthy Bostonians such as Amos A. Lawrence had helped fund the Massachusetts Emigrant Society, which supplied Brown with cash and guns to fight proslavery men on the Kansas frontier. In Boston, Brown met with the physician Samuel Gridley Howe, the Unitarian ministers Thomas Wentworth Higginson and Theodore Parker, and the manufacturer George L. Stearns; they would become part of the "Secret Six," bankrolling his ill-conceived plan to raid a federal arsenal and thereby incite a slave rebellion all over the South.[20]

Brown launched the raid on Harpers Ferry, Virginia, on October 16, 1859, and over two days fought against a local militia company and US Marines who had been stationed nearby under the command of Brevet Colonel Robert E. Lee. Sixteen people lost their lives, including ten of Brown's men; two of them were his sons. Badly injured, Brown was captured and tried, and the jury rendered a guilty verdict on November 2. He was hanged one month later.

In Boston, some activists saw in the wounded and defiant Brown a martyr for the ages, while others expressed shock at his bloodthirsty tactics. Predictably, in any case, he had failed miserably in his aim to provoke a slave uprising. On the day of Brown's execution, the members of Boston's Black community closed their shops, observed a fast, and gathered in Twelfth Baptist for services. The Reverend Grimes led the group in prayer "that God would be with him who was today to hang upon a gallows, to swing between heaven and earth, a sacrifice of their cause." Murmurs of unease greeted antislavery activist Charles Lenox Remond as he took the pulpit; he acknowledged that his presence might not be welcome, since he was a fierce critic of churchgoers and others who put their faith in God exclusively. Remond declared that John Brown "had essentially and practically made himself a black man" because he had "died for the colored race." Subsequent speakers rose in angry response, arguing that only God could effect the destruction of slavery. Rev. Grimes cut the speeches short and adjourned the gathering until later in the day.[21]

That afternoon of Brown's hanging, a large crowd gathered in Tremont Temple to hear leading abolitionists mourn his death. And yet six days later the same venue was host to another packed meeting, this one organized by conservatives, who billed it a "Boston Union" meeting. The city's Democrats blamed their own neighbors for the upheaval Brown had caused, indicting the smug, despicable fools who had egged Brown on and opened their wallets for him and all those now mourning the passing of a mass murderer. At the meeting was Levi Lincoln, a former Massachusetts governor; Edward Everett, a former US senator; and other well-known dignitaries, all eager to reassure the slaveholding South that Brown and his fanatical supporters did not represent the good citizens of Boston.

In fact, events over the next few months provided ample proof (as if Black leaders needed it) of the racist nature of the city's major religious denominations and white political culture. Boston's largest Protestant churches had long deplored abolitionists as ungodly busybodies. In 1854 the Reverend Nehemiah Adams, pastor of the Union Congregational Church, wrote a proslavery tract titled *A South-Side View of Slavery*. In it he argued that bondage proved beneficial to descendants of Africans because it introduced them to Christianity and cultivated their religious sensibilities. Seven years later, Adams responded to his critics by following up with the publication of *The Sable Cloud, a Southern Tale with Northern Comments*. He predicted that emancipation would leave southern Blacks adrift and defenseless, unable to provide for themselves and useful to no one. Lydia Maria Child, an abolitionist and women's rights activist, lamented that Boston's booksellers eagerly distributed this sort of pro-southern material rather than, in her sarcastic words, "soiling their hands with an Anti-Slavery book," such as Harriet Jacobs's *Incidents in the Life of a Slave Girl*. Child blamed the Edward Everett "aristocrats, who make loud complaints of republican institutions, and fret a deal about servants not keeping in their proper position."[22]

In April 1860, Governor Nathaniel Banks vetoed a bill that would have removed the word "white" from the state's law books. In July Boston Democrats offered a hearty welcome to US senator Stephen Douglas, a Democrat from Illinois, who denounced the northern and southern factions of his own party and argued that each new territory should decide the slavery question for itself. Douglas would return in October, right before the presidential election, and receive the endorsement of the editor of the Catholic archdiocese's paper, *The Pilot*. The mass of Irish laborers had been loyal members of the Democrats for decades. To counter all this anti-abolition agitation, Boston's Blacks held hastily called meetings, appealed repeatedly to the state legislature to eliminate "white" legal provisions—for example, those that outlawed Black militias, and those that stipulated the race of voters on registration lists—and formed their own "West Boston Wide Awake" club. Led by John P. Coburn and attired in black caps and capes, the club's members processed through the city, campaigning for Republicans.[23]

Abraham Lincoln, a Republican, won the election because the Democrats had split their votes among three different candidates. Stephen Douglas represented northern Democrats and the principle of "popular sovereignty" in the territories. The John Bell–Edward Everett Constitutional Union ticket, which also attracted Democrats, advanced the long-discredited idea of compromise on the issue of slavery. John C. Breckinridge, the incumbent vice president under James Buchanan, a Democrat, spoke for southern planters and ran on a platform that would preserve slavery at all costs. Nationwide, just under half of all voters cast a ballot for Lincoln, but with the support of the populous northern states he easily won the electoral college. Vote tallies in Boston and its immediate suburbs (Suffolk County) suggested the strength of local working-class white Democrats. Although Lincoln won 63 percent of the Massachusetts vote, in Suffolk County his support amounted to only 49 percent, with Bell and Douglas together receiving almost the same proportion of votes (49 percent). In January 1861, Boston elected a Democratic mayor, Joseph Wightman.[24]

Lincoln promised to leave the system of bondage in the South intact, but slaveholders regarded his platform of "free soil" in the territories as an existential threat to that system everywhere in the nation. After the November election, Black activists faced an ever more intense backlash, with whites infiltrating their meetings and physically attacking those in attendance.[25]

BOSTON'S TREMONT TEMPLE was an unlikely setting for a brawl, and the city's white merchants, bankers, and attorneys made for unlikely brawlers. *The Liberator* termed the chaotic affair on

December 3, 1860, a "mobcratic assault" on antislavery men and women, mayhem instigated by "well-dressed rowdies" to squelch debate on the great issue of the day: "How Can American Slavery be Abolished?"[26]

Built in 1827, the Greek Revival–style "temple" had for the past seventeen years served as a Baptist church on Sundays, its integrated worship services welcoming all and accommodating as many as six hundred people. When Black and white abolitionists reserved the venue's main hall for that Monday morning, they fully expected a large crowd eager not only to pay homage to the martyred John Brown, who had been hanged exactly one year before, but also to discuss strategies for emancipation. However, their recently publicized "Call for Convention" only served to aggravate the conservative Boston establishment. The fact that some of the meeting's sponsors failed to appear at all—William Lloyd Garrison and Wendell Phillips among them—suggests the problematic timing, coming as it did so soon after Lincoln's victory; or perhaps anti-abolitionists had signaled their intention to interfere with the proceedings. Yet the stalwarts Frederick Douglass and William Wells Brown showed up, and they were prepared to do battle—rhetorical or otherwise—with their proslavery antagonists in Boston's own civil war.

Also present that morning were several leaders relatively new to the city's antislavery activism. The Virginia-born carpenter John Oliver, thirty, had returned from his studies at Oberlin College; his political acumen was winning him leadership positions at indignation meetings and other protests. Another newcomer was the Reverend J. Sella Martin. Born in North Carolina in 1833, Martin, the son of an enslaved woman and her owner, had been sold eight times by 1856, when he managed to escape while working on a boat. First he went to Cairo, Illinois, and three years later he found his way to Boston. Impressive for his rhetorical skills, he assumed a temporary pastorate at Tremont Temple. In the summer of 1861, he would become the minister of the First Independent Baptist (Joy Street) Church.[27]

The meeting began inauspiciously. At 10:00 a.m., as soon as its sponsors emerged from an anteroom and ascended the platform, they could see that they were badly outnumbered by men who were decidedly hostile to the stated purpose of the event. Indeed, their chief antagonists, Richard S. Fay and J. Murray Howe, were leading lights in the John Bell–Edward Everett Constitutional Union wing of the Democratic Party; in the recent presidential election, this ticket of former Whigs had won 12 percent of the popular vote and the states of Kentucky, Tennessee, and Virginia. Fay was a Lynn lawyer, businessman, and breeder of sheep and cattle, and Howe a Brookline attorney. Like other wealthy Bostonians, they feared that a handful of abolitionists given to vitriolic screeds were antagonizing southern slave owners and jeopardizing a vibrant trade that had produced great riches for the whole country.

When the abolitionists tried to call the house to order, they were met with a barrage of catcalls, hisses, stamping feet, cheers for the Union and the Constitution, groans ("as if in great agony of the spirit," according to one reporter), and cries ("Put him out!"). Pandemonium ensued. The hall's manager summoned the police, who, arriving in force, added to the confusion. The several dozen Black and white women looking on from the balcony refused to budge from their seats, despite calls for them to leave; they applauded and yelled their approval of the abolitionist speakers "to the echo." When Martin tried to nominate meeting officers, his opponents outvoted him three to one and installed Fay as chair.[28]

Douglass tried to dissuade Fay from accepting the honor, and the white man responded by removing his overcoat, as if in anticipation of a fight. Then, encircled by his supporters, Fay offered several resolutions, including that John Brown should be condemned "for his piratical and bloody attempt" to foment a slave rebellion in Virginia; that "no virtuous and law-abiding citizen of this Community should sympathize with or hold communion with" apologists for Brown; and that "at this perilous juncture" everyone should coalesce around the Union, "alike important to the free labor of the North, the slave labor of the South, and to the interests of the commerce, manufacturers, and agriculture of the world." Fay declared that for far too long he and other respectable citizens had endured the demagoguery of deranged abolitionists; to describe them, he used a word usually applied to backups of sewage in the city's privies—"a nuisance."[29]

Douglass raised his voice above the din, charging that the interlopers had launched the most outrageous assault on free speech "that I have ever witnessed in Boston or elsewhere." He continued, "Shall we obey the blood-hounds of the law who do the dirty work of the slave-catchers?" to which someone replied (after "Knock him down! Sit down!"), "There is a law which we are bound to obey." At that point men on both sides seemed poised for a fight, with canes raised, arms bared, and fists clenched. Reporters hastily pocketed their notes, preparing to flee, and some attendees climbed onto tables and cushioned seats, hoping to avoid the tossed chairs and tumult below. Douglass appeared to be in his element, standing his ground and taunting his tormenters with "You are afraid of your Southern masters." They responded with shouts of "Put all the niggers out! All out! Blow them up!" and "Down with the niggers!" The police eventually escorted Douglass to the organ loft, to quiet and probably also to protect him. At one point he declared that he felt "no more embarrassment by this uproar than if I had been kicked by a jackass." The epithets and insults had flown for three hours or more by the time Mayor Joseph Wightman (the city's first Democratic mayor and no friend of the enslaved) finally ordered the meeting dissolved and the hall closed. The "John-Brown men" called upon their supporters to adjourn; they would reconvene later that evening in the African Meeting House (Rev. J. Sella Martin's Joy Street Church). That

This drawing by the artist Winslow Homer shows a scene from the chaotic Tremont Temple meeting organized by abolitionists and disrupted by anti-abolitionists on December 3, 1860. Black and white women gesticulate from the balcony, Black and white men engage in fisticuffs, and police officers join the melee. A white man seeks to prevent a Black man (probably Frederick Douglass) from speaking. *(Library of Congress)*

meeting, too, would be attacked by angry white men and women, who threw bricks and rocks at those trying to enter the building. A local paper likened the church gathering to a "fire-brand thrown into the combustibles"—a provocative, incendiary move calculated to foment violence.[30]

The aristocratic rabble-rousers at Tremont Temple had made their point and won the skirmish. The white professional classes, together with the mayor and city council and backed by the police, held the reins of power, vastly outnumbering local antislavery forces. Crude expressions of anti-Black sentiment were the order of the day, especially now that the Union—and with it Boston's prosperity—seemed at risk because of a misguided group of Black abolitionists and their odious white allies. The Republicans had swept the November elections, with John A. Andrew elected governor of Massachusetts and Lincoln president. Massachusetts gave Lincoln 63 percent of its vote, an impressive showing indeed. Yet many Bay State whites were coming to consider all Black people sources of disunion.

On January 7, 1861, the Boston City Council instructed Mayor Wightman to demand that state legislators repeal the personal liberty law of 1855. That measure had sought to nullify the 1850 Fugitive Slave Act by prohibiting state officials from cooperating with federal and private slave-catchers and the lawyers who represented enslavers. The council maintained that the 1855 law was unconstitutional and placed "our revered Commonwealth in a false position in regard to the rights of other States." This resolution came soon after South Carolina had seceded from the Union (on December 20) and issued a Declaration of Causes, explicitly condemning Massachusetts and thirteen other states that had enacted similar statutes.[31]

Amid these disorienting events, work and family life went on. Children of the original Edloe Sixty-Six came of age. On December 26, 1859, Thomas Selden, now nineteen, married Elizabeth Maddox, eighteen, daughter of the activist-businessman Stephen Maddox. Earlier that year the couple had had a baby, named William H., though his maternal grandparents had initially claimed parentage. No doubt Stephen, so keen to hire young men of excellent moral character in his tailoring shop, had insisted on a wedding. In the summer of 1860, the young couple were living with her parents in Cambridge, where Thomas, now a laborer and waiter, was working for his father-in-law.[32]

By 1860 Peter Randolph and his family had taken up residence in Charlestown. In 1856 he took charge of what he called "a small struggling church" in New Haven, Connecticut, but found the group there "in a deplorable condition and much discouraged." The congregants resisted joining the Baptist denomination, and they paid him an annual salary of only $200; he left after a year as "the church was not able to support a pastor." In 1858 he answered another call, this one in Newburgh, New York, but this church too was poor, and, as Randolph put it, "the confused state and condition of the colored people in Newburgh prevented the growth and development of the spiritual fruit that one had a right to look for." He returned to Boston to preach part time and start a small newspaper that turned out to be short lived.[33]

In 1860 Randolph became a pastor for the newly established Home for Aged Colored Women in Boston. The charity had been founded by Grimes and the Unitarian minister James Freeman Clarke, whose mother, Rebecca, had wanted some way to provide for one of her longtime Black servants, Rosanna Miller, now too old to work. (The Home for Aged Women on Charles Street accepted only whites.) It was no doubt Grimes's influence that got Martha Thurston the job of the home's matron; she was a member of Twelfth Baptist, serving with his wife in the church's Ladies' Society. Thurston presided over meals and led the group in daily prayers, and she made certain that the residents obeyed the home's rules—bedtime at 10:00 p.m., and no leaving the premises without permission. Randolph later said he "received no compensation" for his two years of service to the home. However, Thurston, whom he considered "a devout Christian woman," assured him, "'Brother Randolph, we will never be able to pay you for your services here, but the Lord Will reward you.'"[34]

The home was located on Southac Street within its community of constituents. In April 1860, the first ten elderly women took up residence there, all suffering from the ill effects of long years of physical labor and from the lack of kin who could care for them. In the words of the home's founders, these were women "whose age and feebleness deprive them of the means of gaining a support, and who are solely dependent upon a precarious charity for their subsistence." The demand for places at the home always far outstripped the supply; in the winter of 1859–1860, Leonard Grimes and Rebecca Clarke had canvassed Ward 6 and identified more than two dozen destitute Black women over the age of sixty who were suffering from cold and hunger.[35]

Despite the provocations in the form of the Supreme Court's Dred Scott decision and John Brown's raid, few Bostonians anticipated the shocking events of the spring of 1861. In Boston, in the months leading up to that time, the persistent and even deepening anti-abolitionist fervor on display boded ill for Black people and their hopes for a just future for themselves and for enslaved southerners. Anti-Black feeling seemed to pervade critical elements of the city's body politic, from the lowliest white laborers to the wealthiest merchants and bankers. Yet few could foresee the devastating price that secession and war would exact from Black men and women laboring for their country and receiving no fair reward in return.

PART II

1861–1865

7
The Politics of Wartime Work and Charitable Assistance

The withdrawal of South Carolina from the Union prompted ten other states to secede, and on February 8, 1861, together they formed a would-be new nation, the Confederate States of America. Ultimately the Confederate states had a population of 9,103,332, about a third of whom were enslaved. Confederate troops seized Fort Sumter, a federal installation in Charleston Harbor, on April 12, and three days later President Lincoln called for suppression of the rebellion. In Boston, native-born white elites rallied around the new president, shocked that their southern counterparts would go to such extreme measures in pursuit of the chimera of independence, and, along the way, forfeit lucrative trade relations with the North. On April 15, the city council expressed alarm that "the authority of the government of the United States [was] opposed and resisted with armed forces by the inhabitants of some portion of the Country." The councillors welcomed the governor's call for 1,200 to 1,500 men to assemble the next day on the Common to be mustered into military service.[1]

Yet well before the surrender of Fort Sumter, the Boston economy had begun to slow down: political uncertainty was bad for business. Early in 1861, the previously vibrant East Coast packet routes linking Boston, New York, and Philadelphia to Richmond, Charleston, and Savannah had begun to shrivel and disappear. Northern ship owners now quickly recalled their vessels from southern ports, and northern bankers refused to extend credit to southern borrowers. That spring, commercial seamen had few ships to sail, and Boston's wharf workers had few ships to load or unload. New York was monopolizing grain traffic, and so, according to one local paper, "our pilots, stevedores, shipwrights and mechanics, traders, ship chandlers and wharfingers have nothing to do." With the threat of war and the onset of hostilities, the "dull and lifeless appearance" of the city's wharves and commercial areas extended well into the fall of 1861.[2]

The ensuing recession produced ripple effects. Out of work, Bostonians frequented eating places less often and bought fewer small luxuries. Well-to-do men who joined the military dismissed their valets and coachmen. Modest households could no longer afford to hire domestic help, and now they did their own laundering, gardening, cooking, cleaning, and caring for children. In Cambridge, Joseph Lesley proposed letting the family's two domestics go. He pointed out that the women, Mary Walker and Mary Cashmore, "[had] been in one place as long as they would expect," and that "few domestics live as long in the same place, & they can hunt up others." His wife, Susan, objected: "They have been the bridge that have carried us through eight trying years, and Mary Walker has been invaluable." The two servants stayed.[3]

The prospect of war ate into the livelihoods of many Black people. Black barbers saw a drop-off in their business, as did many Black men who worked as porters, tenders, and other types of laborers. Waiters, cooks, laundresses, and other servants found fewer places in private homes and commercial establishments. Patron-employers took to advertising in the local papers, seeking positions for Black workers to whom they felt some obligation: "Wanted: A situation for a colored man, about 25, one who perfectly understands indoor work, as a private servant, and has superior taste and judgment in the management of horses, is also a most excellent groom and careful driver." On the other hand, the North End retained its vitality as a site of illicit activity, with prostitutes, cardsharps, gamblers, con men, pickpockets, and grog shop owners profiting from an influx of volunteers awaiting deployment.[4]

A decline in commercial activity, accompanied by a dramatic increase in the cost of living, swelled Boston's already considerable impoverished population. In March 1860 the city council noted an unusually high demand for charity owing to "a diminution of business activity" and a consequent spike in unemployment, placing extraordinary burdens on the Overseers of the Poor. Eventually the Charlestown Navy Yard and the shipyards in East and South Boston would come alive with activity as the federal government fitted gunboats and placed orders for ironclads, sloops-of-war, frigates, and ship engines; but those jobs went mainly to skilled men, and the misery of the unskilled and their families persisted and deepened.[5]

The war seeped into every crevice of the city's being, transforming the meaning of work. Suddenly the capital of the commonwealth turned itself into a great military entrepôt. Thousands of volunteers massed in hastily constructed army camps, soldiers drilled on the Common and marched through the streets, and makeshift hospitals sprang up seemingly overnight. Yet wartime mobilization also brought with it public health hazards—the careless disposal of carcasses of dead horses and loads of decayed bones, the stench pervading the city; recruits arriving by land and sea bringing contagious illnesses with them. A pervasive unease affected all the residents of Boston, who feared that the harbor remained vulnerable to attack from, in the words of the Boston Marine Society, "an audacious and ambitious foe [determined] to waste and destroy the property of its people."[6]

On April 19, four soldiers from the 6th Massachusetts Militia died at the hands of a pro-southern mob in Baltimore. When Union forces lost the first battle of the war, at Manassas, on July 21, the shock was palpable throughout the North. Lydia Maria Child wrote that "for days afterwards, I woke in the morning with the oppressive feeling one has when the corpse of a friend is in the house." Expanded death industries that disposed of human remains and outfitted the bereaved would thrive off battlefield fatalities and the ensuing expressions of anguish and grief.[7]

During the war, city and state policies related to military recruitment and public works as well as the priorities of charities exacerbated the inequities affecting Black men and women. The federal government imposed a quota on Black naval recruits and limited them to the lowest classification of service. The city council initiated massive construction projects, using taxpayer money mostly to enhance the infrastructure in South Boston and employ its residents, Irish Americans. Assistance flowed to the families of white soldiers while leaving the families of unemployed Black men to fend for themselves. Yet even as the fight for the Union widened the divisions between Black and white workers, some Black Bostonians seized the opportunity to enter new fields of labor.

DESPITE SHARP DISAGREEMENTS among whites over the institution of human bondage, the United States of 1861 hardly seemed prepared to go to war against itself and sacrifice more than 750,000 lives over four long years. Most northern and southern white people were English-speaking Protestants working the land. They shared a reverence for the country's founders and professed respect for the Constitution and its guiding principles of republican democracy. The vast majority were not slave owners, but they understood that cotton—cultivating the raw fiber in the South, turning it into cloth in the North—was a key component of the American economy. Most whites, regardless of region, accepted the hierarchical nature of their communities, with Black people occupying a caste at the bottom, and a small number of great planters, merchants, and factory owners at the top.[8]

Nevertheless, both the North and the South managed to convince themselves that the other side would not rest until its regional culture was a national one; and in the end, the war was about work. In order to slaughter each other, then, whites in both sections of the country had to concoct a project of demonization, each side portraying the other as alien, unnatural, immoral. This project was clearly fraught. Many influential families had kin scattered up and down the Eastern Seaboard, and the southern masters of the lash and northern masters of the loom existed in symbiotic relation to each other. Still, by 1860, foreign visitors and domestic travelers, writers, and journalists had embellished and expanded supposed regional traits into hardened tropes about work—who labored, how, and under what conditions. Southern elites categorized Yankees as an unsavory mix of peddlers and shopkeepers fleecing their customers; hollow-eyed, weak-willed immigrant factory operatives laboring for fourteen hours a day; haughty mill owners and merchants invoking God's blessing but caring not a fig if their employees went home at night to an empty cupboard and starved to death in their old age; failing farmers seeking to escape the region's rocky terrain and making a ruckus over the introduction of slavery in the western territories; and self-righteous zealots preaching all manner of nonsense, from labor reform to abolition and women's rights. According to this schema, almost all northerners were hostage to the marketplace, an impersonal force devoid of humanity and sympathy, and the few who were not—the zealots—relied on benefactors and aimed only to disrupt the natural order of things. And now that the North had chosen as president a rough-hewn wood chopper—a "rail splitter"—the region's degradation was complete.

In assessing the South, white northerners also used work as a lens. They pointed out that a third of the southern population was engaged in backbreaking toil, spurred to labor not by the hope of a just reward, but by the crack of a whip. Unable to compete against enslaved workers in the field or workshop, landless whites remained mired in poverty, their only hope that they, too, might one day own another human being. Perched atop this rotten pyramid were the lascivious great planters, disdaining an honest day's work as a matter of principle and lording over households of humiliated womenfolk and servile retainers. In sum, in the northern view, neither the ideal nor the reality of industriousness existed in the South.

It remained to be seen whether the conflict would pit (according to southerners) effeminate, malnourished factory operatives against the manly heirs of a southern martial tradition, or (according to northerners) sturdy New England farm lads skilled in riflery against the spoiled, indolent sons of southern aristocrats. It was no wonder, then, that on April 15 Massachusetts's governor, John Andrew, sought authorization from the secretary of war to enlist "Irish, Germans, and other tough men, to be drilled and prepared here for service." That same day, a state Democratic lawmaker called for the recruitment of a thousand longshoremen, "the most stalwart and physically powerful persons to be found in the country." Fighting was a job for "tough men," and the supply of jobs in the US Army seemed infinite. Thus Boston began its lengthy campaign to meet what city officials and politicians considered persistently unfairly high quotas for able-bodied whites.[9]

DESPITE THE BURGEONING crisis, the army continued to maintain its whites-only enlistment policies akin to a fraternal order; soldiering was a task reserved for men of honor. In April, J. Sella Martin and Robert Morris organized separate petitions demanding that Black men be able to fight; they hoped that "the embarrassment placed upon them by the laws of the State may be removed," so that they might at least form a Home Guard. In response to the petitions, a joint committee at the Massachusetts State House proposed to pledge all the commonwealth's "resources, all her hearts, and all her arms,"—except, noted the petitioners, those of the "colored citizens"—to the conflict at hand. At the end of May, a group of Blacks claimed that if the federal government allowed Black southerners to fight, so numerous were they and "knowing the geography and being acquainted with the character of the enemy, [they] would be of incalculable service to the Government." And from Boston, "the colored women would go as nurses, seamstresses, and warriors, if need be, to crush rebellion and uphold the Government," and the men "have their souls in arms, and all eager for the fray." These entreaties to serve went unheeded.[10]

In fact, though, the US Army's all-white recruitment policies did not deter Boston's Black men from volunteering for the US Navy. Aaron Joseph enlisted in October 1861. A boyhood friend of Thomas Selden's, the seventeen-year-old Joseph had been apprenticing to become a currier. Mustered into service, he was assigned the rank of landsman on the steam sloop-of-war *Mohican*. The ship joined Flag Officer Samuel F. DuPont's South Atlantic Blockading Squadron, which bolstered the immense Union Army force that captured Port Royal, South Carolina, and other nearby islands in November 1861. By that time the United States had more than 260 warships patrolling the Confederacy's 3,500-mile coastline along the Atlantic Ocean, the Gulf of Mexico, and the Mississippi River, and 100 more vessels would soon see service. When the *Mohican* was decommissioned in Philadelphia, in July 1862, Joseph reenlisted and joined the crew of the *Wabash*, a steam screw frigate that helped blockade Charleston Harbor.[11]

Of all the northern military personnel deployed during the Civil War, Black and white "bluejackets" (sailors) represented just 5 percent of the total, and they received their proportionate share of the glory—that is, very little. About one-fifth (17,000–18,000) of all Union sailors were Black, and 7,700 hailed from the northern states, including 434 from Massachusetts and 175 who had been born in Boston. Black naval enlistees tended to come from urban areas; their average age was 24, and their service represented a continuation of a tradition. Black seamen had fought for the United States in the Revolution, in the War of 1812, and in the War of 1848, and they had served in the merchant marine since before the nation's founding.[12]

In Boston, Civil War naval officers enforced an 1839 quota that limited Blacks to 5 out of every 100 recruits. Some Black Bostonians, hoping for a better chance, enlisted at ports other than those in their hometown. Joseph Hayden, the only son of Lewis and Harriet, joined at Portsmouth, New Hampshire, on November 30, 1861. Massachusetts's frantic drive to attract volunteers for its army regiments did not extend to navy crews, primarily because seamen did not count toward local military quotas, although that policy would change in 1864.[13]

Some Black men had joined the navy before the conflict began. In the three years leading up to the attack on Fort Sumter, 128 Black men had enlisted in the US Navy in Boston. Nineteen of them had been born in the city out of only 25 born in Massachusetts. The preponderance of men from other parts of New England and the Mid-Atlantic (66), the South (16, mostly Virginia), and foreign countries (18) revealed the enduring if diminished Black presence in the merchant marine during the late antebellum period. The records for some, but not all, of the enlistees in this group included their occupations, but the accuracy of this data is uncertain. An impatient recruitment officer may have made up information on his own, and some applicants may have reported jobs they thought would give them a better chance of being accepted into the service. In any case, the record includes 35 waiters, 13 cooks, 8 barbers, 4 stewards, and 2 masons, along with a baker, a machinist, a cooper, and a shoemaker. The recorded number of waiters was disproportionate to Boston's Black laboring population. Although the entry for Joel W. Lewis Jr., who enlisted with his younger brother Wendell, says he was a waiter, he had been apprenticing with his father, a Chelsea blacksmith. Likewise, Aaron Joseph had been working as a currier before he signed up, and he returned to that occupation after he was mustered out of the service, but he, too, is recorded in the enlistment document as a waiter/servant. The occupations listed for the white men who joined the navy around this time fall along a wider spectrum: there are machinists, coopers, blacksmiths, iron forgers, and painters, along with an apothecary worker, a carpenter, a shoemaker, a clerk, a boiler maker, a mason, a tailor, a roofer, a currier, and a sawyer; one is simply listed as "laborer."[14]

Naval service offered a steady wage, and the amount of pay was based on one's rank and not the color of one's skin. It offered a life apart from the humdrum of wage-labor drudgery, new places to see, and a chance to fight the slave South. Navy volunteers received no cash bonus for enlisting, but the crew of a warship that captured a blockade runner split the bounty, with the federal government taking half, the captain 7 percent, and the crew members dividing the rest. An allotment system allowed naval servicemen to set aside a certain proportion of their wages to be paid monthly to dependents, so a man could support his family while serving. Though usually confined to the lowest ranks on the ship, at times Black men partook of the communal aspects of a workplace that prized courage under enemy shelling or in rough seas and stormy weather.[15]

Like young men everywhere, Black men had various motives for joining the navy. Those who were Boston-born likely knew each other from their Ward 6 neighborhood. John F. Wright was the son of the prominent trader of the same name; with a father active in abolitionist politics, and with younger siblings named after William Lloyd Garrison, Wendell Phillips, and the reformers Lucretia Mott and Frances Wright, the younger John no doubt had grown up in a household that hailed the war as a struggle for Black freedom. Some of his brothers joined, on the same day or at different times. Aaron Joseph's younger brother Isaac was mustered in on March 31, 1862, and assigned to the *Aroostook*. Other men enlisted after a stint in the South Boston House of Correction. Of 372 prisoners (in July 1860), only 16 were Black men, but 6 of them eventually served in the navy; their crimes included running a brothel, assault, and stealing. Perhaps these restless young men saw military service as a way to make a living and stay out of trouble.[16]

Some enlistees found their way onto Union vessels after first living and working at the Charlestown Navy Yard, reflecting the navy's historic reliance on Black menial laborers in these installations. On August 6, 1860, the yard had a total of 385 people working or stationed there, 7 of them Black. One of them, Gad Minot, 16 years old, enlisted (or reenlisted) in the navy at about the same time that summer. However, this group was not mustered into service right away, suggesting that they continued to work in the yard before shipping out. Minot, the son of a father born in Africa, signed up on August 3, 1860, but he did not receive his first ship assignment—to the *St. Mary's*—until 1863.[17]

Sailing had its dangers as well as its appeal, but some of these occupational hazards were inherent to the job even in peacetime—falling from the rigging to the deck below or into the ocean, perhaps in shark-infested waters; enduring floggings and other harsh and arbitrary punishments; succumbing to a contagious disease that roared through close quarters; going down in a shipwreck. Despite formal policies that promoted egalitarianism on board, Black navy men remained at the mercy of white officers and shipmates, with discrimination ranging from exhausting stints in the sweltering engine room to persistent insults ("monkies," "wooly heads") and outright assault and torture. Wartime brought additional deadly hazards—not just gun battles and shelling from shore, but also the threat of being sold on the auction block into slavery, a possible fate for the Black sailors that their white crewmates did not have to face.[18]

The navy automatically assigned a disproportionate number of Black enlistees, as many as 82 percent of the total, to the lowest ranks of "boy" and "landsman." Regardless of their sailing experience, these men filled service positions as servants and stewards, working aboard steamers and ordnance store vessels as opposed to gunships. Together with formerly enslaved workers who found their way to Union lines or who swam or canoed and then clambered aboard naval ships, Black seamen performed the routine tasks of loading and unloading and maintaining vessels—painting and scrubbing and shoveling coal into the engines. Ship captains exercised discretion in promoting crewmen to the rank of petty officer—but that rank obtained for that vessel only, and, when it was (infrequently) bestowed on Blacks, it often mandated what on land would be considered women's work—for example, procuring and storing food or serving as the captain's personal assistant. These Black men were "petty officers of the staff" and not the gunners and sailmakers recognized as "petty officers of the line."[19]

Despite its risks, naval service afforded some Black men a welcome relief from the alternatives—standing on the sidelines during the momentous war against slaveholders, the great collective effort of the age; living at home with one's parents and feeling at loose ends; worrying where one's next dollar was coming from; making one too many appearances in Police Court and serving out ever longer sentences in the House of Correction. For Black people generally, life ashore in wartime Boston afforded few opportunities for steady work or a decent wage.

At 6:00 p.m. on the night of September 11, 1861, an estimated one thousand unemployed white laborers gathered at the waterfront on Second Street, formed a procession, and marched through their South Boston neighborhood, stopping briefly at the residence of

Ward 12 alderman Samuel Rogers Spinney. After giving Spinney three cheers, the men continued on to Independence Square. They strove to make their demands clear: "To obtain work from the city in that ward, . . . in hopes that some public improvements will be undertaken which will afford them the opportunity." With the firm support of Spinney and other local politicians, the demonstrators seemed to occupy a favorable position; in the words of a reporter, "The matter will doubtless be adjusted with the City authorities, so that employment will be furnished as desired." And so it was, for the Irish American laborers of Boston.[20]

Early military mobilization meant increased financial uncertainty for the mass of white workers, most of whom were Irish immigrants, and regular work for the relatively few fortunate men who were highly skilled. Down at the docks, all the "bustle and activity" that accompanied troop send-offs—the frantic loading of barrels of pork and beef, arms and ammunition, and tents and other supplies, enough for two thousand or three thousand men—provided work for some, but only on a sporadic basis; these "short jobs" paid 50 cents a day, half their regular pay. In contrast, the Charlestown Navy Yard, as well as shipyards in East Boston and South Boston, offered full-time employment to carpenters, rope makers, and ship riggers. During the war, the navy yard alone built a dozen ships (sloops-of-war, monitors, gunboats, and frigates), converted more than forty others to battle-ready condition, and outfitted twenty-three more. Private shipbuilders and engine makers prospered, and their payrolls sustained the families of machinists and steelworkers. Meanwhile, many dockworkers languished.[21]

Summertime appeals to the city on behalf of the Ward 12 workers prompted council action in September, when the aldermen took note of the obvious—that "labor is cheap"—and acknowledged "the necessity of doing what was practicable for the employment of the laboring classes by the City." The assumption was that unemployed workers ineligible for military service would "gladly" toil at "reduced rates of compensation" on public works projects. These projects promised many potential benefits: they would enable workers to support their families, relieve pressure on the Overseers of the Poor and private charities, and, it was hoped, defuse the resentment of underemployed longshoremen. A new avenue to South Boston would "give immediate employment and relief to thousands of laborers in the City who will otherwise suffer from extreme destitution in the coming winter," the council noted: "Far better is it to distribute the funds in employment to the poor, than through the medium of the public charities." The fact that many immigrants volunteered to form all-Irish regiments made the works project all the more palatable to city authorities; these patriotic newcomers would help Boston meet its military quotas, and the city gratefully supported the unemployed in return.[22]

Many residents were no doubt puzzled that so much paving, grading, widening, and lengthening of streets and so much digging and excavating was going on at the same time that private businesses were grinding to a halt and hundreds of men were marching off to war. Yet finances and labor-supply factors seemed propitious. A new iron fence for the Public Garden at a cost of $27,000 might seem like an unwise expenditure, but in fact, cheap iron, together with cheap labor—men "begging for work"—presented an opportunity that the city dare not squander. Calls to widen Union Street during a national crisis would seem to falter on a "conservative policy . . . retrenchment," but the council could point to a great supply of willing workers, making the $87,000 price tag a bargain. Moreover, the city could forgo private middlemen and employ white laborers directly. As for the funds to pay for these projects, the city would secure bank loans and hire only taxpayers, ensuring that some of their wages would go back to municipal coffers. Though few menial workers owned their own homes, their household furnishings were counted toward taxable property.[23]

Between 1861 and 1865, Boston built new public squares, a new city hospital and grammar school, new stables, and a new city hall. These major construction projects, together with an ongoing, intensive program of street and sewer improvements, gave employment to hundreds of white men, with the neighborhood of South Boston and its thirty thousand residents deriving much of the benefit. In a related vein, the war marked the first time in the city's history that Irish immigrants or their sons gained a foothold in the police department as officers—they accounted for forty-one of the officers hired between 1861 and 1865.[24]

By the fall of 1862, Boston's city government had identified two major interrelated wartime objectives as it contended with "waves of a gigantic treason" surging across the land. First, the council would spend freely to employ workers. Second, it would encourage white men to enlist in the army by providing for their dependents. The war was only one month underway when Albert J. Wright, a Milk Street printer, appealed to the city council on behalf of a newly formed Committee of Relief for Ward 12, asking that the city supply some direct assistance to the families of soldiers, "in order that the charities of our citizens for such a purpose may be properly organized." The council held a "wholesome prejudice" against charity, but it also assumed the conflict would be of "limited duration." Compared to centralized efforts, presumably local ward committees could better distribute aid by investigating applicants, keeping records, and dispensing money, thus taking care to preserve the work ethic of the residents. Soon, the formation of the Committee of 150, composed of the city's wealthiest citizens, would make this effort a public-private partnership.[25]

The city's Soldiers' Relief Fund paid out $1 a week for a wife, and an additional $1 for other dependents, such as children and elderly parents, but not more than $12 per month per household, a supplement to a private's monthly pay of $13. In September 1861, the council disbursed $9,311 to 963 dependents, a sum and a number of recipients that would grow exponentially over the coming months and years, with an average of less than $10 a month per household. Mayor Joseph Wightman and the council hoped this effort would induce men to take up arms of their own free will so that Boston could avoid a controversial military draft.[26]

With its program of direct assistance to soldiers' families, the city initially resisted subsidizing a private charity run by women to pay for sewing projects that gave work to female dependents of enlisted men. The council declared, in October 1861, that "the wives and daughters of these absent soldiers can easily obtain needlework and are thus enabled to feel the blessing of earning the fruits of industry, rather than being dependent wholly on the public bounty." However, by late 1862, authorities were allocating modest amounts of money from the Soldiers' Relief Fund—$500 to $800 at a time, irregularly—to the Ladies Industrial Aid Association, which provided sewing jobs for the women kinfolk of Boston's army volunteers.[27]

Through the late summer and fall of 1862, the city continued to chafe under the quotas mandated from Washington. Some men were ineligible for service: immigrants who had made a formal declaration that they would not seek to become US citizens; men who had not voted in an election; men with a documented disability; and essential workers in shipyards, not to mention all Black men, regardless of age. The distressing sight of wounded soldiers begging on the street corners and in the squares presented an unwelcome spectacle of those "whose situation oftentimes becomes a direct check upon enlistments." And most vexing of all was the problem of cash inducements for volunteers: on August 18, the council responded to the president's call for three hundred thousand more troops by alluding to the additional costs such a recruitment effort would incur, the "pernicious effects of the bounty." The city would continue to hemorrhage money in a fruitless effort to keep pace with the suburban towns, which set a "somewhat reckless example" by luring Boston men to enlist from their area with the promise of generous cash bonuses.[28]

To city authorities, the purpose of bounties was to "relieve the whole community from the inconvenience and odium of a draft." Yet violent resistance to large-scale recruitment was evident on August 25, when downtown Boston witnessed a "tumultuous assemblage" in response to Governor Andrew's call for another round of volunteers. A day marked by patriotic rallies, parades, and speeches had turned into an angry free-for-all among opponents to recruitment by late afternoon: a mob attacked and looted a boot and shoe store, a fruit dealer, and a hardware store and went on to issue a stern warning to "the 'old clo' men'"—that is, the secondhand clothing dealers, "the colored gentlemen who enjoy almost a monopoly of this branch of business in that section." The following day, the city appropriated an additional $300,000 for the war effort, some of which was earmarked for bounties for members of an Irish regiment.[29]

In September, Governor Andrew called for men to enlist in what would become the 54th Massachusetts Volunteer Infantry Regiment, but failed to attract enough interest. Two months later the council was authorizing another $25,000 for the Soldiers' Relief Fund (quarterly appropriations amounted to $70,000), questioning Boston's quota—for this round, 11,204 men—and expressing gratitude to 100 cavalry enlistees from California, men who agreed to be credited to Boston. But where would the additional bodies come from?

City and state policies to aid the white poor highlighted the vulnerability of Black people. Their families received no cash payments to soldiers' dependents because their menfolk were not allowed to join the army; and, because the aid was calculated to induce enlistments and meet Boston's army quotas, none of the payments went to US seamen of any color. Likewise, the sewing projects created for the wives and daughters of soldiers employed white women only. The city directed most of the public works jobs toward unemployed longshoremen from Ward 12—a potent, emerging voting bloc in local politics. The council appropriated more taxpayer money to private groups, such as the Franklin Fund for the Benefit of Young Male Mechanics and the Massachusetts Charitable Mechanical Association. These were, on their face, race-neutral policies, but ultimately they benefited white people exclusively.

THE WAR RECONFIGURED old jobs and created new ones, unpaid and paid, for the beneficent, the desperate, the talented, and the conniving. Volunteers, mostly women, sought to help supply the troops in the field, sewing clothing and paying for Bibles and prayerbooks. New bureaucracies related to relief and military service spawned "claim agents" who helped impoverished wives and widows apply for city aid, and "experts," legitimate or not, who offered to certify that men were exempt from service for medical reasons. Intelligence offices retooled and catered to the navy: "Wanted immediately: For the Navy, wardroom Cook and Steward; also two colored servants. . . . Call at M. Ingalls, no. 7 North Square." Spiritualists and astrologers promised contact with departed loved ones and news of loved ones far from home ("Madame Wright has astonished thousands with her magic power"). Apothecaries advertised useful articles for soldiers, such as "Union Shaving Soap (most agreeably perfumed)"; "Persian Insect powder" to destroy bugs, as well as medicine bottles and the elixirs to go in them; and Mrs. E. Kidder's Cordial for Chronic Diarrhea ("It will do you good"). The purveyors of the trappings of mourning—widows' weeds and hats, mourning jewelry, black badges and bunting—took advantage of a heightened demand. Gravediggers worked around the clock in cemeteries, where family members gathered, grateful that their loved ones had a resting place near home and not in a mass burial ground in a bleak southern cornfield.[30]

Between 1861 and 1865, Boston's white population grew from 133,653 to 141,083, about a 5.6 percent increase. In contrast, the

Black community grew by only 64 people, from 2,284 to 2,348, a 2.8 percent increase. Moreover, Blacks still made up less than 2 percent of the total population of the city. These figures revealed the lack of jobs, the low birthrates, and the high rates of mortality and out-migration among Black residents. Indeed, emigration schemes enjoyed a brief revival. A white man, James Redpath, author of a best-selling biography of John Brown, used his windfall to start a paper called *Pine and Palm* to stimulate Black emigration to Haiti. The venture gained more favor from Haitian authorities than from Redpath's Black neighbors. He wrote that "all that is needed is laborers, intelligent and industrious, to devote themselves to the work." He considered the Black-governed nation of Haiti as an ideal place for the cultivators of coffee, cocoa, and sugarcane, despite its arid soil; in calling for colonists he specifically ruled out hairdressers, waiters, clergy, and teachers. Boston's Black churches sponsored "Anti-Haytien Emigration Meetings," where those in attendance excoriated Redpath's scheme. In the end, any traction Redpath got derived from the publicity generated by his paid agents; they received $20 a week (plus an additional $2 for each man or woman who signed up) to lecture throughout the Northeast and Canada. William Wells Brown accepted a position as an agent, as did John Brown Jr.[31]

Though many options were denied the Black residents of Boston, a city transformed into a vast military depot did offer new money-making opportunities that they could take advantage of, and they responded. John Bailey, the pugilist and weapons expert, left Boston for Fort Leavenworth, Kansas, and opened a shooting gallery for the federal officers and soldiers stationed nearby; later in the war he became a sutler (supplier) for General Butler's troops in Virginia. Mark DeMortie served in the same capacity on the South Carolina Sea Islands. John A. Mulligan had worked for many years as a blacksmith, but in the summer of 1860 he was operating a seamen's boardinghouse. The following spring, the thirty-one-year-old Black man stated that he had the "men and means" to recover the anchor of the USS *Mississippi*, recently lost in Boston Harbor. Around that same time, Mulligan was also part of a group of "Colored Boarding Masters" brokering jobs for Black cooks and stewards out of an office on Commercial Street. They also promised to deliver these kinds of workers to New York City or to any port in the Canadian Maritimes.[32]

Various missionary and charitable organizations employed Black men and women to appeal to the benevolent. In 1861 the Reverend J. Sella Martin secured a commission as an agent for the American Missionary Association, a group that proselytized on behalf of the Congregational and Presbyterian denominations. Martin set out on a fund-raising tour of Great Britain, where he found much interest in "the American war," but also a field crowded with competitors for money. From London he wrote, to his friend George Lewis Ruffin in Boston, "There is no end to colored people here—'begging' to establish churches and start newspapers and build schools." The rivalry was intense; some respectable Black clergy from the United States were there "doing a first rate business and they partially neutralize the bad influences of the social leeches." Martin had heard that his Boston church had fallen on hard times, perhaps the reason he decided not to settle permanently in the Bay State upon his return from England.[33]

Martin wrote to President Lincoln in July 1862 recounting his efforts abroad—over eight months he had delivered forty-seven addresses informing his listeners of the Union cause. The pastor was hoping to get a paid position from the federal government so he could continue this work at home: "I write this to let your Excellency know, that if I can be of any manner of service here, should your Excellency ever think it best to employ my People, I am ready to work or preach or fight to put down this rebellion." Martin was not the only Black Bostonian to look to Washington for a non-military job during the war. The renegade attorney Aaron A. Bradley appealed to Lincoln in the hope of receiving a diplomatic post to Saint-Domingue and Haiti. The long-shot efforts of both Martin and Bradley were, not surprisingly, unsuccessful; but they suggested a certain resourcefulness born of desperation on the part of ambitious, entrepreneurial-minded Black men seeking a challenge—and a livelihood commensurate with their talents as well.[34]

Another well-known Black Bostonian, Leo L. Lloyd, began to use the money he had raised among the many prominent white men who had taken an interest in him qua "African prince." In 1859 he traveled to Liberia and sold at a considerable profit the $1,000 in goods he had brought with him. Returning to the United States, he spent the profits on a $10,000, 35-horsepower steam engine built in Brooklyn. He shipped the engine to Liberia via the Boston Planters Line and opened Lloyd's Sugar Mill, an enterprise that seemed destined to give him a good return on his money. Lloyd sought to take advantage of a wave of enthusiasm for the mill in the country—at one point he reportedly employed fifty or sixty people—but sugar cultivation waned by the end of the decade. Lloyd told the Liberia *Herald* that "he intended to be heard hereafter in the efforts he should put forth to promote the agricultural interests of the country."[35]

On May 6, 1861, the former leatherworker Edwin Garrison Walker was admitted to the Massachusetts bar after reading the law for three years; he was a living testament to his father's disdain for Black men who held servile jobs. (By this time, skilled "Morocco dressers" were losing their jobs to large companies that utilized machines.) Robert Morris probably served as a mentor and teacher for Walker; in the coming years they often worked together. Morris maintained a steady law practice during the war. Among other clients, he represented John H. Nichols, a white mariner from Chelsea who woke up one morning aboard a holding ship for navy recruits; apparently (as Nichols told his wife Lizzie), he had imbibed too much the night before and unwittingly volunteered for service. From the ship, he wrote to her,

"I Will Promise you I will not Drink a Drop for one year after I get ashore. . . . God knows this is the worst place I ever got into." Nichols was responding to his wife's anger about the loss of income, given the paltry wages paid to seamen. He admitted, "A man had better stay ashore and walk the streets for all he Will make here but do try to get along the Best you Can till I do come home." With Nichols's signature on the enlistment papers, there was little Morris could do, and the father of two shipped out as a "quarter gun."[36]

John S. Rock persisted in his quest for a stable income and a position equal to his talents; now, on September 14, 1861, he, too, joined the ranks of Boston attorneys. He began to advertise his services as "John S. Rock, Counselor at Law," with an office at 6 Tremont Street (news that was reported as far afield as Macon, Georgia). Rock's first two cases involved retrieving two young men who had signed up for military service without their father's consent—a white seventeen-year-old who had joined the First Battalion, and a Black sixteen-year-old who had joined the crew of the USS *Vermont.* (Said the latter, "I saw other boys enlisting, and I thought I would like to go too.") Soon after he was admitted to the bar, Rock had the added distinction of being appointed a justice of the peace for Boston and Suffolk Counties. He also offered his services to men seeking military exemptions; according to one of his ads, these men "can obtain full instructions and have their blanks filled and sworn to by calling upon JOHN S. ROCK, Counselor at Law and Justice of the Peace, No. 6 Tremont St." Rock's entry into the ranks of attorneys must not have paid well, at least initially, for in the spring of 1862 he once more took to the road to make money, giving lectures in Philadelphia and in Paterson and Camden, New Jersey.[37]

Deacon Cyrus Foster continued to promote his annual concert, adjusting his lecture topic and music to the times. It now featured the "Grand War Speech" and the "Contrabands March: Oh Don't Carry Me Back [to Virginny]." His concerts were always an incongruous mix of musical talent and farce. During his February 1862 performance, he declared, "This war will never come to an end till the President of the United States proclaims liberty to the whole country"—an enlightened assertion but one followed by "an immense cabbage" rolling across the stage, prompting guffaws among the audience. The deacon was then presented with a salted fish, "which he promised to have for his breakfast," and more hilarity ensued. He played to sell-out audiences, and these wartime concerts evidently placed "quite a comfortable sum in the pocket of the worthy Deacon."[38]

The denizens of the North End saw an uptick in activity, as an influx of sailors and soldiers into Boston meant ready cash for illicit workers of all kinds. The practice of targeting out-of-towners for their money knew no color or gender lines; two Black women, Olive Clark aka Hogan and Mary Jane Ross, robbed "a gentleman from the country" by feeding him "oysters and fixins" before lifting his wallet. Some enterprising souls would row out to ships in the harbor and sell liquor to the crew in return for all the junk, cast-off clothing, or purloined articles that could be sold. The city council complained about those seeking to take advantage of sailors' "wants and temptations," and also those "runners and dishonest persons who prowl about the harbor in search of plunder." The Black woman seeking donations who claimed to be the agent of a local missionary carried on a time-honored custom of scamming the unsuspecting. Unlicensed peddlers clogged the streets hawking metal, secondhand clothing, and fruit. Although petty crime had no skin color, the police might define as "disorderly" someone like Mary Fulton, a white woman whose chief offense was "[keeping] company with colored persons," an infraction that landed her in the House of Correction.[39]

Boston's growing population of lonely men away from home would seem to have been a boon for Joseph Clash's businesses, including the Grand Calico Dress Balls at his American Hall. Managers of the Boston Seamen's Friend Society admitted as much when they lamented the various "homes" away from home for the seamen—not only the miserable apartment rented at an exorbitant rate, but also the brothel, the dance hall, and the rum shop: "A woman invites him to go with her, and she leads him like a lamb to the slaughter, drugs his drink, steals his watch, and with stinging words bids him go!" Yet in early 1862 Joseph Clash gradually withdrew from the dance-hall business and went back to running a barbershop full time. Rumor had it that rheumatism and old age had slowed him down; but he had also suffered a terrible shock in March 1861, when his bride, Mary Ann Thacker Clash, died. She was thirty-two years old. Although her obituary gave no cause of death, she might have died in childbirth.[40]

Despite the new money-making opportunities the war afforded Black workers, life in wartime Boston offered no respite from injustices and insults. Joshua B. Smith maintained a sterling reputation as a caterer of large affairs, and in the spring of 1861 he was hired to prepare a variety of meals—from breakfasts to elaborate "collations"—for troops posted nearby en route to the front. On April 22, 1861, Governor Andrew commissioned Smith to provision the 12th Massachusetts Volunteer Infantry Regiment while they camped out in Boston. The agreement promised Smith 50 cents for each private and 75 cents for each officer. By the time the regiment left for the South, the state owed Smith $40,378 for 93 days' worth of food. He presented his bill to Andrew in July, but the governor refused to pay it, saying that the legislature had not authorized him to do so (though he did pay other military caterers at the time). Smith believed that Andrew knew the costs of provisioning "were just, fair and reasonable according to the market value of the substance furnished." A subsequent appeal to Washington would net Smith only 30 cents per ration, "to his great loss," he noted. Almost twenty years later the commonwealth still had not reimbursed Smith for his services, leaving him deeply in debt.[41]

With thousands of white men coming into or leaving Boston as part of the recruitment and deployment processes, the streets were more dangerous than ever for Black residents. In January 1862 two soldiers stationed at Camp Cameron used a bayonet to assault (seemingly randomly) two Black men who were walking along Commercial Street. Howard Athenaeum, the Academy of Music, and other venues made clear in their notices of upcoming events that they would continue to segregate Black patrons in the upstairs gallery. In July 1862, another Barnum Baby Show featured hundreds of "colored picaninnies" for the amusement of white patrons. Meanwhile, Police Court reporters persisted in ridiculing Black defendants and transcribing their statements into dialect. White-run employment agencies sought places for "good American, Nova Scotia, Scotch, English, Irish, and colored cooks, chambermaids, table and general housework girls," suggesting that "colored" workers were not "Americans." Many whites resented what they considered the abolitionist roots of the war. Responding to the insistent antislavery rhetoric of the Republicans, in early 1862 towns in Plymouth and Worcester Counties submitted petitions signed by hundreds of men to the US House of Representatives, urging Congress to "drop the negro question, and attend to the business of the Country."[42]

Many white fraternal organizations found themselves embroiled in controversy over whether to admit Black men to their organizations; often their members would object when Blacks were accepted, no matter how impressive their credentials or lofty their aspirations. In October 1862, fifty-two members of Boston's "Grand Division" of the Sons of Temperance "bolted" when the Charlestown Division accepted the newly minted attorney Edwin Walker as a member; the dissidents contemplated seceding from the national body and forming a new group for "those who don't care to be compelled to meet with the negro on equal footing," according to the *Herald*. They claimed that the issue of slavery was irrelevant; the only "true question" was whether Blacks and whites would meet together or in segregated divisions: "That while we recognize the 'Fatherhood of God,' and the 'Brotherhood of Men,' we do not recognize the negro as the equal to the white man, either by the 'laws of God' or the 'Constitution and Laws of the United States.'"[43]

No matter how much white Bostonians tried to distance themselves from slavery, the war brought the institution to their doorstep. Several Confederate officers held as prisoners of war in Fort Warren in Boston Harbor had managed to keep their bondsmen with them. A feeling of revulsion swept over abolitionists when they learned that John A. Emery, a Black seventeen-year-old from Salem, had been captured by rebel forces in Virginia and sold as a slave. Lieutenant Colonel Arthur F. Deveraux of the 16th Massachusetts Volunteer Infantry Regiment had hired Emery as a servant, and during General George B. McClellan's Peninsula Campaign in the summer of 1862, the young man fell ill. When the 16th retreated, Devereaux left him behind in a field hospital; the Confederates then captured the hospital and sold Emery on the auction block. John Rock made a strenuous effort to free the youth, a victim of an official Confederate policy. In a way, it was fortunate that Emery was hospitalized; if he had been caught bearing arms he could have been shot. It is unclear how he made it back to Massachusetts, but after the war he was on the North Shore working as a shoemaker and a mariner.[44]

In August 1862, Rock took the occasion of West Indian Emancipation Day to reprise what had become for him a stock speech. The war had not improved the status of Black working people in any meaningful way. In fact, according to Rock, the conflict had only proved that "the whole nation seems to have entered a conspiracy to crush" the Black worker, for "we are oppressed everywhere in this slavery-cursed land." Rock was preoccupied with his own struggle to support his family—he and his wife, Catharine, had lost their first son, Toussaint, but welcomed another, John Jr., now three years old. Rock reminded his listeners that

Massachusetts was undeserving of its reputation as a beacon of liberty, "anti-slavery and progressive": "While colored men have many rights, they have but few privileges here." Not only were proslavery employers refusing to hire Blacks even as menials, but white abolitionists continued to patronize establishments that refused to serve Black customers: "Do not our liberal anti-slavery politicians dine at the Revere House, sup at the Parker House, and take their cream and jellies at Copeland's?" From the lowliest worker to the most well-educated Black person, "we are colonized in Boston," denied decent employment and housing, and turned away from places of amusement, Rock said. He offered what was by now a standard refrain to his speeches: "Who is taking our boys into their stores at a low salary, and giving them a chance to rise? Who is admitting them into their work-shops, or into their counting-room?"[45]

THE BLACK COMMUNITY of Boston attempted to provide for its own. Yet even informal, modest forms of aid—a meal delivered to a needy person, a penny pressed into the hand of an elderly woman selling apples on the street—could tax the resources of families on the thin edge of distress. Most formal charitable assistance was dispensed by city or private associations that prioritized destitute whites, although one agent of the City Missionary Society regularly visited an elderly Black couple: Davy Mead and his wife, Martha (Patsy), part of the Edloe Sixty-Six. The couple—he a jobber, seventy-four, and she a domestic, eighty-two—were living in Ward 6. Davy had had a hard life, the missionary wrote, contending with "rough men in the streets" who harassed him, prompting him to respond, "I know where I am; I have been in the Gospel these forty odd years." Into his old age he had pieced together a living sawing wood, making fires, and clearing sidewalks, but now that he was "old and cold and stiff," he could no longer make any money. After his death in 1862, his widow entered what the missionary called "that excellent institution, the Home for Aged Colored Women."[46]

In early 1862 the *Herald* put forth the dubious premise that "Boston is brimful of charity for the poor, without regard to color," citing the home on Southac Street as proof of the city's benevolence toward all. As soon as the home opened, it had a long waiting list. Martha Mead qualified as a respectable woman "whom years and sickness have reduced to poverty." The large number of women in need spoke not just to the plight of older domestic servants but also to the destitution of their younger kinfolk and the wider community. The board approved the application of seventy-four-year-old Sarah Osborne in May 1860 because she had lived in Boston for many years, and "her daughter and grand-daughter are unable to take proper care of her and provide for their own support, & she lived in the utmost dread of being carried to the alms-house." Her fears were well founded, for, according to the home's directors, white inmates of public institutions "would not associate with them [Blacks]," leaving many "dependent on the precarious charity of an occasional benefactor, or of friends nearly as poor as themselves." In any case, the matron, Martha Thurston, had no compunction about expelling those whom she judged troublesome or insufficiently grateful; there were so many other desperate applicants.[47]

The Reverend Leonard Grimes continued his close association with the home, recommending women for admission and testifying to their good character. During the war, his congregants were pulled in different directions. They were still trying to pay off Twelfth Baptist's debt—more than $2,500—charging a small fee for events billed as "Union meetings." At the same time, they came together to send cash and supplies south as part of an emerging freedpeople's relief effort. In the early fall of 1862, Grimes returned to Washington (slavery had been abolished there that April) to investigate conditions among the refugees. On September 25 he addressed a mass meeting held in the church to celebrate the president's dramatic announcement, three days earlier, that he would issue a national emancipation proclamation on January 1. The audience recoiled at Lincoln's stated intention to colonize Americans of African descent in foreign countries. However, Grimes took the occasion to give a lengthy account of the sufferings of escaped slaves, who came into Union lines "with bare and bleeding feet, . . . in many instances half starved and nearly naked." Out of this meeting came the Fugitives' Aid Society of Boston.[48]

The new society was affiliated with the National Freedman's Relief Association of Washington, DC, organized by Elizabeth Keckley. A Black servant for First Lady Mary Lincoln, Keckley was touring the North on behalf of "contraband relief"; Mary Lincoln had provided $200 in seed money. Attendees at the September meeting appointed Octavia Grimes as president of the new society, which was to be a local branch of the national group, and Eveline (Mrs. John P.) Coburn as vice president. A finance committee included five women, each representing one of the major Black churches in Boston. Joy Street Church sponsored a subscription series of six lectures at 50 cents each, featuring Frederick Douglass and other speakers, to aid the "aged and infant contrabands."[49]

Meanwhile, white Bostonians began to take note of the South's deployment of Black manpower for wartime purposes and contemplate its eventual disposition afterward. On October 24, *The Liberator* reprinted an article from the *New York Independent*, which assured its readers that they need not fear an exodus of freedpeople out of the South: "The true Southerner has a sympathy for the black man's easy and shiftless ways." In the North, Black people faced unremitting prejudice, barred from the mechanical trades by whites who refused to work with them. According to the author of the article, no Blacks would want to move to a region where they were hated and where "they may not even carry the hod or blow the bellows, or push the drudging saw!"[50]

Boston's white laboring classes dreaded the possibility of an apocalyptic influx of former slaves. Members of the Black community were inclined to welcome long-lost kin among any southern newcomers, but they feared that even more rivals for Black jobs would depress already starvation-level wages. Meanwhile, a migration in the other direction was taking place, one that claimed the energies of both Black and white Bay Staters. As emissaries of Boston, with its divergent views on Black labor, these military officers, ordinary soldiers and seamen, cotton agents, missionaries, teachers, and relief workers promoted a range of policies; but virtually all of them agreed that clashes on the battlefield signaled only one aspect of a wider war—the transition of millions of Black men, women, and children from slavery to an uncertain freedom. What these northerners saw and did in the South would reverberate throughout the South, and throughout Boston, for years to come.

8

Boston Diaspora I

In Boston's Black community, formal announcement of the Emancipation Proclamation prompted a celebration that stretched over three days, with participants alternately ecstatic over the presumed imminent destruction of slavery and skeptical about President Lincoln's ultimate intentions. On December 31, 1862, Black men, women, and children crowded into churches for the customary New Year's Eve sacred "watch meetings"; but at midnight, those services partook of "a grand Jubilee shout" as congregants offered up prayers of joy and thanksgiving, for, in the words of the Reverend Leonard Grimes, the proclamation heralded "the beginning of a new era, towards which all their eyes had been so long directed." The following day he presided over a daylong ecumenical gathering in Tremont Temple.[1]

Not until the late evening of New Year's Day did official word come over the telegraph that the president had indeed signed the proclamation, which declared that all enslaved people in Confederate-held territory were henceforth free. It lacked the references to African colonization included in Lincoln's initial statement in September. At Tremont Temple, the long-awaited announcement saw (in the words of one observer) "the whole audience rising to their feet and shouting at the tops of their voices, throwing up their hats, and indicating in every conceivable manner symptoms of gratification that the hour of deliverance had at length arrived." Attendees then repaired to the Twelfth Baptist sanctuary, where a series of speakers declaimed until well into the early morning hours. Afterward, everyone went downstairs to the vestry and enjoyed refreshments prepared by the ladies of the church. Yet many remained, rejoicing, until daylight.[2]

At Tremont Temple just two years before that event, the question "How can American slavery be abolished?" had ignited a rhetorical and physical melee pitting conservatives against abolitionists. Now the focus was on a post-emancipation future. William Wells Brown stated that the slaves-becoming-freedpeople would be "as well able to care for themselves as any other class of laborers." He hailed the bonds linking the welfare of southern Blacks to northern capitalists and workers alike: "Set him [the slave] into liberty and he will consume $50 or $75 worth of northern manufactures yearly." Brown predicted that the former slaves would spend their cash wages on all manner of goods, giving a "tremendous impetus" to textile factories and to the national economy overall.[3]

Speaking at Twelfth Baptist, Frederick Douglass "thanked God that to-day he was living to see the beginning of the end of slavery," as a *Boston Herald* reporter put it. He was certain that bondage would cease to exist in the United States. At the same time, according to the reporter, Douglass admitted as an aside that such a happy state of affairs might leave him "worse off now than before; he was used to opposition; he had always had something to fight." Indeed, the proclamation had "taken the wind out of his sails. He was an Abolition lecturer, but now his occupation was gone, and he did not know what to get about." No doubt his comments elicited chuckles from the audience, but Douglass understood that in this new world his fierce antislavery writings and speeches would have little or no currency. Still, he would adapt.[4]

To bolster their optimism, several speakers pointed to news coming out of the South. William Cooper Nell declared that five thousand people in Tidewater Virginia had gathered to mark the proclamation. Union forces had occupied much of the region since May 1861 and were now relying on the labor of Black refugees, people called "contrabands of war." Edward Atkinson, a Brookline, Massachusetts, cotton-mill entrepreneur and insurance-company executive, brought greetings from the South Carolina Sea Islands. With a flourish, he held aloft a specimen of raw cotton and declared that the "gentleman" who grew it had made a profit of $4,000 (for the US government) from the 1862 harvest. Of course, the "gentleman" to whom he referred—probably Edward S. Philbrick, another Bostonian—had not actually grown the cotton: Black men, women, and children had done the planting, hoeing, picking, ginning, and packing, at times working under severe duress. Yet to Atkinson and Philbrick, Black field hands would not prove their "fitness for freedom" until they produced a bountiful crop for the market.[5]

A dramatic reading of a New Year's speech delivered by General Rufus Saxton to the Black people on the Sea Islands was "received with rapturous applause." Unionists there were marking the Emancipation Proclamation with a solemn ceremony at Camp Saxton near Beaufort. Dressed in their Sunday best, Black people arrived from all over the islands, many traveling in small skiffs wending through marshy creeks and into open water. Also gathered there, in a grove of gnarled oak trees, were several natives of Massachusetts—Edward Philbrick; Colonel Thomas Wentworth Higginson, commander of the 1st South Carolina Volunteer Infantry Regiment; members of the clergy; labor superintendents; soldiers; and missionary-teachers. On this fine January day, the roses were blooming and the birds singing. Wafting through the air was the smell of a dozen immense oxen roasting on an open-fire spit. The day was a triumph for the Boston diaspora, the men and women who had journeyed south with their own notions about the freedpeople and their future work.[6]

The city's sojourners in the South came from diverse backgrounds, but many of the whites shared the view that the problem of labor overshadowed all other challenges of the post-emancipation period. On January 12, the Emancipation League of Boston petitioned the US Senate calling for the federal government to create a "Bureau of Emancipation." The league, founded in September 1862 in response to Lincoln's pre-proclamation, brought together prominent white men, militant abolitionists as well as aggressive capitalists. The two groups agreed that Black people's claim on the nation was "simply, justice." Granted "fair play, and fair pay," they would not need charity. Policies toward Black labor varied in Union-controlled areas, but a region-wide, comprehensive federal program putting the freedpeople back to work would prevent Lincoln's actions from becoming either "fruitless or only a proclamation of anarchy." Labor was the "great source of wealth in a large part of our country," and the formerly enslaved must not become a burden to taxpayers.[7]

In Massachusetts, the Emancipation Proclamation also spurred the organization of two regiments of Black soldiers. On January 26, Secretary of War Edwin M. Stanton authorized Governor Andrew to begin a multistate recruitment effort for what would become the 54th Massachusetts. In March, the US Congress passed the Conscription Act, generally acknowledged as the North's first draft law. In May and June of that year, 83 of Boston's total 7,320 draft registrants were Black men, with 9 hailing (originally) from Massachusetts, 16 from other New England states, 18 from the Mid-Atlantic, 33 from the South (22 from Virginia alone), and 7 from abroad. Andrew assured the Black enlistees that they would receive the same pay as white soldiers. Elated, Douglass put out a recruiting broadside: "Men of Color to Arms: Words are now useful only as they stimulate to blows."

The time for speechifying was well-nigh past. Other Black leaders also eagerly embraced the opportunity to recruit soldiers, not only because they had long supported such an effort, but also because they received financial compensation for doing so. Among those were Douglass and his son Frederick Jr., Leonard Grimes, Charles Lenox Remond, Robert Morris, William Wells Brown, Lewis Hayden, and John S. Rock. Some, including Douglass Sr., received a stipend of $10 a week, but all earned a commission for each man they enlisted. The 54th Massachusetts was mustered into service on May 13, and, once that regiment was filled, the 55th on June 22. These soldiers joined the Boston diaspora, the cotton agents and teachers and missionaries, that stretched deep into "Secessia."

Boston's eclectic emissaries to the South adhered to conflicting views on the political meaning of Black labor. The fugitives who had fled to Boston before the war and now volunteered to go (back) south as civilians focused their energies on immediate relief efforts and schooling; they did not question the capacity of the formerly enslaved for learning or taking care of themselves. The whites, in contrast, often saw the freedpeople as more "primitive" and at the same time more "authentic" than free Blacks in the North. In 1862, the writer Nathaniel Hawthorne visited Virginia and at one point encountered a group of Black refugees on the road. He described the "contrabands" this way: "They were unlike the specimens of their race whom we are accustomed to see at the North, and in my judgement, were far more agreeable." Hawthorne was fascinated by the refugees' simple ways—"so picturesquely natural in manners, and wearing such a crust of primeval simplicity, (which is quite polished away from the Northern black man,) that they seemed a kind of creature by themselves, not altogether human, but perhaps quite as good, and akin to the fauns and rustic deities of olden times." To Hawthorne, the Black Bostonians' "polish" was only a veneer that hid a deeper, truer "racial" character.[8]

Whites who went south were eager to conduct a great experiment not unlike the one Samuel May Jr. had identified when the Edloe Sixty-Six arrived in Boston in the fall of 1847. In their view, most ordinary Black folk had never had their fundamental abilities completely tested, so devastating to body and soul was the institution of slavery. In the words of the *National Anti-Slavery Standard* of November 1861, "Here, within the protection of the arms of the United States, might a new experiment of tropical culture by free labor be tried." The success of the experiment would have national implications. This testing of the freedpeople had more than theoretical significance to Boston and its environs, considering the many groups with a vested interest in a robust cotton economy, among them merchants and bankers; factory owners, bosses, and operatives; teamsters and dockworkers; and commercial ship captains and crew members.[9]

In early 1863, a visitor to Boston might have mistaken the city as besieged by enemy combatants. Recruitment tents had sprouted up in the parks and squares, and the streets were clogged with fresh enlistees who had arrived by train from the hinterland. At least some docks were once more humming, now with workers loading lumber, gun cartridges, ammunition, army uniforms, and shoes into vessels bound for troops at points south. Coming in from western Massachusetts were military supplies such as army flannels, rubber cloth, sidearms, and swords, and, in February, 200,000 pounds of army pilot bread. From Maine came shoes, from New Hampshire textiles, from Connecticut guns, and from Rhode Island fish. The harbor was crowded with gunboats, tugboats, and ironclads making their maiden voyages, with receiving vessels processing recruits, and with transport ships taking men to war. Funeral processions from church to cemetery had become a sadly familiar sight. By January 1863, the war's casualty toll stood at more than 480,000, with 270,000 Union soldiers and 212,000 Confederates dead or wounded.

A year and a half into the conflict, the Boston City Council was reeling from the demands imposed upon it. Costs were mounting—another $100,000 was needed for harbor defense, and the annual price tag for the Soldiers' Relief Fund had risen to $350,000. They faced a torrent of other expenses related to bounty payments, rents for armories, the new city hospital and new city hall—all on top of escalating expenditures for the Overseers of the Poor. The soldiers' fund was also supposed to pay the families of wounded men transferred to the Invalid Corps, a unit reserved for whites only. By May, the council wanted to cut back on the overseers' budget, hoping the destitute men, women, and children benefiting from it would be able to survive on their own in the warmer weather.[10]

At the same time, inflation heightened the anxieties of white workers, who feared they might someday soon lose their livelihoods to Black southerners seeking jobs and safety in the North. Indeed, the threat of Black replacements for striking workers was already much in evidence. Throughout the spring of 1863, the caulkers at the Charlestown Navy Yard staged periodic walkouts. In January they struck for higher pay, and on April 1 they got a raise—from $2.50 to $2.75 a day—but eight days later, about 200 of the 250 of them announced they would not return to work because the yard had hired a Black southerner to work beside them. Newspapers reported that this new employee, Forrester Thompson, had aided the Union cause near his hometown of Savannah. The Journeymen's Caulkers Association resolved that they would accept the raise and resume their duties "as soon as the obstacle of that colored person" was gone; they felt his presence compromised "their dignity as 'North End boys,'" and "want[ed] the *dark* obstacle removed from the gang when employed on the caulkers' stage and on the deck of a naval vessel." In June the War Department raised the caulkers' wage to $3.00 a day but began to lay off men; as a newcomer, Thompson was probably one of those who were let go.[11]

While the war years brought economic hardship to many of Boston's unskilled workers, Irish immigrants and their adult children began to exert their influence in the workplace and at the ballot box. They were gaining political clout as key members of the Democratic Party and as volunteers for all-Irish regiments. (Military service provided an expedited path to naturalized citizenship for the foreign-born.) Though still largely impoverished, the Irish American community now had the means to create their own institutions, such as Boston College and the Home for Destitute Catholic Children. Through sheer force of numbers, they put pressure on the public schools to abandon the reading of the King James (Protestant) version of the Bible, and on the city hospital to allow Catholic priests to attend the ill and dying. Boston authorities considered these concessions necessary if immigrants were to fight for the Union and help the city meet its quota of enlistees.[12]

Many Bostonians, whether Black or white, immigrant or native-born, followed news of the war, rendered in graphic detail by individuals in a variety of media. Several Boston dailies published timely dispatches from the front—"Latest by Telegraph!" read the headlines. The *Boston Journal* had a reporter embedded with forces in the Gulf of Mexico, and the *Boston Traveller* with forces at Virginia's Fortress Monroe, a federal installation located on the tip of the peninsula between the York and James Rivers. The *New York Tribune* sent back dispatches about the 54th and the 55th from Port Royal, reports that were reprinted in Bay State papers. In early 1863 Generals David Hunter and George B. McClellan both made visits to Boston—the former, an advocate of Black soldiers, received warmly by abolitionists; and the latter, recently relieved of his command of the Army of the Potomac by the president, hailed by Democrats. Travelers to the South wrote to newspapers and private correspondents about their impressions, and the missionary-teachers kept up a running commentary in the form of letters to editors and friends and family, as well as in lectures upon returning home. And fugitives were still making their way to Boston, bringing news about Confederate troop movements and life behind enemy lines.

On April 23 the famously renditioned fugitive Thomas Sims arrived in Boston from Vicksburg, Mississippi. He had managed a daring moonlit escape, rescuing his wife and eight-year-old daughter via canoe and on foot. Sims recounted his adventures for curious audiences. After his forcible removal from Boston in 1851, he had remained in a Savannah jail until a series of sales (to Augusta, Georgia, then to New Orleans) landed him in Vicksburg. There he worked at his craft, bricklaying, for ten or eleven years, biding his time. When war broke out, he hired himself out and peddled goods among the soldiers defending the city from a months-long siege. That work allowed him to gauge troop deployments and his chances for freedom. A Boston reporter noted he brought little of material value with him, except for daguerreotypes "of dear relatives, still in bondage." He had come back to Boston apparently because his thirty-four-year-old sister Cornelia Sims Sykes had been living there, with her two sons, since at least February 1860. Now Sims announced that he intended to settle his family in Boston.[13]

Thomas Sims was so skilled a bricklayer that upon his forced return to Savannah in 1851, his owner James Potter had decided to sell him rather than allow the authorities to execute him. His new Vicksburg owner eventually let him work as a wage earner as long as he paid the white man a set amount each month. Yet when Sims made his dramatic reentry into Boston, no one suggested that he take up his trade, even with so many new buildings under construction; everyone, Black and white, understood that he had little chance of success in workplaces dominated by white tradesmen. So he began to give lectures on "The House of Bondage (The Returned Bondman of 1851, the Welcomed Freedman of

1863)," with his sponsors charging 15 cents for single admission, 25 cents for double. His two-hour presentation at Tremont Temple on May 6 attracted an audience estimated in the hundreds, and even a *Herald* reporter admitted the thirty-four-year-old was "possessed of considerable intelligence." The proceeds from the lectures were supposed to enable Sims to buy his own business and "earn an honest livelihood." This prospect failed to materialize in Boston, and before long Sims decided to look elsewhere for work that would support his family.[14]

Bostonians devoured the news that Sims and others brought north with them, including firsthand accounts of the South's Black refugees and workers. In February 1863, the *Boston Journal* posed several hypotheticals: Would those throwing off the chains of bondage rise and slaughter their masters and mistresses? Would Boston have to contend with "a general invasion of the North by the 'contrabands,' which was to fill our almshouses and penitentiaries, after deranging all departments of labor by their injurious competition with our present workmen"? For most whites, the main question was whether formerly enslaved people would work at all, responding to the inducement of cash and avoiding dependence upon charity and the largesse of the federal government. Ultimately, these issues were interrelated, for presumably the promise of wages would encourage southern Black field hands to remain in their familiar surroundings without "deranging" northern labor.[15]

Bostonians also followed news about early efforts to deploy free men of color and enslaved men as soldiers—for example, in September 1862, accounts of General David Hunter's abortive attempt to raise a brigade on South Carolina's Sea Islands, an effort that Lincoln quashed. The following month, General Benjamin Butler formed the 1st Louisiana Native Guard, a regiment composed of free men of color as well as fugitive slaves, but consigned the men for the most part to fatigue work. In November came reports about the 1st Kansas Colored Volunteer Infantry Regiment fighting Confederate guerrillas. These reports, combined with the never-ending task of filling military quotas for Boston and Massachusetts, would prepare whites for the novel sight of Black soldiers mobilized for war.[16]

At Fortress Monroe, the Emancipation Proclamation had little practical meaning, since the area remained under Union control throughout the war; the proclamation freed only those still in Confederate territory. Thousands remained enslaved. Nevertheless, the first real chink in slavery's armor appeared here. It was not, however, because of eloquent speeches delivered in Tremont Temple, or fervent pleas in *The Liberator*, or mass petitions gathered by the faithful foes of slavery. Instead, General Benjamin Butler (a Democrat and cotton-mill owner from Lowell) intended to deprive the Confederates of Black labor and divert it to the service of the Union. Three runaways who sought refuge in the fort on May 24, 1861, were soon followed by hundreds fleeing Confederate "press agents," officials authorized to seize enslaved men from their owners and force them to work for the South. Northerners demanded to know why the rebels should profit from the labor of bondsmen. The ugly truth, according to one Boston paper, was that "the enemy are wiser than we are in this respect, as they are in some other ways; and they employ colored men by thousands, to labor, to navigate, and to fight in their public service."[17]

This observer was wrong in thinking, first, that the Confederacy had allowed enslaved men to serve as soldiers, and second, that the labor of Black people was "free" to the military. Impressment agents dragged enslaved workers off the plantation, but they had to pay owners to do so. Still, here were men who toiled not only on fortifications, but in a lead factory (Petersburg); in an iron foundry (Richmond); on docks, loading and unloading transports; and in rivers and streams, dumping obstructions to halt Union vessels. Enslaved women relieved Confederate soldiers of cooking for themselves and washing their own clothes. The First Confiscation Act, passed by Congress in August 1861, allowed Butler to hold within Union lines any runaways who had been used by the enemy for military purposes, "employed in or upon any fort, navy yard, dock, armory, ship, entrenchment, or in any military or naval service." In July of the following year, the Second Confiscation Act included no such stipulation; any Black fugitive who sought refuge was freed. Butler was eager to put the so-called contrabands to use, which meant "arm[ing] them with working tools," there in Virginia and after his transfer to Louisiana.[18]

The area around Fortress Monroe highlighted the multiple roles that Bostonians and other Massachusetts natives would play in reconstructing the post-emancipation South. Charles B. Wilder, a merchant and abolitionist, arrived as an agent of the American Missionary Association (AMA). The association's aggressive proselytizing found little favor among members of Black Methodist and Baptist churches, and deeply offended their preachers. Edward L. Pierce, an attorney and abolitionist from Milton, a suburb of Boston, and now a private in the 3rd Massachusetts Regiment, served as a labor superintendent, organizing Black work crews for the military. Two white sisters from Worcester, Sarah and Lucy Chase, took up residence on Craney Island, where military officials exiled many refugees: women and children as well as the disabled and the elderly. Butler and Pierce worked for the federal government. Wilder was paid by the AMA, and the Chase sisters were sponsored by the New England Educational Association, which lauded the two: "On one side [were] squalid wretchedness and ignorance—on the other the high civilization of heart & intellect reaching out a willing hand to comfort & to elevate!" Drawn mostly from modest households throughout the North and Midwest, the missionaries and teachers relied on a small stipend from a sponsoring society. Freedmen's work was work, no matter how idealistic the goals.[19]

Boston's John Oliver served as both teacher and relief worker in Tidewater Virginia. Over the years he had become an ever more visible activist in abolitionist and anti-colonization circles. In late January 1862, he attended a talk by William Davis, one of the first enslaved Black men to escape to Union lines and seek safety at Fortress Monroe. An AMA missionary took Davis on a speaking tour of New England; the Black man impressed audiences with his account of his conversion to Christianity, juxtaposed with vivid descriptions of the abuse endured by his mother, "whipped until the blood ran down her back to the ground." Admirers praised his oratorical abilities and emotional power on the platform. Davis received a weekly salary of $7 from the AMA, with the rest of the proceeds from his lectures going to the association. He raised cash and brought in donated supplies for the "contrabands."[20]

Oliver applied to the AMA for a commission the day after he heard Davis speak. Over the coming years he would put his considerable talents to work advocating for the civil rights of Virginia freedpeople; but now, he had other reasons for leaving Boston. In late January 1862, he and his estranged wife, Louise, went through a messy divorce. A reporter covering a hearing on February 2 noted that "the parties are colored persons, of some education and respectability." She hired Robert Morris as her lawyer; he hired a young white attorney. John's prolonged absences in California and Ohio meant that it had been five years since they had lived together. Now a lecturer of some renown herself, Louise ridiculed her husband's peace offering of money, declaring "that she could earn as much as he could." In the end, the proceedings freed the two of them from each other. Louise took back her maiden name, DeMortie, and continued to win plaudits for "her rich, full, and musical voice, [and] the exquisite skill with which she modulated it, and the fire and pathos which she infused into all her pieces." In 1863 she moved to occupied New Orleans, where she opened an orphanage for Black children.[21]

Born to free parents in Norfolk, Virginia, in 1833, Louise DeMortie moved with her new husband, the carpenter John Oliver, to Boston in 1853. Under the name Mrs. L. DeMortie Oliver, she soon opened a business shampooing, dyeing, and dressing women's hair. When she and Oliver divorced in 1862, she took back her maiden name and continued a successful though short-lived stage career as an elocutionist, reciting poems by Whittier, Browning, Longfellow, and other literary lights of the day. *(Boston Athenaeum)*

In his February 5 letter of application to the AMA, John Oliver listed the Reverend Leonard Grimes as a reference and invoked the suffering masses on the peninsula: "I have felt a desire to go and help teach them. And with my knowledge of both Slavery and the Slave, and the condition in which the former has left the latter, I Believe that I would be of great Service to that people."[22]

When Oliver arrived at Fortress Monroe in the fall of 1862, one hundred thousand Union troops were stationed in the vicinity. Preparing for a drive up the peninsula to the Confederate capital of Richmond, the soldiers were living off the land, ransacking nearby slave quarters for food and livestock, and leaving devastation in their wake. Most Black people, whether enslaved or free, had sought to provide for themselves by hunting, fishing, oystering, growing vegetables, and hiring themselves out. General George B. McClellan did nothing to intervene in the destruction caused by his troops, and he sought to force every available Black man to work for the army. In this respect he resembled the Confederate "press masters" whose inhumane tactics had spurred the mass migration to Fortress Monroe in the first place. The Union pay scale was paltry—$4 a month for women and $8 for men.[23]

In late 1862, Oliver visited Craney Island. He had started a school in Newport, but the crush of refugees had overwhelmed the area, and Union authorities ordered an evacuation of all but the able-bodied men to the island; there he found six hundred people crammed into three barracks. Though many had worked

This drawing is titled *Morning Mustering of the "Contrabands" at Fortress Monroe [Virginia], on Their Way to Their Day's Work*. Local Black men employed as fatigue workers march under the direction of a mounted Union officer. They are shouldering not guns but pickaxes, rakes, and shovels. The image evokes antebellum scenes of enslaved workers on their way to the fields. Though promised a daily wage by military officials, many of these men received no pay for their labors. *(Getty Images)*

building a federal hospital all summer, most had received no pay at all. Meanwhile, soldiers were stealing ("confiscating") what little these people had. Using "Irish" as a generic term for pillaging Union soldiers, Oliver adopted the prejudices of Boston's Protestants and wrote, "Every house was robbed by these Irishmen, of both clothing and money, where it could be found." Food shortages and torrential rains added to the misery and grew the death count. The general in charge believed the people could earn money by "picking oakum" (pulling the fibers out of old rope) and by fishing, though the fact that soldiers had seized the people's boats made that an impossibility. At the same time, the local quartermaster was profiting by selling food and clothing sent south by sympathetic northerners. He was also withholding the workers' wages—as of May 1862, $10,000 worth. Oliver wrote that this official had "both starved, and beat them [the refugees] with wagon whips." The camp on Craney Island enforced an unnecessary dependence on the government and, in Oliver's words, gave license to "bad men . . . bringing forward their old measures of compromise and colonization." He wrote, "A General without pity is a barbarian."[24]

As the number of refugees on the mainland swelled, one army officer was so disgusted at the prospect of having so many extra mouths to feed that he devised a scheme to send the children and non-able-bodied to the North; but when that plan failed he sent them to Craney. Now an estimated 1,625 desperate people there needed the bare necessities. All the Black women knew how to sew, but they lacked materials: "A perfect mania for thread rages among our Islanders," wrote Lucy Chase in late January. Yet Union policy thwarted the people's efforts at self-sufficiency. Another missionary-teacher expressed outrage that both officers and ordinary soldiers were "fighting the ex-slaves, determined if possible to prevent them from making an honest living." Assured of a just system of payment and the possibility of marketing the products of their own labor, the refugees were initially "all eager to enter the field." Now some were wondering whether the price of "freedom" was just too high.[25]

John Oliver had joined a small coterie of northern Black men and women who went south during the war; most could not afford to go on their own, and the northern societies favored white applicants for sponsorships. Harriet Jacobs was unusual in that by this time she was well known as the author of the 1861 memoir *Incidents in the Life of a Slave Girl.* She went south first as a correspondent for *The Liberator* and then as a teacher supported by the New York Yearly Meeting of Friends. Her own compelling life story amounted to a refutation of white northerners' doubts about what enslaved people could and could not do once they were free. And she, along with John Oliver and a goodly number of white women teachers and nurses, believed that it was essential first to provide for the refugees' immediate needs—food, clothing, shelter, reunions with loved ones—before demanding that they respond to vague platitudes about the blessings of waged labor. The word "charity" held no terror for Jacobs; she believed that the refugees had earned federal and private assistance.

In mid-April 1862, Jacobs traveled to Washington, DC, to distribute clothing, blankets, and shoes to the refugees, and then returned to Boston to raise more money. In a long letter to *The Liberator*, "Life Among the Contrabands," she described scenes of frightened, ragged, and hungry men, women, and children seeking refuge in the city, many ill with measles, diphtheria, scarlet fever, and typhoid, or grieving for loved ones lost to death or separation. White soldiers were commandeering Black labor, promising paltry wages that in most cases were never paid. Conditions were equally chaotic in nearby Alexandria, Virginia. Jacobs was alarmed at the many orphans, their numbers growing by the day. She ended her account by imploring her readers, "If you cannot take one [an orphan], you can do much by contributing your mite to the institution that will open its doors to receive them." Her patron Lydia Maria Child said Jacobs "harrowed up my soul with accounts of the suffering she had witnessed."[26]

Jacobs spent the fall canvassing Massachusetts, New York, and Pennsylvania. She attracted audiences curious about the author of *Incidents*; the book had received favorable notices, for the most part, but some readers doubted her account of her long years in hiding, and others were scandalized by her frank discussion of sexual abuse at the hands of her owner. In addition to honing her prowess as a fund-raiser, Jacobs held several other jobs during her time doing relief work: she gave lectures and solicited cash and in-kind donations; she kept northern readers informed of conditions in the South, writing lengthy, detailed articles for *The Liberator* and other northern publications; and she sorted and distributed supplies as the donors intended. By the end of 1863 she and her daughter Louisa were teaching in a new school she had started in Alexandria.

Harriet Jacobs found the work exhausting but exhilarating, and the chronic ailments she had endured as a domestic servant and governess seem to have diminished and then disappeared. In December 1862, she wrote, "My health is better than it has been in years. . . . The good God has spared me for this work & the last six months has been the happiest of all my life." Whether enslaved or free, Jacobs had always found service debilitating; now that she was moving to her own rhythms, she felt her labors had taken on a whole new meaning, full of purpose.[27]

Returning to the refugee community in Alexandria in January 1863, Jacobs did battle with the Reverend Albert Gladwin, an agent of the American Baptist Free Mission Society. Gladwin insisted on charging the refugees exorbitant rents for cramped, windowless quarters as well as for food, coal, and donated supplies—this while a smallpox epidemic raged through the barracks. Jacobs and her coworker, a white woman named Julia Wilbur, dutifully but reluctantly charged for pieces of clothing, all the while resenting "such an *extensive business.*" Gladwin separated families and sent orphans to live in a squalid smallpox hospital. He denied aid to individuals he considered dirty, telling them to go home and wash, no matter how cold the day, though there was little soap to be had. Meanwhile, he occupied commodious quarters and exploited his own servants, Peter and Susan Washington. Susan did most of the cooking, cleaning, and washing, but earned nothing for her labors. In May, Jacobs noted that "many of the Refugees have worked steadily for the Government since last October, and have not received a dollar." She lamented, "O, when will the white man learn to know the hearts of my abused and suffering people!"[28]

One of the many Bostonians on the Virginia Peninsula wrote to the *Boston Evening Transcript* assessing the situation: "The colored people are as active and industrious and capable as the Irish. They are much more easily managed, and as the Irish are at the North and the negro in the South, each in their more native latitude so let it be. . . . It is almost the universal desire of the colored people to go South instead of North, if moved at all." In this view, members of both groups would have to work hard to prove their worth. Perhaps this correspondent was the same one who reminded readers of the paper what was at stake with the southern "experiment": "Here the colored race are being tested as to their desire for freedom and adaptedness to it."[29]

In Virginia, and throughout the South, the destruction of slavery depended less upon pronouncements coming from the White House or the War Department than on military orders issued from individual officers in the field. In their rush to put refugees to work, northern whites often ignored or actively undermined Blacks' efforts to eke out a mean subsistence on their own. Military policies yielded not "experiments in free labor," but forced-labor projects under the guise of a free-labor wage system.

Beginning in the spring of 1862, Boston's cotton-textile manufacturers sought to shape the South's post-emancipation economy. Massachusetts factory owners had their own representatives on the South Carolina Sea Islands, which were home to approximately ten thousand Black people. In early March, a group of entrepreneurs and teacher-missionaries departed Boston for the islands. On Port Royal Island, Edward S. Philbrick assumed the role of General Rufus Saxton's labor agent, collecting and shipping the 1861 cotton crop to the north. A wealthy engineer, Philbrick brought with him $1,000 of his own money and took day-to-day charge of three plantations on St. Helena Island. He immediately became impatient with Edward L. Pierce, the attorney from Milton, who was now a US Treasury Department official and had been sent from Fortress Monroe to oversee the planting of the 1862 crop. Philbrick found willing assistants in fellow Bostonians William C. Gannett and Charles P. Ware, along with Ware's sister Harriet, who supervised housekeeping matters on the Coffin Point plantation. These and forty-nine other so-called Gideonites (a mildly disparaging term referring to their religious fervor) went south to teach habits of industry to people who had literally worked as slaves all their lives. The Bostonians exhibited their customary chauvinism: according to Philbrick, "the party from Boston stand eminent in talent and earnestness, as compared with those from New York." The only Black person in the Boston "delegation" was Charlotte Forten, daughter of a Philadelphia sailmaker and a resident of Salem who had lived with Charles Lenox Remond and his wife.[30]

Philbrick declared he was "determined to see if something can't be done to prove that the blacks will work for other motives than the lash." This was the "great work" to which he personally would attend. He felt strongly that any form of charity would discourage people from laboring; instead, he would introduce them to a new institution, the plantation store. There they could buy the supplies that had been furnished them as slaves—meat, salt, molasses, tobacco, coffee, and cloth, blankets, shoes, and clothing, with most of the goods donated by northerners. Lacking enough cash to buy what they needed or wanted, they would presumably work harder and grow more cotton. Visiting in the spring of 1862, J. Murray Forbes, a Boston shipbuilder and railroad magnate, ventured the opinion that Sea Island Blacks were now "materially worse off than under their old masters." Yet most whites remained focused on the viability of Black field labor, the major precondition for a revived cotton trade in the not-too-distant future.[31]

The Boston group took up residence on abandoned plantations; the wrecked houses, with remnants of Egyptian marble mantelpieces and mahogany furniture, stood as mute testimony to the vanished glory of the slaveholding elite. Harriet Ware existed in a constant state of exasperation, trying to introduce her servants to New England standards of housekeeping. Ware found in Rose, the cook, a great source of entertainment, amused by her "jabbering away in her outlandish fashion," and her "comical" demeanor in the presence of visiting dignitaries. Rose showed gradual signs of progress, though, according to Ware: "She has regular days when she goes home to wash, changes her 'linen' twice a week, takes a warm bath every Saturday, and keeps her head and feet in a condition to which they were strangers previously." One day, Ware complained that "it would be easier to keep house in a small country house at home and do my own work (minus the washing) and live better than we do here."[32]

Like other white northerners, the Bostonians were constantly comparing the former slaves with Irish workers back home (but not with Black workers back home). Noted Harriet Ware, "Dirty and ragged they [the Blacks] all were, but certainly no more so than poor Irish, and it seems to me not so dirty." Her brother concurred: "I find the nigs rather more agreeable, on the whole, than I expected . . . much to be preferred to the Irish." For Bostonians of means, it hardly seemed possible to sympathize with one of these two impoverished populations without denigrating the other. At the same time, like John Oliver, many northern Blacks in the South tended to identify marauding soldiers as inevitably Irish immigrants, a dubious assumption.[33]

The freedpeople finished their allotted daily "task" in the cotton fields after four or five hours. This traditional system allowed them a modicum of control over their productive energies, as they could devote the rest of the day to fishing and tending their own garden plots, the "negro grounds"; but Gannett and Philbrick were none too pleased. Such examples of personal and collective initiative would mean a lesser cotton harvest. Privately, the two men grumbled that Limus Anders, fifty, a former driver whom they described as an energetic "black Yankee," neglected his cotton crop, preferring to "earn money for himself."[34]

Other developments threatened the Bostonians' aims. Army officers hostile toward Philbrick and Gannett entangled them in reams of so-called red tape. General Hunter periodically raided the quarters and dragooned men for an army regiment he was assembling (Lincoln eventually disbanded it). White soldiers stationed nearby took off pigs, chickens, and other livestock and goods accumulated by the people. The towns of Beaufort and Hilton Head and the many military encampments scattered about the islands offered wage-earning opportunities that lured men and women from the fields. Wives and mothers refused to put in a full day's work planting, hoeing, or picking cotton; they wanted to stay home and care for their children. The people remained resentful of having to pay for basic supplies—whether labeled "necessities" or "luxuries"—and they refused to work on Saturday. Philbrick resorted to cajoling and threatening: "I tell them they must work or I shall report them to Massa Lincoln as too lazy to be free."[35]

Soon after the war began, white Bostonians began to set the stage for a great drama—or concoct a laboratory for a great experiment—that they believed would reveal southern Black people's willingness and ability to labor. These whites agreed among themselves that, once freed, men and women must continue to till the soil and serve their former owners as cooks and servants. Poverty would function as an incentive to escape it by honest means. Back in Boston, it was no wonder that the only significant charitable enterprise sponsored by whites on behalf of Blacks was the Home for Aged Colored Women, the physical infirmities of its elderly inmates testament to their admirable commitment to industriousness.[36]

Yet another kind of work among the freedmen remained an intense subject for debate—whether they might shoulder arms in the military campaign against the South. Then the question changed yet again: Was Black soldiering an affair of honor or just another form of backbreaking labor?

9

"A Higher Standard of Courage"

On November 5, 1862, Thomas Wentworth Higginson, captain in the 51st Massachusetts Volunteer Infantry Regiment, received authorization from General Rufus Saxton to raise an all-Black regiment on the South Carolina Sea Islands. A Unitarian minister, a writer, and a militant abolitionist, the Bay State native aimed to test Black men's fitness for battle. His goal was to have "eight hundred men suddenly transformed from slaves into soldiers, and representing a race affectionate, enthusiastic, grotesque, and dramatic beyond all others." He kept careful track of the various "tests" he administered to these raw recruits.[1]

In the early weeks of his command Higginson asked a series of specific questions: Can the men appreciate justice? Learn to drill in an acceptable manner? Serve credibly on picket duty? Remain at their posts as ordered? Withstand enemy fire and return it in kind? According to Higginson, daily exercises yielded answers all in the affirmative. Still, he seemed suspended between two competing ideologies—the first holding that soldiers should be "treated like children" and trained to obey without question, the second that military service was an exercise in "manliness," one reserved for men of honor, courage, and integrity.[2]

More generally, Higginson intended to investigate the great mystery that animated so much northern interest—whether Black people would remain "sluggish and inefficient in labor!" He took satisfaction from the events of November 30, when the soldiers put in "a hard day's work" unpacking guns and putting up tents, but then had to unload lumber from a steamboat by the bright light of the moon. Worried at first that the men "would grumble at the night-work," he thought this remarkable "jolly scene of labor" worth recounting in detail: "Tugging these wet and heavy boards over a bridge of boats ashore, then across the slimy beach at low tide, then up a steep bank, and all in one great uproar of merriment for two hours. Running most of the time, chattering all the time, snatching the boards from each other's backs as if they were some coveted treasure, getting up eager rivalries between different companies, pouring great choruses of ridicule on the heads of all shirkers, they made the whole scene so enlivening that I gladly stayed out in the moonlight to watch it." By unloading thousands of feet of board "quicker than any white gang could have done it," the newly minted regiment had not only spared their white comrades the hard task, but also confirmed in the minds of their white officers the inherent "suitability" of Black men for fatigue work.[3]

Army camps and naval vessels were peculiar workplaces, producing their own occupational hazards, status hierarchies, mandated tasks, ladders of upward mobility, forms of compensation, and social cultures. Many white officers assigned Black military men the drudge work that freed white soldiers from doing the same. Those discriminatory assignments, combined with lesser pay for Black troops, mirrored conditions in the civilian workforce. On the Sea Islands, Black and white women and men from Boston were part of a larger drama related to the meaning of "race" as it related to the meaning of work nationwide.

The recruitment of Black soldiers added urgency and political resonance to the question regarding the future of southern Blacks. In March 1863, Secretary of War Edwin Stanton appointed a three-member commission to study the status of enslaved people freed by the Emancipation Proclamation and to make recommendations for their transition from bondage to freedom. Issued from New York at the end of June, the preliminary report of the American Freedmen's Inquiry Commission (AFIC) sought to reassure anxious white northerners. It predicted that the freedpeople "need not be, except for a very brief period, any burden whatever on the government." Those currently in refugee camps and otherwise behind Union lines were proving to be "docile and easily managed," willing to work "as long and as hard as white laborers, whether foreign or native born." Black southerners embraced marriage and schooling for themselves and their children with "lively gratitude." They had no interest in moving north, for they possessed strong "local attachments . . . and the Southern climate suits [them] far better than ours." The commissioners did, however, warn that, should emancipation prove a temporary measure, and slavery be reinstituted at some point, Blacks might flee en masse to the North. In that unfortunate event, "the fears of competition in labor sought to be excited in the minds of Northern workingmen will then have some plausible foundation."[4]

The commissioners recommended that Black men take the places of thousands of white troops now working in the quartermaster and commissary departments and hospitals, performing guard and garrison duty, digging trenches and building forts, and providing intelligence as guides and spies. And, too, formerly enslaved men had the qualities to be good soldiers—"docility, earnestness, the instinct of obedience." The refugee camps in the South should serve as "places of reception and distribution only," where men could be deployed to surrounding areas, and women and children could support themselves by laboring for the troops.

Given the incentive of eventual landownership, the freedpeople should pose no threat to taxpayers or northern white workers but stay rooted to the southern soil.[5]

In the spring of 1863, the AFIC conducted interviews in Boston, where abolitionists were monitoring developments in the South with keen interest. On May 28, Harriet Jacobs attended the city's annual meeting of the New England Anti-Slavery Convention. She had with her two little orphan girls, living embodiments of the toll that war had taken on the Black population. Later in the day members of the audience found the sight of the girls "a touching one," and offers to adopt them were forthcoming. Jacobs said she would return later in the summer "with more of the orphan girls, for whom she desired to obtain homes," according to a report of the meeting. To Boston whites, the children were future cooks, laundresses, and maids. It was ironic that Jacobs, who detested domestic service, would want to funnel Black people from the South to the North for that purpose; but she was no doubt hoping to find loving adoptive parents for the children.[6]

That morning, before this touching scene unfolded, however, the meeting's attendees had adjourned to see the 54th Massachusetts regiment assemble for a dress parade on Boston Common, where Governor Andrew reviewed the troops. The historic all-Black regiment, 1,007 strong (with 37 white officers), included men from fifteen states, with barbers, waiters, and seamen predominating. Among the 43 Bostonians were a carpenter, a coachman, a sign painter, a printer, a cook, and at least 11 fugitives from slavery, 5 from Virginia. Accompanying the 54th was its sutler, who sold supplies to the troops—Mark DeMortie. He had been nominated for the position because he was a shrewd businessman and a loyal Republican.

To the strains of "John Brown's Body," the soldiers then paraded through the streets of Boston to the wharf, where the *DeMolay*, a military transport, waited. The timing and circumstances were propitious: nine years ago to the week city police and militia forces had marched a fugitive to the dock and forced him aboard a southbound vessel that returned him to bondage. Today, as one delegate to the antislavery meeting noted, "The entire police force of the city turns out to pioneer and escort one thousand colored soldiers to march to the defeat and overthrow of these very slaveholders to whom poor Anthony Burns was sent back!"[7]

The crowds that cheered the 54th as the soldiers passed through the streets offered up a mix of emotions. (The size of the send-off was indicated that day by the robust activities of several "professionals of the light-fingered game"—pickpockets.) To abolitionists, Black and white, this thrilling sight represented the culmination of decades of organizing, writing, speaking, and petitioning on behalf of Black equality generally, and Black manhood particularly. To city officials, the 54th provided a much-needed boost for their local quota—and the out-of-staters among the regiment were inexpensive, eligible for neither a Massachusetts bounty nor Boston relief funds for their families. To some of the white laboring classes, the Black men's march toward full citizenship raised the specter of renewed demands for better jobs and treatment—privileges the whites feared would come at their own expense. As Frederick Douglass's twenty-three-year-old son Lewis was about to board the *DeMolay*, he suffered a terrible assault at the hands of thugs, who beat and spat on him. (Lewis's brother Charles also joined the 54th.) Whites also attacked two Black women who had been following the procession through the streets. For the men of the 54th, their pride mingled with anger proved prescient.[8]

Several weeks after the send-off for the 54th, on July 21, 1863, Thomas Selden once more rounded the tip of Cape Cod, this time on a ship headed south; he was aboard the Union's *Cahawba*, carrying the 55th Massachusetts. With its 1,226 men, the 55th owed its existence to the oversubscribed 54th. Unlike the 54th, which had a strong contingent of men from Massachusetts, most of the troops for the 55th came from the Midwest; governors there refused to authorize Black regiments but tried to apply the number of recruits bound for Massachusetts to their own quotas (a move rejected by army officials). Selden was one of the regiment's 247 former slaves who had made their way north before or during the war. In July a "Committee of Colored Young Ladies of Boston" raised $58.20 for the regiment, and the Ladies Fugitive Aid Society of New Bedford presented them with towels, handkerchiefs, ration bags, and socks.[9]

Sixteen years had passed since the Edloe Sixty-Six had journeyed from Richmond to Boston. Now the twenty-four-year-old Selden was married, and he and his wife, Elizabeth, twenty-one, had two children, William H., three, and a baby, Lillie G., born the year before. The Seldens had been living in Chelsea with Elizabeth's parents. Thomas registered for the draft in May, giving his occupation as waiter, and then enlisted on June 19; he was a private assigned to Company F and received a $50 bounty (not the $100 he had been promised and that members of the 54th received). Selden's friend Aaron Joseph had joined the navy two years before, and Elizabeth's brother Stephen Maddox had enlisted in the 54th in the spring. Despite Governor Andrew's promise of equal pay, these Black army enlistees would receive $10 a month, minus $3 for clothing expenses, for a total of $7, a little more than half the pay of their white counterparts ($13).

Selden's Company F included 34 men from the Midwest (25 from Ohio); 32 from Massachusetts (24 from Boston); 4 from other New England states; 3 from the border states of Missouri and Maryland; 23 from the Mid-Atlantic; 10 from the South (Selden was one of 6 born in Virginia); and 1 each from Canada and England. Of the men who listed their occupations, 30 worked in service (cook, waiter, groom, barber, porter, or teamster) and 11 were skilled (blacksmith, bricklayer, butcher, engineer, printer, shoemaker, plasterer, glass grinder). The largest category—59—was that of farmers. Selden was an acquaintance of James D. Ruffin, the son of George W. Ruffin, who had moved his free family from Richmond to Boston in 1853. James would become one of the most prolific correspondents for the company, writing for New York's *Weekly Anglo-African.*[10]

The 55th had originally planned a ceremonial march through New York City on its way south, but the recent draft riots there made that move imprudent. In June President Lincoln had called for 100,000 more men for the army. New York's Unionists took heart from federal victories earlier that month in Gettysburg, which halted General Robert E. Lee's attempted invasion of the North, and in Vicksburg, which secured the Mississippi River for Union forces. Yet from July 13 to 16, hundreds of whites in New York had viciously attacked individual Black men, women, and children, as well as an orphan asylum and a seamen's home. If the Civil War was now a war of liberation, whites would hold all Black people responsible for the bloodshed on the battlefield. The assault left more than 100 people dead (11 Black men lynched) and 2,000 wounded. Officials had to divert troops from Gettysburg to quell the violence. Thousands of Blacks fled the city.[11]

Boston witnessed its own contemporaneous draft riot, one with far less deadly consequences. Its quota of recruits that summer amounted to 3,300 men. In the early afternoon of July 14, two assistant provost marshals were making their way through the North End, serving draft notices at individual residences. One wife took the news badly; she chased the marshals into the street, and, in the words of Police Chief Edward Savage, began "hurling at their heads every article within her reach, and screeching like a raving maniac." Local residents gathered and armed themselves with clubs, paving stones, bricks, muskets, and pistols, eventually reaching an estimated several hundred people, young and old, male and female; but, noted Savage (with emphasis), "*there was little diversity of color.*" The crowd was purposeful, menacing the Hanover Street police station and then attacking the Cooper Street armory.[12]

The armory's commanding officer maneuvered a cannon to the front door and fired, instantly killing a twelve-year-old boy and a seventy-two-year-old man, a bystander. As many as eight other people later died of their injuries. That evening the crowd reassembled and moved on to the downtown area, where they looted hardware and cutlery stores of rifles, pistols, and Bowie knives. Consisting primarily of North Enders, the mob made its grievances clear with calls of "Give the dam' Yankees hell!" By this time the mayor had deployed the Light Dragoons and other volunteer militias as well as federal troops stationed nearby; he ordered them to dispense with the customary martial music, which would presumably attract unwanted attention.[13]

In his use of troops on July 14, the mayor had pointedly excluded the 55th, which was camped south of the city in Readville. Still, on July 21, the regiment received a rousing farewell, presenting arms in front of the State House before marching down to the harbor. The *Cahawba* left Boston in a heavy downpour, and before long many of the passengers became seasick. After a few days in North Carolina, the troops arrived on the barrier island Folly Island, South Carolina (east of Port Royal), joining 50,000 Union soldiers stationed off the coast not far from Charleston. En route, the regiment had lost one member who died of measles. In fact, for the 55th, disease would be a far more deadly foe than any rebel force, with typhoid claiming the most lives—33 out of the 121 noncombatant fatalities.[14]

The immediate mission of the 55th was to capture the notorious battery Fort Wagner on the northern end of Morris Island, where many of their comrades in the 54th had fallen on July 18. Confederates had buried the regiment's commanding officer, Colonel Robert Gould Shaw, in a mass grave "with his niggers," in the words of a Confederate officer. The 54th suffered 270 (out of a total 1,515) casualties and men captured, among them Lewis Douglass, who was badly wounded. At the time and since, observers have rightly cited the battle as proof of Black men's courage under fire; but it was also notable as one of many poorly planned assaults against a heavily fortified position, an attack that relied on inexperienced troops and resulted in horrific fatality rates. Neither the men of the 54th nor other Black soldiers had signed up to become cannon fodder. One Union officer reportedly said before the battle, "Put those d___d negroes from Massachusetts in advance, we may as well get rid of them, one time or another."[15]

Boston's Black community now saw the conflict as a righteous war of liberation. Yet if Thomas Selden and his comrades expected to bask in the reflected glory of a noble cause, they were soon disabused of that notion. An array of discriminatory policies and assignments seemed calculated to thwart the men's drive for equality and respect. The War Department enlisted Blacks under the Militia Act of 1862, which initially allowed them to work for the military, but not to serve as soldiers—hence the lesser pay, a glaring injustice once they took to the battlefield. For many months Secretary of War Stanton refused to commission Black officers except as chaplains and surgeons, though these two groups were not part of the regular chain of command and had no authority over whites. Throughout the war, Robert Morris pressed for Black officers, arguing that such appointments served a dual purpose: they recognized men of ability, and they constituted "the only efficient way of developing [southern Blacks'] confidence in the purpose of the government to help them not only to secure but to maintain their rights."[16]

In late May 1863, Union officers were insisting that Massachusetts's Black troops perform heavy work details in the heat and humidity to ensure the "health & General efficiency" of operations—i.e., the comfort of white soldiers. The 54th's Corporal James Henry Gooding, a mariner from New Bedford, noted the arrival of the 55th by observing that they were "introduced to Messrs. Shovel and Spade, a firm largely interested in building rifle pits, breastworks, and batteries." By August, the fatigue duties imposed on Black men had become a scandal. One white officer complained about the situation in no uncertain terms to the regimental commander of the 3rd South Carolina Volunteer Infantry Regiment: "My men are nearly used up. . . . In addition to regular details they have been furnished for drawing sand, loading wood, water, and pumping out vessels. . . . The duty performed is of the hardest kind." These tasks left the men exhausted and susceptible to disease, with some wounded by accidents and all left with torn and ragged clothing.[17]

On Folly Island, the heat was intense, the water polluted, the sandstorms disorienting, and the sand fleas, stinging gnats, and mosquitoes relentless. Sinking in the sand, the men wrestled heavy artillery into position to fire on Fort Wagner. In describing the scene for northern readers, James D. Ruffin noted that preparations for this assault on the fort amounted to "the most dangerous and disagreeable duty that a soldier is ever called upon to perform." Despite constant shelling from the mainland and the "galling fire of artillery and sharpshooters" from the fort, the unarmed men of the 55th were supposed to maintain "a cool and soldierly manner." Meanwhile, under these harrowing conditions, the troops were "doing their duty without complaint." Accordingly, Ruffin asserted that "it requires a higher standard of courage to perform fatigue duty under fire, than to go into battle."[18]

Perhaps the most humiliating assignment visited upon the 55th was their deployment in the service of a New York regiment, setting up camp for the white soldiers on Morris Island—leveling the ground, digging wells, pitching tents, and all other tasks that soldiers normally did for themselves. According to one officer, James Beecher (the brother of *Uncle Tom's Cabin* author Harriet Beecher Stowe), the unremitting fatigue work "has been incessant and trying." He believed that forcing Black soldiers to perform menial work that white soldiers should be doing for themselves "simply throws [the Black men] back where they were before and reduces them to the position of slaves again"—that is, as "hewers of wood and drawers of water" for whites. Soon after this incident, orders from on high sought to limit such blatantly exploitative forms of labor, but some individual commanders persisted in the practice because "the interests of the service necessitated the discrimination."[19]

On October 11, Selden's Company F (consisting of about one hundred men) was sent to Botany Bay Island to emplace cannon aimed at Charleston, four and a half miles away. This kind of work, which had been ongoing for months, was fiendishly difficult. The men positioned armaments atop a platform built on twenty-foot pilings sunk into the soggy ground. The cannon, weighing almost fourteen tons, could send forth a three-hundred-pound ball. (After two months of constant shelling, Wagner fell to federal forces on September 7, the corpses of many of its defenders buried within its walls of sand, the skulls of soldiers from both sides littering the ground around it.) While Company F was on Botany Bay, it lost one of its soldiers, captured by Confederates; he was probably either executed or sold into slavery.[20]

On or about October 14, Thomas Selden was lifting heavy munitions. The sergeant in charge, Boston's Henry Johnson, knew he needed "the heaviest men" to lift the gun; he had called for volunteers, and one of the first to answer was Selden, whom Johnson described as "a healthy hearty strong man." (At five feet eight he was probably among the tallest in his company.) At one point Selden strained to steady the cannon, but he faltered as the gun fell and slipped into the muck. Collapsing, he cried out in pain. Several of his comrades laid him on the grass and ripped open his shirt; they saw a "bunch just above his naval," one of the men later recalled. It soon became clear that he had suffered a hernia, an injury too severe for him to continue working.[21]

The following day, Selden's commanding officer recommended him for duty at the local military hospital, which was treating soldiers for a variety of maladies—mostly, though, for diarrhea. Selden no doubt performed such tasks as changing bedding and disposing of amputated limbs. After two weeks at the hospital, he was called back to duty. The agent in charge of hospital workers commended the young man in a letter to his superiors in early November: "I have the honor to report that the services of Private Thomas Selden Co. F of the 55th Massachusetts Volunteers (colored) have been found very useful by . . . this commission in discharge of the business of this agency." He asked that Selden be allowed to return to work in the hospital sometime in the future.[22]

Several Bostonians knew about Selden's injury because they visited with him around this time. Aaron Joseph saw him in camp soon after his injury and found him in severe distress. At the time, Joseph, a ship steward, was part of a detachment of sailors and marines from the *Wabash* looking for food to buy from the Black refugees on the islands. Joseph had greeted Selden when the 55th arrived on Folly Island that summer.[23]

Around the time of Selden's accident, the 55th's James Henry Gooding sent a letter to President Lincoln from Morris Island. Gooding demanded to know, "Now the main question is, Are we *Soldiers*, or are we LABOURERS. We are fully armed, and equipped, and have done all the various Duties, pertaining to a Soldiers life, have conducted ourselves, to the complete satisfaction of General Officers . . . have shared the perils, and Labour, of Reducing the first stronghold [Fort Wagner], that flaunted a Traitor Flag; and more, Mr President." The government should respect Black troops "by paying them as american SOLDIERS, not as menial hirelings."[24]

Gooding saw a bright line between fighting for the Union and laboring, a line that in fact did not exist. In Boston in 1864, one Black man thought he could exchange laboring for soldiering. Isaiah Price, twenty-four, from Cincinnati, had enlisted in the 55th Massachusetts in late 1863; instead of heading to Hilton Head to join the rest of the regiment, he found himself assigned to the Draft Rendezvous on Gallops Island in Boston Harbor. There he waited on officers and worked as a barber for the white soldiers. Soon after, he went on furlough and failed to return to his post. He was charged with desertion, and a court martial trial in December 1864 resulted in a guilty verdict. He was sentenced to death.[25]

A lawyer for Price saw fit to write to President Lincoln and beg for mercy for his client, and Price himself pleaded his case in a letter to Stanton. The soldier explained that for four months after he enlisted, he had been kept as a servant by the provost marshal in Boston. He deserted, he said, "for the purpose of getting into active service." Price continued, "Being tired of this dull kind of life and wishing to go into active service," and foolishly not knowing "the enormity of the crime" he was committing, he had proceeded to enlist in the 5th Massachusetts Colored Volunteer Cavalry Regiment. He wanted to be released from custody to join his regiment (whether the 55th or the 5th is not clear). A supervisor at a hospital where he was working affirmed his "general good character and faithful performance of his required duties." Eventually Price received a commuted sentence of two years at Fort Columbus in New York Harbor, with loss of pay and allowances for the remainder of his enlistment. Price thought he could trade the monotonous life of a servant for the thrilling life of a fighter, understanding neither the concept of desertion nor the reality of a Black soldier's military duties as defined by his superior officers.[26]

VIEWED AS WORKPLACES, military sites both resembled and differed from those places in Boston, bringing together diverse work crews in fellow-feeling while enforcing established patterns of white authority—all this with the ultimate aim of inflicting harm on other human beings. Army camps and naval vessels were staffed by formerly enslaved men and by free-born northern whites and Blacks, the illiterate and the well-schooled. On the Sea Islands, the Black men of Higginson's 1st South Carolina Volunteer Infantry Regiment—most of them former rice and cotton field workers—joined with the northern regiments consisting of fugitive artisan-blacksmiths who had settled in Boston before the war and highly educated men who had been born or raised in the North. Of the former fugitives in the 54th and 55th, several were now returning to the state of their birth, South Carolina. Some of the soldiers would go on to illustrious careers or encourage their sons to do so—for example, in the 55th, James Monroe Trotter, father of the editor-activist William Monroe Trotter, and Joshua Dunbar, father of the poet Paul Laurence Dunbar. A few Black soldiers achieved the rank of second lieutenant, but this form of recognition was bittersweet, as the men were not mustered in at that rank until July 1865. Among them were James Trotter; William H. DuPree (a plasterer from Chillicothe, Ohio, whom Trotter described as "the most soldierly and accomplished military colored man in the regiment, and . . . acknowledged to be superior to many of our officers"); and Charles L. Mitchell of Boston (who, wounded at Honey Hill, had his right leg amputated above the ankle).[27]

Issues of pay and authority converged in overall systems of discrimination within the northern military. In August 1863, the Reverend Leonard Grimes led a delegation of eleven Black Baptist ministers to the White House, where they spoke to the president about the need for Black chaplains in the Union Army. Grimes's group represented several East Coast cities, and all the men expressed a desire to "minister to their brethren" in the service. Lincoln approved their request in principle; however, local paymasters felt free to deny chaplains the standard salary because they were "of African descent." Governor Andrew wrote to Lincoln protesting this policy, averring that it was "alike in violation of the rights of the Christian churches and the laws of Congress." One chaplain of the Massachusetts 55th described his humiliating dependence on his comrades, from whom he had to borrow money while he remained underpaid by hundreds of dollars: "I am in exceedingly embarrassing circumstances."[28]

Neither Black chaplains nor physicians had any authority over whites, and their superior officers often expressed their contempt for them. Dr. John V. DeGrasse of Boston, a graduate of Bowdoin Medical School, received a commission as a surgeon for the 54th and then the 1st North Carolina Volunteer Infantry Regiment, one of the few Black men to hold that rank during the war. He was the first Black doctor to be admitted to the Massachusetts (or any state's) Medical Society. In November 1864, an all-white military jury convicted him of excessive drinking, and he was discharged from the army. Many white officers drank whenever they had the means and opportunity to do so. A white physician for the 55th noted "the general habit of using liquor upon the slightest occasion; it is dangerously common among officers, as far as

Dr. John V. DeGrasse was born in New York City in 1825. In 1854 he moved to Boston and a year later became a founding member of the Massasoit Guards. As surgeon for the 35th US Colored Infantry Regiment, he faced unrelenting hostility from white officers. He died in 1868. *(Boston Athenaeum)*

I can learn." Whether or not DeGrasse's behavior in this regard was particularly egregious or his conviction warranted, his punishment was humiliating.[29]

Almost all soldiers suffered from the horror of it all—the sound and sight of comrades blown to bits; the grassy field or sandy beach littered with body parts and bloated corpses; the anticipation of pain or death; and the combat's physical and emotional aftereffects, which could linger for years. However, most of their time was spent with their comrades in marching, pitching tents, and downtime. Boston's William Aiken was probably unusual in recalling, of his years in the 55th: "I kept to myself, mostly." For many men, food remained a major preoccupation. John H. Jenkins, a Black porter from Boston, wrote to his wife in January 1865 with the news about a box she had sent: "The pies was all spoilt and hard as a stone, the cake was a little mouldy, but we ate it; the can of peaches was good and a Godsend to me." He was otherwise subsisting on fat pork and a few crackers each day. Northern men expected brown bread and beef, southern men pork and corn bread, and soldiers and seamen alike foraged, fished, and in some cases raided the stores of local folk to supplement their bland and meager diets. Jenkins also reminded his wife to send a "can of good whiskey," which he promised to share with his friend, another Bostonian, John Little, formerly a cook and now serving in the regimental band.[30]

Military life represented a new beginning for the thousands of refugees who donned a uniform. Far from Black Boston, the Sea Islands were now home to freed slaves who retained West African cultural traditions; these people aimed to support themselves while contending with imperious labor superintendents such as Edward Philbrick, William Gannett, and Charles Ware. When Savannah's Susie Baker, who was just fourteen when she married Edward King of Company E, 1st South Carolina Volunteer Infantry Regiment (33rd US Colored Infantry Regiment), joined him at Camp Saxton, she started a school for the formerly enslaved men, teaching them to read and write; she also cleaned muskets and worked as a laundress and an assistant to the regimental physicians. Of her students, she wrote, "Nearly all were anxious to learn." The survivors would create a post-emancipation Black community there on the coast and the Sea Islands, one that moved to the rhythms of the tides and the growing season, quite different from the service economy of downtown Boston.[31]

Regardless of background, Black soldiers maintained old connections and forged new ones. On September 3, 1863, Prince Hall Lodge members of the 54th organized a "traveling lodge" that met in a rude wooden shelter. (By 1860, eighteen northern and midwestern states along with Maryland, Virginia, Louisiana, and Canada had Prince Hall Lodges.) In January 1864, the Freemasons of the 55th Massachusetts and the 1st North Carolina Volunteers joined together to offer resolutions honoring their fallen comrade Sergeant John Bird of Ypsilanti, Michigan, saying, "In his death we have lost a kind friend and true brother, our sacred and ancient institution [has lost] a noble and worthy member, whose charity knew no bounds to a friend and brother in distress, and whose love for his fellow-man were among his many virtues." Members erected their own "Masonic Temple" of canvas on Folly Island. There, they and other Black Freemasons could join in familiar rituals in unfamiliar territory.[32]

Black servicemen formed a subset of all servicemen, enduring varying degrees of homesickness, elation, and existential dread. All soldiers at some point engaged in fatigue work. Gunboat crews spent long periods of enforced inactivity interrupted every few weeks or months by encounters with blockade runners. Close quarters, whether on a ship or in a camp, put military men at risk for epidemics that had no respect for skin color or age. In 1864, crew members in the South Atlantic Blockading Squadron suffered when yellow fever swept through their ranks. All men assigned to ships in the Mississippi River were vulnerable to malaria.[33]

Compared to soldiers, sailors generally had advantages over army troops on the move in terms of diet, shelter, clothing, and medical care. Crew members of roving ships saw a wider world—the *St. Mary's* Gad Minot, for example, traveled to Panama Bay and Valparaiso in 1863 and 1864. For fourteen months, beginning June 1864, the *Niagara* made ports of call throughout the United Kingdom, France, Belgium, and Spain, from Cork to Cádiz. One of the men on board, William B. Gould, a literate mason formerly enslaved in North Carolina, preferred the seafaring life to life in army camps ashore, as did, no doubt, many others. Soldiers suffered higher casualty rates than seamen and routinely had their pay garnished for lost equipment—bayonets ($2.33 each), equipage (45 cents), sword and accoutrements ($3), haversack and canteen ($1.12). Still, raw naval recruits were likely to be subjected to hazing, a time-honored initiation that soldiers did not have to endure. And work as a steamship fireman (a "coal passer") was hot and dirty.[34]

For Black servicemen, wartime jobs on terra firma and on the high seas were similar in certain crucial respects. Black soldiers and seamen spent more time than their white counterparts engaged in grueling physical labor, loading and unloading vessels, shoveling coal into steamship boilers, digging trenches, scrubbing and painting surfaces, erecting fortifications, and preparing and storing food. In contrast to Black soldiers, for the most part Black sailors received the same pay as whites according to their rank, but with most of them hired as "boy" or "landsman," they made the lowest wage the navy had to offer. Blacks, regardless of regiment or vessel, served under white officers. Some ships did include Black gun crews, while army camps had few Blacks assigned to special tasks other than cooks or hospital aides. Whether in the army, the navy, or a civilian workplace, the social dynamics of meal preparation and personal service mandated that Black men have direct contact with unpredictable whites. One white man, William Crane, threw a plate of hot food in the face of an unnamed

Black cook because, according to Crane, the cook was in the habit of giving crew members "sauce instead of victuals," and failed to have the coffee ready on time. Such were the liabilities faced by Black men relegated to domestic service work.[35]

Numbers tell a larger story of comparative hardship and danger for Black military men regardless of service. The Massachusetts 55th lost 175 (out of a total of 822 men), 121 of those from disease. Selden's Company F, of 122 men, lost 14 from disease (pneumonia, typhoid, tuberculosis, and inflammation of the brain) and 3 from wounds or unknown causes. Seven (including Selden) sustained serious wounds, and 4 deserted. Union soldiers overall had a 1 in 9 risk of dying during the war; the chances for Blacks were 1 in 5. One out of 15 white Union soldiers succumbed to disease, compared to 1 out of 7 Black soldiers. And Black men captured in war faced immediate execution or sale on the auction block.[36]

Like an increasing proportion of employees in the civilian sector, Black soldiers and sailors labored under close supervision, with the commissioned officer as boss. These white men varied in temperament and politics, leading to a kind of day-to-day unpredictability at odds with the strict protocols that lay at the heart of military life. At one extreme was the commanding officer who respected his subordinates, offered them at least verbal encouragement, and sought to make the best use of the individual and collective talents of his men. In August 1864, Colonel Edward N. Hallowell, commander of the 54th, fired off an angry letter of protest to the head of the Morris Island Ordnance Department, which had allowed only white soldiers to serve as clerks, consigning Black soldiers to the jobs of cook and laborer. Officers such as Hallowell earned the gratitude of their men. However, more typical was the white man who saw a Black regiment as a vehicle for his own career advancement. These white officers disciplined their troops in unduly harsh ways, provoking resentment and even violence in return. One member of the 55th, probably James Ruffin, noted that many of the white officers of the Black troops were "sporting characters," men who ingratiated themselves with members of Congress and received commissions, to "the utter exclusion of intelligent soldiers (both white and colored, whose capacity no one for one moment can doubt)." Some officers devised sadistic forms of correction akin to that inflicted on enslaved workers, striking soldiers with whips or swords.[37]

Although it is possible that white Union soldiers in general became more antislavery in their convictions over the course of the war, that stance did not guarantee fair or even humane treatment of Black men in uniform. Adamant opposition to the idea of Black officers infected the white military establishment from the secretary of war on down to the lowliest private. White lieutenants refused to sleep in the same tent or eat at the same table with a Black man of the same rank. A white officer told James M. Trotter "that it was 'too soon,' that time should be granted white officers *to get rid of their prejudices.*" In a letter to his friend Francis Jackson Garrison (son of William Lloyd Garrison), Trotter observed, of the failure to promote Black soldiers, "Yes, Franky, there is really more turning up the noise on account of the commissions *in our very midst* than elsewhere; *and no other reason is given except Color.*"[38]

Regardless of their branch of service, Black men often had to contend with whites who saw them not as fellow soldiers but as sources of entertainment. The white crew of the gunboat USS *Braziliera* put on regular and, in some cases, elaborately staged performances that featured minstrel singers and risible Black characters. Army regiments constructed immense stages for such shows. One white Massachusetts soldier wrote home that the Black people he saw in the South "look just like our minstrels on the stage. You don't see any true darkies in the North." At times whites forced Black men to dance and sing and "pat juba" for the white men's amusement. Such an impulse among whites could take a seemingly more benign form, too. One white artilleryman, describing performances on the *Constitution* as it left Boston

After the Civil War, James M. Trotter settled his family in Boston. In 1878 he wrote *Music and Some Highly Musical People*, a study of music in the United States. The book featured "remarkable musicians of the colored race," including some of Boston's instrumentalists, singers, and church organists. *(Courtesy National Park Service, Gettysburg National Military Park, Museum Collection, GETT #38208)*

Harbor, wrote, for example, "After tea the colored waiters of the ship gave us a rich treat, by singing, most beautifully, a number of popular melodies. Their voices accorded most harmoniously, and they attracted many listeners." Nevertheless, this scene positioned Black men as singing retainers and not as comrades-in-arms.[39]

The dynamics of military workplaces reflected official War Department policies, white officers' priorities, and enlisted men's individual personalities and personal relationships. No unit was the same for all who were part of it. Yet, in general, Black seamen and the soldiers of the 54th and 55th Infantry and 5th Cavalry Regiments returned to Boston having labored under conditions that were significantly different from those of their white counterparts.

At the same time, the service created and solidified bonds among Black men who had come together from all over the country and from many backgrounds. Most took from their experience of military work not one single truth, but multiple lessons as complex and contradictory as life itself.

While Higginson recruited Black soldiers on the Sea Islands, Edward Philbrick and other planters engaged in a tug-of-war among themselves and with military officers over Black men's labor. Some men had abandoned the cotton fields to shoulder a musket, and white officers felt free to try to coerce those still at work there into service. Philbrick was relieved, though, in March 1863, when the federal government proceeded to sell off plantations to those who could afford to buy them. He knew that the times demanded hard-headed entrepreneurs, writing, "I don't believe in putting Reverends in places where prompt business men are required." Together with other investors he bought large tracts of land, mostly on St. Helena—eleven plantations for a total of $7,000—and leased two others, ushering in a new, systematic plan of wage labor that he could control. He hired superintendents he felt he could trust, including his uncle and fellow Bostonian Richard Soule Jr. Philbrick was an abolitionist to the extent that he believed free labor was cheaper than slave labor. One teacher-missionary expressed her disgust that Philbrick and his agents had "only changed the mode of compulsion," adding, "They *force* men to prove they are fit to be free by holding a tyrant's power over them." Philbrick held out the promise of selling some of the land to Black workers, but first they would have to earn enough money to pay market prices for it.[40]

By late spring, Philbrick thought the prospects for his land-holdings were promising. Planting proceeded apace, with the use of plows made in Groton, Massachusetts, "astonish[ing] the negroes by their efficiency," he wrote. Nevertheless, some workers continued to stage slowdowns in the fields, and others set out for the town of Beaufort on the island of Port Royal, where, in the words of Charles Ware, jobs for cash wages attracted the so-called loafers, or those of "general worthless character." A new policy that rewarded tractable workers with bonuses, making invidious distinctions among family members and friends, failed to have the desired salutary effect. Philbrick threatened to evict those men and women who refused to pay a tax on the corn they grew. In the North, the shirkers would be fired from their jobs; in the South, with federal agents still looking over his shoulder, Philbrick felt constrained in his combined roles as employer, landlord, store owner, and agricultural supplier. At the same time, his tenants had just produced a most profitable crop, making, in his words, the "enterprise a permanent thing and tak[ing] it off the hands of philanthropic benevolence, which, though well enough for a spurt, can never be relied on to civilize the four millions of darkies likely to be on our hands." Philbrick sought to stiffen the resolve of Ware, who feared the bad publicity from making money off the backs of former slaves. Philbrick reassured him, "The fact is just this. Negro labor has got to be employed, if at all, because it is *profitable*, and it has got to come into the market like everything else, subject to the supply and demand which may arise from all kinds of enterprises in which it chances to be employed." No one should ever have to apologize for obeying the "natural" law of supply and demand.[41]

On October 20, 1863, Harriet Ware was preparing dinner when her brother Charles asked if she had "'any prejudice against color,' as he had asked the steward of the *Wabash* [Admiral Samuel Dupont's flagship] to dine." Charles described their prospective guest as "a Boston boy who speaks English as well as you do." Harriet assented, the guest arrived, and the meal proceeded pleasantly, after which she rendered this verdict: "We found him a very bright, intelligent young fellow and very modest and unassuming withal—gave his name only as 'Joseph' both to Mr. Soule and C[harles]." Their dinner companion that evening was Aaron Joseph, on the island "foraging for the Admiral." He had regaled his hosts with tales of a US navy vessel he had recently served on (Harriet heard it as *Mohegan*) that had captured a "slave-pirate" carrying a human cargo of nine hundred souls off the coast of Africa. In fact, as of October 1, 1861, Joseph had indeed served on the steam sloop-of-war *Mohican*, but only after its days of plying the waters off Africa were over. The thrilling tale he told the Wares and their other guests recounted the 1860 capture of the slaver *Erie*, but it was a tale that Joseph had heard secondhand from his crewmates. As a steward of the *Mohican*, though, Joseph had taken part in the October 1861 battle that had pounded the Sea Islands into submission and secured a number of the other islands for the Union—the Battle of Port Royal.[42]

The freedpeople in and around the Coffin Point plantation found Aaron Joseph to be a curious figure. According to Harriet Ware, one of the local women, Amaritta, caught herself calling him "Maussa [Master]" because he walked with and talked to whites as an equal. Yet the Wares and the other guests hardly knew what to make of this young Black man, as dark in color as the field hands they saw every day. They could not reconcile as members of a single "race" Joseph, this "very bright, intelligent young fellow," and Robert, the retainer they knew only by his first name and described as "utterly undemonstrative before white people and . . . only gradually thawing into a little more communicativeness."[43]

Few white Bostonians in the wartime South thought deeply about their own views on "race," perhaps because the whole concept seemed so perplexing. Both Aaron Joseph and Robert had dark skin, but they seemed to come from two different worlds if judged on the basis of their speech, self-presentation, and history; and certainly not all Black people had the same phenotype. Some whites could see that over time the descendants of enslaved men and women who had made their way to Boston had lost their southern accents and embraced city life, sharing much with their white counterparts. Nevertheless, whites' preoccupation with the smokescreen of race blinded them to the specific constraints under which Black people north and south lived and labored.

In the spring of 1864, the Wares encountered another Black Bostonian who muddled their "racial" ideas—forty-six-year-old Mary Walker. Long restless in her job as a servant to a series of white women, Walker sailed to the Sea Islands in April. Hoping, in her words, to attend to "the welfare of her race," she took up residence with Harriet and Charles Ware at Coffin Point. The Ware siblings and William Gannett welcomed her with the understanding that she would take over housekeeping when Harriet returned to Boston for the summer. Alluding to Walker's light skin color, Gannett described her as "a white runaway slave from Cambridge."[44]

By this time Gannett and Charles Ware had been handsomely rewarded for their management of the 1863 cotton crop, earning about $4,000 each. Mary Walker no doubt heard the chronic complaints of the white men—that the workers were ungrateful and untrustworthy, that they were inveterate liars and ultimately inscrutable. Before she arrived, Charles had caused a scandal by viciously beating a young unmarried Black woman who had recently given birth, punishing her for what he considered her immoral behavior.[45]

Once on St. Helena Island, Mary Walker realized that she had walked into the middle of an uproar. In March, nineteen laborers working Philbrick's Fripp Point plantation had petitioned President Lincoln to "be relieved from Mr. Philbrick's oppression!" according to Harriet Ware. In mid-April, Treasury Secretary Salmon P. Chase sent Special Agent Judge Austin Smith of Chautauqua County, New York, to investigate the workers' complaints. Walker, who served tea to Smith and other visiting dignitaries, no doubt heard at least part of the discussion. The workers' petition, written by John H. Major, with eighteen other men signing their marks, detailed the betrayals they had endured over the previous two years.[46]

In their list of grievances against Philbrick, the petitioners said he had bought up several plantations under false pretenses, promising to sell the land to the freedpeople at $1.00 an acre, but was now demanding ten times that price, a sum none could afford to pay. (Philbrick and his investors currently owned 6,030 acres, home to 900 Black men, women, and children, about 370 of them adult field hands.) "Wee have work'd for Mr Philbrick the whole year faithfully, and hav received nothing comparatively, not enough to sustaine life if wee depended entirely uppon our wages." And then there were the stores: "He has Stors here chargeing feerefull prices for every nessary of life, and at last the People have become discouraged, all most heart broken."[47]

After interviewing several of the principals—superintendents and laborers alike—Smith conveyed his findings to Secretary Chase on May 15. The judge wrote that he believed Philbrick to be an honorable man, and that, together with "the eminent philanthropists he represents," he did intend to sell the freedpeople land at reasonable prices, but only "*when the war should close*"; that, at least, was his original intent. Yet Smith's report was not a complete vindication of Philbrick. The judge noted that the St. Helena workers' wages of 47 cents a day were "not equal to the wages paid to white people at the North for the same character and amount of labor, while the groceries, and other necessaries furnished them, are much higher here than at the North." He contrasted the value of the 1863 cotton harvest, which netted the whites a profit of $70,000, with the workers' "hardships & exposure in raising it" and the high prices they were charged for food and clothing. In fact, Smith wrote, these field hands deserved higher pay than their northern counterparts, who averaged about a dollar a day. Moreover, he pointed out, the store charged its "customers" 25 percent more than what it cost to import the food and supplies and made a profit of 10 percent on everything sold. At the end of the year it had about $10,000 worth of goods on hand.[48]

Smith anticipated the Bostonians' justification for paying their workers so little and charging them so much at the store. He understood that the former slaves raised chickens and eggs and pigs "for their own use & for sale." Their "cheap mode of living & dressing" contrasted with that of northerners, who expected a higher standard of living. Still, noted the judge, these workers—and their forebears for many generations—had toiled for years for no pay at all. They had built the plantation dwellings and produced the plantation's crop, all of which amounted to "an equitable lien upon the lands of their masters." Smith concluded that all these factors meant that the freedpeople should expect to pay a "reasonable price" for the land. The investors' huge profits should allow them to do the right thing, and "if the law does not hold these men to the fulfillment of their promises, public opinion will." In the end, Judge Smith's report did not affect conditions on the islands in any meaningful way. After the investigation, according to Harriet Ware, the workers "were silenced, but not convinced."[49]

That summer Mary Walker spent much of her free time visiting the quarters and speaking to the people there. She had come south with no firm purpose in mind, and it was difficult for her to forge a connection to the Sea Islanders, who spoke in the Gullah dialect and followed West African worship practices. The unfamiliarity cut both ways: The servant Rose was not sure what to make of Walker, with her New England airs and easy conversations with whites. In July, Charles Ware recounted an "amusing" chat he had with Walker: "She understands all the peculiarities of affairs down here with wonderful quickness and penetration; I have learned to respect her judgment and opinion. To hear her rail at these people, and slip out sly hints about the conduct of the 'friends of the freedman' is a treat." Perhaps Walker and Ware did share a laugh over the self-assured Gideonites. Or perhaps Ware himself was one of the "friends of the freedman" whom Walker found amusing in his own arrogant way.[50]

The day that Judge Smith issued the findings of his investigation, the American Freedmen's Inquiry Commission released its final report on the status and future of formerly enslaved southerners, focusing mainly on the problem of agricultural productivity. According to its first sentence, "The greatest social and political problems of the world connect themselves more or less with the subject of labor." The commissioners indicted southern elites for their disdain for honest toil; a society was civilized only to "the degree of estimation in which labor is held there." Once the former slaves were granted basic political and civil rights ("without which they are but laboring as a man labors with hands bound"), the evidence indicated that they would be able to support themselves. Northern Black men and women would gladly migrate (back) to the South, as "the personal prejudice against negroes is stronger in the Northern than in the Southern States." Overall, southern Blacks should depend on government aid and private charity only temporarily, and after that, "the natural laws of supply and demand should be left to regulate rates of compensation and places of residence." Presumably a system of annual contracts would bring together planters with their land and Blacks with their labor to restore the basic features of the antebellum staple-crop economy.[51]

Two contingents of the Boston wartime diaspora—white cotton agents and Black teachers and relief workers—had radically different ideas and aims in mind when they journeyed to the wartime South. Philbrick and his acolytes placed a priority on restoring the southern cotton economy to its central role as an engine of prosperity for the entire nation. The former slaves must continue to toil in the fields as their forebears had for generations, in the process proving their worth as free workers, if not full citizens. In contrast, John Oliver and Harriet Jacobs put into practice their own notions of freedom, focusing first on providing refugees with the basics of food, clothing, and shelter, and then on starting schools that would instruct children and adults alike in literacy skills. Thus did representatives of Boston's merchant and manufacturing elite, together with the city's Black community, enact the pre-politics of Reconstruction.

In September Mary Walker sailed for Boston. Charles Ware wrote that she was "almost sick of this country," though comments she made later to friends suggested she was sick of the planter Philbrick as much as anyone or anything else. As she left South Carolina, Boston's Family Mourning Store on Winter Street was placing ads for a new line of "Fall Goods for Mourning," including "black dress goods, in large variety," and plain and trimmed mourning shawls. Given the ongoing high demand for their wares, Boston clothiers would seem to welcome Mary Walker's skills; but in fact, once she returned to Cambridge she had a hard time finding a job. The wartime labor market prized speed and efficiency over careful handiwork, and Walker eventually resumed work as a domestic servant, joining the ranks of other Black women struggling to make a living.[52]

10

Hardship on the Homefront

From the summer of 1863 through the early fall of 1864, the soldiers of the 54th and 55th Massachusetts Volunteer Infantry Regiments wrote to friends, loved ones, government officials, and newspaper editors condemning the War Department's discriminatory policies, particularly those mandating lesser pay for Blacks. These letters, petitions, and articles rank among the most eloquent pieces of literature promoting the historic Black struggle for justice. Yet in their writings, the protesters made clear that more than principle was at stake: their families at home were suffering from the loss of breadwinners, from the lack of jobs for Black people generally, and from the indifference of city authorities and (white) charities. Indeed, the plight of soldiers from Boston in the pest-infested marshlands of the Sea Islands had a direct bearing on the Black community on the western slope of Beacon Hill.

Wartime always brings social upheaval at home, including, in some cases, expanded economic opportunities for those excluded from certain peacetime jobs; but the American Civil War did not in any permanent or meaningful way open the doors to all-white workplaces for Black men and women. In Boston, Black wives and mothers endured the ravages of price inflation and the lack of employment possibilities, swelling the ranks of the city's enlarged impoverished population. After the announcement of the Emancipation Proclamation on January 1, 1863, President Lincoln recast the war as a fight against slavery, a move that hastened the recruitment of Black soldiers but did not relieve them of the grinding fatigue work that set them apart from white men in uniform. The war gave rise to a class of Black brokers mediating between sea captains and Black sailors, between aid applicants and state officials, and between southern migrants and northern employers, but for the most part these jobs were only temporary. Black workers in Boston would emerge from the conflict the way they entered it—shut out of machine jobs and relegated to manual labor and domestic service. The war years represented not a reconfiguration of the division of labor, but a brief recalibration of it, yielding little in the way of a new day for the Black laboring classes.

In April 1864, First Sergeant James D. Ruffin of Boston explained to the readers of the *Weekly Anglo-African* why for the past nine months he and his comrades had refused to accept their lesser monthly paychecks of $7—even after November 1863, when the Massachusetts Legislature passed a bill to make up the difference. Ruffin acknowledged that the men had been sent $7 a week all along; but that was "money," he wrote, not "pay," or compensation, for the work they did: "The United States knows our value as soldiers too well to suppose that we will sacrifice the position we have gained by most arduous labor," he wrote, and he and his comrades must stand up for their rights, "come what may." Those who doubted the courage of Black soldiers need only look to the graves of men who fell under fire in the Battles of Fort Wagner, Port Hudson, Milliken's Bend, Olustee, and Fort Pillow. (In the aftermath of this last battle, in early April 1864, Confederates executed captured Black soldiers and buried the wounded alive.) If the heroic actions of these men "do not settle [the matter] in our favor," wrote Ruffin, "then it is because our enemies *will not* have it settled in that way." Meanwhile, "MANHOOD IS OUR

MOTTO. 'TIS WRITTEN IN OUR EVERY PURPOSE AND SEALED IN OUR HEART OF HEARTS."[1]

True men provided for and protected their families. Ruffin wondered how elected officials and military officers could evince so little concern for the welfare of soldiers' dependents back home: "But aside from the recognition of our title to equal rights with the white soldier, who suffers no more for his country than ourselves, have they no care for the heart-rending appeals of the wives, children, and other relations, to the soldiers, for aid in their suffering—yes, in some cases starving condition?" Ruffin condemned the federal government for abdicating its responsibility: "How the authorities expect our families to live without the means to buy bread, pay house rent, and meet the other incidental expenses of living in these terrible times, we know not; but if it [the government] does not exert its well known power it certainly will not be felt guiltless in this matter." Bitterly, he asked, "Are our parents, wives, children and sisters to suffer, while we, their natural protectors, are fighting the battles of the nation?"[2]

Sergeant James M. Trotter, with Thomas Selden's Company F, reported that the pay issue had "impelled many to grow disheartened." Hardship at home had a devastating impact on troops in the field: "You know how hard it must be for a husband and father to retain his evenness of mind and spirits when he knows that his loved ones suffer for his aid while he is so bound that he cannot give it." Unlike Ruffin and Trotter, Corporal Thomas D. Freeman of Company H of the 54th was not writing for publication when he contacted attorney Robert Morris in April 1864. A thirty-year-old upholsterer from Boston, Freeman implored Morris to help, reminding him that Black soldiers wanted the "Same Equality as they [the whites] do." The unjust pay system meant "there is men here whose familys are Suffering to day for want of means to get along with[;] they cannot live this way nor can you." Freeman also informed Morris that at least some of the men had never received the bounty (or part of it) promised them: "Tis nothing more than fraud that had been practiced on us—Shame oh Shame." Wounded at a failed Union incursion, the Battle of Honey Hill later that year, on November 30, Freeman died in 1866 after returning to Boston.[3]

It was not only in Boston that family members were hurting, and it was not only the unequal pay issue that caused distress at home. Isaiah Price, spared execution after he deserted from Gallops Island, wrote to President Lincoln in early 1865 and pleaded on behalf of his wife and children in Illinois. Price had volunteered for the 55th and helped Massachusetts make its quota of men; but his wife lived in Cairo, Illinois, and so was ineligible to receive aid from the commonwealth. He detailed her labors: "The children being small she cannot leave them to go out to work[;] she has to go out and gather up her washing, & do at home the best way she can." His offer to reenlist for three more years went unanswered, and he remained in prison until 1866.[4]

From the first call for Black soldiers in early 1863, Robert Morris resisted the idea of Black men serving a country that demeaned them. Morris's futile, years-long effort to secure authorization for a Black militia, combined with the Lincoln administration's policy of denying Black men military commissions, left him seething: "I want you to understand I am not going to the war; God forbid, that I should ask any man to go. . . . But if anyone chooses to make a fool of himself he can do so." Frederick Douglass and Governor John Andrew took the soldiers' case directly to Washington. (Douglass met with Lincoln in August 1863 and again a year later.) Before the deployment of the 54th and 55th, Lincoln justified the unequal pay by arguing that the Black men had not yet proved themselves in battle. After they demonstrated bravery in several engagements, he argued that the lesser pay was a compromise necessary to allow the men to serve at all.[5]

Boston's Austin R. Lewis, a twenty-five-year-old married man in the 55th who had been a mason, was among the seventy-four members of Company D who petitioned President Lincoln on

July 16, 1864. The month before, Congress had passed an act equalizing pay—at least for Black men who had been free before the start of the war—but the funds had still not arrived (and would not until October, when the men of the 54th and the 55th promptly repaid the $14,000 they collectively owed to Mark DeMortie and his sutler-partner, who had extended them credit to buy postage stamps, food, and other supplies). The men of Company D wrote, "We came to fight For Liberty, justice, and equality. These are gifts we Prise more Highly than Gold. For these We left our homes our famileys, Friends & Relatives most Dear to take as it ware our Lives in our Hands To Do Battle for God & Liberty." The signatories resolved, "If imediate steps are not taken to Relieve us, we will Resort to more stringent mesures." Lewis was killed in the Battle of Honey Hill.[6]

Reports circulated within the ranks of despairing wives who had been deprived of their husband's pay and in some cases the bounties and allotments promised them. Wrote Ruffin, "Our debasement is most complete. No chances for promotion, no money for our families, and we are little better than an armed band of laborers with rusty muskets and bright spades, what is our incentive to duty?" He answered his own question: "Yet God has put it into our hearts to believe that we will survive or perish with the liberty of our country."[7]

In late 1864, the Bay State began to assemble a new Black regiment, the 5th Massachusetts Colored Volunteer Cavalry. Presumably men who worked as grooms, coach and buggy drivers, farriers, and hostlers would make good horsemen. Among the early enlistees was Joseph H. Elisha, the incorrigible horseback joyrider from Boston. The twenty-four-year-old had joined the navy in the summer of 1862 and served until October 1863, assigned to the aging USS *Ohio*, a receiving ship anchored in Boston Harbor. Elisha apparently never sailed out of the harbor. On various documents he listed his occupation as shoemaker, printer, barber, and, after 1863, seaman; during his months on the *Ohio* he probably worked as a barber, a cook, or a menial. Now, as an enlistee in the 5th, he received a third of his bounty of $100, with the rest promised him at the end of his service. Joining him in Company C was his brother James F. Elisha, a barber.

No doubt Joseph Elisha could imagine himself astride a magnificent steed, waving his sword and charging some rebel stronghold—he was an excellent horseman, as several Boston police officers could attest. He must have found the prospect of serving his country on horseback much more appealing than toiling as a servant-laborer aboard the *Ohio*. Yet he was to be sorely disappointed. The 5th Cavalry (one of seven Black cavalry regiments in the Union Army) remained dismounted for the duration of the war. Wherever horses were to be had—and they were increasingly scarce by the third year of the conflict—they went to white cavalrymen.[8]

James Elisha apparently immediately became disillusioned by the prospects before him. In March 1864 he deserted, though he returned to his unit soon after, his pay docked $30. He served as a cook for Company C. In fact, the cavalry regiment had much in common with both the 54th and the 55th—inferior supplies, endless fatigue work, battle action (on the Virginia Peninsula) before the troops had undergone extensive training, harsh punishment inflicted by white officers whose highest priority was their own career advancement. The 5th's commanding officer, Boston's aristocratic Charles Francis Adams Jr., initially expressed doubts about his own men's abilities: "After all a negro is not the equal of the white man. . . . [H]e has not the mental vigor and energy, he cannot stand up against adversity." Soon, though, he changed his mind and admitted the men "[took] readily to discipline" and were "decidedly soldierly in their bearing."[9]

On June 15, the 5th took part in an assault on rebel-fortified earthworks at Baylor's Farm, Virginia, as part of a Union drive toward Petersburg. They made their way over forested terrain and through thick underbrush under a hail of shot and shell. Some of the men retreated amid cannon fire, causing the whole regiment to be condemned for cowardice. In August 1864, the men were forced to watch as an officer had one of their own tied by his thumbs to a pole, with his feet barely touching the ground. (This soldier had failed to appear when called to clean up the trash in the camp.) When he lost consciousness and fell to the ground, the rope ripped off part of the skin on his fingers. According to Philadelphia's *Daily Age*, "A cold shudder would have run through the veins of the most hardened mortal witnessing the scene." (The source for this story might have been Charles Douglass, Frederick's son, who by this time had transferred from the 54th Massachusetts to the 5th Cavalry.) One officer worried that the incident might become widely publicized and incite a mutiny. In his eyes, the punishment amounted to a public relations disaster, not a craven failure of leadership. The 5th spent much of the rest of the war consigned to guard duty and other jobs normally assigned to wounded soldiers. Joseph Elisha's love of horses proved poor preparation for service in the cavalry.[10]

The compelling grievances of Black soldiers and the hardships endured by their families depressed enlistment efforts to some extent. Black recruiters embraced the opportunity to bring more young men into military service and to earn some money in the form of commission fees in the process. They fanned out—the Reverend Leonard Grimes to New Bedford, Charles Lenox Remond to Illinois, John S. Rock to Providence and Philadelphia. Yet Grimes encountered outspoken defiance at some meetings, such as the one in New Bedford where a speaker "insisted that until justice, full justice, was done to the colored man, and he was placed on an entire equality with the whites, he could not be expected to enlist." Rock believed that much was at stake, delivering stirring words of encouragement to the 5th US Colored Heavy Artillery Regiment, urging his audience to "remember that the colored soldier has the destiny of the colored race in his hands."[11]

THE WAR YEARS provided new job opportunities for certain Black men and diminished the incomes of others, especially preachers who relied on their congregants for a salary. A favored few men would get jobs as public servants, preceding subsequent generations who would rely on the lifeline of government employment in the face of private-employer discrimination. Late in the war, Mark DeMortie was appointed a messenger for the Boston Custom House, joining William Cooper Nell and Lewis Hayden as Republicans rewarded by state and federal officials for their organizing efforts in Ward 6. Nell became one of the nation's first Black postal clerks.[12]

Some men, such as those who worked at the Chelsea Naval Hospital, became nurses. Hundreds of wounded men arrived in Boston via transport ship on a routine basis. William B. Gould, the mason from North Carolina, had joined the navy in 1862. He first set foot in Boston in March 1863, when his ship, the USS *Cambridge*, docked in the city. At one point, when he was assigned to the *Ohio*, he marveled, "Here we meet with all Kinds and all classes of men." Enjoying a leave for two weeks in April, he dreaded going back to the holding vessel—"Now again for Prison life," he wrote. At the end of May he contracted the measles, but after recovering from the illness he stayed on in the hospital and worked as a nurse. He took satisfaction from caring for the ill and keenly felt the loss of his patients who died. Gould enjoyed his relative freedom outside work hours, going ashore often, especially in the evening, and taking time off to visit kin in Nantucket and receive them in Boston. Released from duty in the hospital and assigned to the frigate USS *Niagara*, he seemed eager to take to the sea again, "to be afloat once more." He wrote, "There is nothing like the whistling wind and the danceing Bark on the Bounding Billow bearing its precious treasure to the shores of some distant clime."[13]

Having grown up in a small town in North Carolina, Gould took special pleasure in his perambulations around Boston, scouring local markets for food (he was a steward), and taking in big-city sights and sounds. Yet the streets and shops remained sites of danger for some enterprising Black men who were well known around town. One of these was Joseph Clash. By early 1863 Clash had returned to his job as a barber full time. He had leased his American Hall to a local missionary, the Reverend Perez Mason, who conducted worship services there. Mason was described in the press as "constantly employed in some labor of love among the poor, distressed, and unfortunate." He was no doubt grateful for the meeting space despite its tainted past.[14]

On February 2, 1863, Clash had just finished shaving two white men, John Rogers and Michael Sweeney, when he noticed that a songbook was missing from a table in his shop. He ordered both men to leave but they refused. Clash then pulled out a rusty six-shooter and shot Rogers in the chest, killing him. The papers announced breathlessly that "the celebrated Joe Clash" was once again in custody, this time for "Pistoling an Unruly customer." Though possessed of a household name, Clash was now "somewhat venerable" (at the age of fifty-four), having abandoned his dance hall, "where fast young men, white and black, met the sable belles of that locality in free and easy intercourse, untrammeled by the ordinary restrictions of the ball-room." The patrons of his former business of "unrivalled notoriety" expressed regret about the repurposing of the hall, now used for more elevated ends, though Clash retained his reputation as a "remarkably smooth, easy and rapid shaver." Clash's murder trial was held on March 12 and he was acquitted of manslaughter the next day. He had given up his hall but kept his influence among (presumably all-white) jurors.[15]

The wartime fortunes of Boston's Black preachers for the most part tracked the fortunes of their congregants—which is to say, they declined during these years. The Reverend J. Sella Martin had departed for London with great fanfare in late 1863. The following spring, he returned to the United States—not to Boston and the Joy Street Baptist Church, which had fallen on hard times, but to New York City, where he took up preaching at the Shiloh Presbyterian Church. New York, with its Black population of 12,500 (in 1860), offered larger churches and more possibilities for advancement compared to Boston.

Peter Randolph continued his own quest for a congregation and a stable livelihood to provide for his growing family—his wife, Amelia, and three children: Mary, nine; Charles, four; and Thaddeus, one (his daughter Sophie had died). And so in 1864 he took tentative steps to read law with Edwin Walker, although there is no evidence he was ever admitted to the Massachusetts bar. Instead, he returned to the lecture circuit, at times reprising his speech on "Idleness," so well received by white patrons. One Boston paper suggested that attending his lectures was one way sympathetic persons might aid his family: "With a wife and children dependent on him for support, he entered upon his career of freedom, and by energy and perseverance, has succeeded in acquiring a fair education, a little property, and a large number of friends, who respect him for his moral worth and upright conduct."[16]

Another would-be preacher made his first appearance in Boston in January 1864, when Thomas Sims's brother, James, escaped from Savannah and joined his brother and sister in the city. (James spelled the family name with two "m's.") The reunion of the Simms/Sims siblings—Thomas, James, and Cornelia—was not permanent. James, a carpenter, had been teaching a clandestine school in Savannah; reports that authorities were planning to shut it down prompted him to flee to the Bay State. A member of the Black Freemasons, he took great pleasure in meeting Lewis Hayden, grandmaster of the Prince Hall Grand Lodge. Within a month of his arrival, Simms was attending meetings of the Massachusetts Anti-Slavery Society. He donated $1 to the group; this gift suggested a certain amount of discretionary income, perhaps derived from his work as a carpenter. No doubt he had to grease the palms of a ship captain and crew members on the navy gunboat or supply ship that he boarded along the occupied Georgia–South Carolina coast.[17]

On Sunday evening, March 20, 1864, James Simms became an ordained minister of the Baptist Church. (By this time, Thomas was in Nashville working as a recruiter for the Union Army.) The special ordination service featured the Reverends Randolph and Grimes. Simms had received the blessing of an ecclesiastical council that had convened the week before; its members expressed their approval of "his Conversion, call and views of doctrines." He remained in Boston another several months, giving talks to the Freedmen's Aid Society, Sunday schools, and church congregations, but he did not make his home in the Bay State. Returning to Savannah, he pursued a variety of careers—as a labor agent and politician, for example—in addition to that of his new-found calling in the ministry.[18]

Overall, the war laid bare the precarious nature of breadwinning among the city's Black clergy. One distressed *Christian Recorder* correspondent wrote an indignant article titled "How a Minister Is Treated in Boston," claiming that the Bethel AME Church preacher "does not get paid for his labor . . . [and] does not get enough to pay his board [lodgings]." He had to get by on one meal a day, "and poor at that," and his congregants did "not care whether he is clothed or not," leading to the conclusion, "The people in Boston are not worthy of a good minister." Yet Leonard and Octavia Grimes would have begged to differ. Predictably, their actions to promote the Union cause, support Republican politicians, and aid the freedpeople blended seamlessly with their church work. Twelfth Baptist, still trying to pay its debt ($2,000 in 1865), continued to host fund-raisers as well as gatherings devoted to the Union war effort and Black troops. Around this time, the Grimeses' daughter Emma, twenty-three, married Miles R. Robinson, a restaurateur living in Philadelphia. At some point Leonard Grimes had turned down Governor Andrew's offer of an army chaplaincy. Perhaps the preacher felt he could do more for the Union cause while at home in Boston than in an army camp, or maybe he was reluctant to leave his family and his congregation.[19]

DURING THE WAR, intermediaries of all kinds remained in high demand from workers, job-seekers, applicants for aid, draft resisters, and the grief-stricken—all seeking to make their way in a new, tumultuous world. A few Black men and women became brokers helping clients navigate confusing rules and regulations, a job that sometimes provided a handsome living and other times ended in tragedy. Institutional intermediaries were of a different order: labor unions, corporate monopolies, and charitable organizations engaged in fraught efforts to bridge the interests of employer and worker, business and consumer, rich and poor.

Some brokers prospered, and others lost their jobs. During the war, Boston City Hall dispensed with independent labor contractors and hired workers directly, making Boston, for the first time in its history, a large employer. Black Bostonians found the everyday sight of white men working on the streets particularly galling. (These workers were probably drawn from the overlapping ranks of older men, those ineligible for the draft, and recent immigrants.) Employees of the Paving and Internal Health Departments and other beneficiaries of the city's public works projects served as a constant reminder of the overt favoritism that animated municipal authorities. Frederick Douglass resented the privileges enjoyed by what he called "drunken Irishmen" and the "ignorant Dutchman [i.e., Germans]."[20]

Throughout 1863 and 1864, the city council faced persistent demands for wage increases from what it no doubt considered insufficiently grateful public employees. The police, lamplighters, steam-fire-engine drivers, janitors, removers of night soil and cleaners of privies, and city printers besieged the council with petitions ranging from plaintive to furious, pointing to inflated prices for rent and food and demanding higher pay. The Internal Health teamsters, street shovelers, and offal removers joined this chorus of what the council considered a group of malcontents. So it came as no surprise that in late 1864 the city authorized the committee overseeing these workers to travel to Philadelphia and inspect a new mechanical street sweeper with an eye to buying one. Each quarter, the Boston budget bled more and more red ink: building contractors reported the inevitable cost overruns and billed the city for more money. Annual expenses for hay, grain, straw, lumber, harnesses, and other supplies were increasing exponentially. Meanwhile, as conditions among the poor worsened, the council curtailed expenditures for their relief—from $90,000 in 1863 to $39,000 the following year.[21]

Complaints poured in about the disgraceful treatment of men, women, and children employed by the city in its residential facilities, though council members were largely dismissive. The House of Correction, they sniffed, "is not an hotel, but a penal institution," with necessarily strict, enforced hierarchies akin to the military. (Authorities reported that the women there were "more difficult to control than the men." At least, they said, that was "the universal testimony of all who [had] an opportunity of testing their comparative docility under restraint.") The principles of deprivation and stern discipline also applied to the Boston Almshouse, the Boston Lunatic Hospital, and the Boston House of Reformation of Juvenile Offenders. Authorities in charge of the House of Reformation reportedly denied the children sufficient food, fed them moldy bread, and meted out punishments harsher than those in the state prison, including whippings and solitary confinement. Children were required to work (but not attend school) while incarcerated; one boy assigned to wash windows on the fourth floor of a building fell and broke his wrists, hip, and ribs and shattered his elbow. Another youth died when an earthen embankment on which he was working collapsed. Though youngsters were toiling even "where life or limb is in danger," the imperative for child labor prevailed. The city also boasted a new workshop for female convicts at the House of Correction, built at a cost of $10,000. As usual, the old and infirm were at most risk, leading one paper to urge its readers to support private charities so that elderly women did not have to throw themselves on the mercy of the unforgiving matrons at the Deer Island almshouse.[22]

The city's much-vaunted Soldiers' Relief Fund was spending about $70,000 a quarter, or almost $300,000 a year, but this amount was not enough to fend off hardship for large numbers of Boston's women, children, elderly, and disabled. Many factors shaped whether soldiers and their dependents ever saw the aid promised to them by various programs. Some officials appropriated for themselves the cash and goods intended for the needy. The criteria for awarding enlistment bounties were ever shifting, complicated by the competing and overlapping jurisdictions of city, state, and federal government. Applicants who could not prove residence in a particular locale faced rejection. City agents subjected wives and widows and their children to intense scrutiny to locate only "worthy" recipients. Authorities objected to increased benefits, even with runaway inflation, on the theory that the high cost of living was only a temporary challenge. For some families the decline in earning power would be permanent, however. Men who had marched off to war in 1861 were returning three years later, their regimental ranks decimated by as much as 90 percent by deaths, wounds, disease, and desertion.[23]

As mediators between employers and employees, labor unions did not fare well during the war years. Employers and city officials denounced them as a hindrance to the war effort and threatened to quash (white) workers' collective action. In early 1864, when New York City had captured a sizable portion of Boston's foreign trade in flour, pork, bacon, and beef, longshoremen faced reduced working hours and struck, demanding 60 cents an hour or $5 a day. Employers responded in well-placed news articles. The *Boston Herald* reported, "The plan among several leading merchants is to send South and procure some 2000 negroes." Later that year a protracted strike among newspaper printers led to the firing of some members of the Printers' Union; others returned to work at the same wage and joined new hires—women compositors and men living outside Boston, both groups barred from joining the union. Such exclusionary practices were bound to hobble the union's effectiveness. For their part, Boston newspaper publishers considered the Printers' Union a monopoly that aimed to control their business. More generally, the city council felt it was its responsibility to protect the public against "combinations" of any kind, whether a monopoly of ferry service from East Boston, price-gouging entrepreneurs, or labor unions.[24]

In 1864, shortages and the high price of coal helped to revive a dormant Labor Reform Association (LRA) composed of several different crafts. For each ton they bought, Bostonians paid eight times the cost miners charged to dig the ton out of the ground, with the railroads and other middlemen reaping the rest. The combined effects of railroad monopolies and government contractors purchasing large quantities of coal for war purposes put the ordinary householder at a distinct disadvantage. The LRA proposed to divert an oversupply of the fuel from Philadelphia to Boston and offer it to customers at a radically reduced price. The association hoped that by selling cheap coal to its members it might bring additional craft unions or guilds into its ranks.[25]

The proposed coal cooperative was an opening wedge in a new kind of abolition movement—the effort to end the twelve-hour workday in favor of an eight-hour day. The leader of this movement was a young Boston machinist, Ira Steward, who chafed under the rigors of the dawn-to-dusk regimen that was the lot of most skilled and industrial workers. In 1863, Steward won approval for the eight-hour day from his union, the International Machinists and Blacksmiths Union, then meeting in Boston. Hired by the IMBU as a paid agent, Steward set about creating an alliance with Boston's reformers to pressure the state legislature to effect change. He aimed to overcome the historical animosity between the city's antislavery and temperance advocates, on the one hand, and white workingmen, on the other. He scolded reformers, reminding them that too often men and women of privilege "ignore the *poverty* and *labor* side of the story." Arguing that the excessively long workday was the baneful consequence of an inefficient marketing system, Steward pointed to Boston's eighty coal dealers, who, he believed, might be reduced easily to one, saving the workingmen an estimated $5 million a year. His cry was "the discharge of all useless middle men; and the abolition of all useless hours!" as he launched the eight-hour movement to promote a shorter workday.[26]

So-called useless middle men and war profiteers were the bane of Bostonians up and down the social ladder. Fishermen in the North End and on the islands took matters in their own hands when they bypassed retailers and set up informal markets on the north side of Commercial Wharf. Each day a flotilla of small boats brought the fish directly to crowds of buyers. Reported one local paper, "No one can estimate what an advantage this is to the poorer classes at such times as the present, when all kinds of provisions are so enormously high." Indeed, opined the *Traveller*, many unemployed wharf workers might consider taking up fishing and, in the process, do "two useful things—keep out of idleness themselves and help their neighbors and countrymen, by furnishing them with abundant supplies of fish. They need not fear an overstocked market."[27]

THE CHALLENGES FACED by three Black workers illustrated the promise and peril of wartime brokerage. John Mulligan, the agent who placed seamen with captains, was a victim of his own commercial success. John S. Rock mediated between civilians and newly enlisted men, on the one hand, and military authorities, on the other, at times caught between policies he did not support.

And Octavia Grimes embarked on a new career in response to an emerging mass migration of refugees out of Virginia and into Boston. Together these three came up against the limits of a demanding kind of work where the interests of employers, government officials, and applicants for jobs and aid all collided.

The seamen's boardinghouse operator John Mulligan could match Joseph Clash for ambition, but he lacked Clash's political connections with the police and judicial establishment, and evidence of his success put him in harm's way. Mulligan had gained some renown as, in the words of a local paper, "one of the most intelligent colored men of the city." In 1864 he was operating the Colored Boarding Masters of Boston, an employment service. He was good at what he did, and he had an impressive horse and buggy to show for it. On July 14, he drove his rig up Commercial Street, parked it, and went into a nearby store. Coming back outside, he found a white man, a longshoreman named O'Neil, sitting in the buggy. When O'Neil refused to budge, Mulligan threatened the man, reportedly remarking that "he would shoot any white ______ who drove his team away." Mulligan then took out his pistol and fired a warning shot into the air. At that point, apparently, "the friends of the intruder" began to chase Mulligan, yelling "Hit him! Kill him!" They pelted him with stones and bricks (this on the one-year anniversary of the 1863 draft riot), and the Black man turned suddenly and fired his gun at one of his tormentors, mortally wounding him.[28]

Charged with murder, Mulligan claimed self-defense and hired attorneys Robert Morris and Edwin Walker to represent him. That trial ended in a hung jury. A subsequent trial, now with Mulligan accused of manslaughter, resulted in a guilty verdict; however, the jury cited "mitigating circumstances" and urged the judge to show clemency and dismiss the charges. Instead, the judge sentenced Mulligan to a year in prison. His public display of prosperity (his buggy) had provoked white men of modest means. Yet the trial was also a reminder that of all the Black brokers, the criminal defense lawyers Morris and Walker were likely to enjoy a steady stream of customers for their services.[29]

Military service and a constellation of related activities yielded business opportunities for enterprising brokers—savvy civilians, whether lawyers or not. John S. Rock handled paperwork related to bounties, exemptions, pension claims, and naturalization status. Applicants had to present all manner of certified documents—birth and marriage certificates, doctor's reports, proof of citizenship—to enlist, qualify for assistance, or secure a substitute or otherwise avoid service.[30]

As ever, Rock remained principled in his defense of the rights and dignity of Black soldiers. He excoriated the Boston-born colonel Charles Sawyer Russell, a white man organizing the 28th US Colored Infantry Regiment, the only Black unit from Indiana. According to Rock, Russell had demonstrated no previous commitment to abolition or Black rights generally: "I did not feel at liberty to urge any one to fight under an officer who I had never heard of before, and (so far as I know) had never expressed any sympathy with the race who have been so long outraged and who are obliged to fight against fearful odds." Rock had heard that Russell called the men under his command "a set of Jack___ and blockheads." Russell angrily defended himself to Rock, who countered, "You have no right to insult me. . . . I was not employed by you."[31]

Rock *was* employed by the city and state, fulfilling multiple roles as an agent for women applying for public assistance and for men seeking bounties and deferments. In 1864 he was advertising as a "Licensed Government Claim Agent." Among his references were Governor Andrew and a paymaster who disbursed funds for Boston's Office of Soldiers' Relief. The latter offered high praise for Rock, calling him "an honorable and trustworthy man . . . familiar with the laws and the requirements of this office," and said he was "careful and correct in the preparation of his cases." Alluding to Rock's success, the paymaster wrote, "We are paying him large amounts every month and have every confidence in his honor and integrity."[32]

In his role as military recruiter, Rock received a fee for signing up each Black man—whether in Boston's Ward 6 or in Philadelphia (his mother's hometown, where he was canvassing for the 5th Cavalry in the spring of 1864). Discriminatory policies imposed by the commonwealth proved a barrier to recruitment, and he expressed his frustration to Governor Andrew, who had promised bounties to the new enlistees in the 5th. However, the governor insisted on deferring full payment until the men had finished their terms of service; he feared that paying men right away would cause more desertions. Rock thought that proportionately fewer Black men deserted than their white counterparts, but, more to the point, he considered Andrew's policy shortsighted, arguing that it would be better "to lose a few to gain a great many." With "a more liberal policy," he thought, he could have enlisted three times as many men in the 5th as he was able to do under the deferred bounty system. It was around this time that he also explored the possibility of representing veterans and the widows of veterans in their claims for US-sponsored pensions: "I have been intending to commence this business for about a year," he wrote a fellow attorney, noting that he must advertise widely to pursue this new line of work.[33]

Drafted soldiers could claim exemptions if they had varicose veins, lacked teeth, cared for motherless children, or suffered from defective vision and general disabilities. Wealthy men could afford the $300 to pay a substitute who was a foreign alien or a non-Massachusetts resident. However, all these conditions and family situations had to be documented and certified, providing Rock and other agents with a steady, and at times handsome, stream of income during the war. Still, competition for business was fierce.[34]

Rock's various enterprises depended on the patronage of impoverished men and women, Black and white. Hester Jane Cooper, a thirty-eight-year-old Black woman, was eligible for state aid when her husband, William, enlisted in the Union Army, but she was very "needy." In the summer of 1864 Rock felt obliged to advance her at least part of the amount she hoped to receive. When she wrote later and told him she had not received the money, he advised her to go to the attorney to whom he had sent the money, but added, "Keep your temper [and] don't have any words with him. Don't make any threats." Rock was appalled at the brokers who provided a $40 advance on a $100 bounty, but then demanded $60 from the discharged soldier—an interest rate of 50 percent. The wife of one seaman wanted to ensure that her husband received his "prize money" from the sale of the cargo of a captured Confederate vessel, but she placed the claim in the hands of a man whom Rock feared had absconded with the funds.[35]

Unscrupulous bounty brokers not only denied servicemen and their families the funds promised to them, but also added to their misery. In making his appeal to John Andrew for bounties paid up front, Rock reminded the governor of the sacrifices made by ordinary people committed to the Union cause. In April 1864, Rock managed to enlist five men in the 5th; they traveled one hundred miles to Philadelphia at his expense and had to rely on another broker for living expenses while they awaited deployment. Lacking funds, "they declined to go farther." Around the same time, two men on furlough from the unit found themselves "in a very uncomfortable position," taken advantage of by agents who deceived them "and caused them to leave their families to suffer." Rock also reported that three other men, on furlough from the 5th, should now be returning to their unit but lacked the means to do so. They faced harsh punishments—charges of desertion even—if they were not able to make their way back to Virginia on time. Rock worried that these men and others with similar stories would discourage others from serving. They wanted to fight for their country, "but the men are poor," he wrote in a letter, "and cannot afford to leave their families destitute for months."[36]

That summer and fall, Rock was representing soldiers and their wives in various cases related to enlistment at the same time that he was arranging for his mother to move from Philadelphia to Boston. He took time out from his work to attend a convention of Black leaders in Syracuse from October 4 to 7. There, the delegates acknowledged evidence of wartime progress in the fight for Black rights. The president and Congress had abolished slavery in Washington, DC, struck down the law prohibiting Black men from working as postal clerks and mail carriers, recognized the independence of Haiti and Liberia, and promised retaliation for the "unmilitary and barbarous treatment" of Black servicemen captured by Confederate forces. The delegates offered thanks to Senator Charles Sumner and General Benjamin Butler, "and to all other noble workers, both in our legislative halls and elsewhere."[37]

As one of the featured speakers at the meeting, Rock characteristically focused on the issues of unequal pay and the lack of promotions for Black soldiers; but he also recounted the case involving a member of the 54th Massachusetts, "a splendid penman" detailed as a clerk. The white officer in charge sent him back to his company saying "that no Negro will be allowed to hold any position in this department except that of a cook or a laborer." To his credit, Governor Andrew had intervened. Declared Rock, "They [Black soldiers] have not gone to the battle-field for the sake of killing and being killed, but they are fighting for liberty and equality." The men resented that they were being cheated out of the glory they had earned, a reward for valor on the battlefield and hard work off of it. The convention concluded by forming a National Equal Rights League. Yet, as Rock well understood, constitutional rights could never guarantee true equality if splendid penmen were consigned to the job of cook or laborer.[38]

A few days after Rock arrived back in Boston from Syracuse, on October 12, 1864, Roger B. Taney, chief justice of the US Supreme Court, died at the age of eighty-seven. The death of the man responsible for the infamous Dred Scott decision left Rock hopeful for his own future. Rock had learned earlier that year that Senator Sumner planned to recommend that he be certified to argue cases before the high court (Rock himself had initiated the process with a letter to Sumner in December 1863). However, Rock confided to a correspondent, "Mr. Sumner thinks I had better do nothing with my matter while Judge Taney occupies the bench." Taney's successor was to be Treasury Secretary Salmon P. Chase of Ohio, a Lincoln appointee and abolitionist-minded Republican. The decision regarding Rock was Chase's to make. Within a few months, John Rock would become the first Black lawyer to be admitted to the bar of the US Supreme Court.[39]

Sumner believed this appointment would send a loud message to employers of all kinds: "The admission of a colored lawyer to the bar of the Supreme Court would make it difficult for any restrictions on account of color to be maintained anywhere." The senator adhered to an outsized faith in the power of the "Black First," an honor bestowed on a few that, however, failed to transform larger patterns of discriminatory hiring or the prejudices of white workers.[40]

IN 1864 LEONARD and Octavia Grimes began to place southern refugees in northern homes. On August 5, the steamer *George Leary* sailed from Fortress Monroe with two hundred Black women and children bound for Philadelphia, New York, and Boston. By this time an estimated ten thousand refugees had settled in the area around the fortress. Living in sheds and barns, they had no fuel, food, or clothing. Federal agents blamed this disastrous situation on military officials, who aggressively recruited Black men into the army but made no provision for their wives and children. Captain Charles B. Wilder, a Boston abolitionist in charge of contrabands at Fortress Monroe, believed that sending these dependents north would accomplish several goals—it would take starving people off his hands; provide domestic servants, always in demand, for white northerners; and allow the former slaves to get an education "in the atmosphere of freedom." However, Wilder and other officials overseeing this nascent mass migration north were distressed to learn that not all wives wanted to go and leave their husbands and other kinfolk behind.[41]

The day the *George Leary* departed Virginia, Octavia Grimes began taking out classified ads for her new business: "Colored servants, women, and girls may be found at Mrs. L. A. Grimes's, 28 Grove Street, if immediate application is made." For a $5 fee paid by the employer, she would place one or more of the southern migrants in a Boston-area household. With the help of her husband, who greeted the newcomers as they disembarked at the Boston docks, Octavia had become the operator of an intelligence office. She joined other placement agents in New York and Philadelphia, some more honest than others. One agent in Brooklyn offered to find jobs for one thousand Black workers in an unusual way: he proposed to sell tickets for $1 to all potential employers, with each ticket entitling the bearer to board the ship and pick one person, an adult or a child, as an employee. An echo of the "scramble"—the process by which whites had formerly purchased enslaved workers in southern ports—this scheme was soon abandoned.[42]

The Grimeses were not the first to channel southern women and children into northern households. At some point, John Oliver left his school in Virginia and went to Philadelphia, where, in September 1863, he was operating an "employment office for colored persons" out of Clarkson Hall. He assured Wilder that he could get "good homes" for both men and women sent from Norfolk and Fortress Monroe. Oliver noted, "The demand is very good at this time and all the more since the New York riots." It was unclear whether he meant that the large number of Black residents fleeing that city had left a shortage of servants, or that some whites sought to make amends for the violence by hiring Black refugees.[43]

In addition to running her new intelligence office, Octavia Grimes had other work to do. That spring she began to plan for a grand fair that would benefit Black soldiers and their families. It is significant that the group sponsoring the fair called itself the "Colored Ladies Sanitary Commission," indicating that Black troops could not count on aid from the national US Sanitary Commission (SC) and its local branches. A private agency, the commission aimed to raise funds to provide soldiers in the field with medical care, food, and clothing.[44]

In fact, the robust charitable effort on the part of wealthy white women apparently did not extend to either Black soldiers or their families. The New England branch of the SC sponsored fairs like those developed by antislavery associations before the war. These benefits also raised money that went to aid Union prisoners of war, virtually all white. The fair of December 1863 included tableaus and displays of paintings and sculptures from the Boston Athenaeum. According to a local paper, the fair was notable for "the display of rich and costly articles, many of them imported for the purpose." The event was certain to "surpass anything of the kind ever exhibited in America." Indeed, it raised $146,000. The following year, a benefit for a new (all-white) sailors' home brought in even more money. It attracted large crowds to the Common, where replicas of the ironclads *Monitor* and *Merrimac* floated on Frog Pond. An enormous ox nicknamed "General Grant" fetched $2,000.[45]

The Colored Ladies fair explicitly linked their own fundraising effort to the issues of Black soldiers' unequal pay and the plight of their family members on the home front: "Hundreds of the [54th and 55th troops] have fallen in defense of the American Flag," the organizers noted, "leaving here in our midst their poor, suffering and destitute wives and children." They wrote, "As we have just sent into the field another brave regiment, the 5th Cavalry, and their families are left with us, while their husbands, brothers and fathers have gone to uphold the honor of the flag, there will be a demand for all our friends may assist us in raising." Besides Octavia Grimes, leaders of the effort included Christiana Carteaux Bannister, the well-known entrepreneur specializing in hair products and services. In August 1864, Bannister criticized the recruitment of Black men: "She did not want any more to go to aid a government that had treated them so cruelly," according to the *Weekly Anglo-African*. "She would rather beg from door to door than that her husband should go to war."[46]

The soldiers' fair sponsored by Boston's Colored Ladies Sanitary Commission took place from 10:00 a.m. to 10:00 p.m. in Mercantile Hall from Tuesday, October 18, through Saturday the 22nd, with tickets 25 cents apiece and "season admission" 50 cents. The theme was "Boys, the dear old flag never touched the ground," a reference to the heroic actions of New Bedford's William H. Carney of the 54th. Though wounded, Carney had kept the American flag aloft during the assault on Fort Wagner (in 1900 he would become the first Black soldier to receive the US Medal of Honor). Organizers rented the hall, placed ads in local newspapers soliciting cash and goods, sorted the donations, arranged for different towns to be represented by tables, and shipped aid south. They printed tickets, selling some ahead of time and more at the door. They asked for and got favorable replies from some prominent whites: Senator Henry Wilson delivered an address the first evening, and Elizabeth P. Peabody, a noted educator and Transcendentalist, presided over a table "expressly devoted to the benefit of colored orphans." Chickering Pianos and Mason and Hamlin Organs donated instruments. The artist Edward Bannister's portrait of the fallen Colonel Robert Gould Shaw was valued at $200. Black women contributed baked goods and various pieces of needlework. The net proceeds amounted to $3,600, about $66,300 in today's dollars, a sizable sum but far less than the white women had raised with their own fair.[47]

THE LAST TWO months of 1864 brought decisive political and military developments. The presidential election pitted Lincoln against a former Union general, George B. McClellan, a Democrat and a proponent of immediate peace talks with the Confederacy. Lincoln scored an overwhelming victory, winning 72.22 percent of the Massachusetts vote to McClellan's 27.77 percent. In Boston, incumbent mayor Frederic Lincoln Jr. received seven out of ten votes cast in a contest with Democratic attorney and author Thomas Coffin Amory. The Black voters of Boston added to the tallies for both Lincolns (the mayor was a Boston-born businessman and unrelated to the president).

In the fall of 1864, George Lewis Ruffin surveyed the city's voter registration rolls and compiled a list of more than three hundred Black names; he was contemplating a political career for himself someday. The registrants had paid a poll tax of $1.50; the vast majority did not own real estate, but they did possess some personal property, mostly in the form of furniture and housewares. Among those seeking to affirm their citizenship in this tangible way were well-known figures such as John S. Rock, Henry L.W. Thacker, John P. Coburn, Rev. Leonard Grimes and his son John, William Cooper Nell, Robert Morris, and George Lewis Ruffin himself. Also on the list were a surprising number of laborers and waiters, including the porter Carter Selden and the laborer Charles Fountain, members of the Edloe Sixty-Six. Of special note were fugitives who had made their permanent home in Boston—not just the famous Lewis Hayden, but other formerly enslaved men from Virginia, Kentucky, and Maryland. Ruffin also noted that some men were "out of town"—the pugilist John Bailey had temporarily relocated to Kansas, and other men on the list had left Boston permanently. Still, Ruffin's list would provide a starting point for Black Republicans' robust postwar organizing campaigns.[48]

And now the end of the war indeed appeared to be in sight. With the city of Atlanta liberated in early September, General William Tecumseh Sherman began his famous march to the sea on November 15. Fifteen days later, the 54th and 55th, together with white troops from Ohio and New York, attacked a Confederate force at Honey Hill, South Carolina, to cut off rail supply lines between Charleston and Savannah. The federal forces suffered heavy losses, including 746 dead, wounded, or missing, in contrast to the South's total losses of 8 killed and 39 wounded.

The fall of Savannah on December 22 represented a turning point in the war, presaging a Union victory. Sherman had bisected the state of Georgia, and his army, 60,000 strong, encountered no resistance when they marched into the river port. Rather than torch the city, which held little military value, Sherman and his officers took up residence in its elegant townhouses. They also discovered stockpiles of cotton: 25,000 bales in dock warehouses and an additional 5,000 scattered in private homes throughout the city. The future of Black workers in both Boston and Savannah hung in the balance, with precious few white allies in either place.

11

"False and Exaggerated Ideas of Freedom"

Bostonians of means prided themselves on what they considered the city's enduring spirit of civic-minded generosity. They pointed to the many private and tax-supported institutions designed to house, heal, and reform the city's poor, ill, and wayward; to the public library and the public schools; and to the Common, a manicured slice of the city maintained for the enjoyment of all. And so, in early January 1865, reports of fellow Americans in distress prompted the city's white citizens and officials to act with alacrity. The *Daily Advertiser* approved: "The appeal made to our humane sympathies is by itself a call which is never addressed in vain to this community." Still, this new object of Boston's benevolence was somewhat surprising—the city of Savannah, Georgia. Union military officials reported that its proud people were now destitute and demoralized, its once elegant parks and byways crumbling and choked with weeds. In response, Boston's elite organized a major relief effort to feed their erstwhile enemies deep in the heart of the still-defiant Confederacy.[1]

On January 9 in Faneuil Hall, James C. Converse, president of the Boston Board of Trade, presided over a large, enthusiastic meeting dedicated to suffering Savannah. The organizers expressed confidence that the river port would soon repent of its role in the rebellion; before long it would "welcome the old [US] flag" and do so "without the sullenness and bad temper which disgraced other Southern cities." In fact, time would tell that Bostonians had mistaken Savannah's war-weariness and dilapidated condition for its leaders' remorse about secession. For now, though, the Boston City Council would oversee a massive effort to send south bacon, pork lard, brown sugar, Irish potatoes, cornmeal, beans, and hard bread, a grocery wish-list helpfully submitted by Dr. Richard D. Arnold, Savannah's mayor. The Boston owners of the steamer *Greyhound* offered to transport the supplies free of charge.[2]

In March, the relief committee wrote directly to Mayor Arnold, inquiring about Savannah's stored cotton bales and their ultimate disposition. The nearly twenty million pounds of the fiber was worth about $38 million. Arnold, a physician, was receptive to the Bostonians' queries. He appreciated the historical relations between the two places and remembered with fondness his visits to the Bay State city—especially his last, in 1860, when he attended the fourth National Quarantine and Sanitary Commission meeting. He as well as anyone understood that ties of kinship, trade, and cultural exchange bound the two places together.[3]

Though grateful for the aid, Arnold felt compelled to remind his benefactors that a reconfigured system of Black labor would determine the fate of both North and South: "Unless labor, the source of all well-being in this world, shall be re-organized in some practical form, a dreary future awaits the South." Now, in early 1865, he anticipated the end of slavery and the end of the war. For their part, the Boston benefactors feared that, if left to their own devices and the uncertainties of the marketplace, the former slaves might find themselves "crush[ed]" by the "necessity of capital and labor." They warned that the emancipation of almost four million enslaved workers would present a challenge, one that had "never been equaled in magnitude in the history of any nation, and will require all the sagacity, wisdom, and philanthropy of every statesman, patriot, and Christian to meet it."[4]

If Boston cotton magnates had hoped to ingratiate themselves with Mayor Arnold and lay early claim to the stockpiled cotton, they were greatly disappointed. The secretaries of war and of the treasury squabbled over jurisdictional issues, and the government of the Confederacy weighed in on the matter as well. By late April, most of the bales had been shipped to New York City, where they were auctioned off to the highest bidder. Nevertheless, Boston had made its postwar priority clear: a swift revival of trade with the Cotton South regardless of the working conditions for former slaves. In promoting this goal, textile-mill owners and shippers would enjoy the support of both the Republicans and the Democrats, who envisioned a postbellum future in which most Black people would continue to toil in the cotton fields.

In early 1865, with the occupation of Savannah and the capture of Charleston, the imminent destruction of slavery seemed to be a foregone conclusion. On January 31, Freemason to Prince Hall Freemason, Governor Andrew presented Lewis Hayden with two items that signaled the passing of an era—a gavel made from a Hampton, Virginia, whipping post, and a rude boat made of straw, the means by which a fugitive named Jack Flowers had made his way from the interior of South Carolina to Union picket lines and freedom on the coast. On February 1, Congress passed the Thirteenth Amendment to the Constitution, abolishing slavery, and sent it to the states for ratification. (The measure would not win the requisite state approval until December 1865.) Also on that day, at a formal ceremony in his courtroom, Chief Justice Salmon P. Chase admitted Dr. John S. Rock as a member of the Supreme Court bar. Two weeks later, a grand "Freedom Jubilee" held in Cambridgeport brought together Black and white men and women from all over the Boston area, old warhorses of the abolitionist movement such as William Wells Brown and

Wendell Phillips as well as newcomers such as the Black poet and orator Frances Ellen Watkins Harper from Maryland.[5]

Finally, that spring, came the long-anticipated results of several southern so-called experiments testing Black people's ability to work in a post-emancipation economy. Basing its findings on reports from Port Royal, the New England Freedmen's Aid Society noted in its journal that, despite the awful system of slavery, "the American Negro has had, however, one advantage, which though far from neutralizing all the ill effects of his bondage, gives a favorable augury for his future. He has been trained to *labor*." Edward Philbrick testified that Sea Island freedpeople were ginning twice as much cotton as their enslaved selves had just a few short years before. And General Rufus Saxton rendered a final verdict on the potential of the former slaves, reporting that "the experiment has been entirely satisfactory. It has demonstrated beyond controversy, that, under the usual inducements of free labor, they will be industrious and efficient laborers."[6]

The freedpeople were not the only group of workers to figure in late-wartime debates on the "labor question." Republican "free labor" ideology exalted employees acting as unfettered individuals; if employers failed to pay fair wages, they risked losing their workers to someone who would. In Boston, Ira Steward, the proponent of the eight-hour workday, tried to reconcile traditional republicanism with a modern free market; both notions seemed to rule out the need for collective action among wage earners. He lectured and wrote on the topic "The Eight Hour Movement: A Reduction of Hours Is an Increase in Wages." A shorter workday would afford the laborer time to read a book, entertain visitors, and take a bath. Decent pay would increase the employee's purchasing power, which would stimulate production of and demand for fine goods previously available only to the wealthy. Employers would have to hire more workers, now that some were on the job for only eight hours; the resulting labor shortage would push wages higher for all.[7]

Wendell Phillips, recruited by Steward, brought an antebellum reformer's sensibility to the cause, calling for workers to be educated "on the question of relations of labor and capital &c, by lectures," the way temperance and antislavery activists had been instructed. Phillips disapproved of strikes, believing them to be harmful and counterproductive. For his part, Steward turned the notion of a strike on its head and defined it in terms of employers' refusal to raise wages: "That resistance would amount to the folly of a 'strike' by *Employers themselves*, against the strongest power in the world, viz., the *habits, customs*, and *opinions* of the masses."[8]

Steward spoke for white workingmen; presumably higher pay would free the honest toiler's wife or daughter from the drudgery of wage earning. At the same time, the war had profound consequences for white working women, opening nursing and school teaching to large numbers for the first time in American history. Signaling a new era in women's work were the nurses in both Union and Confederate hospitals (including Massachusetts's Dorothea Dix and Louisa May Alcott) and the northern teachers, "soldiers of light and love," in freedpeople's schools (Harriet Jacobs and hundreds of others). This gender-based ideology held that, by virtue of their tender nature, women were better than men at caring for the ill, the dying, and the young—though the custom of paying women less than their male counterparts contributed to employers' willingness to hire them.[9]

In their pronouncements on the social division of labor, white congressional representatives, local school boards, missionaries, reformers, and union members tended to identify discrete groups—the former slaves in the fields, white mechanics in shops and operatives in factories, and white women in the "helping" professions and (unwaged) charitable and church work. Largely missing from these discussions were northern Black men and women. An exception was a *Boston Evening Transcript* article in February 1865 addressing the future of Black workers in an increasingly industrial age. The article, signed "Housekeeper" and titled "Call for

Schools for Colored Servants," claimed that such schools "would be handmaid to Victory"—that is, they would represent a fitting way to end the war. Young white men should abandon their jobs in dry-goods stores and join the army for a final "vigorous campaign" that would bring the conflict to a close. These seemingly effeminate store clerks, "who have been contented to sell pins and tapes to women," must redeem their manhood. Into their places would step white women fleeing paid housework, a job that tended to disorder the temperament of those with a nervous or delicate condition. In turn, the white women's places "can be admirably filled by colored servants," whose abilities as cooks and maids would be enhanced by formal training. Under this scheme, all Black men and women could aspire to become "accomplished and artistic house servants."[10]

The "natural" order of things would have white men producing, white women selling and nurturing, and Black men and women serving. While the clock managed the workday for whites, the whims of employers and the rhythms of the seasons determined the workday for Blacks. Thus in the "modernizing" North, Black people would move goods; scrub floors; clean clothes, windows, and dishes; cook; and care for other people's children, gardens, and horses. In fact, in the coming decades, immigrants from Eastern Europe would also take these jobs. Nevertheless, this racialized division of labor amounted to a kind of social glue binding together elites north and south in the form of shared assumptions about the meaning of Black work. Neither massive industrial transformations nor the war's tremendous loss of life need change the traditional duties of Black people in the fields, on the streets, and in white households.

In late January 1865, James Trotter reported that the deployment of the 55th Massachusetts Volunteer Infantry Regiment so near to Savannah "create[d] much sensation among the

Georgians. They have great fear of colored troops and are trembling because of our proximity and the expectation of our coming to town to them was [as] Belshazzar reads the handwriting on the wall." Trotter speculated that the regiment had not marched into Savannah itself because of the bedraggled condition of the men: "The campaign has caused nearly all to wear fleshcolored clothing," he observed, referring to their tattered uniforms. However, on February 18, 1865, the soldiers did make a triumphal entry into Charleston. Together with the 21st US Colored Infantry Regiment of the United States Colored Troops (USCT), they sang "John Brown's Body" to the cheers of Black men, women, and children, some of them weeping for joy. James Redpath was there to record the scene: "Imagine, if you can, this stirring song chanted with the most rapturous, most exultant emphasis, by a regiment of negro troops, who have been lying in sight of Charleston for nearly two years—as they trod with tumultuous delight along the streets of this pro-Slavery city." The procession was especially sweet to those soldiers who had trod those streets as slaves.[11]

Still disabled by a hernia, Thomas Selden might not have partaken of this celebration. In any case it marked neither the cessation of hostilities nor a respite from labor for the 55th Massachusetts. The regiment left Charleston the following month en route to Summerville, South Carolina (twenty-four miles to the northwest), along the way foraging for food (cattle were grazing along the route and easily accessible), building bridges over creeks, dismantling rebel guns, and engaging in periodic, deadly skirmishes with the enemy. For at least part of this march, Selden rode in a wagon, too weak to walk. In March he was sent back to a hospital in Charleston to recover from an acute bout of diarrhea.[12]

That spring, for five months, the men of the 55th became subjects in a new kind of experiment—this one focused on supposed physiological differences between, on the one hand, soldiers of color—"Full Blacks," "Mulattoes," or "Indians"—and, on the other, white soldiers. The regimental physician, Burt Wilder, took his orders from the American Association for the Advancement of Science (AAAS), which supplied him with an array of scientific instruments to measure individual men's weight, strength, and lung capacity. Wilder remained mystified by some of the instructions—for example, how to gauge the percentage of "black blood" in each man. He decided that, "in order to show the amount of colored blood," he would record information about the men's parents and grandparents. Later the AAAS used his data to argue for the inferiority of Blacks, a conclusion that Wilder rejected.[13]

After months of toil, the 5th Massachusetts Cavalry, too, had its moment of glory. The Elisha brothers were with the unit when it was among the first regiments, and the first with Black troops, to enter Richmond on April 3, 1865. They were greeted by cries of "God bless you! We have been waiting for you and looking for you for a long time!" Colonel Charles Francis Adams Jr. described the scene later primarily in terms of his men's deportment, reporting "that the conduct of the recruited portion of the Regiment on this occasion was most exemplary. Not only were they guilty of no desorder or act of pillage, but not one man left his rank & not a single case of intoxication, even, came under my notice. Both in its appearance & conduct the Regiment did credit to itself & the Commonwealth." Adams considered this event as the one "which I should most have desired as the culmination of my life in the Army."[14]

The following day, the 5th Cavalry served as an escort for President Lincoln and his entourage in their visit to newly occupied Richmond. Soon after, its members went back to fatigue duty, only now assigned to Texas; but the sacrifices of Black soldiers throughout the war had made a deep impression on Lincoln. He set aside his colonization plans, which he feared would interfere with the ongoing recruitment of Black manpower, and began to contemplate suffrage for all Black men.[15]

The liberation of Richmond, the Confederate capital, signaled one stage in the end of the war, and on April 9 General Robert

E. Lee surrendered his Army of Northern Virginia to General Ulysses S. Grant at Appomattox Courthouse, Virginia. These dramatic events did little to alter the everyday routines of Black regiments in the coming weeks.

And then came the news in the early morning of Saturday, April 15, that the president had been murdered, cut down by an assassin's bullet while he was watching a play in a Washington theater the night before. Black people everywhere reacted with shock and grief. Boston draped itself in mourning bunting. A general meeting of citizens took place in Faneuil Hall on Monday, followed by services in the individual churches on Thursday. John S. Rock delivered remarks at Twelfth Baptist.[16]

On June 1, 1865, in accordance with a proclamation from President Andrew Johnson, the City of Boston observed "a day wherein 'all shall be occupied at the same time in contemplation of the virtues, and sorrow for the sudden and violent end, of Abraham Lincoln, late the president of the United States of America.'" In a massive procession that began that morning on Cornhill Street and traversed much of the city, hundreds of men marched in groups according to their station. The mayor and chief of police served as marshals. Next came the fire department; the city council and the school committee; trustees of the public library and hospital; Overseers of the Poor; and various chapters of the (white) Sons of Temperance, Freemasons, and Odd Fellows, all interspersed with military regiments and marching bands. These were followed by members of labor unions and guilds, headed by delegates to the Workingmen's Assembly—the carpenters, coopers, painters, upholsterers, bricklayers, steam boiler makers, sailmakers, tailors, and more—on and on they came, forty unions and workers' benevolent societies in all, in solemn formation. Also included were white veterans' groups, the American Society of Hibernians, the Boston Catholic Relief Society and a variety of other Irish Catholic groups, and representatives of various German and Scandinavian mutual aid and cultural associations. The day's events culminated in services at Music Hall and a concert by the Handel and Hayden Society. Senator Charles Sumner gave the eulogy, and the Reverend Leonard Grimes offered the benediction.[17]

Grimes occupied a place of honor on the dais, but his role in the afternoon service amounted to a token Black presence. The state's Black regiments—the 54th, the 55th, and the 5th Cavalry—were still in the field, not to be mustered out until the summer. By featuring various crafts as represented by their labor unions or guilds, the organizers of the parade ensured (intentionally or not) that Black workers would have no place in it. The procession featured no gardeners, servants, stable hands, or waiters. The city failed to extend invitations to the Black churches, the Prince Hall Freemasons, or the antislavery groups. In mixing ritual and spectacle in this way, the city of Boston made manifest an idealized social order, one that rendered Black Bostonians invisible and unworthy of public recognition: not only the Black soldiers whose sacrifices had helped to win the war, but also Black waged and unwaged laborers of all kinds. Yet it was these citizens who had the most to fear now that Lincoln was dead.

IN THE SUMMER of 1865, a Charleston correspondent for a Boston newspaper discerned the "growth of a bitter and hostile spirit between blacks and whites" throughout South Carolina. Who was to blame? Some identified the culprits as the unrepentant rebels, others the unsettled freedpeople, and still others "Boston busybodies, who have gone South and stirred up animosities of race." Whites would always be the "dominant race," the correspondent said, and for some to claim otherwise, adopting the mantle of the "exclusive advocates and admirers of the negro race," was a criminal act. If constantly told that their wages were too low, Black workers would be "transformed into a vast body of worthlessness, degradation and wretchedness." Misguided Bostonians were peddling fantastical notions of "freedom" among the gullible.[18]

These supposed busybodies included not only the Gideonites on the Sea Islands, but also men of the Massachusetts 55th. James Trotter, for example, was serving in a newly created federal agency, the Office of the Commission on Labor, in Orangeburg, South Carolina, seventy-six miles northwest of Charleston. Trotter was responsible for ensuring that former slaveholders were abiding by written annual labor contracts with men and women now free. He surveyed Orangeburg's plantations and expressed satisfaction with the reception he received: "The Chivalry all treated me with respect and were skillful in concealing whatever bitterness they may have felt when seeing a 'nigger' with shoulder straps riding along the road to Columbia visiting their plantations in order to see that they were treating properly the colored people." Trotter could hardly gauge compliance with the order for contracts in one short visit to a plantation; still, he noted, although his "duties" were "quite arduous," he felt the job was worthwhile, writing, "I am very glad to be here, as I have ample opportunity to be of service to the freedmen."[19]

Around June 12, a young white officer of the 55th, Charles C. Soule, took it upon himself to address the newly freed people of Orangeburg. The twenty-three-year-old was a graduate of Harvard College and the son of Richard Soule Jr., Philbrick's partner on St. Helena Island. When Charles assembled the local freedpeople, he had been in the Orangeburg district for about a month. He considered conditions there disorderly in the extreme, and he knew whom to blame. He told his superiors that Blacks, who outnumbered whites by five to one, "already excited by the prospect of freedom, were urged to lawlessness and acts of violence by the colored soldiers" (men of the 55th Massachusetts): Black northerners, he said, were giving the local people "false and exaggerated ideas of freedom." Acknowledging that the workers trusted only people of their own color, Soule nevertheless intended to instruct them in how to live and labor, especially now that the crops were "in the most critical stage." He knew they thrilled to the dress parades of the Black troops: as Burt Wilder put it, people "of both sexes and all ages . . . rejoiced to see a regiment of their own color presenting such discipline and skill." So the 55th was probably there for his talk that day.[20]

Soule was his father's son. The speech amounted to a callow young white man hectoring Black women and men about the virtues of work, people who had literally slaved their whole lives. Soule's advice came in largely negative terms: Do not expect a life substantially different from slavery—"you must know that the only difference you can feel yet . . . is that neither you nor your children can be bought or sold." Do not "ask for more pay than free people at the north get." Do not forget that the house you live in, the land you till, the seed you plant, the ploughs and hoes, do not belong to you. Do not ask for Saturday off, and do not leave the plantation, even to visit your wife or children. Do not grumble because you are hungry. Do not "stop work on any account, for the whole crop must be raised and got in, or we shall starve."[21]

Remember: "When you work, work hard." Understand: "why some of the white people who used to own you, do not have to work in the field. It is because they are rich." This outcome was only right: "Some people must be rich, to pay others, and they have the right to do no work except to look out after their property." No doubt echoing his father, Soule believed that workers should not be allowed more than a little garden, some chickens and pigs, and a share of the crop: "Were the freedmen to receive more, the relation between capital and labor would be disturbed, and an undue value placed upon the latter." Soule's admonition channeled Boston's cotton magnates and merchants, as had his father's work on the islands.[22]

Still weak from his hernia, Thomas Selden might not have heard Soule proffer his advice to the freed folk of Orangeburg. Selden was detached from service on June 21, 1865, but not mustered out until August 29. He probably spent the intervening weeks in a military hospital in Charleston. Formal discharge came in Boston on September 23. His final reckoning with the army included $47 in pay and a $100 bounty that he had not yet received; but he owed the government $33 for a gun and equipment, "lost carelessly."[23]

In August Thomas Selden once again rounded the tip of Cape Cod en route to Boston. He came home a wounded man to a family in mourning. For many soldiers, a series of reunions was the signal experience of homecoming—in Thomas's case, with his wife, Elizabeth; their children, William and Lillie; and the extended Selden and Maddox families. His brother-in-law Stephen H. Maddox, who had enlisted as a private in the 55th and earned promotion to corporal, had died of pneumonia on Folly Island on January 31, 1864.

Anticipating Thomas's imminent return, Elizabeth Selden told a Massachusetts census-taker on May 1 that she and her husband were living together with their two children under the same roof as her parents, Elizabeth and Stephen, and her four siblings: Jane, seventeen; George, fifteen; Isaac, nineteen; and Keziah, nine. However, within a few weeks or months of Thomas's discharge, he and Elizabeth divorced, or at least separated in a way that preceded her remarriage the following year. The Seldens' son, William, stayed with his mother, while Lillie went with her father. Several possible factors account for the breakup. Because of his injury, Thomas would never again be able to work full time; perhaps that made him resentful and despondent and left his wife frightened for the future. She later recalled that Thomas "was in needy circumstances during all his life after his return from the war, owing to his poor health and inability to work." He could not afford to pay for a physician's care. Or perhaps in Thomas's absence Elizabeth had taken a lover and felt no need to settle for a husband who could no longer satisfy her. And yet, as a newly married man, Thomas had gone to live with his in-laws in 1859, when he was nineteen; the decision to leave might have been his, to get out from under the Maddox family once and for all. Or maybe husband and wife simply agreed that it was time to part ways.[24]

In any case, Elizabeth soon remarried, now to another veteran of the 55th—in fact, a member of Selden's Company F—Albert Revaleon (or Revalion), a hairdresser (like his father) who had grown up in Charlestown. For the official record, the bride gave her last name as Curtis, her mother's maiden name, and reported that this was her first marriage. It is possible that she and Thomas did not obtain an official divorce, or perhaps she did not want to embarrass her parents by giving her full name as Elizabeth Maddox Selden. In 1865, Albert was living in Chelsea with his mother, Margaret, sixty-five, and his two mariner brothers. Their home was just a few doors down from the extended Maddox-Selden household.[25]

Mustering out meant getting married for many returning servicemen, and Rev. Grimes officiated at a number of such weddings. Although Thomas Selden's own marriage was disintegrating, he forged a new connection with the Maddox family when his former wife's younger sister Jane married Aaron Joseph in Chelsea on October 13, 1865. Friends since childhood, Aaron and Thomas were now brothers-in-law, at least briefly. Discharged from the navy on May 11, Joseph was in Boston to welcome Selden back home on the day of his discharge, September 20, and later recalled that his friend "was never a well man after he got out of the military." The two subsequently visited each other frequently, with Joseph remarking that Thomas "could not do a man's work on account of his rupture, bothering him so much." No longer employed by Stephen Maddox, Thomas would work as a porter, a janitor, and a laborer—in other words, jobs for which he was decidedly unsuited, given the severity of his injury.[26]

That summer of 1865, virtually everyone had a story to tell about love or loss, or both. It was then that, for the first time in seventeen years, Mary Walker laid eyes on her long-lost son Bryant, twenty-one, and daughter, Agnes, twenty-eight. The two had recently arrived in Cambridge from Raleigh. In March, one of that city's occupying Union generals, Oliver O. Howard, arranged the initial communication between the children and their mother. (Howard would soon be named head of the new Freedmen's Bureau, and he and his younger brother Charles H. Howard would prove to be avid proponents of sending former slaves north.) Mary's elation at seeing her children was, quite literally, indescribable. Bryant's wife had stayed behind, but Agnes came with her husband, James Burgwyn. Catherine Robbins, the sister of Mary's former employer Anne Jean Lyman, was impressed by Bryant's upright appearance. A formerly enslaved house servant, he seemed to lack the degraded and "demoralized" countenance of so many southern Blacks, she thought. Robbins wrote that if "slavery trains people to be as he appears, it does better than our [northern] institutions for his race." Still, the joy that forty-seven-year-old Mary felt was tempered by the fact that she now had to face a new worry—helping to find jobs for three Black adults in postwar Boston.[27]

Indeed, many Black workers, including veterans, faced an uncertain future. William Aiken of the 54th had married right before he enlisted (in March 1863), and his employers, Brown & Robertson, offered him his old job back—or some job (he was a plasterer). Aiken had worked for them for a dozen years before the war, and he was particularly grateful for the work, because he had been wounded twice in his legs—at Fort Wagner and at Boykin Mill. His wife was shocked at his "broken up" appearance when she first saw him at a mustering-out ceremony on the

Common in August: he was so stooped over that she feared "he would never be so good as he was before he went away." Similarly, Thomas Cannon's wife, Caroline, remembered that when he came back from the war Thomas "apparently suffered so much pain he had to lay in bed a part of the time"; when he was up, he used a cane.[28]

These men came back to a city transformed. The Twelfth Baptist congregation had grown rapidly over the five years they had been gone and now had three hundred members. The new city hall on School Street, the expanding area of the Back Bay landfill, and countless other rearrangements of stone, brick, and dirt had enlarged and reshaped the city. Bostonians born in Ireland had begun the war as immigrants, but had emerged from the conflict with a claim to full citizenship. Though for the most part still confined to jobs for unskilled laborers, they felt little connection to Blacks as fellow soldiers or workers. The Republicans promoted economic nationalism, subsidizing commerce via grants of land to railroads and tariffs on foreign-made goods. The purposes of the nation-state were to defend the country and encourage the private accumulation of capital.[29]

Meanwhile, a jarring disjuncture existed between a city seeking to regain its prominence in the firmament of nations, on the one hand, and contending with large numbers of men and women shattered by the war, on the other. The wharves showed a reassuring busyness, but at the same time the remnants of battered regiments, the men footsore and battle-scarred, trudged through the streets on their way home. Visible reminders of the horrors of the conflict, many men, regardless of skin color, found the city all too ready to move on and forget, while they and their families proved casualties of peace as well as war. It was around this time that the Society for the Prevention of Pauperism released its report for the past year, noting it had received applications from 655 men and 1,904 women—returning soldiers and seamen, and, more numerous than the men, the wives of wounded soldiers and widows as well as women in-migrants to the city. "George," a southern "contraband," received mention, but otherwise all or virtually all the beneficiaries appeared to be white.[30]

The society divided Boston's workers into two categories—the skillful and the slothful. Those men who had followed manufacturing or mechanical pursuits had no trouble finding work. In contrast, those who were simple-minded, addicted to vicious habits, or averse to labor remained unemployed for long periods of time. As for the unskilled men, the report said, "the farm or their trade is repugnant to them, and they are looking for some kind of place in a store, a hotel, or bar-room, or they want to drive a horse-car or an express." In other words, these were men competing with Blacks for jobs as teamsters, porters, or drivers. Boston's male laboring population remained bifurcated, with machine operatives and skilled tradesmen constituting a relatively privileged group compared to the impoverished, the underemployed, and casual workers.[31]

Despite grim prospects in Boston for ordinary Black men and women and their families, several veterans of the 54th and the 55th decided to move to the city permanently after the war. James M. Trotter set up housekeeping with his bride, Virginia, and took in William DuPree as a boarder. Both veterans would be rewarded with jobs at the US postal service for their loyalty to the Republican Party. William B. Gould married a young woman from Nantucket, gave up the seafaring life, and settled in Dedham; his aunt in Boston helped expand his contacts with Black leaders in the area. Selden's Company F included men who had lived in Pennsylvania, New York, Ohio, and Georgia and now decided to become Bostonians. Though these men relocated for any number of reasons, including proximity to kin and new Boston-based friends, the city's integrated public schools served as a particularly potent inducement.[32]

BLACK LEADERS CONSIDERED the ongoing struggle for justice to be nationwide, not limited to the South. In Boston, Lewis Hayden, the grand master of the Prince Hall Grand Lodge, focused on enduring patterns of segregation that affected Black Freemasons. On December 27, 1865, he delivered a public lecture, "Caste Among Masons." In his lengthy discourse he decried discrimination by the (white) parent body but said nothing about his son Joseph, who had died of disease six months earlier at a camp in Mobile Bay. Joseph had been born in Detroit soon after his parents escaped from slavery in Kentucky. The young man had joined the navy before Black men were permitted to serve in the army and served for three and a half years in the Gulf Blockading Squadron. Together with countless other Black parents and sons, the Haydens had made the greatest sacrifice to the cause of freedom.[33]

For Lewis Hayden, the South's surrender was incomplete: "Although the dark and damning curse of slavery is disappearing, yet its hissing may still be heard." In other words, for seekers after justice, the work was not yet finished: "This causes us truly to feel, when we look over these fields of labor, that the harvest is great, but the laborers are few." Branches of the Grand Lodge were being established in the South—in Richmond by Peter Randolph and in Savannah by James Simms, among other places. Yet freedpeople continued to toil under the yoke of that modern-day pharaoh, President Andrew Johnson, and his neo-Confederate minions. Together with the defeated rebels, Johnson was a vociferous opponent of both Black civil rights and the members of his own party who supported those rights. He evinced little interest in reining in southern whites' efforts to institute a system of neo-slavery throughout the South. Hayden went on to remind his listeners that God had created "of one blood . . . all nations of men," and so the prejudices Blacks faced were those based on skin color, nothing more: "Color, not intelligence; the hue of the skin, rather than the merit of the man." Hayden focused on the discriminatory stance of the white Masons, proxy for barriers based on color everywhere. However, by eliding the subject of white men's prejudice in the workplace, he avoided a topic that would have been anathema to any Republican possessed of political ambitions—including himself; in 1872 he would be elected to the state legislature.[34]

In Boston, an unlikely white man offered historical context for Hayden's call for justice, at the same time issuing a stern reminder about what the nation owed to the South's Black workers. The Reverend Charles L. Woodworth was district secretary of the New England region for the American Missionary Association. During the war, the Connecticut-born Woodworth had served as chaplain to the 27th Massachusetts Volunteer Infantry Regiment stationed in Newbern, North Carolina. In late 1865, he was soliciting cash and clothing for the benefit of the freedpeople, whom he greatly admired for their intelligence, piety, and "conscience void of offense."[35]

Yet Woodworth was no sanctimonious missionary. He took a long view of American history and produced a powerful statement outlining the debt the nation had incurred to formerly enslaved men, women, and children. He titled his tract (or sermon) "The Full Enfranchisement of the Negro," signaling his support for what at the time was considered a radical position. Yet Woodworth went beyond the Republican Party's call for Black suffrage and legal rights generally. Instead, he focused on the institution of bondage as critical to the economic foundation of the nation. Of the southern freedman, he said that "the gains which we have made out of his unpaid labor, demand on our part an equal restitution. . . . More than any other man he has produced the raw material out of which the wealth of the country has been created." For over two hundred years this worker had not received any share of his rightful earnings. Woodworth elaborated, "His labor has furnished the seed from which have sprung the manufacturing villages of the country. From the cotton raised by his hand, thousands have spun their fortunes; while every class and every industry among us has felt the quickening impulse, and the whole land has smiled under an unexampled thrift and plenty." Nevertheless, the earnings of Black people remained in the hands of white men. Woodworth's plea was to "give him back that of which we have robbed him, that which he would have been but for our injustice, and he is no longer a slave, but a man and a citizen." Woodworth was blunt: "Capital has made sure returns. . . . Disguise it as we may, we have grown rich by robbing the poor, and mighty by tasking the energies of the weak." Added to this great injustice was the shameful treatment accorded Black soldiers, especially since their courage had helped win a Union victory. Now it would be unseemly for the North to congratulate itself for arming the man of color, because "neither party in the war meant any good to him."[36]

Edward Philbrick and other whites claimed Black men owed *them*—a debt of gratitude to the Union for freeing them and their families, a debt incurred for supplies purchased at the store and for land rented or sharecropped. In his own statement, Woodworth argued that, to the contrary, it was the nation that was in arrears—for centuries' worth of Black people's unpaid labor. Except for Charles Sumner and a handful of other Radical Republicans, few white men and women in Boston or elsewhere could comprehend this national balance sheet: it enumerated enormous amounts of Black people's credit extended to white America, with virtually none of it repaid.

Most northern whites, regardless of party, were satisfied that, by destroying slavery, the nation had fulfilled its obligations to Black people. Northern Republicans insisted that Black men must be able to vote and run for office, and that the freedpeople must be empowered to use their labor as leverage with southern white landowners. Annual sharecropping labor contracts would achieve equilibrium between whites' need for workers and Blacks' need for work. In envisioning a future where southern Black peasants would till their own soil, the Republicans remained true to their focus on small producers unencumbered by the heavy hand of the state—a vision that was becoming increasingly irrelevant in an era of large corporations and sprawling factories. And by focusing on Blacks' civil rights in the South, Republicans largely ignored the conditions endured by Black job-seekers in the North.

The year 1865 began with the white people of Boston extending the hand of friendship to the white people of Savannah, sending south tierces of sugar, half-chests of tea, drums of hake, and barrels of smoked shoulders, cornmeal, onions, and potatoes, among other supplies. Now, almost a year later, hundreds of Virginia refugees began to arrive in Boston. The city's white laboring classes had long expressed their dread of an incursion of southern Blacks; yet this mass migration of refugees prompted no protests or petitions in opposition. The demand for domestic servants seemed limitless.

PART III

1865–1875

12

Their Suffering Housekeepers

In the years immediately following the war, the federal government sent hundreds of freedpeople from Virginia and Washington, DC, to Boston. This massive relocation project was carried out by the US Bureau of Refugees, Freedmen, and Abandoned Lands—the Freedmen's Bureau—established by Congress in March 1865. Conceived as a way to address the human misery endemic to southern refugee settlements, a bureau transportation program sought to funnel Black servants into white households. Presumably these formerly enslaved people now scrounging for work in a town or in the countryside would find plenty of wage work (as domestics) once they disembarked on a Boston wharf.

The program consisted of two overlapping initiatives: one, out of Washington, overseen by General Charles H. Howard from 1866 to 1869 (his brother General Oliver O. Howard served as bureau head); the other, out of Fortress Monroe (and Norfolk, Richmond, Petersburg, and Hampton), coordinated by General Samuel C. Armstrong during the same years. Between May 1866 and December 1867, as a part of the latter effort, the bureau paid the tickets of 579 freedpeople bound for New England, mostly to

Massachusetts, and most of those to Boston. About three-quarters of the migrants were between twelve and twenty-five years old.[1]

During the war, the Virginia Peninsula proved a reluctant host to thousands of Black refugees streaming in from nearby areas as well as from other states. Many endured crowded, chaotic, life-threatening conditions in temporary, makeshift camps. Nevertheless, formerly enslaved people gradually created freed communities, drawing upon limited resources to organize churches, build schoolhouses, and search for long-lost loved ones. Poverty afflicted almost all: some families continued to live in the slave quarters and work the land of their former owners, now as renters, while others squatted on abandoned property only to be displaced by Union troops or civil authorities. Among the most pervasive forms of labor exploitation was wage theft—a white employer's refusal to pay a Black person's wage after an agreed-upon task was completed. In the words of Worcester's Sarah Chase, now working at a hospital in Richmond, "Not a few hard workers are growing thin and weak by trying to live on promises to pay," and even those who could find jobs such as coal-heaving were forced to subsist on "a dinner of half-baked corn bread and coffee." Women walked for miles to secure a half-day's washing. With the approval of local judges, white landowners "apprenticed" freed children, virtually enslaving them, running roughshod over the protests of parents. Bureau agents sent orphans to orphanages despite the offers of relatives to care for them. Whites sought to continue to profit off Black labor, but they had an aversion to Black political activity and schooling; their resentment triggered random physical attacks on individuals and the burning of Black schoolhouses and bureau offices.[2]

Local almshouses were overwhelmed by the crush of refugees; civil officials expressed contempt for the in-migrants, described as a "very large destitute colored population not legitimately belonging to us and we have no power under the law of removing them." Bureau rations and northern donations of shoes, clothing, and blankets were unequal to the need. In Washington, refugees took shelter in huts that afforded no protection from the elements and found themselves preyed upon by pawnbrokers offering easy loans. It was not surprising, then, that the bureau saw as one of its major functions the swift reduction of the local Black population. Officials focused on sending freedpeople not only to the North, the South, and the Midwest, but also to their former homes. Pressured to leave, many hesitated to go north. According to Charles Howard, families wanted to provide for themselves, but "the cold is a bugbear and the fact is that they are totally ignorant of that part of the Country and its people[,] making them prefer the hard lot here to the uncertainties and apprehended evils of going away."[3]

The bureau transportation program combined a hardheaded assessment of local demographic conditions with an idealistic fervor. General Armstrong possessed a strong moralistic streak. Born in Hawaii of Presbyterian-missionary parents, he believed that the program was essential to the reconstruction of the South and the well-being of the refugees—a boon to those who stayed behind as well as to those who left. In the summer of 1866 he encouraged local bureau agents to scour the countryside around Hampton and advertise the program widely, in order "to use every effort to induce those especially females to remove to Boston"; he was interested in finding "indigent or unemployed freedpeople, who are already, or are liable to become dependent upon the Bureau for support." He discouraged agents from rounding up the poor indiscriminately, however: each person granted transportation should be a "person of good character and honesty." No doubt some might apply "for the most improper purposes"—a reference, perhaps, to those who would take advantage of the bureau's goodwill and then prove to be malingerers, or worse, prostitutes. In sum, "As getting homes in the North is believed to be an excellent thing for the freedpeople, it is hoped that no effort will be spared to make this enterprise a success."[4]

In sending people north, bureau officials relied on a mix of requests for workers from individual northerners and standing orders from contacts, such as operators of "intelligence" (employment) offices. Civilian labor agents were crucial to this relocation effort, and rivalry among them was fierce; in the DC area, one Boston agent competed with twenty other people seeking a commission for each person they could get on a train or steamship. Most would-be employers requested a single domestic servant, general laborer, or farmhand; but in January 1867, the town of Glastonbury, Connecticut, wanted nearly a dozen woodchoppers. Some northerners could be specific about their needs, even presumptuously so, and apparently word spread widely throughout New England about the migrants. From the Piper & Haskins confectionery and fancy-goods store in Concord, New Hampshire, came this order: "We would like to have you Send us a Colored Cook as soon as possible. We want a good frugal woman, and honest, and of good disposition, one of good judgment, and quick to learn. We want a first class cook. . . . We would like to have you use all possible dispatch, our cook was taken suddenly sick so we are without one."[5]

Requests came into the bureau from a variety of prospective Boston and area employers—bank managers, lawyers, judges, physicians, mayors (of Lawrence and Chelsea), hotels, warehouses, furniture dealers, milliners' shops, merchants, and owners of dry-goods stores, among others. Fifteen-year-old William Smith went to Harvard professor Louis Agassiz, though it is uncertain whether Agassiz put him to work as a servant or forced him to participate in some kind of "scientific" experiment related to "race." A goodly number of the wealthy men and women requesting freedpeople already had live-in Irish servants working for them; some of these employers were looking for a cheaper alternative, some wanted to rid themselves of Catholics in their household, and others saw Black workers as objects of charity.

The four- or five-day journey north was fraught from beginning to end. Migrants usually traveled via regular schooner service, which ran on Tuesdays and Saturdays starting from Richmond or Norfolk with stops at Fortress Monroe. At times family members ended up going separately, when some in their party got lost on the way to the dock or a particular ship's passenger list was full. More than one person landed in Boston only to learn over the next days and weeks that close kin had had a change of mind and decided to stay in Virginia. In some cases, passengers stopped in New York City, a layover that caused its own problems. Once a ship anchored in that city's harbor, labor agents or other resourceful types tried to entice those bound for Boston to try their luck in New York (usually under false pretenses of gainful employment). Transfers on land came with their own challenges. In July 1867, E. P. Williams, a bureau representative in New York, enlisted the police to escort forty-six passengers from one boat to a different one that would take them on the final leg to Boston. The frightened men, women, and children endured taunts and insults as they made their way along the docks. Stopping in New York was a "beastly business," according to Williams, made even more "villainous" because any delay meant that the ship's captain would only grudgingly provide more rations than he had anticipated, although the bureau had to pick up the tab for the extra food.[6]

Armstrong expressed apprehension against "exposing young women to the approaches of any parties in New York or elsewhere along the route." He feared unscrupulous agents would take advantage of migrants, especially those traveling without close kin: "Every means that ingenuity and the prospect of profit could suggest would be employed." He was also aware of instances where crew members, as well as labor agents, used girls and women for "base purposes." Once in Boston, all bureau-sponsored travelers should be met at the dock by a certified agent, but he knew there was "an occasional escape." In some cases, relatives and former acquaintances swooped in and spirited away migrants promised to specific employers.[7]

The summer of 1867 was the high-water mark for migration to Boston. One day bureau agent James J. Gardner had trouble fetching the day's arrivals from Central Wharf. He knew from experience that passengers would "leave the boat etc off at the representation of any one, frequently, or by false inducement held out, or by making false statements themselves [the migrants] of having paid their fare, or received special direction." The boat had sailed into Boston Harbor at 4:30 a.m., much earlier than usual, and though Gardner rushed down to the dock and arrived, breathless, at 4:40, he was able to collect only seven of his fourteen charges. One woman had hurried away after telling Gardner that her husband was in Boston, and she had directions to the place where he was staying. Two others left the boat, and in the "mist of the morning had vanished away." And indeed, despite the bureau's plans, the best-laid placement efforts often went awry.[8]

ON THE MORNING of Wednesday, March 20, 1867, the house at 67 Joy Street was full of commotion. Wallpaper hangers, plasterers, whitewashers, and carpenters were making repairs, preparing what was to be called the Joy Street Freedmen's Asylum, a temporary home for Black migrants from the South that would become part of the Freedmen's Bureau transportation program. The home was apparently the brainchild of Ralph Haskins, a wealthy white real estate broker and auctioneer. Haskins was planning to pay rent on the place, no doubt anticipating a tidy profit accruing from the local demand for servants. (Employers would pay him a placement fee.) Gathering there that morning were at least some of the ten newcomers from Fortress Monroe who had landed at Central Wharf the day before. Curious neighbors showed up. The well-known chimney sweep Joseph Scarlett wanted to see how the repairs were going. A Mr. Bailey was hoping to find some of his Virginia kinfolk. However, conversation quickly turned to the newcomers' complaints about their breakfast that morning, and when and how it had materialized. In fact, within a few days this scandal would trigger an investigation initiated by bureau officials hundreds of miles away.[9]

When the migrants had arrived at the wharf, they had been met by a man who had advised them to seek out Maria Smith, the twenty-seven-year-old Black proprietor of an intelligence office on Beacon Hill. The captain had summarily ordered them off the vessel, saying he was responsible for neither feeding nor housing them once they reached Boston. Now in a strange city, with no kin or friends to greet them at the dock, the party had little choice but to find their way to Smith's.

Caught by surprise, Smith did not know what to do with the group once they appeared on her doorstep. The unplanned element of it all aggravated her. Together with her husband, H. L. Smith, she matched freedpeople from the DC–Tidewater Virginia area with employers in Boston. The Smiths' methods were unusually aggressive. H. L. worked out of Washington, where he handled the paperwork for people requesting or agreeing to transportation out of the area. His wife lived in Sears Place, an alley off Anderson Street in the West End; she received the travelers and then charged prospective employers a fee, at least part of which she was supposed to return to the Freedmen's Bureau. In this way the Smiths collected commissions at both the point of departure and (once the migrant was placed in a job) the point of arrival.

As for this group that had left from Fortress Monroe on March 15, Maria Smith later claimed that bureau officials always alerted her before sending anyone, but in this case she had not received the requisite notification. Nevertheless, here were five men in their twenties, two teenagers, and three women in their twenties—and someone had to put them up for the night. Smith could accommodate the women, but not the men and boys. Presumably, before too long the Joy Street asylum would be able to handle groups of this size while she looked for work for them; but right now, she was running an employment agency, not a home for migrants.

Without room at her own place, Smith dispatched her son to Eliza Casson's nearby boardinghouse at 18 Blossom Court. Casson, forty-seven, and, like Maria Smith, Black and Virginia-born, had resided in Boston for more than two decades. Smith had arranged for lodging for previous groups of freedpeople with Casson, paying 12½ cents a night for each person. Helping with the boardinghouse was Eliza's husband John Casson, also forty-seven, who worked alternately as a waiter, whitewasher, and general laborer. The seven men and teenagers could stay at the Casson place for one night.

Casson agreed to take in the weary travelers with the understanding that Maria Smith would reimburse her; but the following morning, Casson sent word that the men would not receive breakfast without assurance from Smith that she would pay for their food. This Smith refused to do; she had to worry about her own rent and business-related expenses, including advertisements in the local papers: "Mrs. H. L. Smith, agent of the Freedmen's Bureau . . . has constantly on hand help, both male and female." Casson reluctantly proceeded to feed her famished guests a meager meal.[10]

The arrival of the ten migrants in March 1867 brought long-standing tensions between the two businesswomen to the surface. Eliza Casson took a dim view of Maria Smith, who, Casson charged, routinely neglected those she placed. Casson told Howard that this past winter two men had come from Washington, and although Smith sent them out to work, she did not bother to attend to one of them when his feet got terribly frostbitten. (He probably lacked the sturdy footwear necessary for a job that involved working outside in freezing temperatures.) Casson was concerned about her own reputation: word could spread rapidly within the tight-knit Beacon Hill community, and she did not wish to be implicated in the less-than-hospitable reception of the recent arrivals. She asked several of the migrants, plus others who had heard the news, to write "certified statements" that she would submit to Howard; she intended that these statements would assign blame to Maria Smith for any negative reports he might receive.

Among those who wrote complaints was twelve-year-old Peter Thomas, one of the new migrants, who claimed that Smith would not "give him a mouth full of bread to eat" when he arrived at her home. Several neighbors also wrote, charging that the newcomers routinely taken in by Smith were forced to subsist on a pint of meal and one-half a herring per day; and that Smith treated Mr. Bailey badly when she implied that he had shown up that morning at the Joy Street home only because he was soliciting for prostitutes among the women. Erastus J. Jones, himself a recent arrival, was disillusioned with Boston in general and Smith in particular. Back in Virginia he had been told "we would have good time [in Boston]," but once he got to the city, "we found [those promises] Contrary all to gather."[11]

DESPITE PREPARATIONS TO ready the Joy Street residence as a waystation, it never served its intended purpose, and in fact by the end of May funding for it had evaporated. The asylum was a victim of clashing personalities, economic realities, and disapproval on the part of some white and Black Bostonians. Ralph Haskins appreciated the financial potential of the venture, but first he needed the bureau's financial backing. That support was never forthcoming.

Haskins did his best to convince bureau officials that he was an honest broker and that the home was worthy of support. He worried that Howard was unable "to appreciate the kind and extent of opposition [to the house] encountered here." Among those hostile to the enterprise were people "evidently jealous of the success of the Joy St. Asylum . . . industriously striving to make for it and for those interested in its welfare all the trouble in their power." In addition, Haskins wrote, he detected "a fear among our native colored people that the influx of freed people will have a tendency to reduce wages." And, too, "there are many (colored) Intelligence offices in Boston," all competing for the same job-seekers. Haskins believed that Mrs. Smith's office was the object of a particularly mean-spirited envy, "it alone being aided by the Freedmen's Bureau." He also felt defensive in responding to Howard's suggestion that placements should be managed by one of the charities in the city, and not by women and men (such as himself) trying to run a business. Haskins reminded Howard of the logistical difficulties that would prevent the Joy Street house from hosting migrants for any length of time; and, indeed, it was better that the officer send only women and girls, who could be placed relatively easily, rather than men and boys, who often languished for weeks after their arrival with no prospects for gainful employment in sight.[12]

The complaints of some of the migrants went beyond pangs of hunger. Around this same time, Charles Coffin Jewett, head of the Boston Public Library (from 1858 to 1868), wrote to Howard. Jewett was a proponent of the bureau's Boston efforts, and now he sought to exonerate Maria Smith of what he considered scurrilous charges. He acknowledged that not all the migrants sent north had found satisfactory jobs: in a recent case, on the day of their arrival, two men had "peremptorily" refused the places offered to them, "saying that they were promised employment on public works." Jewett made subsequent inquiries to the city's "master mechanics," but received only disappointing news: "They generally said that they were employing Irishmen, that they could not mix the two kinds of workmen without great danger of exciting quarrels, but that they hoped to change their whole workforce before too long." This latter point was perhaps a veiled reference to employers' constant but mostly unfulfilled threats to hire Black southerners permanently in the places of white workingmen, who were always clamoring for higher wages. As for Peter Thomas and other members of his party, they apparently wanted to stay together in the city rather than going to the countryside. In Boston, they believed the women could "take in washing" and the children could go to school. Jewett made it clear to Howard that the local demand was for Black women domestics and Black men farmworkers. Freedpeople contemplating removal to New England should expect nothing more.[13]

Meanwhile, Maria Smith was none too happy with some of the people sent to her. Not only did she have to contend with the complaints of neighbors, who worried about the effect of her placements on the already depressed job market for Black men, but the supposed bad manners of the newcomers left her exasperated. People she called "Rowdies and Loafers" hung around her office, refusing to show what she considered proper deference to prospective employers who came to look them over: "When the employers come into the office to see the people they will not get of[f] the Chairs and give them to the Ladies and Gentlemen without I ask them." These migrants seemed determined not to reenact the protocols of the southern slave market.[14]

Indeed, while Smith was complaining about the migrants, some Blacks and whites were comparing the whole Freedmen's Bureau transportation program to slavery. At times, labor agents separated husbands from wives, or children from parents, without securing the necessary consent. Agents packed men, women, and children onto steamer decks "like cattle," denying them beds and exposing them to the elements. Too often the most vulnerable migrants fell prey to con men and rival intelligence offices. Once in the north, the newcomers could find only menial work, regardless of their talents or ambitions. Finally, critics charged, agents simply oversaw the process by which Black men and women traded one unfeeling taskmaster for another. Even the language of the placement services evoked the slave market: one northern agent promoted the importation of Black women servants, "for which commodity he anticipated a brisk demand." Regardless of the aptness of the analogies to slavery, many of the migrants suffered from a trauma akin to that felt by fugitive slaves—in this case, they had endured the brutality of slavery, the physical deprivations and sense of dislocation of the refugee camps, and the risks and uncertainties of the journey to Boston.[15]

Octavia Grimes sought a bureau commission so that she could receive bureau-sponsored migrants, but officials soon broke with her (in July 1866), apparently because of her refusal to turn over the fees employers paid her ($5 per placement). She and Maria Smith had close ties to major Boston church congregations—Grimes, of course, with Twelfth Baptist, and Smith with the Reverend J. McKay's Revere Street Methodist Church. Congregants might be potential employers themselves or serve as valuable contacts for men and women seeking work. The Reverend Leonard Grimes received at least some migrants around the time the bureau was "relieving [Octavia] from care of freedpeople arriving in Boston." A notice placed in the *Boston Traveller* of June 26, 1866, announced that groups of "young colored Virginians" were arriving in the city, and that Rev. Grimes was "engineering the matter and hope[d] sooner or later to supply the demand." The notice added, "Among the girls were several of very light color." Octavia would persist in her work without the bureau's blessing.[16]

The bureau transportation project encountered obstacles from several quarters. Despite the humanitarian impulses behind the placement services, some Boston workers and their families feared that an influx of Black southerners would inevitably cheapen all Black labor in the city, in the process straining the charitable resources of an already impoverished community. Neither Boston nor Cambridge felt any obligation to assist freedpeople who lacked a livelihood, whether able-bodied or disabled, young or old, man or woman. Commonwealth authorities decided that Bay State taxpayers need not foot the bill for services provided to people who could choose to stay in the South. And so whatever assistance the migrants might receive in Boston must come from private efforts, leavened with bureau money if possible.

Unmentioned by Haskins in his letter to Howard was the name of the person most determined to see the Smiths' enterprise fail—the formidable Anna Lowell, a white woman who ran a rival operation across the river in Cambridgeport on Walnut Street. She called it the Howard Industrial School (HIS). Lowell was convinced that Maria Smith routinely waylaid migrants, "intercepting" them at the Boston docks, regardless of other plans made for them. Lowell leveled the most damning charge she could think of against the Smiths—that their underhandedness stemmed from "their desire to make money."[17]

Unlike the Black agents, who saw the bureau-sponsored transportation and placement program as a source of livelihood, Anna Lowell did not aim to make money from the venture. She hoped to do well by the migrants and also to fill the demand for domestic servants with pliant women and girls. Yet her missionary impulses ill prepared her for the task at hand. Lowell's critics claimed that she unceremoniously forced women out of the Walnut Street residence if they did not find work soon enough, that she routinely separated mothers from children, and that she failed to adequately screen potential employers. She freely admitted that the house could not board large numbers of people, and that the teachers there did not offer much in the way of instruction in the domestic arts. In fact, her "school" was more like a waystation for migrants. The only acceptable long-term residents were the children of live-in domestic servants whose employers refused to allow babies and toddlers to remain with their mothers.

Many Black women migrants to Boston relied on the Howard Industrial School for their start as wage earners. Lowell's "school" found favor with both Armstrong and Howard and derived its name from the substantial aid that Howard provided for two years, beginning in late 1866. The driving force behind the school and its mission, Lowell lived a life that offered a stark contrast to the future she envisioned for the objects of her benevolence. She had been born in 1833 to an illustrious Boston family—her uncle James Russell Lowell was a famous poet, and her older brother Charles Russell Lowell III, a general in the Union Army, had died from battle wounds in 1864. Anna had volunteered as an army nurse, first on a hospital ship in the James River and then at the downtown Washington, DC, Army Square Hospital from November 1862 to August 1865.[18]

Lowell had grown up in a rarified world of literature and high-minded ideals, her family and extended kin well known for their commitment to abolitionism. Her mother, Anna Cabot Jackson Lowell (1819–1874), had published several books before the war, including poetry and volumes on pedagogy, astronomy, and rules of grammar. *Thoughts on the Education of Girls* (1853) posited a young woman's special "world to work in" but also her need for a rigorous curriculum: "Let her mental discipline, also be sharp and well directed; let each stroke tell; let no moment be wasted . . . that her elasticity may not be impaired, nor the rest of her nature neglected." This paean to women's intelligence and imagination played no role in the project developed by her daughter for Black migrants from the South.[19]

Anna the younger eschewed the life of a cloistered bookworm. During the war, she had worked at the Armory Square Hospital to help care for the hundreds of severely wounded soldiers streaming in, men who went under the surgeon's knife without even a glass of brandy to dull the pain. She was not reluctant to criticize those physicians and administrators above her who seemed to be caught up in their own "miserable jealousies" to the detriment of the patients' welfare. Drawing on her family's connections, in 1863 she had the temerity to write to Senator Charles Sumner to complain about squabbling superiors and the lack of supplies. At the end, she acknowledged, "I have expressed myself rather thoroughly."[20]

Lowell's Howard Industrial School was riddled with ironies. She herself appreciated the novelty of a woman of her station descending to the level of intelligence-office manager, a position associated with slightly shady men and women. Lowell had founded the HIS just as white native-born women were leaving domestic service in droves. Prominent authors were denigrating paid housework as a particularly exploitative, retrograde form of employment. Moreover, despite the elevated rhetoric surrounding the project, the day-to-day business of running the home left Lowell impatient and exasperated. The intense demand for domestics did not necessarily guarantee a smooth transition for young women moving from a Virginia refugee camp to a Boston parlor. Lowell's charity was premised on labor contracts between two parties vastly unequal in power and material resources. And, too, she eventually ran up against the bleak reality of Massachusetts politics and the reluctance of state authorities to provide the aid she needed once bureau funding ran out. In the end, the HIS lasted only a little over two years, despite Lowell's hope that one day it would become permanent and self-supporting.

A simple ad placed in a Boston newspaper spoke to the degradation of domestic service in the postbellum era: the employer wanted a Black cook "of obliging disposition, and willing to do a part of the washing" for a family. Servants hired to do a specific job—as a cook, a parlor maid, a laundress, or a governess to the children—could now expect as part of their duties to wash windows, scrub floors, beat carpets, and carry firewood into the house. Native-born white women voted against the job with their feet, favoring places as machine operatives or department store clerks—jobs with set hours and a set pay scale—rather than household "help." In the words of a popular song, a domestic was "the general slave around the corner," with little money or time to call her own. Making the job even more repulsive was its association with dirt—not just the removal of it from surfaces, but also the soiled hands, faces, and garments of those who scrubbed all day.[21]

A postwar chorus of white female voices denigrating domestic service (as opposed to the housework that married women performed for free) only served to heighten the fact that Black employees were outliers in the emerging modern world of work. Postbellum writers and labor-reform activists offered biting critiques of the job, stressing the dignity of work and the rights of the individual. Jennie Collins, a white woman, began her work life in a Lawrence textile mill when she was fourteen. In 1850 she moved to Boston and took a job as a domestic servant. By the postwar period she was actively organizing Massachusetts white women wage workers. In 1871 she wrote *Nature's Aristocracy: Or, Battles and Wounds in Times of Peace*. Part memoir, part investigative journalism, part political theory, the book reserved special scorn for the mistresses of Boston's households. Often active in ministering to the poor, these penny-pinching women drove their servants mercilessly, according to Collins. She relayed anecdotes, probably based on composites of stories she had heard or knew firsthand, including one about a woman who fired her laundress and then forced her domestic to wash, iron, and stack piles of linen in addition to the regular housework. According to Collins, this employer's husband thought nothing of donating thousands of dollars to a local charity while his wife refused to pay her servant $2 a week. In Collins's view, the typical mistress was "not only ignorant of household duties, but unrefined in all her ways and tastes . . . arrogant and disagreeable, quick-tempered and vain." Within the tidy Victorian cottage and elegant townhouse raged everyday class warfare.[22]

In 1875 the popular writer Louisa May Alcott (of *Little Women* fame) wrote a novel, aptly titled *Work*, that explored the options available to white native-born women at the time. Alcott's orphan-heroine, Christie Devon, takes a picaresque journey through New England, trying her hand at different kinds of employment. She works briefly as a domestic, but chafes under the imperious management of a woman who "took no more personal interest in her servants than if they were clocks, to be wound up once a day, and sent away the moment they got out of repair." Christie has her standards: "I like to work for people whom I can respect." She eventually finds emotional fulfillment and modest material success as a Jennie Collins–like speaker for women's labor reform and a cultivator of flowers and fruit, living in a commune with like-minded people. According to Alcott, New England was full of Christies, women "willing to work, yet unable to bear the contact with coarser natures which makes labor seem degrading, or to endure the hard struggle for the bare necessities of life when life has lost all that makes it beautiful."[23]

HOWARD SCHOOL GREW out of the Soldiers' Memorial Society, a group founded in 1865 by white men of Boston who had served in the Union Army and white women who had worked on behalf of its soldiers. Now these well-to-do Bostonians joined together and turned their attention to the postwar South, distributing clothing and sponsoring teachers in Virginia, the Carolinas, and Florida. By late 1866 the society was lending rhetorical if not financial support to the Howard Industrial School, a new institution founded by one of its own members, Anna Lowell: "This undertaking," the society declared at its third annual meeting, "[is] a most valuable instrumentality in the adjustment of the disturbed condition of affairs [in the South]." The school won the approval of other local reformers as well. In October 1866, in an annual report, the Industrial Aid Society for the Prevention of Pauperism anticipated the founding of the HIS by a couple of months, stating, "Our female domestics are becoming absorbed by the various manufacturing establishments; and there is not sufficient emigration to Massachusetts to supply their places. We want well-trained servants, as a domestic comfort and necessity;

and we think that colored women from the South would supply this want."[24]

To justify the HIS, promoters invoked the imperatives of supply and demand. Directors of the Soldiers' Memorial Society opined, "While there is great want of labor here, particularly of domestic servants, there is an overplus of such labor at the South. It is as certain, as that water runs downhill, that the overplus will come into the vacant place, where it is needed." This situation called for equilibrium: "If the supply of servants could be made more nearly equal to the demand than at present, many and the worst of the evils to which our housekeepers are now subject would be obviated." Those "evils" no doubt included a diminishing number of fickle immigrant women servants. One journalist described households where they worked as "tyrannized over by domestic despots from over the seas."[25]

In appealing to support from the public, Lowell presented her project as an opportunity for those who could not go south but still wished to minister to freedwomen and at the same time address the needs of "our [Boston's] suffering housekeepers." In calling for missionaries to venture south, groups such as the American Missionary Association had declared that the "greatest obstacle in the way of reform among the freedmen is the low standard of morality among the women." The remedy? "This is an obstacle which can only be removed by the personal influence of the pure Christian women." Presumably white women might exert such "personal influence" in their own kitchens just as well as in the South.[26]

The *Boston Daily Advertiser* announced the opening of Lowell's school by asking its readers a familiar question: "*Are the freed people able and willing to be self-supporting?*" Lowell conceived her project as a transformative one that would produce "valuable and trusty servants" out of former field hands. It would simultaneously rescue Black women from sexual abuse in households lorded over by men of low morals and meet a desperate need for "help" in the kitchens of Boston. Respecting Black family ties was not in keeping with the mission: Here was Jane Jones, twenty-three, employed by Mrs. R. W. Lawson in Cambridge, and her daughter Susan, two, adopted by a white woman in Cambridgeport. Here were several little children staying in the HIS while their mothers lived and worked elsewhere. For Lowell, such separations were an unfortunate but necessary byproduct of the labor market for live-in domestics.[27]

The HIS depended on the substantial aid that Howard provided beginning in late 1866—rent for the building, the salary of a matron, and transportation for the freedpeople. From November 1, 1866, to August 1, 1867, the school received 3 men, 174 women, 47 girls ten years and older, 32 boys ten years and older, and 100 girls and boys under ten. Almost all came from Virginia. Lowell preferred orphan girls and able-bodied young women unencumbered by husbands, sons, infants, or indeed relatives of any kind. The freedwoman Virginia Nelson gave her "free will and consent" to let her eleven-year-old daughter Lillie go from Alexandria to Cambridgeport, "to enter the Industrial School of Miss Lowell at that place." Nelson eventually took her son John and followed her daughter to Boston. (Back home, the mother had lodged a "complaint of abuse" with the Freedmen's Bureau, accusing her husband, George, of "improper intimacy with other women.") While Lowell welcomed these children, she remained adamant that her efforts had no use for boys, men, and others impossible or difficult to place. When she found out that a recent party included infants and disabled people, she begged Armstrong to send "some of the good ones as a 'reward'" for her willingness to receive the unemployable.[28]

Lowell oversaw the daily management of the home with the help of her mother and several matrons, teachers, and Sunday school instructors who rotated in and out; supporters of the HIS lauded them as "well known for their judicious and self-sacrificing benevolence." Lowell appreciated the assistance of a woman whom she called "Auntie Tyrell," probably Lucy Tirell, herself a recent migrant from Virginia along with her husband, who was a laborer, and their children. Yet, to her annoyance, Lowell soon realized that she could control neither the movements nor the prospects of those who passed through the HIS. Dissatisfied employers returned women to the home, and youngsters at times ran away from it. Virginia Nelson, who had sent her daughter Lillie north in 1867, a year later placed an ad in the *Herald* seeking information about her son John, age ten, who had been admitted to the school the previous March but soon afterward went missing: "He wore a grey suit, no hat, was about 5 feet in height and very straight. Any information of his whereabouts left with his mother at the School in Cambridgeport will be thankfully received. Virginia Nelson."[29]

William H. Cheeseman presented Lowell with a challenge of a different order. The fifteen-year-old arrived from Hampton in May 1867 and remained at the HIS for nearly two months. Lowell disapproved of his comportment with the other residents, commenting, "It is always an evil to have girls and boys together." In June he found work with a physician, a Dr. Cullis, and his wife, Lucretia. Lowell was relieved, as it was difficult to find jobs "for such lads." However, William soon disappointed his employers by lying to them, and they sent him back to the HIS. Lowell convinced the Cullises to give William another chance, which they did; but then he stole some money from them. Confirming Lowell's appraisal of him as "cunning," William bought a watch with the money he stole and sent it to himself through the mail, claiming it was a gift from his brother in Chicago.[30]

In December, Lucretia Cullis was appalled when William asked her and her husband for a character reference; she recommended that he be sent to a reformatory, as it was "unsafe to have such a boy at large." It was around this time that William wrote to bureau headquarters in Washington, DC, pleading with officials not to send any more people to the HIS, "as they are thrown out in the street. Miss and Mrs. Lowell are the ones responsible." Though a bit shaky, his penmanship and spelling were decent, and Armstrong took the charge seriously enough to ask for a response from Lowell. Now quite aggravated, she confronted William and demanded to know if he was not grateful for all she had done for him; and then, she told Howard, "he began to cry." His subsequent fate is unknown.[31]

Lowell grappled with other unanticipated difficulties: Who would pay for medical care if any of the women became ill and could not work? If their children became ill? Who would support those who secured only seasonal work, leaving them jobless for part of the year? What responsibility did Lowell and her matrons have to help track down a woman who "ran away from the first place she went to"? Or the ten-year-old boy who absconded from the HIS and then returned, only to be fired from "a good place"? Or to those whom, like William Cheeseman, Lowell judged to be lazy, incorrigible, or of "poor character"?[32]

Nevertheless, in September 1867, Lowell sent Howard a report on the school declaring that "the experiment has been a most successful one." She had seen rapid gains in the demeanor of the migrants who were gainfully employed: "Many of them who came up last winter would not be recognized. Now they have improved so much in every way, and even in a short time, their expression becomes brighter and more intellectual. Instead of living in poverty and dependence, they are all supporting themselves by honest labor, and their children will be even more benefited than they." Still, there were storm clouds on the horizon: the school would not be able to survive without additional substantial bureau funding. At times the building housed forty to sixty persons, though it "[could] hardly hold 30 comfortably." The residents lacked a suitable place for bathing and washing their clothes.[33]

The financial underpinnings of Lowell's effort were problematic. The HIS charged employers $1 to $3 to help defray the costs of boarding as many as dozens of people at a time. (Employers were warned not to take the fee out of a servant's wages.) For a "capable, able-bodied woman," the charge was $3, though boys and girls were placed free of charge. The venture was supposed to be a charity, not a business, and the hope was that "those who take these people into their service and are patient with the faults which slavery has encouraged in them, will not have reason to repeat their kindness." Still, the accumulated fees were not sufficient to sustain the project. In late November 1867, the school sponsored an evening fund-raiser, "A Musical and Literary Entertainment" at Cambridge City Hall, featuring songs, dramatic readings, and instrumental music.[34]

The November soiree—and also the "private theatrics" at Lyceum Hall in December—were necessary because, in April, the Massachusetts Legislature had denied the HIS the ability to incorporate, and thus become eligible for public funding. The vote was 18–13. Speaking against the bill was Senator Joseph Tucker of Berkshire County. No doubt voicing the concerns of many of his white colleagues and constituents, he said, according to the *Boston Post*, that "he could see no good reason why Massachusetts should expend money to provide schools for negroes who are to be imported hither, when our school houses are already too few and too scarce to accommodate our own children." If the supporters of their legislation had their way, the commonwealth would just as likely have "to provide for the education of poor whites in Tennessee, and the destitute all over the world, as for those who are supposed to be specially provided for in this bill." Nevertheless, at this point Lowell was just hoping to construct a wash house on the premises, not establish a conventional school.[35]

In January 1868, the HIS sent out an appeal for donations to clergy all over New England. By this time the school was branding itself as a home for "the children of freedwomen who come to the North in search of employment"—in other words, primarily a residential child-care facility and "depot," or "temporary resting place," for their mothers. Lowell acknowledged that the original plan—to provide instruction in sewing and cooking as well as reading and writing—was impractical and unpopular with the migrants, who preferred to find work immediately rather than learn skills and earn more later. In looking for enough money to buy the building, Lowell suggested that such a donation was "a safe investment" for "some benevolent person."[36]

DESPITE THE HOME's difficulties, Virginia migrants found live-in service positions in neighborhoods all over Boston. In her detailed report of August 1867, Lowell noted that 231 migrants had been placed in families, and that 76 "have taken care of themselves." Of this latter group, many had connected with kinfolk already in the city, either fugitives from slavery who had arrived before the war or recent migrants. Such familial support was often crucial, but it was not always enough to get and keep the newcomers on their feet.[37]

On October 9, 1869, the Home for Aged Colored Women admitted one of the bureau-sponsored migrants, a Mrs. Henderson, who gave her age as sixty-two. The directors encapsulated her recent history this way: "born & bred a slave in Va., sitting with the crowds of fugitives through the Union lines, stationed for a time at Hampton; but driven from there by return of the property to rebel owners, she came North to find employment." In Boston, Mrs. Henderson worked "far beyond her strength," presenting "a very pathetic case of destitution, helplessness, friendlessness." Her daughter, who had come with her or already resided in Boston, was working; but unable to care for her mother, she promised to provide $1 each week from her own wages to help support her. Admitted to the home, Mrs. Henderson felt "joy . . . unbounded to find herself 'after grubbing life-long' [in her words], welcomed to such peace & comfort." Yet within a few days of her arrival she suffered "a grave disease of the chest," and died in Massachusetts General Hospital. How many other migrants were "wandering about homeless and hopeless" like Mrs. Henderson is unknown, but certainly not all could count on a reliable support system once they arrived in Boston.[38]

By the late fall of 1868, the HIS was on the verge of collapse. That year, Anna Lowell married Dr. Henry E. Woodbury, a prominent Washington physician, and her commitment to the effort was waning. The task of keeping the home going fell to one of the matrons, A. E. Buttrick. Buttrick wrote increasingly frantic letters to Howard, claiming that if they could not raise $2,000 from donors by January, the building would have to close. A bureau appropriation of $5,000 would sustain it through the following year. Meanwhile, recent events confirmed that the school's original plan was untenable, owing to the unpredictable health and personal proclivities of the migrants. Buttrick had sent a Mrs. Reback, who was suffering from tuberculosis, to the local Consumptives' Home, prompting the ill woman to accuse Buttrick "of turning her out of doors and many other very ungrateful remarks." A Mrs. Tolliver, also failing in health, was "irritable and unreasonable." Buttrick hoped that Howard would pay for her trip back to see her son in Washington before she died. The matron suggested that instead of trying to maintain the home, the bureau might pay for the rent of several small rooms that would shelter "the orphans and stray girls." Winding down its own operations in 1869, the bureau never followed up on this idea, and by the summer of 1869 the HIS had closed its doors.[39]

Anna Lowell began her placement project at a time when no northern public entity took responsibility for the welfare of formerly enslaved men, women, and children. In the South, the Freedmen's Bureau represented a historic, initial foray of the federal government into the realm of social welfare; but in its brief existence it could not begin to address the basic needs—let alone the long-term prospects—of millions of freedpeople. Viewed within this context, the HIS stands out as the project of a white woman of goodwill, a project dependent on private largesse and ultimately inadequate to the task at hand. Nevertheless, the southern refugees who eventually made their home in Boston entered a vibrant community with deep Virginia roots.

THE STORY OF Aaron and Roberta West illustrates variations on the themes of luck, pluck, and patronage affecting the fortunes of some freed families. Aaron was born a slave in Stafford County, Virginia, in 1835. In 1862 he and his wife, Roberta, eight years his junior, had a daughter, Rebecca; another daughter, Georgiana, followed within a year or so. In late 1863, West joined the 1st US Colored Volunteer Cavalry Regiment in Norfolk; he listed his occupation as "servant," and perhaps had had some experience with horses. Like Joseph Elisha, though, he would never mount a horse during his time in the army. For much of his first year he was stationed in Virginia, first at Camp Hamilton and then at Wilson's Landing. In the spring of 1864 he served as a teamster in the quartermaster's department. His regiment met up with the 5th Massachusetts Cavalry during operations around Petersburg and Richmond in May, and a year later, the men of the 1st Colored Cavalry sailed from City Point, Virginia, to the Rio Grande Valley of southern Texas. In February 1866, West was mustered out in Brazos Santiago, a port on Brazos Island in the Gulf of Mexico.[40]

West returned to Virginia and, together with four other men, rented land from a former slave owner near Elizabeth City. Before too long, though, he had made his way to Massachusetts, alone. He likely relied on contacts he had made with men from that state, either Black soldiers or white officers, during his stint in the army. He settled in Lexington, west of Boston, apparently with the aid of a white man, Abner Stone. The Stone family was well-to-do, and Abner's wife, Ellen, had been active in abolitionist and women's rights circles in Lexington before the war. Aaron West was anxious to have his wife and daughters join him, inquiring of Armstrong about their well-being and sending the general the fare for their journey. On July 1, 1867, Armstrong wrote to West, assuring him that his family would be sailing for Boston that day. If West could not meet them immediately upon their arrival in five or six days, he could find them at the HIS—"Miss Lowell, who goes with this party from here having kindly agreed to take charge of her [and the children] for a day or two."[41]

West was due $70.65 from the army—a bounty and pay—and for a while bureau officials could not locate him. One day his mother appeared at one of the offices to report that her son was ill and that she would accept the money on his behalf. Hearing of this, on November 27, 1867, West wrote from Massachusetts, pointing out that his health was excellent, and that the money should be sent directly to him and not to his mother.[42]

In 1870 the West family was living in Arlington, near the Lexington line. Aaron was working as a laborer, Roberta was "keeping house," and Rebecca and Georgiana were attending school. Two younger children, three-year-old Hattie and one-month-old Roberta, had been born in Massachusetts. The Wests were living with two other couples from Virginia, the men both laborers. Over the next few years the Wests would move around within a circumscribed area—Boston, Somerville, Lexington, Arlington—and Aaron would eventually become a clothing dealer.

Aaron West's journey of four years took him from enslavement in Virginia, to service as a US soldier in Virginia and Texas, then back to his home state and, as a migrant, on to Massachusetts, where his young family would be reunited. Helping him to establish a new life in Lexington were funds he earned as a soldier along with the aid of his patrons, Abner and Ellen Stone. West kept his family intact, and, by staying for the most part on the periphery of Boston, he avoided the city's high rents and the intense competition among Black men for menial jobs.

Not all southern migrants came north on transportation provided by the Freedmen's Bureau, and not all who moved to Massachusetts settled in Boston. Migrants who found themselves in rural areas, or who traveled north singly, suffered from a social isolation that compounded the difficulties of performing heavy manual labor in the fields or the workshop. In the summer of 1865, a concerned resident of Bristol County wrote to a newspaper, the *Boston Express*, to expose the ill treatment his neighbor had wrought upon a Black man, a native of North Carolina. The author contended that the Bay State, "the pilgrim settlement, furnishes a sample of brutality scarcely equalled in our land or indeed any country reclaimed from barbarism." In the summer of 1863, an enslaved man named John S. Anthony Jr. had run away from his owner in New Bern, North Carolina, probably soon after the arrival of the 55th Massachusetts there. Anthony found his way to Fortress Monroe, where, likely in his capacity as a laborer, he met Brigadier General Ebenezer Weaver Peirce, an officer in the Massachusetts militia and a resident of Freetown, Bristol County. In the fall of 1863, Peirce promised the twenty-two-year-old that if he would come north to work, he would pay him $12 a month. According to the neighbor, once on Peirce's farm, the freedman "did a considerable part of raking and pitching of hay and the baling both in garden and field, cut the wood in the forest for home consumption and some for sale, did the chores, attended on a horse, cow, bull, hogs, and in addition thereto was required to wash the wearing apparel for the family [Peirce and his wife and son], and sometimes the dishes, and there is abundant evidence to prove that he did all this faithfully."[43]

Anthony toiled for two years, earning $258 but receiving only $72, most of which he had to spend on clothing for himself. His food was meager and of poor quality. Forced to sleep in the cellar during the winter, he requested that he be allowed to move to the potato crib, which furnished more warmth. He was the only Black man in the area. At the same time, Peirce was prospering as a real estate speculator, and gaining some renown as a historian and genealogist. John Anthony eventually returned to North Carolina, and in 1882 he married a Black woman named Brenda Louise

Bynum and began life anew. Anthony's ordeal on the Peirce farm was not unusual in terms of the loneliness, the estrangement from his employers, the broken promise of compensation, the physical deprivation, and the heavy work demands. For all its hardships, the city would always afford a more varied and vital existence.[44]

THE GRIMESES' AND Smiths' intelligence offices outlasted both the Freedmen's Bureau and the Howard Industrial School. In 1870, Maria (Mrs. H. L.) Smith could afford to take out an ad in the Boston city directory identifying her home-based business as "U.S. Freedmen's Employment Office, 3 Garden St."—"Best of help furnished at short notice" (this even though the bureau had ceased operations in 1869). Octavia Grimes was living in Somerville but working with Elizabeth (Mrs. Joseph) Jamieson, a dressmaker, on Anderson Street, with an office at 43 Phillips (formerly Southac) Street. They called their business "Grimes & Jamieson." With their deep connections to the Black community, Maria Smith and Octavia Grimes had advantages compared to Anna Lowell, even though the white woman came from a prominent family and forged mutually respectful connections with bureau officials in DC and Virginia.[45]

The bureau-sponsored transportation program responded to the needs of Boston's "suffering" white women employers, but in the process cast into sharp relief the suffering of Black southerners, both as refugees and as workers new to Boston. It is unknown how many of the migrants regretted leaving the home of their forebears, despite all its hardships, and how many gladly embraced a new life in the Bay State, with its schools for their children, rich associational life, and famous, outspoken activists. Still, as some Blacks traveled north to Boston, others went south to partake of the great work of Reconstruction.

13

Boston Diaspora II

In the years immediately after the war, the gracious parks and busy streets of both Savannah and Richmond witnessed a remarkable confluence of Bostonians. Their motives for going and their tribulations while staying were as varied as their backgrounds—formerly enslaved men and women hoping to provide immediate material assistance and literacy instruction to the freedpeople, children and adults alike; clergymen and missionaries aiming to bring the gospel to the unconverted or to the misguided members of another denomination; doctors and lawyers with professional credentials expecting to find expanded possibilities for their talents; and, overlapping all these categories, men and women harboring strong personal ambitious, political or otherwise. Despite the wide differences in their means and ends, virtually all had to raise money, not only to fund their initiatives but also to pay themselves a salary. Some Black sojourners saw in the disordered South a place to make a living permanently—this in contrast to Boston, where stable employment eluded many of even the most highly educated and determined. For most, however, neither the impoverished freedpeople nor the federal government, neither the former rebels nor the sponsoring missionary agencies, could offer them a viable livelihood. Even idealists needed to pay the rent.

In December 1865, the firebrand lawyer Aaron A. Bradley left Boston and returned to Georgia, where he had been born a slave. His turbulent tenure there would become the stuff of nightmares come to life for embittered whites. Within a few days of his arrival in Savannah, Bradley spoke at a mass meeting at Second African Baptist Church. The fifty-year-old attorney took the pulpit after a pastor, the venerable Reverend Garrison Frazier, told members of the audience that they must accommodate themselves to postbellum realities. Frazier's injunction "You must not steal!" offended Bradley, who reminded his listeners that the fruits of the fertile Lowcountry Rice Kingdom were the products of their own backbreaking labor; therefore, they should seize the region's plantations and harvested crops by any means necessary. US military authorities—and virtually every other white person within hearing distance—decried Bradley's "insurrectionary" remarks. According to a reporter, he had exhorted Blacks "not to make working contracts, but to retain the lands unless removed at the point of a bayonet, notwithstanding the lands had been restored [on the order of President Andrew Johnson] to their former owners." It was most fitting, in the view of this reporter, that Bradley's Georgia homecoming included his prompt arrest for "sedition."[1]

Tried and convicted in a military court, Bradley narrowly escaped a one-year sentence in nearby Fort Pulaski. He hastened back to Boston, where, in September 1866, he appeared at Tremont Temple, raising money for a new "Colored High School" he wanted to start in Savannah. (In fact, the school never materialized: Bradley was a *provocateur*, not an aspiring teacher.) Within a few months he was once again in Georgia and making news, this time by casting himself as a leader of rice workers in South Carolina who were staging a militant revolt against white landowners. According to reports, Bradley urged these men and women "to resist at the point of a bayonet" any attempt to evict them from the land. Over the next few years, the Derringer-pistol-packing, Bowie-knife-toting Bradley managed to bring together groups of varying political loyalties in shared outrage, including Freedmen's Bureau officials, US military officers, local Black leaders, northern missionaries and teachers, and civil authorities. He relished public spectacles of his own making, in one breath quoting the Constitution and in the next counseling armed resistance against white planters. Not long after issuing a written screed against "all bad men in the city of Savannah"—in his view, an eclectic lot of northerners and southerners, Blacks and whites, Republicans and Democrats—he was once more in Boston, appealing for contributions. Derided by whites of various stripes as the "Great Wahoo," an "incubus" of torture, and a "narrow-minded colored pettifogger," Bradley nevertheless offered Bostonians a disingenuous message predicting, "at an early day, the best of feelings on the part of the [white] inhabitants of that Commonwealth [Georgia] in favor of the Union."[2]

The Boston press maintained an enduring fascination with Bradley as he moved back and forth between that city and Savannah, money on his mind. His uplifting speeches in Boston offered a sharp contrast to his angry rhetoric and actions in Savannah; yet he understood that the most effective way to get northerners to donate was to predict a chastened rebeldom. Lacking any other source of income, the "Boston negro," as he was sometimes called, intended to monetize his adventures in the South by seeking out audiences in New York as well as Boston. Troublemaking as a source of livelihood faltered at times, though. Wading into the middle of another rice workers' uprising in January 1866, he offered to send a petition on their behalf to Washington, DC, a document that he (wrongly) claimed would help win back their land. He proposed to charge each signatory one dollar, with the fee to go toward postage. One elderly woman said she would not sign, noting that she could send a petition to Washington herself for a mere 3 cents (i.e., the price of a stamp). Bradley's plan to raise money from impoverished rice hands fell far short of his objectives.[3]

In contrast to Bradley, Harriet and Louisa Jacobs remained committed to schooling for the freedpeople. Fund-raising for the Jacobs school in Alexandria was going well, as Harriet received and then resold articles left over from northern Freedmen's Aid Society fairs. Higher-ups had finally dismissed the odious Albert Gladwin, considered by Jacobs to be heartless toward the freedpeople in the extreme. After Samuel May Jr. visited the school, he showered it with praise in a report he sent to supporters. Harriet arranged for a photo of the school building, with one hundred pupils, along with their teachers, posing outside; it was distributed as part of a fund-raising campaign to northern churches and benevolent societies. Louisa had always wanted to be a teacher, and she delighted in her pupils: "Slavery has not crushed out the animal spirits of these children," she wrote. "Fun lurks in the corners of their eyes, dimples their mouths, tingles at their fingers' ends, and is, like a torpedo, ready to explode at the slightest touch." Despite the pleasure she took in their eagerness, teaching seventy-five abecedarians every day left her exhausted. In 1865 she achieved a respite of sorts when she took over the school's Industrial Department, offering instruction in cooking and sewing.[4]

Nevertheless, by May 1865, mother and daughter decided that they would seek a new field of labor, though the way forward remained unclear. The struggle against prejudice seemed endless, the needs of the former slaves infinite. Returning from a brief sojourn in Richmond and boarding a boat, Harriet found herself confronted by a guard who turned her away, saying, "No niggers allowed in the cabin." The light-skinned Louisa marched on straightaway, but to gain access Harriet had to claim to be the nurse of a white woman companion—a sign that the war, in some form, at least, was far from over.[5]

The Jacobses arrived in Savannah in November 1865, just a month before Aaron Bradley, and promptly secured a place for a schoolroom. Harriet probably considered Savannah a most promising place to open a school because of the Savannah Education Association (SEA), organized by Black residents soon after Sherman liberated the city in late 1864. James Simms, a leader of the new group, might have been the conduit through which she learned of the association and its goal of providing a common-school education for all Black children. While in Savannah, Harriet remained a keen observer of Lowcountry political and labor relations. She described a scene in the city where "crowds of [refugees] huddled around a few burning sticks, so ragged and filthy they scarce look like human beings." She decried whites' determination to keep Blacks from owning the land they had tilled as enslaved workers, and from keeping pigs and chickens, tending gardens, and owning muskets and boats. She sang the praises of Simms, who was now cobbling together a living as a teacher, preacher, politician, and agent of both the Freedmen's Bureau and the American Home Baptist Missionary Society. Simms had assisted William Wells Brown in writing a new edition of *The Black Man*, published in 1865 with a Savannah imprint (but produced in Boston). Harriet and Louisa set about teaching, but the mother hoped to become a matron in a home for elderly Blacks, and the daughter hoped for the same position in an orphan asylum, though neither institution yet existed. Louisa summed up the situation in Georgia by noting, of the former slaves, "The chains have fallen off from them, but justice has not yet found an echo in the hearts of their old oppressors."[6]

Other Black teachers from Boston followed. The Virginia-born Hezekiah Brown had grown up in Pennsylvania, but before the war he worked as a barber in Boston and lived in a boardinghouse with John Oliver. After studying theology at Lincoln University, from 1865 to 1867, Brown went south, because, he wrote, "we are an oppressed and despised race, as well as poor and in need, . . . My heart is in the work, and my head, and my hands." He taught for the American Missionary Association (AMA) and started his own "Brown School," which offered a classical education and included subjects such as orthography, grammar, and geography, reflecting his own college education.[7]

Before long, Harriet and Louisa Jacobs, Hezekiah Brown, and other Black teachers in Georgia all ran up against the juggernaut of the AMA, the aggressive missionary arm of the Congregational and Presbyterian Churches. The AMA considered schooling not only a means of building a self-sufficient Black peasantry in the South, but also an entering wedge to proselytize among Black Baptists and Methodists. Working closely with Freedmen's Bureau officials, it set out to undermine the SEA and install white northern teachers in its schools, in the process either dismissing northern and southern Black teachers altogether or retaining a favored few, but only as classroom assistants. The AMA commissioned white women from New England, with a strong contingent from Massachusetts. Their tasks included teaching children during the day and adults at night, leading Sunday school classes, distributing clothing and other supplies to families, and writing so-called begging letters to prospective donors. Crafting these letters proved to be a delicate task, for they had to balance the children's enthusiasm for learning with a bleak picture of conditions in the South—this in a way to keep the neo-abolitionist dollars flowing southward even after the war had been won. Meanwhile, many of the white teachers, dependent on the paltry $15-a-month stipend (such as Boston's Hannah C. Bullard, whose piano-maker father had abandoned the family), deeply resented their well-to-do coworkers who could use their own money to supplement their monthly food budgets. Most teachers stayed only for a year or two; they saw no future for themselves in the South.[8]

A little over a year after its founding, the SEA collapsed, the victim of the AMA's rival tuition-free schools. By charging a modest monthly fee to pay its teachers, the SEA had priced itself out of reach of freed parents who had little or no cash. In July 1866, the

Jacobses, discouraged by mounting anti-Black violence and the AMA monopoly on Black schooling, returned to Boston. Over the next couple of years, the AMA pushed out most independent Black teachers. By 1869, Hezekiah Brown had moved with his wife, Marion, also a teacher, to the small town of Dittsmerville, outside of Savannah, and opened a new school. After the war, the laundress-nurse-teacher Susie Baker King had started teaching in the city, but in the fall of 1866, the AMA siphoned off the pupils from her small school; her attempt at night classes met the same fate in 1868. Now a widow, she, too, retreated to the nearby countryside, where she taught, but without much success, and besides, "country life did not agree with me," she wrote. Eventually she found she could not support herself and her son through teaching and went to work for a white family.[9]

OTHER BLACK BOSTONIANS made their mark on the postbellum Richmond cityscape. The widow Rebecca Davis Lee graduated from the New England Female Medical College in 1864 and married Arthur Crumpler, a wartime fugitive from Virginia, the following year. Crumpler, who had worked as an enslaved blacksmith and showed a flair for inventing mechanical devices, had made his way to Newton, a suburb of Boston, and found a patron in a white schoolmaster there. He and Rebecca probably met at Twelfth Baptist, where both were members. Soon after the end of the war, Rebecca spent at least a year in Richmond, where she advertised her services in the Black community and assured potential patients that she was "a regular of Mr. Grimes's church" and "sent by no society or party." She made a connection with the Freedmen's Bureau and, working with an indigent population, specialized in diseases among women and children; but her patients, desperately needy, could not sustain her medical practice. Back in Boston and living on Joy Street, she worked as a "doctress" while her husband worked as a porter.[10]

Several people returned to Richmond or its environs because they had been born there or in the vicinity. The Reverend Peter Randolph traveled back and forth between Richmond and Boston frequently between 1865 and 1870. (Though exhausting, the journeys had their upsides, such as the day he met and talked to Frederick Douglass on a train.) In the spring of 1865, Randolph wanted to celebrate Richmond's fall by returning to his native state, but, as he recalled later, "I had not the necessary means to undertake the work." Just barely able to provide for his wife and children, Randolph was giving guest sermons for a modest fee. Still, the Reverend Leonard Grimes urged him to go. One day, one of Randolph's patrons, the dry-goods merchant J. H. Lester, asked him how he managed to make ends meet. When Randolph admitted he lived in a perpetual state of financial distress, Lester gave him the cash equivalent of a barrel of flour, enough money for the preacher to make the journey to City Point, Virginia. Searching for a viable congregation, Randolph was disappointed to see that the people there were "in a confused state, and [they] wanted more than I was able to give them." He moved on to Richmond and found a desolate city, with charred buildings and scores of wounded and maimed men on the streets. The freedpeople, though, were rejoicing, "Slavery chain done broke at last."[11]

Randolph soon realized that his restrained style of worship was not to the people's liking. Of a local divine, he wrote, "His preaching was much more excitable than mine, and seemed to effect [*sic*] the people in a way I could not." Then, Randolph made the acquaintance of several men who had been free before the war, and one of them donated land for a new church. On May 21, Randolph became the first minister of Richmond's new Ebenezer Baptist Church. (He would return periodically to Boston to see his family and give talks on the "condition and prospects of the Southern Freedmen," enlisting Samuel May Jr. in the effort.) Randolph also formed a branch of the Prince Hall Grand Lodge of Freemasons, which he named "The Pocahontas Lodge."

At an annual preacher's salary of $200, however, he needed to find additional work. He became an agent of the Freedmen's Bureau, issuing tickets to applicants for food and clothing, marrying couples, and seeking justice for the many men, women, and children who were being abused by their vengeful former owners—such as the young girl "shamefully whipped and her back burned with a hot iron."[12]

Randolph was appalled by the violence inflicted on Blacks, not only by white southerners but by Union military officials. He therefore became an "instigator" in helping to organize a meeting between a group of prominent Richmond Black leaders and President Andrew Johnson. The gathering took place in Washington on June 16, 1865, and featured the detailed testimony of several men who had been witness to, or victims of, Union soldiers' brutality: "Our present condition is, in many respects worse than when we were slaves, and living under slave law. Under the old system, we had the *protection* of our masters, who were financially interested in our physical welfare. That protection is now withdrawn, and our old masters have become our enemies." Richmond was in a chaotic condition, with the Confederate mayor holding onto power and Union officers and civil authorities wielding unchecked authority over the Black population (not unlike the situation in Savannah). The requirement that all Blacks carry passes had given license to provost marshals to enter "our buildings and workshops, and have taken men from the workbench and put them into prison because they had no pass."[13]

One of the men providing evidence about Richmond at that June meeting was John Oliver. (As for his former wife, going by the name of "Mrs. Louise DeMortie," she had become the matron of the New Orleans Orphan's Home located in a mansion on Esplanade Street; General Nathaniel P. Banks, himself a native of Massachusetts, supported her effort. After the war, the orphanage moved to the US Marine Hospital, and, to raise money, DeMortie went north and continued to lecture and recite patriotic poetry from memory at events in Boston, Poughkeepsie, Philadelphia, and New York. Yet her work came to an untimely end when, in October 1867, she "of the voluminous voice, and elocutionary powers wonderful and puzzling to describe," in the words of an admirer, died of yellow fever in New Orleans at the age of thirty-four. Her friend William Wells Brown eulogized her as "a remarkable gifted and brilliant woman," with "refined manners, and possessing energy which always brings success. . . . Louise DeMortie was one of the most beautiful of her sex."[14])

At some point John Oliver had abandoned his job as a Philadelphia employment agent and decided to move to Richmond. There he pursued a political career and advocated for the rights of the freedpeople in opposition to both northern and southern authorities. In his statement to President Johnson, he recounted a recent disturbing incident. While he and a friend were walking on the street, a Union Army guard challenged and detained them, using "abusive and vulgar language." The guard would not accept Oliver's pass ("signed by the Secretary of State of the Commonwealth of Massachusetts") and assaulted his friend: "While he was standing in the street the officer of the day told him that he had given insolence to the guard, which [the friend] denied, whereupon the officer dismounted and beat him with his fist." Richmond remained a dangerous place for Black pedestrians, whom whites routinely shoved and pushed off the sidewalks in an effort to preserve antebellum norms of public decorum.[15]

In immersing himself in Virginia postwar politics, Oliver would find a vocation equal to his talents, though not always equal to his financial needs. Determined to live a life of public service, he pieced together several jobs. In June 1866, the *Richmond Times* disparagingly noted that he "made a living by hanging about the Freedmen's Court and charging to ignorant applicants to that tribunal fifty cents to write about their complaints, petitions or applications as the case might be." (Peter Randolph had done the same thing.) The enfranchisement of Black men under the Reconstruction Acts of March 1867 opened a new realm of political activity for Oliver and others. (The legislation also provided for the military occupation of several former Confederate states, a measure that Congress had hoped would provide protection for Black voters and lawmakers.) Oliver quickly climbed the ranks of the city and state Republican Party, and his willingness to work with whites earned him a series of appointed positions and some notable "firsts" for a Black man—first Black notary public appointed in Virginia; first Black registrar for the 16th Military District in Richmond; and first Black "messenger" of the Richmond City Council, a municipal job that involved managing deliveries and pickups. The *Richmond Examiner* called him "a man of character and a considerable ability," prompting the *Boston Traveller* to note that he was "a very different man" from that other Boston headliner active in the South, Aaron A. Bradley.[16]

The ballot came at a cost to Oliver's fellow citizens. In November 1867 he and other Radical Republicans condemned "the untold hardships and sufferings necessarily entailed upon so very many of the laboring classes of this city by their discharge from employment avowedly because of the free exercise of the elective franchise at the late election." In other words, voting could get you fired from your job. Was the right to vote worth one's livelihood? Following a political trajectory like that of other Black leaders, Oliver, over time, became disillusioned with the party of Lincoln. In Virginia, some of its most outspoken white members favored segregated schools, and they urged Black families to forget about their confiscated lands and go back to work. White party leaders unabashedly marginalized Black men, their largest constituency. One observer noted, in the spring of 1868, that while Oliver was a member of the Republican Party's state executive committee, representing 100,000 Black constituents, the eighteen white members among them could claim only 1,000 followers of their own color.[17]

In 1870 Oliver was elected president of the Richmond chapter of the National Colored Labor Union, founded in 1869. In accepting the honor, he recalled his days as a master carpenter, saying, as a reporter recounted, that "if there was anything he could do, it was build a house." He also referred to the many political meetings that he and other Black Republicans had held since the war, and yet "nothing good has been achieved." He urged his listeners to seek out an alternative strategy to achieve justice, one that rested on "a firmer basis than politics."[18]

For a while, in the wake of Appomattox, Boston newspapers provided extensive coverage of conditions in the South. The periodic visits back home from agitators, teachers, and preachers, combined with their eyewitness reports, held the attention of virtually every segment of the city's population. The commercial classes took note of strikes among Black stevedores at major southern cotton ports. The Black community reacted with horror to stories of lynchings and mass murder perpetrated by unreconstructed rebels. White and Black laborers pondered the consequences of an in-migration of Black southerners, willing workers. Neo-abolitionists and other reformers debated the merits of land distribution. Indeed, so intense was Boston's interest in the events unfolding in the South that some charities feared for the city's unfortunates, now that philanthropists and former abolitionists were directing their attention and cash toward the freedpeople. In October 1866 the Industrial Aid Society for the Prevention of Pauperism acknowledged that "the war made many and pressing claims, and they were promptly answered"—at times in a trade-off with the many and pressing claims of the Boston poor. Black southerners would continue through the years to stake a claim to the energies and financial resources of committed Bostonians. As Harriet Jacobs noted, a paper freedom was not enough for Blacks regardless of where they lived; it was "a priceless boon, but its value [would be] enhanced with some of life's comforts"—comforts that remained out of reach amid persistent labor exploitation and hardship in both the North and the neo-Confederate South.[19]

PETER RANDOLPH'S RICHMOND church, Ebenezer Baptist, grew rapidly, but following a now familiar narrative, its impoverished congregants were unable to pay their minister a decent salary. Randolph therefore went north and threw himself on the mercy of old friends, speaking often at Twelfth Baptist and relating the sufferings of the freedpeople. Announcements of his talks included testimonials from Virginia whites, including the mayor of Richmond. In October 1866, R. M. Manly, Virginia's secretary of education, wrote that Randolph's "influence is wise and conservative, and wise and safe counsellors are too few among this [Black] people." The members of Ebenezer Church were too poor to help themselves now, Manly said, but "when general prosperity shall return to the city, they will have no occasion to ask for assistance from abroad [i.e., the North]." Apparently, he felt that people were more likely to provide aid if they felt the need was temporary.[20]

Randolph had tried to impose his own notions of Baptist worship on the Ebenezer congregants, but in the process, he wrote, he had been "brought immediately face to face with strange customs and trying difficulties." He did away with gender-segregated services and allowed women to take some role in the leadership of the church. Between 1865 and 1869, the membership roll swelled from 600 to 1,400, which increased donations accordingly. In addition, some of the Boston whites who visited—including Randolph's patron Isaac Fenno—dropped generous donations in the collection plate.[21]

Besides raising money, Randolph had other reasons to divide his time between the two commonwealths of Virginia and Massachusetts. His family had remained in Boston, and his wife, Amelia, was bearing a heavy burden. On June 25, 1866, his son

Thaddeus Walker died, a month after the birth of another son, Peter. And then, on August 1, Peter died.[22]

Randolph resigned from Ebenezer Baptist on December 13, 1869. He felt it was time to go. Back in Boston, his wife was ill and grieving. In Virginia, conservative whites had recaptured the state's political machinery, depriving him of the contacts he had made in high places, and making life even more miserable for the Black population. Also, in the end he was probably voted out by his own church members in favor of a local minister, someone who practiced a decidedly southern style of preaching. When Randolph returned to the Bay State, he embraced missionary work on behalf of the temperance cause, another itinerant position that would deprive him of the stable pulpit he had been seeking all his life.

In 1870 Randolph founded a new Baptist church, also called Ebenezer, on Washington Street in Boston's South End (it received official sanction in 1871). Many of the Virginia migrants had settled in this part of the city, eschewing the densely packed Ward 6 (one Boston newspaper estimated that 700 southern migrants had moved to the South End since the war). Randolph was convinced he understood the needs, both spiritual and material, of these newcomers. He appreciated what he called their "sympathetic element," emotional intensity. Among the names of Black Virginians arriving in Boston during the five years after the war were Selden, Griffin, Whiting, Webb, Bailey, and eight other common ones (Scott, Harrison, Jones, Lee, Clark, Carter, Richardson, and Taylor) that matched those of the families in the Edloe Sixty-Six.[23]

Assisting Randolph in starting the new church was Jefferson Ruffin, son of Torrington and Harriet Ruffin, one of the original Edloe families, and Martha Ruffin, Torrington's sister and a recent arrival from Virginia (this branch of Ruffins was not immediately related to the George and Nancy Ruffin family from Richmond).

A reporter for the *Herald* no doubt got his story from Randolph when he wrote, "Much credit is due to the women whose zeal largely contributed to the success of the enterprise." This new congregation occupied one room of a tenement building; services were disturbed by the sounds of a card game next door, with men calling out "I pass" or "trump" or "jack," evidently trying to rattle the earnest clergyman in the adjoining apartment.[24]

Randolph remained suspended between two constituencies—on the one hand, his Black congregants in Richmond and more recently in Boston, who expected ecstatic worship services, and, on the other, his white patrons, and at least some northern Black churchgoers, who insisted on more sedate practices. In his writings and speeches, he took pains to remind northern whites of the horrors of bondage, expressing solidarity with those who had recently been liberated; but he also felt grateful to Massachusetts, which he regarded as his true home. He disapproved of the "rough and uncultivated" worship practices of the freedpeople, "the meetings carried on till a late hour, the groaning, and shouting, the getting happy, and falling over benches." Nevertheless, he tried to explain to his white readers that such emotions revealed both the desire for communal sustenance and a profound faith deserving of respect: "In the South, their great social and religious enjoyment has come through their church life." He could at times offer gentle rebukes to even the staunchest of white allies, as when US senator Henry Wilson of Massachusetts addressed Black people in Virginia, offering them advice about living free lives: wrote Randolph, "They were not looking for advice, however, but land to plant corn and potatoes, for their wives and children."[25]

Randolph's conflicting emotions manifested themselves in subtle ways. At a festive gathering of Unitarian clergymen in Boston in May 1867, former governor John A. Andrew paid tribute to his friend Peter Randolph, recalling the arrival of the Edloe Sixty-Six nearly two decades before. Andrew told his audience that his initial impression of the travelers—as "a very crooked sort of old men," reluctant to engage in honest labor—turned out to be wrong. Within three years, "every one of these crooked men were straightened out and walked as if they had been trained by an orderly sergeant and had got out of the awkward squad and allowed to appear at a battalion drill." Inspired by Peter "the blacksmith and preacher," Andrew had kept track of them. He could now report that they were hard workers, and several owned their own houses.[26]

In reminiscing, Andrew recalled that he had once asked Randolph why he had become a minister. The Black man responded by telling of an admonition from his mother soon after his father died: "Now your father is dead, and you are only a poor little black slave boy; when I am gone, unless you make Jesus your friend, you will not have a friend on earth." This awful prediction had driven the distraught young Peter to wander the hills and fields, where he began "praying for some sign that Jesus was willing to be my friend." It was then that he heard the voice of God, proclaiming that indeed Jesus would befriend him. Puzzled, Andrew asked, "Do you mean that the impression or conviction came so suddenly and with such an intensity into your mind that it was to you as if a voice had spoken those words?" Randolph demurred. "You educated men can never comprehend this, for God is so good that he takes pity on us poor slaves and *accommodates himself to our understanding*." According to Andrew, a "divine spirit" had sustained enslaved people for over two hundred years and revealed the power of faith of the humblest of beings, such as that widow and her little boy. Yet, in seeking to make a hard and fast distinction between the literal and the spiritual for his Unitarian listeners, Andrew expressed his own confusion about the former slaves' ways of believing. That incomprehension represented an enduring, if unacknowledged, estrangement between the two men and the two political and religious cultures they represented.[27]

LIKE MANY OF their white antebellum abolitionist counterparts, white Republicans in the postwar period saw northern and southern Blacks as belonging to distinct laboring populations. According to this view, freed agricultural workers were integral to a revived cotton economy; they were destined to work in the fields and abide by their enslaved forebears' cultural sensibilities. In contrast, northern Blacks were supposedly peripheral to the postwar economy, though they might form a newly appreciated constituency of the Republican Party. It was not surprising, then, that a customary northern racial division of labor remained intact after 1865, even while the civil rights of Black men expanded and, on the surface at least, seemed to herald a new day of equality. This triumphalist narrative had little relevance to labor relations in Boston.

14

White Men Demanding Their Own Rights, but Refusing to Concede to Others Theirs

On December 3, 1866, Dr. John S. Rock died of tuberculosis. He was forty-eight years old. The funeral service, conducted four days later by the Reverend Leonard Grimes at Twelfth Baptist, drew a throng of mourners. Members of the Prince Hall Grand Lodge of Freemasons attended in full regalia. Obituaries highlighted Rock's "firsts": he was the first Black lawyer admitted to argue before the United States Supreme Court, and the first Black lawyer to be received on the floor of the House of Representatives. These honors capped his career but did not encompass it. Over the years he had worked as a dentist, physician, public lecturer, activist, essayist, and lawyer. With his death, the city of Boston and the nation lost an insistent, outspoken proponent of Black people's full and equal access to all kinds of employment.[1]

Suffering from poor health for many years, Rock endured a series of devastating personal losses. Toussaint Lewis Hayden Rock, the son born soon after Rock and his wife, Catharine Bower Rock, moved to Boston, died in March 1857 at the age of three; another son, Julian McCrea Rock, born in October of that year, died in infancy. Between the birth of Toussaint and the death of Julian came another son, John S. Rock Jr., in 1856. Catharine Rock succumbed to TB in 1864.

Rock died at his home on Phillips Street. (The city had recently renamed Southac after Wendell Phillips.) The large dwelling had once hid fugitive slaves; it was still a boardinghouse, now operated by Rock's seventy-year-old mother, Maria. Rock's will revealed a sizable estate, a goodly part of it no doubt a result of his work as a lawyer and claims agent during the war. He left his mother all his worldly goods—furniture, clothing, and library—and stipulated that she receive $120 a year for two years. To his son, John, he bequeathed $2,000, to be invested in real estate within five miles of Boston, plus the rest of his assets. Should his son die before him, the money would go to the Institute for Colored Youth in Philadelphia, for gym apparatus or books "or some such other things as said trustees may deem proper for the physical development of the pupils in said Institute."[2]

At some point—probably in 1865, soon after Catharine's death—Rock had sent John Jr. to Philadelphia to live in a household that included the youth's maternal uncle and aunts. John Bower was a tailor and purveyor of secondhand clothing. Sarah Bower Bell was a dressmaker. The widow Henrietta S. Bower Duterte had taken over the business of her late husband, Haitian-born Francis Duterte, becoming the first Black woman in the country to serve as an undertaker. In 1870, twelve-year-old John Jr. was attending the institute cited in his father's will, a private school founded by a Quaker philanthropist. It offered students vocational training as well as a classical education in trigonometry, chemistry, and Latin: Boston had no equivalent. However, in 1877, after a lingering illness, the youth died while still a student.[3]

After the war, the issue of workplace discrimination largely receded from Boston's public discourse, yielding a vacuum when it came to larger discussions of a central, lived experience among Black men and women. City authorities congratulated themselves on the recent gains in Black political rights, implying they believed the struggle for equality was won. In the Black community, many leaders turned their attention from slavery to the future of the South, where freedpeople were bearing the brunt of the wrath of defeated secessionists. And, too, partisan politics became a consuming issue of the day. Now the sanctuary of Twelfth Baptist rang with forceful denunciations of retrograde white politicians, the Republican president Andrew Johnson among them, and echoed with a contentious debate over the Fourteenth Amendment.

In August 1865 the physician Dr. John B. Smith presided over a mass meeting of Black Bostonians. The group resolved that they would "never be satisfied with any thing short of perfect and absolute equality before the law and . . . regard[ed] any attempt to inhibit them from that equality as dishonest, unmanly, and wicked in the extreme, come from what quarter it may." The drive for "equality before the law" animated many Black leaders, who saw partisan politicking as a pathway to that goal. In the process they placed the interests of the Black laboring classes at the mercy of feckless white men of both parties.[4]

For leaders of the Boston and national Black communities, suffrage was a—if not *the*—key pillar of citizenship, the foundation of all other aspects of legal equality. The end of the Civil War intensified the claim of Black men to the vote; only a federal amendment to the Constitution could guarantee it. Black soldiers had served with distinction in the conflict, and Black Republicans had become a key constituency of their party. Presumably any residual effects of the antebellum slavocracy could be eliminated at the ballot box. Well-organized and possessed of time-tested leaders, Boston's Black community focused on winning political power and dismantling discriminatory laws in the South as well as the North. Yet legal rights were no guarantee of economic opportunity.[5]

Black women pressed for the right to vote. Together with white women and male allies, Louisa Jacobs and others went public with the case that the vote belonged to all adult citizens, not only men. Some suffragists argued that women had made substantial contributions to the Union effort as nurses, wartime wage earners, suppliers of food and clothing for the troops, and relief workers. In Boston, the Republicans drew from a cross-section of neo-abolitionists and prominent lawyers, fugitive slaves and northern-born old-timers, army and navy veterans, and recent southern migrants. Black women and white women of reformist sensibilities identified with the party and pressed the men in it to support their enfranchisement.[6]

The postwar Black political project was fraught from the beginning. Black men represented only 14 percent of eligible Ward 6 voters, and though they constituted a key swing bloc, they had little choice but to rely on the promises and patronage bestowed by whites. In Boston, the Republicans were a majority party representing the well-heeled elite—industrialists, lawyers, and other business owners and professionals—while the Democrats' largest constituency consisted of working-class whites, and especially Irish immigrants. Class as well as Black-specific interests did not necessarily align along party lines, and Black voters themselves ran the gamut of janitors, porters, and waiters to lawyers, physicians, and businessmen. Still, the successes of Boston's Black politicians in the decade after the war were the envy of their counterparts throughout the North, as the city's voters began to send Blacks to both the city council and the state legislature on a regular basis. In 1866, Charles L. Mitchell, a printer by trade and a veteran of the 55th Massachusetts (from Ward 6), and Edwin Garrison Walker, the leatherworker and then lawyer by trade (from Charlestown), were the first Black men elected to the Massachusetts House of Representatives, and indeed, the first Black men to be elected to any state legislature in the country.[7]

As lawmakers, both Mitchell and Walker refused to endorse the commonwealth's ratification of the Fourteenth Amendment (in 1867), which guaranteed all Americans due process under the law. They believed the measure treated the former Confederate states too leniently and failed to provide for Black male suffrage. More generally, they and other Black leaders demanded federal guarantees of citizenship rights—national mandates, not the patchwork of state-specific measures that had prevailed in the antebellum period. In 1870, the ratification of the Fifteenth Amendment, which guaranteed all male citizens the right to vote, mollified the critics to a great extent and pointed toward a more hopeful future in the eyes of many. At a grand event celebrating the amendment in April 1870, Charles Lenox Remond referred to the financial sacrifices he had made over the years in the service of freedom. He declared the day to be Black people's "Fourth of July," and added that he "went into the anti-slavery movement thirty-five years ago, poor, and was now poorer, in dollars and cents, but the largest millionaire in the land in his feelings."[8]

Still, the debates over the Fourteenth and Fifteenth Amendments signaled troubled intraparty relationships among Black Republicans. With emancipation, the social cohesion characteristic of the West End Black community, with its single, overweening purpose, dissolved; in its wake arose fractious debates over national policies and personal feuds over nominations for elected office and convention delegates. Stark class differences emerged to challenge the notion that all Black people agreed on specific group-based interests. A geographical split between longtime residents on the north side of Beacon Hill and hundreds of newly arrived Black southerners who had settled in the South End highlighted and hardened the two groups' divergent cultural sensibilities.[9]

Many Black men saw their allegiance to the Republican Party largely in transactional terms, with civil-service jobs a reward for a few of the party faithful, especially veterans. Newcomers to the city, the veterans James Monroe Trotter and his brother-in-law William DuPree, immediately entered the local political arena. They, together with William C. Nell and his nephew Ira Nell, and other veterans, such as Cornelius Weeden, son of the tailor Henry Weeden, worked for the US Post Office as superintendents, clerks, letter sorters, and carriers. Mark DeMortie and James D. Ruffin got appointments at the Custom House, and Burrill Smith, wounded at Fort Wagner, and Charles Mitchell, wounded at Honey Hill, worked there as weigher and clerk, respectively. George Lewis Ruffin, the first Black person to graduate from Harvard Law School and the first elected to the Boston City Council (in 1876, for two terms), was also the first to be appointed a judge in Massachusetts (in Charlestown).[10]

Patronage positions offered prestige and a good salary and rewarded Black men as a valued constituency of the Republican Party. The most famous Black Republican, Frederick Douglass, received a series of high-profile appointments during the quarter century after the war—as president of the Freedman's Savings Bank, US marshal for the District of Columbia, recorder of deeds for the district, and consul-general to the Republic of Haiti, among other jobs; these positions guaranteed Douglass a level of financial security he had not previously known. Still, for ordinary aspirants, the spoils system had its drawbacks. Lewis Hayden's situation was unique in that he held the position of messenger for the commonwealth's secretary of state for thirty years, until he died. In contrast, almost all political job holders (and seekers) remained at the mercy of national and local elections, and some men were never considered for promotions that their white coworkers took for granted. Nevertheless, prominent Black civil servants had little incentive to berate Republican employers—as John Rock had berated white abolitionists—over their failure to pursue egalitarian hiring policies.[11]

By the mid-1870s, it was apparent that the Republican Party offered few tangible gains for the mass of Black workers. In the South, sharecroppers' annual labor contracts kept an agricultural system dominated by white landowners and landless Blacks intact, with increasing numbers of whites joining the ranks of the landless. In Boston, white Republicans avoided the subject of integrated worksites; if advocating for Black suffrage was considered a radical stance for a northern white politician, calling for expanded opportunity for Black workers would have been a self-destructive, career-ending move.

Republican party politics produced much in the way of disillusionment and ideological differences among Black leaders. Robert Morris believed that "the Republican Party has done nothing for the negroes," making manifest an independent spirit that would pit Black establishment Republicans against dissidents within their own party. Morris and Edwin Walker argued for separate Black political clubs and made efforts to broker Black votes for certain Democratic candidates, both measures intended to remind white Republicans that they could not take Black votes for granted. They urged a protest vote against Republicans and support for the Democratic presidential candidate Horace Greeley, who ran against Ulysses S. Grant in 1872. The disagreement between Black Republican bolters and stalwarts mirrored the one between white men of the party. In the summer of 1872, in a "Letter from Wendell Phillips to the Colored Citizens of Boston," the famous abolitionist declared, "the nation and your race are safe only in the hands of the old, regular Republican party." In contrast, Senator Charles Sumner urged a vote for Greeley.[12]

John A. Mulligan, the seamen's boardinghouse operator, became active in the Republican Party. He had served his sentence in prison for murder, but upon his release, found himself back in court several times, because of his litigious and physically aggressive stance toward both the sailors and the sea captains whom he claimed had crossed him. In 1872 he began calling himself "a Democratic black Republican," deriding his former Republican colleagues as the "barking spaniels of a defunct party." A critic charged that he was acting only as an "irrepressible office-seeker," with self-interest "the alpha and omega of his faith."[13]

At the same time, a decision to ally with Democrats, no matter how tentative or temporary, proved a bitter pill. In the South, the party backed terrorist attacks against Black men and women, supporting the depredations of the Ku Klux Klan and other violent groups. In Boston, the Democrats represented the white laboring classes, including the second generation of Irish immigrants, who began to enjoy at least limited access to occupations previously reserved for native-born white people. In September 1874, a Republican paper expressed disbelief that Morris, Walker, and others would pass resolutions "signifying a loss of faith in the Republican Party," as southern whites continued their rampages against Black citizens. Asked the paper incredulously, "To whom will the colored men look for support—the Democrats?" A question that begged another question: "If not to the Democrats and Republicans, to whom?"[14]

Perhaps the answer was that they must look to each other. Black leaders continued to meet in conventions, as they had throughout the antebellum period; now, the meetings included prominent southerners (James Simms was a frequent presence), with delegates focusing on labor in the South and suffrage in the North. A committee of the National Colored Convention met in Boston in October 1868 and crafted a compelling petition to Congress, detailing the violence and wage theft that afflicted freedpeople all over the South: "Since our enfranchisement all sympathy for us has become extinct, we are abused and cursed. Thousands after working hard through the years have been run off and glad to escape with our lives[,] our years of work lost." The National Convention of Colored Men of America, held in Washington,

DC, in January 1869, focused on the fact that suffrage was not yet universal; indeed, "the heel of the oppressor is still upon the neck of the colored American. That is to say, he is deprived of the *Elective franchise*."[15]

The absence of a postwar, robust discussion of Black economic vulnerability suggests that most Republicans took a discriminatory division of labor for granted. In December 1869, Frederick Douglass came to Boston and delivered a major, hours-long address, but in it he neglected to mention hard-pressed Black wage earners in the North. Though recognizing that southern whites "believed in slavery and they believe in it still," he struck an optimistic note overall, lauding the strength and potential of the United States and denouncing deadly forms of prejudice against Chinese immigrants, so similar to prejudice against Blacks: "Right wrongs no man." Ignoring the lack of Black job opportunity, Douglass said of the United States, "Here, labor is abundant and better remunerated than any where else."[16]

By this time Boston's employment patterns had become fixed, with Blacks excluded from municipal public works projects, factory jobs, and the skilled trades. Soon after the war, Irish immigrants and their children began to find work not only as manual laborers, but also as city police officers, firefighters, and public school teachers. In contrast, a pattern of Black exclusion from whole swaths of public and private employment remained intact until well into the twentieth century. In 1900, the largest job category for Boston's Black men was that of janitor, with most working at either some form of personal or domestic service or in "trade and transportation"; most women remained confined to clothes washing and domestic service. The Republican Party proved a poor vehicle for Black economic mobility.[17]

In February 1867, the Boston City Council approved a petition by Benjamin F. Roberts and twenty-three other Black citizens who demanded that the word "colored" be omitted from lists of eligible voters and taxpayers. The council members noted that the petition was "in accordance with the spirit of the times, as well as in harmony with that republicanism which recognizes all citizens as standing upon the same equality before the law." One by one, the barriers to full equality had crumbled, according to the council; gradually, "the negro pew, the separate school, exclusion from the militia, exclusion from the jury box, denial of a seat at places of public amusement, of conveyance in public carriages, with separation from other residents of the City Directory," had been eliminated. In fact, though, owners of stores, managers of halls and other venues, and conductors on public transportation still decided whether or not to accommodate Black patrons and customers; not until the late nineteenth century, with the passage of legislative mandates, would such practices begin to diminish, if not disappear entirely. Still, the council noted, "[the petitioners] are well-known and orderly persons; . . . they pay their taxes without murmuring, serve on the jury with fidelity, perform military duty when asked with alacrity; [and] are ready to quell riots and insurrections when their services are required." In other words, they had proved themselves worthy of full citizenship.[18]

Had John Rock lived, he no doubt would have noted the irony that although Boston played a central role in pressing for Black civil rights via constitutional amendment, judicial decisions, and legislation, its own hiring and wage practices seemed largely impervious to change. Moreover, the relentless displacement of Black entrepreneurs continued; in 1870, 17 percent of all barbers in Boston were Black; three decades later that figure was 5 percent. By rigorously segregating the workforce, white employers essentially intensified the competition among Black men for a shrinking number of jobs, keeping wages as low as possible. These anti-Black practices were legal and largely accepted by most whites.[19]

In the decade after the war, Boston's elected officials found themselves forced to contend with questions related to the length of the workday and the definition of a fair wage, now that the city itself had become a major employer. (At the same time, a few officials objected to these wide-ranging discussions, on the theory that such talk was only a ploy among politicians hoping to make "political capital" on the eve of an election.) The mayor's office toggled back and forth between Republicans (1863–1868) and Democrats (1868–1873), but regardless of partisan affiliation, few could deny that labor was plentiful and cheap, leading to some moral quandaries. Despite the fulsome nature of these discussions, the plight of Black workers remained off the table and out of sight in city council meetings.[20]

The enduring debate over the "worthy" and "unworthy" poor ran up against postwar realities, for council members admitted that whole categories of Bostonians were suffering through no fault of their own: war widows and orphans; disabled veterans; brutalized seamen who had deserted; job-seekers shut out of a glutted labor market; the frail and the elderly; the children of drunkards; the victims of unscrupulous intelligence offices; laborers who, though toiling for upward of eleven or twelve hours a day, could not make ends meet; and the jobless reeling from disasters such as the Great Fire of 1872 (which destroyed much of the commercial district, leaving twenty-eight dead and twenty thousand jobless) and periodic downturns, such as the Depression of 1873. The respectable classes might rail against the truant boys roaming the city streets, but, according to the council, many youngsters were "compelled to remain from school to gather food or fuel, or to do whatever they can to help their distressed families." In the summer of 1869, the city approved a concert for the entertainment of wounded soldiers and their families, but noted that many of the beneficiaries could not afford the 25 cents admission fee. Moreover, the profiteering of residential landlords created public health hazards that the city could hardly blame on tenants. More and more workers were living in large multiunit buildings, such as the one at 235 Federal Street, deemed "unfit for human habitation by reason of leaky roof, offensive vault and dirty house, and likely to cause sickness among the inhabitants." The residents of the West End Black community remained particularly susceptible to epidemics; in the early 1870s, their neighborhood still lacked adequate sewage and drainage services.[21]

The city government continued to put paupers, juvenile delinquents, and criminals to work. Following wartime practices, it dispensed with expensive contractor-middlemen, hiring men directly for the Paving, Public Health, and Commons and Public Gardens Departments. (Public health workers removed offal from the city streets and night soil from private residences, cleaned privies, and constructed sewers.) This new system was not only "more economical," in terms of labor costs, but also supposedly increased the taxpayer base and decreased the number of poor whom the city was obliged to support. The expansion of public works held the promise of keeping more white laborers within city limits, since many were tempted to move to the suburbs in a quest for cheaper rents and better sanitation. City work could help to cement the partisan loyalties of employees. At the same time, budgetary considerations exerted a downward pressure on laborers' wages, calling into question the penchant among otherwise cost-conscious city councillors for lavish July 4 banquets and champagne dinners at Parker's Hotel at taxpayers' expense.[22]

The council represented a wide spectrum of opinion on labor-related issues: How to deal with the disorder that came with tolerating certain kinds of workers—newsboys, victuallers, owners of billiard halls and grog shops, intelligence agents, and second-hand clothing dealers? Did the residential asylums for the poor promote slothfulness? Ruminating on Boston's robust public correctional and social-welfare institutions, one alderman opined, "If you want to encourage poverty this is the way to do it," arguing that the cities and towns of Europe and of Boston's hinterlands were "emptying themselves into our midst." He did feel defensive, though, adding, "And yet the man who stands up and says a word against it [the almshouse] is said to be hard-hearted."[23]

City authorities were torn between providing worthy men with jobs, on the one hand, and managing the city as efficiently as possible, on the other. Like workers in the private sector, municipal laborers lacked full-time, year-round work. The city reduced the 1,050-strong paving workforce to 750 employees in the winter. Perhaps the major project of cutting down Fort Hill (near the wharves) could be postponed until the off-season, "while there were a large number of workers idle, who would thereby obtain employment and a living." By 1870, though, the council faced a very different decision about how to proceed—whether to remove the earth by steam shovel or continue to pay workers to do it by hand, paying rock-bottom wages. It was a difficult decision, but the former plan won out, because, as the council minutes recorded, "they could see no other way but to accept the lowest bid for the work." The city still eagerly took advantage of the abundance of labor and paid the lowest possible wages, about $1.75 to $1.88 a day.[24]

For the most part, discussions surrounding the "labor question" arose not spontaneously, from the ranks of Boston's political leaders, but in response to the many ways in which groups of public workers (all white) drew attention to them by lobbying, striking, and pleading, especially for higher wages and a shorter workday. Ira Steward's movement continued apace, and he and other reformers persisted in pressing for an eight-hour day for public as well as private salaried and wage earners. Boston was not the only place where these issues garnered attention: in 1868, Congress passed legislation mandating an eight-hour workday for federal laborers and skilled tradesmen (though the measure would be compromised by a wage cut and lax enforcement). Still, most council members remained unmoved.[25]

All sorts of policies had financial implications for workers, but city hall seemed more solicitous toward white child workers than Blacks of any age. For example, in 1871, a councillor pointed out that charging East Bostonians to use the ferry to commute to work amounted to a tax on them, a particularly egregious policy considering the many children who came into the city but earned only a pittance: "The capitalists of Boston were benefited by the labors of these children, who were obliged to labor eleven or twelve hours a day and pay tolls coming from and returning to their homes." He termed the fee "the most outrageous thing the city could ever be guilty of."[26]

Running through these controversies was a dispute among politicians and administrators over the meaning of "reform." Increasingly, running on a "reform ticket" meant committing to saving the city money, as any good businessman would. These new reformers were replacing the antebellum men and women who promoted policies they considered contrary to crass commercial values. One house builder who represented Ward 6 (but clearly not the laboring men there) "said he believed in doing the city's business as he would his own"; given a chance to substitute strikers with two thousand willing, if ill-paid, workers, he would not hesitate to do so. He reminded his colleagues that he had been elected "on a reform ticket, which did not mean an increase in pay" for city employees.[27]

In the private sector, employers countered the demands of white laborers with threats to use Black workers as strikebreakers, and, in a few instances, as permanent replacements. In April 1868, white freight men working for the Boston and Albany Railroad protested a wage cut (from $1.75 to $1.50 a day) and walked off the job. Within two days the company had installed Black men in their places. Mark DeMortie and Lewis Hayden spread the word about the new jobs, a call that netted 120 eager workers. The fired men were enraged. Yet other parties were satisfied with the outcome of the strike—the Black workers, grateful for stable, relatively well-paying jobs; the company, which paid the new men $1.60, and thus secured a cheaper workforce in the process; and the city's white political and commercial establishment, uniformly opposed to strikes. In general, though, bosses found plenty of whites ready to take the places of disgruntled workers.[28]

If Boston's white laboring classes hoped to discourage employers' perennial threats to replace them with Black men and women, a broad coalition among workers of various ethnicities and occupations would seem to represent a necessary first step. Yet most white workers rejected that idea out of hand. In this regard members of the Boston Typographical Union were exceptional. During a lockout in late 1864, they began publishing their own paper, the *Boston Daily Evening Voice*, which advocated for "the rights of labor, without distinction of sex, complexion, or birthplace." Among the editors were skilled workers who had supported the abolitionist movement before the war. The *Voice* and its successor, a weekly, became the official organ of the Boston Trades Assembly. In expressing support for public schools and libraries as well as an eight-hour day, and deploring the fact that "woman is obligated to work like a slave to earn her bread," the *Voice* reflected the aspirations of upwardly mobile, literate tradesmen. Yet, departing from white working-class orthodoxy, the paper supported land-distribution policies in the South and favored admitting Black workers into labor unions in the North.[29]

Invoking the legacy of Black soldiers who had fought to preserve the Union, the *Voice* argued that the fates of all laboring classes were intertwined, and that justice for one group meant justice for all: "Now it is obvious if we demand our own rights as men, we must concede to other men theirs." The paper reminded its readers of the Irish railroad workers who had forfeited their own jobs as a result of a misguided, self-destructive prejudice toward Blacks. Nationwide, other cases made the same point: "If the workingmen have learned anything it is that there can be no hope of their success but in union—the union of all who labor. How mad and suicidal then, to hold up one hand for the degradation of the Negro, while the other is raised for the elevation of the white laborer!" To shun the Black man was to weaken the power of the white workingman, for "he that might have become our cooperator becomes our enemy." The paper also advocated for the rights of freedmen to vote and own land. In this way the paper could take the moral high ground while encouraging the former slaves to remain in the South rather than moving north to compete with whites for jobs.[30]

No other white group or publication made the case for unity with Blacks so explicitly, and when the *Voice* published its last issue in October 1867, the push for solidarity across racial lines died with it. Private employers who had political ambitions took pains to avoid roiling all-white workplaces either by integrating them or by doing away with white employees in favor of Black ones. The Typographical Union remained atypical, perhaps because a few white women and Black men were among the ranks of printers' apprentices and journeymen and women.[31]

Meanwhile, many white labor reformers were coalescing around the eight-hour day as a panacea for all the problems of the white laboring classes. Ira Steward and others formed the Grand Eight-Hour League of Massachusetts in the spring of 1866. Several prominent white abolitionists, including Phillips, Garrison, and others with burnished social reformers' credentials, supported the cause. A Workingmen's Institute, founded in December of that year, provided a forum for speakers determined to "reconstruct" relations between capitalist and laborer, even as textile-mill owners stuck stubbornly to a ten- or eleven-hour workday for their employees.[32]

The factory operatives' long day affected white women as well as men, though white men tended to see workers' interests as distinctly gendered. For the most part, Boston's female wage earners remained confined to the jobs of garment work, retail sales, and domestic service, with smaller numbers working as bookbinders, printers, and teachers. The category of seamstress encompassed a wide range of skills belying a rigid class and wage structure. Most white women workers averaged $3 or $4 a week, and they suffered greatly during the winter months, when expenses for fuel ate into their meager earnings. Those who did alterations for department stores, sewing and standing over hot pressing irons, were nevertheless better off than the needlewomen who worked at home, sewing well into the night for 25 cents a day. Sewing machine operators who used uniform patterns earned much less than the "aristocrats" of the profession. These entrepreneurs catered to the wealthy, employed their own assistants, and eschewed unionization in favor of a proud individualism; they could make as much as $30 a week. Boston's Needle Woman's Friend Society served as a broker between shops and impoverished women; the inmates of the Home for Consumptives and other hospitals and refuges sewed and earned a small amount of money. Most women workers had to pay rent at $2.50 to $4 per week; those who lived with their parents helped to depress wages for everyone.[33]

The Civil War sparked wider discussions about the meaning of citizenship for women, leading to the founding of the American Equal Rights Association (AERA) in New York City in May 1866, which linked the cause of universal suffrage to the interests of all men and all women. Those invited to speak on behalf of the association in 1867 included Charles Lenox Remond and the Black poet and orator Frances Ellen Watkins Harper. Surprisingly, the reserved Louisa Jacobs also accepted an invitation to take to the stump with the group, appearing on the platform in the heady company of Susan B. Anthony and Elizabeth Cady Stanton.

Remond and Jacobs met with a skeptical—if not downright disapproving—reception from the general public, but they also became disillusioned with both the work and the message of AERA itself. In a reprise of the abolitionist speakers' dilemma, neither one could afford to volunteer their services, no matter how deep their commitment to the cause. The association was supposed to pay Remond a salary of $100 a month, but he had to cover his own travel expenses, which left him only half that amount. Owing him money, Anthony acknowledged in February 1867 that "Mr. Remond is very needy. . . . I know his wife & three little ones sadly need it." He resigned as an AERA lecturer soon after, with the association still in debt to him. For her part, Louisa received only her travel expenses, leaving her with nothing to send home to her mother in Cambridge. The young woman also chafed under Stanton and Anthony's constant denigration of Black men as ignorant and unworthy of the vote. Physically and emotionally depleted, Louisa ended her brief career as a public speaker in March 1867.[34]

The overlapping efforts of labor reformers and suffragists reached an apex in 1869, when a range of initiatives challenged the status quo. The New England Labor Reform League served as a high-minded sounding board for ideas. White activists impatient with the league's lofty pronouncements started a rival, the Boston Eight-Hour League, more attuned to achieving results than to theorizing. That summer, the state legislature created the Massachusetts Bureau of Labor Statistics, which accumulated data and advocated for laborers in general. In the fall, the Massachusetts Labor Reform Party presented voters with a short-lived alternative to the two main political parties.

Boston, the site of several postwar women's rights conventions, emerged as a center of suffragist agitation. In 1869, Julia Ward Howe, Lucy Stone, William Lloyd Garrison, Frances Ellen Watkins Harper, and Josephine St. Pierre Ruffin (wife of George Lewis and sister-in-law of James D.) founded the American Woman Suffrage Association (AWSA). The AWSA focused on the issue of the women's vote, but it also supported the Fifteenth Amendment (which enfranchised Black men but not women). The association thus departed from, and proceeded to feud with, the National Woman Suffrage Association (NWSA), a New York–based group led by Stanton and Anthony. Around this time, Jennie Collins and other advocates for white laboring women formed the Boston Working Women's League, another pro-suffrage group.[35]

In April 1869, the New England Women's Club, composed of well-to-do white women, released its "Report of the Committee of Needlewomen" documenting the plight of twenty thousand of the region's women. The report attributed their hardship to an oversupply of labor, which was the consequence of mechanization; the in-migration of women from the hinterland; and the prevalence of out-workers on the countryside. The local Needle Woman's Friend Society proposed a solution to the swollen labor market for seamstresses: "Something must be done to dignify domestic service," it stated, to make that work preferable to both sewing and sex work.[36]

The New England Women's Club hired Harriet Jacobs as clerk to record attendance at meetings and monitor members' use of the rooms. She and Louisa had recently returned from a trip to London, where they were received (in the words of one Englishwoman) as "a poor, respectable-looking mulatto woman, with a handsome, ladylike *white* daughter, and a book with the heart-breaking story of her life." They had hoped to raise money for a Savannah orphanage, but found little interest in the idea among the British public. The home was never built.[37]

AGITATION ON BEHALF of white workers spanned the realms of theorizing, legislative lobbying, public speaking, petitioning, partisan politicking, and labor organizing; but these efforts gained little traction in the last three decades of the nineteenth century. The New England Labor Reform League and the Boston Working Women's League disappeared after a year. Wages remained low, hours long, and women disfranchised. The Republican Party officially and steadfastly opposed women's suffrage. It was no surprise that Boston Democrats and the influential Catholic paper *The Pilot* held the same view. A contingent of Boston's

Black leaders, including William Wells Brown and members of the clergy, also opposed it. An effort to amend the Massachusetts Constitution to allow women the right to vote was defeated in 1871, though women could vote for school committee members beginning in 1879.[38]

Black workers, too, sought to organize in 1869. With local and state labor reformers focused on the working conditions of white men and women, Black laborers had to advocate for themselves, not only in Boston and in Massachusetts generally but at the national level as well. Despite the egalitarian rhetoric emanating from the highest echelons of the white National Labor Union (founded in 1866), most of its constituent unions barred Blacks altogether. As a result, in December 1869, 214 delegates from around the country met for four days at a convention in Washington, DC, and formed the Colored National Labor Union. (An ad placed in the printed proceedings touted the federal-government-backed Freedman's Bank: "SAVE YOUR MONEY! Every Man Can Become Rich if He Will!"—but within five years the bank would fail, taking with it the money of 60,000 southern depositors, affecting nearly half a million family members.) The convention's main speaker was John Mercer Langston of Ohio, a recruiter of soldiers for the 55th Massachusetts. In his address, "The Relations of the Colored People to American Industry," Langston nodded toward a handful of exceptions—a gunsmith, a landscape painter, a sculptress (this last no doubt Edmonia Lewis, a friend of Langston's and resident of Boston at the time). He called for foundries, steamboats, railroads, stores, and factories to be opened to Black men and women job-seekers, as well as for unity: "We are not insensible of our weakness in our disorganized condition," he said. Blacks lacked a "larger opportunity to follow those diversified pursuits of industry which in New England and our Northern States generally have done so much to enlighten, elevate, and bless the people." Concluding, he denounced the white laboring classes, especially "the white mechanic and laborer of the North, so long ill-taught and advised that his true interest is gained by hatred and abuse of laborers of African descent, as well as the Chinaman." "A labor movement based on discrimination," he predicted, "will prove to be of very little value."[39]

While white labor leaders in general remained oblivious to racial injustice, they repurposed eighteenth-century tropes of labor exploitation and compared their own members to slaves. At the first convention of the New England Labor Reform League, its head, Ezra Heywood, declared that "we are all negroes"; but he was not expressing solidarity with Black people. Rather, he saw northern cities as latter-day plantations worked by the impoverished many and lorded over by a fabulously wealthy few. He also denounced the forces that held women in "wretched pecuniary servitude." A white woman labor reformer made a similar point in describing the suffering needlewoman: "Truly she has the privilege of working at starvation prices; of paying for a home, subject to an enforced, and, it may be[,] obnoxious and degrading tenant; of being hunted down and returned to her master like any other slave." The New England Women's Club exclaimed, "How many women, born for better things, have been slaves to the unproductive needle all their lives, because they never had the opportunity to learn the work for which they are best suited by nature!" The words "slave" and "slavery" resonated with white New Englanders indifferent to the descendants of enslaved people in their midst.[40]

Despite the ferment surrounding suffrage, wage, and hour issues, northern postwar reformers emulated the strategies of the abolitionists to argue for "equality" in a strictly legal sense without scrutinizing the dynamics of individual workplaces. Boston's white laboring classes refused to take on Black apprentices, excluded Blacks as coworkers, and denied them membership in all-white unions. A few Black men loyal to the Republican Party could count on patronage positions that lifted them above the mass of Black laborers; but the party itself failed to challenge a social division of labor that relegated northern Black workers to the margins. To many whites, the term "Black worker" referred to a field hand in the South, leaving northern employers free to defer to—and thereby reinforce—the exclusionary impulses of their white employees.

15

Persistent Industry

The end of one's work-life is just as revealing as the early years, for only over time do avenues or barriers to advancement become evident. Some jobs come with a built-in ladder of upward mobility, a way for a wage earner to ascend gradually within a workplace, take on more responsibility, and earn more money. At times, seemingly lowly positions eventually yield proprietorship, such as when the waiter opens a restaurant or the tailor opens a clothing store. Most Black Bostonians, like many working-class whites, lacked access to these ladder rungs in the form of union-sponsored apprenticeships, promotions, capital accumulation, and a supervisor's favoritism. Unlike their white counterparts, though, Black workers rarely saw their children do better than they had done in the workforce. Instead, porters, tenders, waiters, domestic servants, laundresses, and even professionals defined a desirable position as a stable one. And the death of a steady, even highly successful male breadwinner could leave his widow penniless, with nothing of material value to show for a lifetime of toil.

Carter Selden's long tenure with a single employer testified to his work ethic and reliability as a porter. From the 1860s through the 1880s, Selden worked for Joseph Breck & Son, dealers in agricultural implements at 51 North Market Street. The firm, one of the largest of its kind in the region, advertised "Machines of all Descriptions . . . All at the Lowest Cash Prices," and sold cultivators, churns, harrows, mowers, sowers, plows, weather vanes, wheelbarrows, hoes, rakes, and grindstones. The job gave Selden plenty to do: hauling merchandise into the store, moving it around, and then hauling it out. During this whole period, Carter lived at 40 Phillips Street, another indicator of his remarkable stability over the years.[1]

In 1870 Selden was presiding over an extended family in his household and his West End neighborhood. Now seventy, he was living with his wife, Sarah, who was working as a laundress; his daughter Mary, twenty; and his married son Edward, thirty, also a porter. Sometime after the end of the war, Edward and his wife, Elizabeth, had moved their family back to Boston from New York City, where the couple's two children had been born. Also living in the household were John and Virginia Watson, a waiter and his wife born in Virginia. Not far away, on South Russell Street, Carter's son Thomas and his family were boarding with John and Eliza Casson. Thomas, twenty-eight, had remarried in September 1868; his wife, née Louisa Marsden, was from Prince Edward Island, twenty-three years old, and now a bride for the first time.

Thomas was working as a porter at 116 Milk Street. The job seemed to come with some promise of a future—not upward mobility, but at least long-term work for a single employer. The Milk Street building contained several offices and businesses, and it is uncertain whether Thomas worked for one or some of them. In any case, it is probable that his father arranged things for him. Still, working as a porter seemed like an odd job for a man wounded in the war, a man who, in the words of his first wife, had returned from the South in "poor health," with his capacity for manual labor severely compromised.[2]

Sometime after 1870, Thomas and his wife, Louisa, moved their growing family to the suburb of Newton, and three more daughters were born over the next seven years. He had brought with him to the marriage his daughter Lillie, now twelve, and he and Louisa had their first daughter together in 1869. The government pension he began receiving in the summer of 1865—$4 a month—did not even cover one week's rent. By this time Thomas's friend Aaron Joseph and his wife, Jane, had relocated to Plymouth. While Aaron was working in a cotton mill (probably as a custodian), Jane had the company of her sister Elizabeth Maddox Selden Revaleon, Thomas's first wife, who had divorced her second husband sometime in the 1870s and moved with her children and her mother, Elizabeth Maddox, to Plymouth. Elizabeth the younger worked as a servant, while her (and Thomas's) son William, now twenty, had a job as a laborer. She had had three more children with Albert Revaleon. The eventual confluence of the Maddox, Revaleon, Joseph, and Selden families in southeastern Massachusetts would yield some surprises in the early 1880s.

As a young man, Aaron Joseph had learned the craft of a currier. When he joined the navy in 1862, he or someone else listed his job as waiter/servant. After a stint in the Plymouth cotton mill, he moved to New Bedford and once again took to the sea, now as a steward on merchant marine ships. In his peripatetic work history, and in his residential restlessness, he was not unusual among Boston's Black Civil War veterans, or Boston Black laborers in general.

Like their white counterparts, many Black veterans had returned from the war with physical disabilities—amputated limbs and still painful gunshot wounds—but compared to whites, a disproportionate number of Black men had also incurred wounds doing fatigue work. And the fact that menial labor was often the only kind of employment open to them meant that they and their families suffered from their diminished wage-earning capabilities. Moreover, the long-lasting effects of the war exacerbated the normal effects of aging among veterans who were impoverished and condemned to a life of hard physical labor. A wounded veteran put an additional burden on already struggling spouses, parents, siblings, and neighbors. Thomas Cannon, wounded in the left thigh at Honey Hill, felt so much stiffness in his leg he could not stand for any length of time; according to his wife, who now provided for them both, he "suffered so much pain he had to lay on a bed part of his time & when he walk a round he use a cain."[3]

The postwar careers of men of the 54th and 55th regiments and 5th Cavalry highlight the challenges Black men faced. These husbands and fathers possessed few, if any, prospects for job advancement. Some men left Boston and sought opportunities elsewhere. In contrast, Joseph Elisha, the lover of horses, stayed in Boston, and after working as a shoemaker and printer, followed his father's occupation as a barber. William Aiken was fortunate to be able to resume his old job as a porter at a provisioning store. At some point he left to drive his own wagon team, but gave that up and moved to Portsmouth, New Hampshire, where he tried his hand at farming for a while. Of his work history, he remarked, "I worked as a laborer whenever and wherever I could get a job, in stores, loading teams, cleaning snow from walks, in gardens and farming."[4]

Although several veterans married right out of service (with the wedding officiant often the Reverend Grimes), some continued to live in their parents' homes with other adult siblings. James D. Ruffin returned to his mother's house in Chelsea, rejoining John, thirty-seven, a barber; Emma, thirty-nine, a domestic servant; and O'Connor, twenty-five, and Powhatan, twenty-nine, both porters for the railroad. Similarly, Cornelius Robbins, a naval veteran, continued to work as a mariner, with a home base that included his parents and his siblings and their spouses, ranging in age from seventeen to thirty-three—two waiters, three seamstresses, and a porter. Cornelius Weeden married, and, as a laborer, together with his wife, née Matilda Nichols, a laundress, supported their two sons and Cornelius's parents, Henry, now seventy-three and still a tailor and clothing dealer, and Jane, sixty.

Not all veterans adjusted to civilian life. Gad Minot, a sailor working in the Charlestown Navy Yard in 1860, had served on the *St. Mary's*, a guard ship that became notorious for the racist and violent impulses of its white crew members. Minot was a member of the crew when the vessel was deployed to Panama Bay and Valparaiso, Chile. After service aboard another ship, this one the *Bat*, he was mustered out in 1865 in his hometown of Boston, apparently at loose ends. Between 1866 and 1869 he was arrested several times for assault with a razor blade, as well as for stripping roofs of shingles and lead sheeting to sell. In and out of the House of Correction, he was living with his parents in Cambridge in 1870. But in January 1871, a charge of slashing a woman with a razor led to one last jail sentence, this one for eighteen months. Minot died in prison five months later at the age of twenty-nine. He was one of only a few Black people in Boston with an African parent—his father, Odicondo, born in 1811, worked as a chimney sweep and outlived his son.[5]

It seems remarkable that some men who were confined to menial toil—and that, sporadic at best—could afford to free their wives from wage earning, and in many cases keep even their teenaged children in school. In time-honored fashion, households that included several employed adults made this possible. In 1870, Eliza Meeks (Mukes), who came north from Virginia as part of the Freedmen's Bureau migration, was keeping house in Cambridge. Addie, twelve, was attending school. But living with mother and daughter were Eliza's older children and their spouses—eight people altogether, including a laborer, a tea packer, a seamstress, a dressmaker, a clerk, and three waiters. In other job markets, Addie might have been sent out to work as a servant to add to the family's income; however, Boston did not offer enough wage-earning opportunities to lure—or force—young Black men and women into the labor market. In any case, the presence of so many adult workers in the household made Addie's schooling possible, a pattern common to Boston's laboring population in general.

Too, it is likely that a web of mutual aid societies provided just enough assistance in time of illness and death to allow families of modest means the wherewithal to free certain able-bodied household members from paid labor. Fraternal orders such as the Prince Hall Freemasons, the Hancock Mutual Relief Association, and the Ancient Landmark Lodge No. 32 of the Odd Fellows looked out for their own members, most of whom were literate and relatively well-to-do. The April 1870 celebration of the ratification of the Fifteenth Amendment featured a "grand procession" of representatives from around the commonwealth, with several of Boston's Black fraternal orders, including the Rising Sun Lodge, the Olive Branch Lodge of Good Samaritans, the John Brown Total Abstinence Society, and the Lone Star Benevolent Society.[6]

Groups of workers created their own orders—for example, the Benevolent Fraternity of Coachmen and the Head and Side Waiters Association. Yet poorer people probably relied on smaller, more ephemeral societies imported from the South after the war. Assessing members a small amount—perhaps 5 cents a week—these cooperatives paid for members' medical care and burial. Richmond had a multitude of them; together they revealed a tangled web of kin, workplace, denominational, and neighborhood loyalties—all elements of social cohesion that, for any one person or family, might have loosened or dissolved in the move north. The temperance-oriented True Reformers had its headquarters in Richmond and a branch in Boston, suggesting at least some associational continuity between the two cities.[7]

Alternately unemployed and chronically underemployed, a large percentage of Black Bostonians constituted a subset of Boston's working poor, and some integrated worksites, living spaces, and entertainment venues characteristic of the antebellum period endured. The flattening of one impoverished neighborhood, Fort Hill, pushed displaced families into ever more crowded apartments in the city. A huge building in Boston might house as many as 450 people, 54 families in 56 rooms, a mix of native-born whites, Irish immigrants, Blacks, and Indigenous people. The Massachusetts Bureau of Labor Statistics described one of these structures as "without ventilation, without sun, its passages at mid-day dark as mid-night. . . . Filth, want and disease fill the house." In the North End, Black and white seamen were still carousing together, good-natured drunken gatherings at times morphing into street brawls of flying stones and brickbats. Seamstresses ventured out at night to patronize steamy dance halls and theaters with mixed clienteles.[8]

Brothels and streets remained uniquely multicultural worksites, targeted in periodic police "descents" as before the war. A May 1872 raid netted 183 sex workers, "most of whom," according to Police Chief Edward Savage, "were subsequently sent to their friends outside the city." In August the *Herald* described the crackdown on crime as akin to a war: captains in the "Ends"—West, North, and South—"daubed on the war paint, put their most trusty men into the trenches, and opened hostilities in earnest," the men "laying siege to the brothels" along their "front." This was a war the police were bound to lose. In an echo of antebellum reports, the *Herald* described "A West End School of Night Walkers"—"spinsters who are not particular how they walk, where they walk, or who they 'go for,' black or white." In keeping with postwar trends, however, prostitution was becoming more organized, with some women spared time in the House of Correction by prosperous pimps and madams who could pay fines and bail fees running into the hundreds of dollars. In contrast, solo practitioners went to jail.[9]

Despite the intermixing among the Boston poor, the Black community retained distinctive features. It contained large numbers of southerners, as migrants from Virginia continued to move north. After the demise of the Freedmen's Bureau, private agents continued to bring Black men, women, and children from Richmond to Massachusetts to work as domestics and waiters. Responding to reports of a northern labor recruiter signing up hundreds of Blacks in 1870, a Richmond paper mocked Boston for its insatiable demand for "'*helps*' in families, hotels, and public houses generally." Supposedly, "an unfortunate ambition" among young white people in the rural areas prompted them to seek jobs in factories "and follow the pursuits of gain and speculation." White northerners had no interest in Black migrants as farm-hands, according to this writer. Instead, "for housework, boot-blacks, and such drudgery, the negroes are thought in the North to be good." Once New England became a land of "African and Asiatic people," its lawmakers would have to enact measures similar to those in the South meant to control its own non-white populations; presumably, this legislation would put the two former combatants on "a footing of equality."[10]

Boston had few social services that addressed the needs of its poorest Black residents. The City Missionary Society focused its energies on those who professed to be Christians, or who at least were open to listening while an agent read to them from the Bible. At times, wage-earning responsibilities interfered with expressions of piety. One missionary noted with approval the devotion of a "Mr. G., formerly enslaved," who left his work on the docks early every Saturday afternoon at 3:00, forgoing the extra money so he could get home in time to see her: "He says he gets more by doing so, than all the money he could earn; for he gets that which money cannot buy, and which he feasts upon until Saturday comes again." In another case, "a young colored man of some intelligence and unblemished character, but ignorant of spiritual religion," showed interest in the gospel; but he found work outside the city for the summer and could not go to church services then. He returned in the autumn but he had to be at his job as a hotel waiter early Sunday morning, so church attendance was not possible.[11]

The Boston Industrial Aid Society tended to channel its mainly white supplicants into temporary forms of employment—washing, scrubbing, cleaning, and other jobs—making life even more difficult for Black job-seekers. The society encountered relatively few Black applicants for aid but remained ever on the lookout for the unworthy. Its annual report of 1866 highlighted John M., thirty-five, a Black man who persisted in "asking everyone for work whom he thinks will not employ him, so as to make a good case for aid." If offered a job, the authors predicted, "he will shirk it." In contrast, the society looked favorably upon L.B., forty-seven, a Black woman rendered frail from long years of domestic service and "continuous labor" (though she could still do "day work"). Her mother was currently an inmate in the Home for Aged Colored Women.[12]

Although the demand for the services of the home grew, the home's capacity remained the same—ten inmates, a matron, a servant, and a cook. (The Reverend Grimes probably had a say in who was hired—Rachel A. Smith, a housekeeper in 1871, was a member of Twelfth Baptist.) The residents included elderly women scarred by illness and lifelong hardship—Lucy Gardiner, whose five children were all dead; Eliza Richardson, sixty-eight, "worn out with cooking & hard work"; and Jane Moulton, eighty, who resisted admission until, "reduced to extremity, no bedstead, no fire, & mind flickering, she consented to come to us." Elizabeth Thompson, though only forty, was infirm: "Unreasonably hard work having been imposed upon her in her youth while at service, her health was ruined; & she gradually lost the power of supporting herself." She had no known kin. The managers of the house rejected the application of Eunice Deboise, though she was miserable in the Bridgewater Almshouse, surrounded by shrieking patients whose noises left her "sick & depressed." Her daughter was healthy and presumably able to care for her.[13]

The expectation that families and neighbors would gladly look out for these women did not always reflect reality. Rachel Ann

Edwardson, born enslaved in Baltimore, had lived for five years with her brother; but now "his wife is no longer willing to have him give his sister a home." At times even a woman's longtime neighbors could turn on her as she was seeking help. The home's directors were inclined to admit Patience Davis, a native of Virginia, "but many respectable colored people who had known her for years agreed in statements regarding her character and past life which showed her unsuitable for this home." She was denied admission.[14]

The Home for Aged Colored Women made its expectations for residents explicit by describing model inmates. When she entered the home in 1870, Rebecca Davis, eighty-two, had only one surviving child out of the sixteen she had borne. Descended from Pankapoag Indians, she was a native of Canton, Massachusetts. The directors praised her strength of character: "With great energy & Aboriginal independence of will, she has labored industriously to maintain herself & family, justly proud of her freedom and ability to do so." Only when her daughter was unable to support her and a stroke felled her did she agree to be admitted.[15]

Sometime in the 1870s, the home began to sponsor an annual fair to raise money. Members of the city's Black churches were major contributors. Among the items sold were products sewn by the residents themselves, and the directors acknowledged their contribution in the annual report for 1877: "The inmates are already working busily themselves, and there is something truly pathetic in the patience and industry which these poor, trembling fingers bring to their task, and the pride they have in trying to do something which shall reflect credit upon the Home." Around this time, Peter Randolph's twenty-year-old daughter Mary was one of the volunteers who came every week to read to the inmates, offering them a welcome diversion while they did their work.[16]

In their eulogies for deceased inmates, the directors made their own personal values clear and revealed their notions of a good death. The departed were described as good, contented, cheerful, and willing to work, for example. Louisa Williams "won the warm affection [of the staff] by her grateful temper, & her persistent industry while she could move at all. The love of flowers & the care of plants beautified her latest years; and perfect serenity of mind shed a halo round the pillow of the long-suffering, dying woman, which impressed every one with reverence for her."[17]

Not all Black Bostonians died penniless. Some made headlines for their achievements and lived lives of relative privilege; these were the well-known, well-educated, and well-to-do men and women who gave the community its luster and national standing. Few combined all of these qualities, though George Lewis Ruffin, active in Republican politics and Massachusetts's first Black judge, together with his wife, Josephine St. Pierre Ruffin, a leader of the national Black women's club movement, certainly qualified. Prominence in antebellum abolitionist circles, combined with name recognition, did not guarantee an existence free of money worries, as the struggles of Harriet Jacobs and Peter Randolph clearly indicated. Neither did local federal and patronage jobs, which were contingent on the party in power at any one time. In general, the route to financial well-being lay along one of two paths—real estate investments, or a business that garnered a white clientele. John Bailey, the gym owner; Joshua Bowen Smith and George Downing, caterers; the artists Edmonia Lewis and Edward Bannister; and Robert Morris and Edwin G. Walker, both criminal defense lawyers, all established a firm foundation of white patrons and customers. They were able to furnish their homes with Victorian bric-a-brac, dress in the latest fashions, and travel in the United States and abroad. Their glittering success was the pride of Black Boston, even as most men and women remained confined to low-paying menial employment.

Reflecting the larger society, the roughly 2 percent of Boston's Black residents who constituted the community's elite intermarried and passed their advantages and money on to their children. Mark DeMortie, who went on to a successful business career after serving as sutler for the 54th Massachusetts, managed to elude accusations and lawsuits charging him with bigamy and desertion (brought by a woman in Chicago) and married Cornelia Downing, daughter of George T. Downing. Her mother, Serena Leonora, was a daughter of Dr. John V. DeGrasse. The wedding took place in the new Downing residence in Washington, DC. Papers covered "The Grand Colored Wedding at Washington" and trumpeted "the *elite* of colored fashion and high life [who] were assembled in the front parlor." The bride wore a dress of a heavy moire antique round point lace and a headdress embellished with orange blossoms, diamonds, and pearls. The guests brought gifts of china, silver, and cut glass.[18]

In a May 1870 letter to the bride-to-be, Louisa Jacobs wished her friend Cornelia "great contentment and happiness," but added, "I do not say of cloudless happiness for I believe there is no such existence in this life. If we only hold and regulate the sunshine that lives within our reach we shall not be deeply scared by the cloud that will sometimes mar its brightness." That year Louisa and her mother, Harriet, opened a boardinghouse in Cambridge, and Harriet's brother John and his wife Elleanor (a white Englishwoman) and grandchildren arrived from England and moved in nearby. Harriet seemed to be within reach of a long-deferred "dream of my life," in her words, first articulated in 1855: "I do not sit with my children in a home of my own. I still yearn for a hearthstone of my own, however humble." Yet her relief at finally having her own home (albeit a rented one) was short-lived: John died in December 1873.[19]

In Cambridge, the Jacobs extended family lived near another famous fugitive from slavery. Mary Walker continued to work as a seamstress, though her failing eyesight made fancy needlework more difficult. Meanwhile, her children proved both a blessing and a source of never-ending worry. She found sewing jobs for her daughter, Agnes. At first, her son-in-law, James, was able to work as a carpenter, and her son, Bryant, took a job as a gardener for Harvard College and then as a coachman. In 1866 Bryant married a young Irish immigrant, Anne Gorey. James proceeded to work at a series of jobs, as a handyman, valet, and steward. The family rejoiced when Bryant was appointed sexton of the First Parish Church of Cambridge, where he served as a custodian, clerk, gardener, and carpenter, tending the building's fires and doing other chores at the behest of the parishioners. When he was fired from the job in January 1872—for drinking—the burden fell on Mary Walker to double her breadwinning efforts. She and Agnes converted their dwelling to a boardinghouse, and Anne took in washing. In November 1872, Mary Walker died. One of her white patrons wrote, "What a hard suffering life she has had & never harder than the last year, with Bryant's failure & her own impaired health." She was fifty-four years old. She spent her last seven years in the company of her beloved children, finally, but her need to support them and their need to support themselves had overwhelmed her.[20]

While Boston beckoned to some, not all prominent Black people who went there remained. Christiana Carteaux Bannister continued to advertise her special treatments for "all hair and scalp diseases" until 1870; then she and her husband, the painter Edward Bannister, moved to Rhode Island. He became the first Black artist to win first prize (in painting) in a national competition—at the Philadelphia Centennial Exposition in 1876—and identified himself as a resident of Providence. Several men found jobs in the federal government in Washington—John Bailey's son Parker, a graduate of Harvard College, in the War Department; and Richard Greener, the first Black person to earn a Harvard undergraduate degree, in the Treasury Department. Though he had aspired to a political career in Boston, in 1874 Mark DeMortie moved his family to his native Virginia, where he became the proprietor of a sassafras oil distillery.[21]

For some, on-the-road fund-raising proved an enduring form of political commitment if not a viable livelihood. William Wells Brown continued to write, enhancing Boston's reputation as a mecca of Black literature and art. In 1873 he published a study of Africa and the African diaspora, *The Rising Son*. In 1868 he had assumed the presidency of a new reform group, the National Association for the Organization of Night Schools and the Spread of Temperance Among the Freedpeople of the South, a job that required him to proselytize throughout the North. Charles Lenox Remond, too, took to the road again, apparently undeterred by his disappointing time with the American Equal Rights Association. Now fifty-seven, he traveled and spoke on behalf of the Colored People's Educational Monument Association. William Wells Brown also canvassed for the project, which aimed to collect one cent from every Black person in the country; the goal was to erect the Emancipation Memorial, also known as the Freedman's Memorial, in the Capitol Hill neighborhood of Washington, DC. Reporting from New York State in July 1867, Remond believed his mission was "a failure among the colored people" because they lacked the enthusiasm, as well as resources, necessary for the cause. In an echo of his experiences before and after the war, the sponsoring group had provided him with only a modest stipend, just barely enough to cover his travel expenses. Remond's life remained a testament to the privations endured by principled activists working as fund-raisers.[22]

Joseph Clash's tumultuous career was shaped by a complex matrix of factors, including, but not limited to, labor supply and demand and his personal drive. By the end of the war, Clash had abandoned his dance hall and decided to concentrate on his barbershop business, which apparently included an illicit "liquour nuisance" on the side. However, even with a personal history interspersed with gunfights and charges of murder, he still aspired to respectability, as he no doubt did when he married Mary Ann

Thacker. In May 1869, he presented the Boston Shaw Guards, a Black militia established in 1863 (named after Colonel Robert Gould Shaw, commander of the 54th Massachusetts), "with a magnificent portrait of Abraham Lincoln." He received in turn the thanks accorded to him, "a fine member of the corps."[23]

Four months later, Robert Morris officiated at the wedding of Clash and Mary (Nelly) Jones, twenty-seven, a white woman from Gardner, Maine; she was his fourth wife. They took up residence on North Street in a dwelling that contained his barber business. Then, on October 23, 1872, Clash locked the door to his shop, went down to the cellar, and shot himself with a pistol. He left three suicide notes for his wife. According to a death notice in the *Herald*, besides Mary, the seventy-year-old also left seven children, "none of whom lived with him." Over his last decade he had suffered through the death of his third wife, Mary Ann, felt the pains of old age, abandoned his raucous dance-hall business, and finally found himself living alone. His last wife, Mary Jones, either left him or he drove her out. The funeral, according to a paper, was held at the North End Mission (Clash's former hall) and was "largely attended."[24]

Presiding over the service was the Reverend C. M. Winchester, a missionary who within three years would be replaced by another man of the cloth. Few preachers of any denomination enjoyed the remarkably long tenure that was the hallmark of Leonard A. Grimes's time at Twelfth Baptist. By the summer of 1870, he had moved his family out of Ward 6 and into East Somerville, where he purchased a house. After the war his church grew dramatically, doubling its membership from three hundred to six hundred in just five years; its pews were filled with recent southern migrants who went to Sunday school and prayer meetings and got baptized, married, and buried with Grimes as officiant. He also threw open the church doors to regular mass meetings that celebrated the Republican Party, a show of support that did not always meet with universal approval. Some speakers aiming to "vindicate" Republicans provoked hecklers in the audience, bringing an unseemly discord into the sanctuary.[25]

Together Leonard and Octavia Grimes persisted in their work as labor agents, placing southern migrants in Boston jobs through at least 1870. Leonard's parishioners marked each of his passing years and showered the couple with gifts during "donation visits." For his twenty-first anniversary as preacher, they presented him with a marble statue titled *Forever Free* by his friend the sculptor Edmonia Lewis. Three years later they enumerated his accomplishments since 1848—he had delivered 8,573 sermons, conducted 6,438 prayer meetings, officiated at 1,422 funerals, and baptized 1,323 children and adults. The church was accepting 60 new members a year.[26]

Yet, as father and mother, and as pastor and pastor's wife, the Grimeses faced severe tests of their faith. They had suffered the loss of two children before the war, and then, in 1870, they lost their twenty-nine-year-old son John Andrew Grimes to tuberculosis. He was a talented singer, a photographer of some repute in the Boston area, and an emerging light in the Republican Party. Two years later, in September 1872, their married daughter and only remaining child, Emma Grimes Robinson, died at home. According to her obituary, "having lost two brothers and a sister she seemed to long to be with them."[27]

The mismatch between the size of the Twelfth Baptist congregation and the modest resources of its congregants meant that the Grimeses could never free themselves of financial worries flowing from the needs of the church. In March 1867 Octavia was still serving as superintendent of the Sunday school. She spearheaded a committee of other women in sponsoring a fair with the aim of raising $2,000 for a new church organ. By 1869 she had started another fund-raising effort, this for a library and church renovations. Those expenses, combined with the remaining debt on the building, left the church owing $6,200.

One church leader, summing up the dilemma, said that although the congregation was growing, and attendance high, "the income [was] very small": "The society is too poor to build an edifice suited to the wants of the parish, [and] discouragements and difficulties thicken around it."[28]

On March 14, 1873, seven months after Emma's death, Leonard Grimes collapsed and died at home. He was fifty-eight. Rev. Grimes had served the city's "fugitive church" and the antislavery cause with energy and dedication. He was a leader in the national Black Baptist church and a firm supporter of the Republican Party. As a political venue, Twelfth Baptist played a central role in the history of Boston's Black community, and both the pastor and his wife had worked diligently to raise the funds to sustain and grow it. Directors of the Home for Aged Colored Women, which owed its existence to his perseverance, lauded his "unwearied labors in behalf of this institution." The loss of his children had exacted a devastating emotional toll from him. His was a life marked by public triumphs and personal sorrows.[29]

Other preachers as well could attest to the fact that a national profile and appreciative congregation were no guarantee of a comfortable life. The Reverend J. Sella Martin eventually settled in Washington, DC, where he became the minister of the 15th Street Presbyterian, a Black church with well-to-do congregants. Despite his salary of $2,000 a year, and accolades from white Presbyterians hailing him as "one of the most learned and eloquent of our Anglo-African brethren," Washington did not suit him. He resented that his daughter was barred from attending a new school in that city. One paper noted the irony, since "the daughter is a handsome blonde, the father a light mulatto, and the mother being so white that no trace of negro blood is noticed in her face." In 1870 Martin received an appointment from the US Post Office, but within two years he had decamped to Louisiana. In 1872 he won election to the Louisiana State Legislature as a representative from Caddo Parish. When he lost the next election, he secured an appointment with the post office and wrote for a local paper, the *Louisianan*. In the summer of 1876, depressed and unemployed, with his wife and daughter living in Massachusetts, he took an overdose of laudanum and died. He was forty-four. In an obituary, the *New York Times* paid tribute to him as "a remarkable man of his race; a man of great natural ability, and an eloquent and effective speaker." Despite these impressive gifts, his life had consisted of a restless search for a place where he would find both respect and a livelihood.[30]

Peter Randolph never stayed for very long at any one church. On a Sunday in July 1873, he spoke from the pulpit at Ebenezer Baptist, the church he had founded in the South End. He took as his text for the sermon that morning John 16:7: "Nevertheless, I tell you the truth; it is for you that I go away, for, if I go not away, the Comforter will not come unto you; but, if I depart, I will send him unto you." In October, he announced his resignation as minister. The church had just moved into a larger sanctuary in April, but it is possible that Randolph encountered the same difficulties with Ebenezer Boston as with Ebenezer Richmond, with both congregations insisting on a southern style of worship that he disliked. A visitor who attended the dedication ceremony for the new quarters described the church as "a little company of colored people, most of them formerly slaves. . . . They were very poor, and unable to supply themselves with what they wanted"—including, apparently, a preacher. Services featured "such singing as these people were used to in their Southern homes. We need not say it was earnest and heart-stirring, and greatly delighted all present." Although perhaps not the pastor.[31]

After leaving Ebenezer, Randolph kept busy out of necessity. He perhaps earned a modest stipend for serving as grand chaplain of the Most Worshipful Prince Hall Grand Lodge of Masons and the Day Star Chapter, No. 6, Golden Rule Alliance. He spoke on behalf of prison reform, "showing that inmates of prisons are greatly wronged." He was the guest speaker at Sunday services in churches in Boston and its suburbs and participated in the ordination of Baptist preachers around the state. He gave a eulogy at the funeral of his Baptist brother, Leonard Grimes. He filled the pulpit of a church in Providence for a year, and, as he put it, "labored" at a church in Worcester and among the Mashpee Indians on Cape Cod and Martha's Vineyard. In 1880 he was living with his wife, Amelia, and daughter Mary, twenty-eight, in East Boston.[32]

Over the years Randolph retained a keen interest in the fate of his sixty-five *Thomas H. Thompson* shipmates from 1847. Through their stories, the history of the city came into focus—Black people's individual and collective struggles for decent jobs, a stable income, a chance for advancement. The soaring rhetoric of freedom and equality that emanated from Civil War–era Boston provided inspiration to Black people then and to many other people in the long term. Yet men and women exist not in the long term but day by day, and, as even Peter Randolph might have put it, no one can live by constitutional rights alone.

16

"Safely Doing Injustice" to Black Bostonians

On April 17, 1884, Thomas Selden died of pneumonia. For a few months he had been living at the home of his sister Agnes and her husband, George Henson, at 7 Primus Avenue, an alley off Phillips Street, just one mile from where the Edloe Sixty-Six had first stepped onto free soil thirty-seven years before. Thomas left behind a grieving widow—but not Louisa Marsden Selden, his wife of sixteen years, who had died in March 1883. Soon after Louisa's death, Thomas had traveled to New Bedford, where, on November 15, 1883, he had remarried his first wife, who became Elizabeth Maddox Selden Revaleon Selden. By that time Elizabeth had been divorced for a year from her second husband, Albert Revaleon; together they had had five children. Thomas had been receiving a monthly pension of $4, an amount that was increased to $8 on April 3, 1884, just two weeks before he died. Elizabeth would now be eligible for an army widow's pension. Whether their remarriage was the culmination of a lifelong love affair interrupted by detours to new families, or a connection of convenience meant to guarantee Elizabeth a pension in her old age, is not known. What is known is that Elizabeth desperately needed the money.[1]

In 1880, Thomas and his second wife, Louisa, were living in Newton with their four daughters; by early 1883 the family had moved to 38 Phillips Street, next door to Thomas's father and stepmother, Carter and Sarah. At the age of eighty, Carter Selden was still working at 51 North Market. Though his years of toil never yielded the means to buy a house, Carter lived to an advanced age in the company of his wife with three of his children living nearby. George, Agnes's husband of thirteen years, was working as a porter alongside his father-in-law, at 51 North Market. Thomas's brother Edward also lived in the West End. He was active in the Ancient Landmark Lodge No. 32, International Order of Odd Fellows, serving in a high elective position, "Noble Grand," in 1867. Widowed sometime before 1870, Edward lived for a while with his father and stepmother, working as a porter in a hotel. In June 1871 he married again, to Elizabeth Somers of Virginia, bringing to the union his son and daughter.[2]

In 1880, Edward was heading a household typical of that of other Black laborers. It included five boarders plus Edward's aunt Lavinia, sixty-five, and his daughter Sarah, now eighteen and working as a laundress. In this household of eight, six people were employed; at least five were formerly enslaved, and five had been born in Virginia. Edward would enjoy relatively steady work as a porter and "choreman," and, with the aid of boarders, maintain his own household, becoming a "well known West End citizen" (according to his obituary in 1894). In the early 1890s he was rewarded with the position of sexton at the Charles Street AME Church.[3]

While Edward was proving himself a stolid father and worker, Thomas endured a series of tragedies. On February 7, 1882, Carter Selden died. Within the next two years, Thomas would also lose three of his daughters and his wife Louisa. In the months before he died, he suffered sorrow piled upon sorrow, including chronic pain from his hernia and the deaths of several family members from tuberculosis, which is highly contagious. It spread rapidly through the crowded quarters on Phillips Street and the back alley called Primus Avenue.

When Thomas and Elizabeth married each other for the second time, she had been living with her mother and four of her children (ages five to twenty) in Plymouth, working as a servant. The move from Boston was probably precipitated by the death of Elizabeth's father, Stephen Maddox, and her mother's desire to be near the family of her other daughter, Jane Joseph, in Plymouth. Within a year, both the Maddox multigenerational family and the Joseph nuclear family had moved to New Bedford, where Aaron Joseph took a job as a ship's steward. Over his lifetime Aaron had worked as a currier, waiter, cotton-mill employee, and merchant-marine seaman. He had been elected commander of the (segregated) New Bedford Robert G. Shaw Post of the Grand Army of the Republic, and he had served as an officer of the Cumberland Association of Naval Veterans. He had joined Bethel AME Church, the church of sailors.[4]

Thomas Selden was not the only veteran who remarried a first wife shortly before his death: America Barnett of Company D of the 5th Cavalry did the same. These men made one last effort to provide for the mother of (some of) their children. For almost all Black veterans, and especially for those whose wartime injuries prevented them from performing manual labor, the pittance of a pension could make the difference for their families between eating and starving. Because he had been injured in the service, Thomas received a monthly stipend soon after he was mustered out of the army. However, in the early 1880s he began to reapply, claiming that the hernia prevented him from making a living. The prominent Republicans Charles H. Mitchell and James D. Ruffin testified on his behalf, which perhaps helps to explain the increase in the amount he received in the spring of 1884.[5]

Thomas's widow, Elizabeth, filed several times for a widow's pension; after all, she had been married to a Civil War veteran when he died. Although the record is unclear, it appears that she did indeed receive a monthly pension of $8, but not until 1890, six years after Thomas's death. The Dependent Pension Act of 1890, which expanded benefits for disabled veterans and survivors of veterans, may account for her success with the claim. Government agents had been skeptical that Thomas's hernia was the cause of his death, and they needed sworn statements from army comrades who had been there that day in October 1863 to witness the accident that caused his injury. The pension application also called for testimony from longtime acquaintances who could account for his character and his work history. In 1885, forty-three-year-old Aaron Joseph affirmed that he had known Selden for thirty-five years and had visited him regularly before the war: "I have always lived and worked in the same neighborhood with him up to my enlistment and knew him to be a strong hearty and well man." After Selden returned home from service, according to Joseph, he "could not do a man's work on account of his rupture, bothering him so much." His condition was so severe that he had to wear a truss. Other veterans of Company F of the 55th gave detailed accounts of the accident that caused Selden's injury—among them Sergeant Henry W. Johnson, who had been in charge of the men on fatigue duty that day on Botany Bay Island. A Boston physician gave his expert opinion that Selden's hernia was the direct cause of death, for the veteran was in such a weakened state that an ordinary chest cold had turned into the pneumonia that killed him. Testimony was still being taken in 1888, now for Elizabeth's application for a widow's pension.[6]

In 1907 the government discontinued Elizabeth's pension, however, because the year before she had married again, this time to sixty-three-year-old John H.E. Brown, a janitor. After Brown's death in 1915, she once again petitioned for a pension. Now sixty-six years old and still living in New Bedford, she requested $8 a month: "I take in a little work but I am quite poorly sometime." She added plaintively, "I am getting quit[e] old now and feeble and don't think I will need it long." Over the years she had incurred attorneys' fees of $10 to $25 each time she filed an application. Several unmarried women were helping her get by, and she wanted to pay them; with their last names of Maddox and Joseph, it appears that Elizabeth could count on the kindly ministrations of a new generation. In 1916 she was getting $20 a month. She died in New Bedford on October 1, 1921.

Together, Thomas and Elizabeth had struggled with what no doubt appeared to be a confusing and capricious pension system. Other veterans of the 54th and 55th regiments and the 5th Cavalry encountered even more formidable obstacles. Moving from place to place, they might lose track not only of essential documents, such as marriage certificates and discharge papers, but also of friends and acquaintances who could serve as witnesses. For both Blacks and whites in the nineteenth century, instances of remarriage, abandonment, out-of-wedlock births, and long-term common-law marriages were not unusual. For government administrators, evidence (or rumors) of marital infidelity, drinking, or sexually transmitted diseases often took precedence over more basic factors, such as war-related disabilities. Pension applicants needed to secure a doctor's certification that detailed the precise nature of an injury, and they needed documentation about the applicant's current physical condition. Contacting and securing the cooperation of all these people placed a burden on men of modest means, especially those who moved frequently.[7]

Developed in 1833 to assist veterans of the Revolutionary War, the US pension system offered the same level of benefits to all, based on eligibility, regardless of skin color. Nevertheless, pension awards reveal the way that race-blind policies could morph into vehicles of discrimination once those policies were enacted by federal and local administrators and interviewers, as well as physicians called upon to assess a veteran's ability to labor. The application process was arduous and provided administrators considerable leeway in judging a man's character, and hence his worthiness to receive aid. In the initial round of applications (1862–1870), two out of ten Black veterans filed claims, while four out of ten of their white counterparts did so. Among white applicants, about three-quarters received a pension, but only 40 percent of Black applicants had their claims approved. Beginning in 1890, when Congress revised the system to allow for pensions for men disabled after the war, again about three-quarters of white applicants were successful, but only 46 percent of Black applicants. These figures mask the biases of claim agents and also the reasons why many Black veterans did not or could not pursue claims at all.[8]

In applying for a pension, freedmen (who represented two-thirds of all Black applicants) were at a distinct disadvantage. They often lacked the required paperwork, and many had abandoned their slave names and assumed new ones. Wounds incurred while performing fatigue work were more difficult to document than wounds incurred on the battlefield, and many veterans did not know how to contact their former officers. Lawyers' fees alone put the application process out of reach of many men and their dependents.[9]

The travails of Susan Henrietta Potter Hall, widow of 54th Massachusetts veteran Elias Hall, speak to the difficulties of widows seeking to document their own histories. Susan had been born in Boston in 1854 to a Black father and a Penobscot (Indian) mother. Eight years later, after the death of her mother, she moved to Plympton, Massachusetts, with her father and stepmother and soon began working as a domestic and picking cranberries. Her stepmother, also Native American, enlisted the girl in making and peddling Indian baskets in the neighborhood. At age twenty, Susan married a woodchopper, Charlie Jackson, in an informal ceremony; but after she became pregnant he deserted her. In the years that followed, she had three children with Virginia-born Elias Hall while he was still living with his first wife. After his wife died, Elias and Susan married (in 1891). The two lived in Boston, where she worked as a custodian. When Elias died in

1905, she applied for a widow's pension. Pension officials boiled her complicated history down to the fact that she claimed she had been married to and divorced from Jackson but had no documents to prove it, rendering her marriage to Elias Hall invalid and herself ineligible for a widow's pension. Neither the customs surrounding common-law marriage nor the detailed testimony of friends, neighbors, and her children could overcome the lack of formal documentation.[10]

Thomas Selden's mother was not eligible for a widow's pension, but she, too, desperately needed assistance in her old age. In October 1882, a charity worker employed by the city recommended that Sarah Selden, sixty, be approved for "outside aid" sponsored by the Home for Aged Colored Women. The home described the recently widowed Mrs. Selden as "very fat and unwieldy & infirm & unable to work." Her children were doing their best by her, providing food, but she wanted the home to pay for her rent, $4 a month. Thomas and Edward Selden and George Henson lacked the discretionary income to help Sarah—their stepmother and mother-in-law, respectively—on a regular basis. The managers of the home agreed to give her $2 a month. She lived another seventeen years.[11]

Sarah Selden was fortunate to have advocates who would vouch for her. Peter Randolph maintained his connection to the Home for Aged Colored Women and to the Selden family; he had officiated at George and Agnes's wedding in 1871. And, too, the Reverend John T. Jennifer, born enslaved in Virginia, had served as the pastor of Charles Street AME, which had hired Edward Selden as sexton; Jennifer also recommended women for admission to the home. Meanwhile, most private charities and residential programs in the city continued to exclude Black people, and even those that did consider Black applicants at times turned them away for alleged "immoral" behavior. City missionaries denied aid to one widow who took in a male boarder to help her meet expenses, deeming the arrangement unseemly.[12]

In 1900 the Home for Aged Colored Women, still located in the West End on Myrtle Street, housed twenty residents. Aging and infirm Black wage-earning women relied on the home from generation to generation; others relied only on the kindness of kin, neighbors, and fellow mutual-aid society members. It is not surprising that, although the porter Carter Selden had managed to keep his family together over the years, he left his widow little or no cash, resulting in her dependence on their children. Given this pattern of chronic hardship among elderly Black women, the home looked favorably on those applicants who had continued to work despite their advanced age, and, in some cases, physical disabilities. Eleanor Lewis was a blind woman who had left the Cambridge almshouse to try to earn some money by telling fortunes, but she "became convinced that it was deceiving people to do so, & having no other means of support, would either have to return to the Alms House, or starved." She was still able to do beadwork and housework, however. A Mrs. Collins, over eighty years old, impressed the managers by "[going] out washing when she can get to do it." Elizabeth Monroe Hatfield was earning a small wage washing dishes for a white woman but had no place to sleep. Another woman, who had labored for a single family for twenty years, was eking out a bare subsistence and living in a basement room.[13]

However, some of the home's inmates came from what would appear to be relatively privileged backgrounds, suggesting the vulnerability of widows regardless of the status of their husbands. Louisa Gray, sixty, admitted in 1884, was the sister of William Cooper Nell, the prolific journalist, writer, and abolitionist agitator. Her brother had died a decade before, and she had a "bad husband" who could not or would not support her. In 1895 the home took in Catharine Morris; her famous husband, the attorney Robert Morris, had died thirteen years earlier. And there were other examples: In January 1879, the caterer J. B. Smith petitioned the state legislature for the money it still owed him for provisioning the 12th Massachusetts Volunteer Infantry Regiment in April 1861. Smith died six months later, leaving his widow, Emeline, to submit a claim for the $16,617.20 owed to his estate. Forced by her husband's debts to go into service as a nurse and housekeeper, she finally extracted a lump sum of $5,000 from the state, presumably not enough to satisfy her creditors. It was no wonder, then, that some men anticipated the hardships that might be endured by their widows. Lewis Hayden worried about paying off his mortgage and thereby securing some financial security for his widow after his death; in response, a group of his friends got together and raised enough money so that Harriet could (in 1889) stay in the house, which had sheltered so many fugitives years before. For some women, neither a long Boston lineage nor a famous or well-to-do Boston brother or husband was a guarantee of comfort in their old age.[14]

Between the time it opened in 1860 and the time it closed in 1944, the Home for Aged Colored Women provided a lifeline for many elderly women who had few if any resources to fall back on in their advanced years. Born enslaved in Portsmouth, Virginia, in 1792, Charity Green lost her husband and son when they were sold away from her and sent to Alabama. After freedom, she labored in Boston for the daughter of her former (Virginia) owner without pay. She entered the Home for Aged Colored Women in 1877. The managers noted, "She never received any wages, & came to us without a cent." On January 30, 1895, the home celebrated her one hundredth birthday "with music, flowers, & ice cream," and she was in characteristically good spirits: "She was bright and enjoyed it." When she died two years later, the matron confirmed her age—she had been "in the same family for four generations until she came to the Home." The Boston papers ran her obituary and suggested that she might have been the oldest woman in the city, albeit "without kin or kindred." Members of the family who had once owned her were living in Cambridge.[15]

In July 1896, the clergyman Dr. Charles Parkhurst published an essay, "The Race Problem in Boston." Widely reprinted and considered a sensation around the country, the essay first appeared in a periodical that Parkhurst edited, *Zion's Herald*, the magazine of New England (white) Methodists. Born in Vermont in 1845, he had graduated from Dartmouth College and Andover Theological Seminary. He produced much of the paper's content himself, and, according to an admirer, had "a tendency to go to extremes." In the South, local papers indulged in some ill-disguised *schadenfreude*, running summaries of the piece under headlines such as "The Negro Treated Better in the South than in the North."[16]

Certainly, Parkhurst's pointed critique of Boston's social division of labor qualified him as an "extremist" in the turbulent 1890s. He began by acknowledging the city's illustrious history as a haven for fugitive slaves and the center of militant abolitionism: "Boston has ever stood for all that is best in thought, in morals, and in religion in America." Given its potential to promote the advancement of Black people, the city was attracting a surprisingly small number of in-migrants. Still, southerners kept arriving: in 1900, population statistics revealed that six out of ten of Boston's Black residents were southern-born; 28 percent of the total had been born in Massachusetts, and the same number in Virginia.[17]

Parkhurst reflected on his recent trip to the South, where he was surprised to see (in Augusta, Georgia) Black carpenters and masons working on a building construction project. He remarked, "With years of residence in Boston we never saw a Negro with the hatchet or the trowel, nor even with the blacksmith's apron." He contrasted Boston and southern urban workplaces this way: "Here the Negro carries the hod; in the South he lays the brick and mortar; here he shovels out the cellar, there he frames the dwelling; here he whitewashes the fences, there he paints the houses; here he cleans the stable, there he shoes the horses; here he is a common laborer, there he is an artisan." This situation was even more striking given the large numbers of downtrodden, impoverished Black people in the southern countryside.[18]

In Boston, according to Parkhurst, a Black man might go as far as becoming "the smoothest, most obsequious of waiters; he may even attend a soda-water fountain in a first-class drug store"; but Harvard-trained lawyers and physicians could make only a mean subsistence providing professional services to people of their own color. He observed, "Even the colored barber is no more." White customers shunned Black barbers, and white barbers feared they would lose their white customers if they shaved Black men. One Black tailor hired only white clerks because he knew that a public-facing Black staff would cost him his white clientele. Parkhurst quoted Dr. D. P. Roberts, the current minister of the Charles Street AME Church, who said, "Massachusetts opens our schools to us, but she shuts her shops. She urges us to study, but finds us no way to apply our learning"—this in a city where many Black college graduates had no option but to take jobs running elevators, unloading ships, or delivering mail. Trained teachers were told to "go down South, among your own people." The hard truth, he wrote, was that most Black men "are given the work that white folks don't want."[19]

Parkhurst noted Boston's uneven progress toward the ideal of a truly egalitarian city. He highlighted the disjuncture between the opportunities accorded the consumer and those of the laborer when he quoted the remarks of a Black resident: "We can go most anywhere with the white man, and *spend* our dollar, but we cannot go anywhere with the white man and *earn* it." At the same time, many white business owners had failed to heed an 1885 state law that prohibited discrimination in lodgings, transportation, and public amusement and entertainment venues. (This law, resulting from a half century of pressure and petitioning from Black Bostonians, was meant to counter the owners of venues who claimed that since they were not licensed by the city or state, they had no obligation to admit Black customers or patrons.) While venturing out and about on the streets and in the shops and hotels, Black residents and visitors felt an existential dread born of the unpredictability of whites' behavior, the same dread that had afflicted their parents and grandparents. Parkhurst concluded his essay by describing the League of American Wheelmen, an association of bicyclists founded in Newport in 1880. At the insistence of southern branches, in 1894 the national group restricted membership to "any amateur *white* wheelman of good character," arguing that such a move was justified because the league qualified as a "social" group rather than a professional association. Concluded Parkhurst, "Such is the law of the League of American Wheelmen, and such the unwritten but inexorable law of Boston."[20]

The statistics bore out Parkhurst's analysis. Between 1895 and 1905, the number of Boston's Black residents grew from 16,307 to 21,234 but remained less than 2 percent of the city's overall total population. Only 4 in 100 Black families owned their homes by then. As the city became more segregated, so did its public schools. Irish immigrants and their grown children were getting jobs in the skilled trades, in business offices, in factories, and in the civil service (public school teaching and law enforcement). About 5 percent of Black men held clerical positions (as clerks, bookkeepers, and stenographers), a percentage higher than in other cities; still, most of them probably worked in Black establishments, and it was not unusual for a clerk to lose his job and become a waiter, cook, or laborer. Moreover, success in one job did not necessarily lead to a better one, or to advantages for one's offspring. Workplace gatekeepers excluded young Black people from the rungs on a ladder to advancement. These included the department stores that employed only whites as "cash" girls and boys, jobs that led to promotions and positions in sales. Unions decided whom to accept into apprenticeship programs. Factories excluded Black workers. As a general principle, machine-operative jobs went to whites.[21]

But how to explain Parkhurst's point that the law of exclusion and bias in Boston was "inexorable"? He indicted the white Bostonians who failed to challenge the decades-old customs that relegated Black men and women to the lowliest jobs and kept their sons and daughters in those jobs as well. These potential white allies included Civil War army and navy veterans, the Republican Party, labor leaders and reformers, state agencies and the Boston City Council, and social workers and academics. In fact, all these groups, for their own reasons, preserved traditional job categories and shaped new kinds of "modern" workplaces reserved for whites.

Black Bostonians might have reasonably looked to the national association of Union veterans, the Grand Army of the Republic (GAR), for support on the issue of equal job opportunity. Nearly 180,000 Black sailors and soldiers had fought in the Civil War, and they had proved themselves on the battlefront and in military workplaces of all kinds. Yet the GAR remained stubbornly indifferent to the prejudice faced by Black veterans and Black laborers generally—which was not surprising, given the rigid separation of Black and white army regiments during the war. The association segregated its own ranks and, by the end of the century, its members embraced their former enemies at Civil War reunions. Local GAR-sponsored commemorations featured few, if any, Black veterans, as their sacrifices for the Union cause receded from white consciousness.[22]

And so Black veterans established their own posts and celebrated themselves. On August 1 and 2, 1887, three hundred of them met in Tremont Hall for a gala reunion. Sponsored by veterans of the 54th and 55th Massachusetts Volunteer Infantry Regiments, the event was attended by three men who had belatedly won well-earned promotions—Lieutenants James M. Trotter, William H. DuPree, and Charles H. Mitchell. Frederick Douglass's son Lewis, a veteran of the 54th, pointedly contradicted the platitudes of several white officers who spoke. He noted that, despite the veterans' courage while "disaster upon disaster met us on the battlefield of the nation's struggle for existence," the nation had failed them: "The stubborn and colossal fact stands out, boldly, wickedly and cruelly, that Americans of African descent, survivors of their brave dead comrades . . . are today in a large portion of this great nation denied justice in the courts, deprived of the exercise of the elective franchise, the victims of mob violence, an unprotected and outraged people." Yet as a group, white Union veterans remained silent.[23]

Most Black veterans were Republicans, and they continued to press for patronage appointments in return for their loyalty to the Union. They argued that the mere presence of Black men in clerical and managerial positions would impress upon the white laboring classes that Black people were intelligent and capable of taking on responsible positions, opening the way for integrated workplaces. The persistence of the status quo revealed the fallacy of this optimistic proposition, which was dubious from the outset. The appointment of James M. Trotter as District of Columbia recorder of deeds (the first Massachusetts Black man rewarded with such a position), and several other Black Bostonians to positions in the Customs House and the post office, instilled hope among the Black Republican faithful, even in the face of discriminatory treatment when it came to promotions. Nevertheless, white Republicans resisted Blacks' calls for more clerkships. One white Democratic leader pointed out that Blacks' demands for decent jobs inevitably elicited the response from white Republicans that, in the State House, "they had men running elevators, washing windows, working in the restaurant, and in the barbershop, and this was all that is due them."[24]

Beginning in 1878, Edwin G. Walker and others sought to align with Democrats of Irish extraction. For Black leaders, this coalition of convenience probably had less to do with their support for Democrats' specific proposals than with their disgust for a common enemy—Boston's powerful, wealthy, Protestant Republican establishment. In 1885 Walker and other Black independents supported Hugh O'Brien for mayor, the city's first Irish-immigrant and Catholic mayor. O'Brien sought to reward his newfound constituents with city jobs, but Republican aldermen thwarted his attempts to appoint Black men to the fire and police departments, and they rejected his nomination of Walker as city assessor (in 1888). The new mayor did manage to add two more Black men to the city payroll—a police officer and an employee in the Office of Weights and Measures. By the early 1890s, the coalition had dissolved, with Boston Democrats now so well organized they did not need Black votes, and with Black voters appalled at the unapologetic white-supremacist impulses of Democrats in the South. These developments effectively rendered Blacks politically homeless. Meeting in convention in the summer of 1896, they engaged in an angry debate with each other over whether to back the Republican candidate William McKinley or the Democrat William Jennings Bryan for president. Stymied, the convention refused to endorse either.[25]

After the Civil War, the rise of the Ku Klux Klan in the South and the oppressive sharecropping system became issues of vital concern to Black Bostonians. In the last decade of the nineteenth century, newspaper accounts of southern atrocities became an almost daily occurrence, galvanizing the local community. At the same time, discrimination in Boston claimed the energies of both the old and a new generation of activists. In May 1893, the refusal of a Cambridge barber to shave a Black Harvard student, W. H. Lewis, made headlines. The *Boston Globe* reported, of leading Black men and women, "What they deplore most are the difficulties which are thrown in the way of their advancement in business." If there were more Black-owned barbershops, this disgraceful episode never would have happened. Moreover, Edwin Walker averred, "the business portion of the community will not employ our children for anything but menial work." Although another interviewee, Josephine St. Pierre Ruffin (who, with her daughter, Florida Ruffin Ridley, had founded the New Era Club and the *Women's Era* newspaper), condemned bias against local Black homebuyers and renters, she also said it was not "the lot of the colored citizen of Massachusetts" that worried her: instead, wrote the *Globe* reporter, it was "the suffering of the negroes of the South" that was "a source of great pain to her."[26]

Absent the threat or reality of a mass exodus of Blacks out of the South and into the North, organized labor and its advocates showed little regard for the conditions of Boston's Black workers. White reformers celebrated the creation of a Commonwealth Bureau of Statistics of Labor in 1869, but that agency identified its mission chiefly in terms of tracking immigrant laborers in the manufacturing sector. For the period 1865 to 1920, Black men constituted just barely 1 percent of the commonwealth's workforce, and since most of these men were concentrated in day-labor jobs, they were not subject to the months-long chronic layoffs characteristic of factory machine operatives. Together, the Knights of Labor and the Central Labor Union conducted impressive organizing drives and work stoppages, especially during the national campaign for the elusive eight-hour day in the spring of 1886. However, their constituent groups consisted of skilled white workers, with those in the building trades among the most militant.[27]

Frank Keys Foster, a leader of the Knights, worked with cigar maker Samuel Gompers to found the American Federation of Labor, composed of workers in the skilled trades, in 1886. Born in Massachusetts, Foster served as the president of the federation's first Massachusetts chapter. He was a printer by trade and edited the pro-union *Labor Leader* between 1887 and its demise in the 1890s; but he ignored the issue of racial discrimination in its pages. Boston's Black coachmen and waiters formed associations, but, stressing sociability and mutual aid, these were more akin to fraternal orders or social clubs than labor unions. In contrast, Irish American workers played a key role in the city's Knights of Labor Assemblies and Central Labor Union, extending their influence to organized labor as well as the Democratic Party and the Catholic Church.[28]

Whites continued to benefit from public works employment in Boston, which by 1900 functioned as a means of income redistribution, a social safety net, and an old-age pension system. (The city limited the program to citizens, excluding recent immigrants such as Italians.) City employees earned slightly more than they would have as private employees, and they had more job security. According to one estimate, around the turn of the century one-third of all Irish families in the South End benefited from city employment in some way. Political considerations determined virtually all job appointments connected with city services, from menial jobs in the Streets and Paving Department to engineers and clerks. An audit by a finance commission in 1907 condemned these hiring practices for leading to "inefficient and superfluous labor." The report found that the "spoilsmen" on the city council spent too much of their time "besieging the heads of departments to employ men, raise salaries, give out contracts, and order goods for the benefit of their political supporters and constituents."[29]

Although corrupt hiring practices for street work had become the chief offense, city hall employment in general provided "opportunity for enormous waste," according to auditors. Between 1895 and 1907, the population of Boston increased by 22 percent, but the number of city employees increased by almost 60 percent. The man-hours per day worked in 1907 were only half of those worked in 1895, probably because of "an excessive number of men, many of them old," in street work. In sum, "the size of this force was, under political pressure, increased beyond the needs of the department." The finance commission estimated that in the waterworks alone the city had diverted $1.5 million from the department's revenues "to put and keep on the department payrolls men for whom there was no legitimate work." Essentially, the city used public monies to enhance the welfare of white laboring families at the expense of Black families.[30]

In Boston, traditional forms of workplace bias remained intact despite late nineteenth-century economic transformations in the city and the nation—especially the rise of heavy manufacturing, a consumer culture, and the retail sector. At the same time, an emerging academic establishment of white social scientists and social settlement workers added the veneer of scholarly rigor and respectability to old and new exclusionary policies. A group of reformers called Progressives sought to mediate between what they saw as two equally dangerous forces in American life—rapacious titans of industry, on the one hand, and the aggrieved, violence-prone laboring classes, on the other. In the nation's largest cities, Progressives directed most of their attention to housing and job issues that affected immigrants. Presumably the compilation of quantitative data could shape policy initiatives that would address the urban "ills" of poverty, prostitution, intemperance, political corruption, and class conflict.

In 1914, Progressive economist John Daniels wrote a book, titled *In Freedom's Birthplace: A Study of Boston Negroes*, while he was a Fellow at South End House, a social settlement founded in 1891 by the social worker Robert A. Woods. In his introduction to the volume, Woods expressed puzzlement at what he identified as a recent development: "It cannot be doubted that the feeling of aversion on the part of the whites [against Black people] in the cities is increasing."[31]

Accounting for the concentration of Black men and women workers in menial jobs, Daniels cited two main causes: first, the "industrial unfitness of the Negroes themselves," owing to "their inherent traits"; and second, the discriminatory impulses among white employers, employees, store customers, and labor unions (and he might have added Boston city authorities). He then tied himself in intellectual knots, uncertain which "traits" of Blacks were genetic, which the product of historical forces, and which the stereotypes concocted by white employers. Daniels's work showed how the deployment of new theories of scientific racism could justify a traditional division of labor, one deemed "natural" even in the face of rampant prejudice and unapologetic white self-interest.[32]

Daniels suggested that Black people's response to ill-paid, disagreeable work was somehow a function of their "race." If they showed high rates of turnover, refusing to commit themselves to hot, dirty manual labor associated with "servility and degradation," it was because of the "excessive migratoriness which is inherent in the Negro character." If employers were reluctant to hire them, it was because they were "characterized by an easy-going manner of life which borders closely on indolence"—this despite the fact that proportionately more Black men and women were earning wages than were whites. If they were nowhere to be found among factory operatives, it was because they possessed an "aversion for steady work" and demonstrated "traits of irresponsibility, instability, and un-trustworthiness." Among other Black "traits" identified by Daniels was "a lack of independence and initiative."[33]

Daniels based his conclusions on his own observations and on the views of Boston's white employers, who considered Black workers "as a class" to be "unreliable and incompetent." Yet he seemed vaguely aware that a verdict of "industrial unfitness" might be problematic if members of that group were never given an opportunity to *prove* their "fitness" for a particular kind of job in the first place. He admitted that the employers he interviewed had never hired a Black person; indeed, they showed a preference for the friends and relatives of their current employees, a strategy to keep peace on the shop floor and maintain the loyalty of the workers to the company. In essence, conditions in Boston reflected a nationwide trend: employers excluded Black people from jobs such as textile-mill operative, and then claimed that, because no Blacks held these jobs, they were incapable of doing them.[34]

In his book, Daniels included a telling quotation from Edgar P. Benjamin, an attorney who had been born in South Carolina just a few years removed from slavery, in 1871. An 1894 graduate of the Boston University School of Law, Benjamin noted that whites fretting over what they called the "Negro Problem," preoccupied with the "darker races" at home and abroad, were being disingenuous about where the "problem" lay. "There is absolutely no 'Negro Problem,' so-called, in Boston," he told Daniels. It was "only another name for the 'Problem of safely doing injustice to the Negro'."[35]

AMONG HIS OTHER talents, the Reverend Peter Randolph was a gifted memoirist. His two books, *Sketches of Slave Life: Or, Illustrations of the "Peculiar Institution"* (1855) and *From Slave Cabin to the Pulpit: The Autobiography of Rev. Peter Randolph: The Southern Question Illustrated and Sketches of Slave Life* (1893), offer searing firsthand accounts of enslavement in antebellum Tidewater Virginia. The title of the latter volume, like the title of Booker T. Washington's *Up from Slavery* (1901), suggests a personal lifetime trajectory from poverty to Victorian respectability, from degradation to dignity. Both men hoped to refute, at least subtly, the notion that Black people were born with certain immutable "racial" characteristics that would inhibit their ability to thrive and prosper over the course of their lifetime.

Randolph liked to recount reunions with old friends and acquaintances; such meetings provided him with an opportunity to reminisce about his own history. While serving as the pastor of the Ebenezer Church in Richmond, he met "Uncle Philip Jones," whom he remembered from the time in Virginia when both were enslaved. Randolph described a moving encounter: "The old man approached me with head white as cotton, tottering feet and trembling hand," he wrote, and then Jones burst into "tears and sobs" at the sight of Randolph, who had been a child when Jones had last seen him. In another instance, preaching in Hyannis on Cape Cod one day, Randolph met an elderly man who was "one among the crowd" that had greeted the Edloe Sixty-Six when they disembarked from the *Thomas H. Thompson* on the Boston wharf in 1847.[36]

Despite Randolph's penchant for reminiscing, he wrote virtually nothing about his sole surviving older brother, Anthony, who had been living in Newport, Rhode Island, since he first arrived in the North. (The other Randolph brothers, Richard, born in 1825, and James, born in 1837, both died sometime between 1847 and 1855.) Anthony worked as a waiter for many years at Newport hotels; he had begun his life in the seaside town residing onsite in the Bellevue Hotel with the other waiters, most but not all of them Black. By 1860 he had married a Rhode Island woman, Martha, who worked as a washerwoman. Anthony seemed to exemplify the kind of hardworking southern migrant that Peter admired. Newport was not a long journey from Boston, by land or water, making visits between the two brothers at least a theoretical possibility. And both men were Freemasons, with Anthony a charter member of Stone Mill Lodge No. 3 in Newport.[37]

However, sometime in the early 1880s Anthony became ordained as a minister—there are references to "the Rev. Anthony Randolph of Newport" in the local press—but in the African Methodist Episcopal, not the Baptist, Church. At that point he seems to have given up working as a waiter, picking up odd jobs as a whitewasher and a laborer. He and Peter were in the same place in Boston in September 1884, when the Most Worshipful Prince Hall Grand Lodge of the Freemasons hosted a celebration marking the centennial of its founding. The day's festivities included an elaborate procession, a banquet, and a concert. Members of other lodges from New England and from as far away as Savannah came for the event. Occupying a place of honor in one of the carriages was the Reverend Peter Randolph, worshipful grand chaplain, and the Reverend Anthony Randolph represented his own lodge. It is unknown whether the brothers shared a warm embrace in literal fraternal fellow-feeling, studiously ignored each other, or gave each other a greeting somewhere in between.[38]

On September 15, 1887, Peter Randolph wrote to Samuel May Jr. reflecting on all that had transpired over the past forty years and acknowledging their "acquaintance and friendship" through the decades. Randolph reported that his health was as good as could be expected, but his wife was feeble. He commented on the tangible evidence of his history of enslavement: "I bare on me now some of the ills that I received in the house of bondage and must feel and suffer more as age grows upon me." He mourned the passing of other "coworkers" who had "gone to there Reward." Randolph added, "I am happy to say I am still trying to do what I can to make the world better." Of the original Sixty-Six, very few of those who came as adults were living, and indeed, Torrington Ruffin had died just two months earlier at the age of seventy-seven.[39]

In response to this letter, May requested information about the original migrants. On September 21, the preacher wrote and listed fourteen of them, including himself, his wife, his daughter, his brother Anthony, and Sarah Selden and her children Mary and Edward. The list was incomplete, for it omitted many who came as children, now heading their own households, as well as all those who had moved away from Boston. In addition, the reach of the initial group had grown with kin who arrived later, including Edward Selden's aunt Lavinia and Torrington Ruffin's sister Martha Jones, a laundress who had helped Peter Randolph found the Boston Ebenezer Church. Randolph added a postscript: "Any little [sum] sir that you please to send will be very thankfully Rec'd." It is uncertain whether Randolph considered himself an object of charity for May or a person whose lifetime of toiling in the vineyard of the Lord had earned him a small reward from a white man he called his friend.[40]

Randolph remained active in the Freemasons into his old age and continued to participate in indignation meetings—such as the one in West Springfield, Massachusetts, in May 1892, commemorating "their outraged dead"—Black lives lost to violence at the hands of white men and women in the South. The meeting took note of the broken promises of the previous quarter century: "The black man is free, but to what does it amount? Daily tales of bloodshed and murder are brought to us from the South. We are still oppressed; we are a race persecuted and left without a hope." Randolph was a featured speaker at a retrospective recognizing "Anti-Slavery Workers" sponsored by the Danvers Historical Society in April 1893; organizers hailed him as "represent[ing] the slave race." Four years later he was still officiating at ordinations and funerals, presiding over political meetings, ministering to the Mashpee Indians, and offering the invocation and the benediction at gatherings of Prince Hall Freemasons.[41]

Peter Randolph died on August 7, 1897, at the age of seventy-two, from kidney disease. The following year, his only surviving daughter, Mary Frances Randolph Vannible, also died. Amelia outlasted her husband by ten years. Randolph's obituary claimed he had "the record of founding and preaching over more Baptist churches than any other Baptist clergyman in New England"—a nod to his itinerancy, a way of life that kept him apart from his family for long stretches of time, and one that he never fully embraced.[42]

Among Randolph's last observations, published in *From Slave Cabin to the Pulpit*, was this reminder to his white readers: "The colored man is not only plantation hand, but he is a mechanic, tradesman and banker; he is a preacher, teacher, editor, lawyer and doctor." Randolph himself had worked as a blacksmith, tender, newspaper editor, preacher, writer, temperance reformer, and advocate for the Richmond freedpeople. In material terms, at least, he received little or no compensation for these jobs or for a lifetime of struggle and thwarted dreams; presumed white allies failed him, and justice eluded him and his fellow workers, men and women, North and South.[43]

THE CITY OF Boston, like most other places in the United States, lacked mechanisms to ensure that equality of economic opportunity was a fact and not a rhetorical flourish invoked at Fourth of July dinners and political campaign rallies. By the late nineteenth century, most white Bostonians accepted Black men at the ballot box and in the jury box; but by then, antebellum employment patterns had hardened into an ossified system of discrimination, limiting many Black workers to casual, ill-paid, dead-end jobs. A cascade of incremental decisions on the part of individual city officials, factory owners and merchants, shopfloor bosses, and labor leaders shut Black people out of a wide variety of employment possibilities; white-run voluntary associations, religious organizations, and entertainment venues reinforced these decisions outside the workplace. Many whites came to believe that the ideals of a free society could coexist with everyday systems of inequality now deemed "natural"—predetermined, immutable. By 1900 an industrializing United States flexing its muscles on the world stage was a far different country than it had been in 1850; and yet Boston's social division of labor had largely remained static over that half century.

The prescience of John Rock's words in his 1860 address upon the anniversary of the death of Crispus Attucks—"Words are easy, like the wind"—remained evident long after his own death. In that speech, he had gone on to denounce Boston's abolitionists for ignoring the plight of their Black neighbors. A talented orator, Rock appreciated the power of words to inspire people of goodwill to action; but he also understood that it would take a great deal more than words, a great deal of hard work, to create a truly just society.

Acknowledgments

I OWE AN enormous debt of gratitude to many people I have never met. In the era of COVID-19, a time of hazardous travel conditions and shuttered reading rooms, a large number of archivists and librarians provided me (and countless others) with critical assistance. Special-collections curators responded to my requests for material from specific boxes and folders. Interlibrary loan staff tracked down books, articles, and pamphlets. Reference librarians located statistics and other vital information.

I would like to thank Emily Walhout, Houghton Public Services, Harvard University; Michael Austin, Houghton Library, Harvard University; Marta Crilly, Archivist for Reference and Outreach, Boston City Archives; Kaitlin Connolly, Reference Department, State Library of Massachusetts, State House of the Commonwealth; Caitlin Jones, Head of Reference, Massachusetts Archives; Donzella Maupin, Archives Manager, University Archives, Hampton University; Phillip Cunningham, Head of Research Services, Amistad Research Center, Tulane University; Sonja N. Woods, Archivist, University Archives, Moorland-Spingarn Research Center, Howard University; staff at the National Archives and Records Administration (Civil War Pensions Division); and, at the University of Texas at Austin Perry-Castañeda Library, Adriana Cásarez, Diversity Resident and Interim US History Librarian, and the Interlibrary Loan and

Reference Librarians. For image reproductions and permissions, I would also like to thank Anna Clutterbuck-Cook and Hannah Elder, Massachusetts Historical Society; Shawn P. Quigley of the National Park Service; Courtney Matthews and Kenneth Johnson, Library of Congress; Will Evans, Boston Athenaeum; Donna E. Russo, Historic New England; Lisa Uhrig, Ross County Historical Society, Chillicothe, Ohio; and Sherri Jackson, Bridgeman Images. I would also like to acknowledge the private and public entities that have digitized such a wide range of historical resources; the recent proliferation of online materials has meant that, in certain fields, at least, historians were able to continue to mine the archives and explore the (virtual) library stacks despite the pandemic.

I began this project while teaching at the University of Texas at Austin. I am grateful to College of Liberal Arts Deans Randy Diehl and Ann Stevens for granting me a year of leave to complete this study. In the History Department, staff members Arturo Flores, Jacquelin Llado, Courtney Meador, Martha Gonzalez, Michael Johnson, Judy Hogan, and Eilis Keeley helped me with my departmental duties in countless ways. Gabriela Camarena, Sara Beshai, and Nick Roland (now Dr. Roland) provided research assistance. I thank the many wonderful faculty colleagues, friends, and neighbors who made my thirteen years in Austin so meaningful and productive.

Writing this book also coincided with my tenure as president of the American Historical Association. I was fortunate to be able to work with Executive Director Jim Grossman and Deputy Director Dana Schaffer and the rest of the superb AHA staff; they made my time as president incredibly rewarding, as we contended with new and old challenges facing professional historians at home and around the world.

Friends and colleagues gave generously of their time to read all or parts of the manuscript. Ellen Fitzpatrick, Joe William Trotter, Robert L. Hall, Elizabeth Hafkin Pleck, and Jim

Sidbury drew on their own wide-ranging knowledge of US history and historiography and gave me extensive comments on an initial draft. I also appreciate the suggestions offered by Paula Giddings, Elizabeth Herbin-Triant, Jacqueline Goggin, and Bill Childs, as well as Bill Cain's enthusiasm for the project. Leslie Rowland of the Freedmen and Southern Society Project put me in touch with James Michael Schruefer, who located a great deal of fascinating archival correspondence emanating from Massachusetts during and immediately after the Civil War. My brother Kent Jones helped me access information from the archives of his alma mater, Oberlin College, and Theda Skocpol shared her broad knowledge and detailed findings related to the history of Black fraternal order and mutual aid societies. Kate Blackmer did a terrific job with the maps.

This study builds upon the extensive scholarship on nineteenth-century Boston, and I regret I do not have enough space here to acknowledge all the excellent historians who have written books and articles on the freedom struggle in the city, the Commonwealth of Massachusetts, and New England. However, I would like to single out for special mention four people. Katherine Clay Bassard did an excellent job editing Peter Randolph's writings and chronicling his life. Elizabeth Hafkin Pleck conducted an extensive study of Boston in the post–Civil War era. James Oliver Horton and Lois Horton published numerous books and articles on the Black community of antebellum Boston, work that provided me with both inspiration and foundational material: they bequeathed to the historical profession a powerful legacy of rigorous scholarship and generosity of spirit.

This is my fifth book with Basic Books, and I am proud to be associated with the editors there. I would like to acknowledge publisher Lara Heimert for her ongoing interest in my work and her determined efforts that I reach a wide audience for it. Once again, Brian Distelberg managed to find the right balance between supporting the project unconditionally and insisting that

I rethink and revise parts of it. Kyle Gipson gave the first draft a thorough reading and offered a no-holds-barred critique; this book is much better for his insights. I also benefited from Michael Kaler's close attention to the manuscript's stylistic elements, organization, and artwork, and from Katherine Streckfus's expert, meticulous copy-editing.

My former agent, Geri Thoma, helped launch me on this project, and her successor, John Schline, saw it through to completion.

In the midst of all of the upheaval and distress associated with the pandemic, I was fortunate to be able to count on family members and close friends through lockdowns and successive waves of viral variants. From afar, the Abramsons in Philadelphia and Randy and Barb Jones in Raleigh Zoomed a most welcome family-feeling. Sarah Abramson and Steven Halloran, Amelia and Henry, and Anna and Erica Abramson offered love in the time of COVID, and, together with Tonya Price and Kent Jones, Ellen Fitzpatrick, Karin Lifter, and Nina Tumarkin, made our Massachusetts homecoming a happy one.

Forty-five years ago I met my husband, Jeffrey Abramson, at the Wellesley College Library card catalog. Those hulking wooden drawers full of index cards have long since receded into history, but our love has endured through it all. My debt to him is the greatest one of all, and the most difficult to repay.

Concord, Massachusetts
August 2022

Abbreviations

A-ANYLH .... *Afro-Americans in New York Life and History*
AAS........................ American Antiquarian Society
AHR .... *American Historical Review*
AT .... *American Traveller*
BA .... Boston Athenaeum
BAANHS............. Historical Research Study, Boston African American National Historic Site
BC .... *Boston Courier*
BCG......................... *Boston Commercial Gazette*
BDA .... *Boston Daily Atlas*
BDB .... *Boston Daily Bee*
BDC .... *Boston Daily Courier*
BDM .... *Boston Daily Mail*
BDT .... *Boston Daily Times*
BE .... *Boston Express*
BET......................... *Boston Evening Transcript*
BG........................... *Boston Globe*
BH........................... *Boston Herald*
BJ............................ *Boston Journal*
BMJ......................... *Boston Morning Journal*
BP............................ *Boston Post*
BPL......................... Boston Public Library
BR .... *Boston Recorder*

BS.......................... *Baltimore Sun*
BS-WA................... *Boston Semi-Weekly Atlas*
BS-W Advertiser.... *Boston Semi-Weekly Advertiser*
BT.......................... *Boston Traveller*
BTJ........................ *Boston Tract Journal*
BWM.................... *Boston Weekly Messenger*
BWR...................... *Boston Weekly Register*
CA.......................... *Colored American*
CC........................ Boston City Council
CE......................... *Christian Era*
CR......................... *Christian Register*
CW........................ *Christian Watchman*
CWH.................... *Civil War History*
DC FB .... Records of the Assistant Commissioner for the District of Columbia, United States Bureau of Refugees, Freedmen, and Abandoned Lands (Freedmen's Bureau), Washington, DC
ER......................... *Emancipator and Republican*
FB......................... Freedmen's Bureau (United States Bureau of Refugees, Freedmen, and Abandoned Lands)
FDP...................... *Frederick Douglass' Paper*
FJ.......................... *Freedom's Journal*
FS.......................... *Feminist Studies*
FSSP .... Freedmen and Southern Society Project
GHQ..................... *Georgia Historical Quarterly*
HEQ..................... *History of Education Quarterly*
HJM...................... *Historical Journal of Massachusetts*
IJHA...................... *International Journal of Historical Archaeology*
JAAH.................... *Journal of African American History*
JAEH.................... *Journal of American Ethnic History*
JAH....................... *Journal of American History*
JCWE.................... *Journal of the Civil War Era*

JIH............................*Journal of Interdisciplinary History*
JNH............................*Journal of Negro History*
JSH............................*Journal of Southern History*
LH..............................*Labor History*
MHR...........................*Massachusetts Historical Review*
MPNEJA.....................*Massachusetts Ploughman and New England Journal of Agriculture*
MR.............................*Massachusetts Review*
MVHR........................*Mississippi Valley Historical Review*
NARA......................... National Archives and Records Administration, Washington, DC
NA-SS.........................*National Anti-Slavery Standard*
NEF............................*New England Farmer*
NEHGR......................*New England Historical and Genealogical Register*
NEQ............................*New England Quarterly*
NHB............................*Negro History Bulletin*
NOT............................*New Orleans Tribune*
NS..............................*North Star*
NYRB.........................*New York Review of Books*
NYT............................*New York Times*
RE..............................*Richmond Enquirer*
RG............................. Record Group
SS..............................*Science and Society*
SSH............................*Social Science History*
VA.............................. Virginia
VA FB .... Records of the Virginia Office of the United States Bureau of Refugees, Freedmen, and Abandoned Lands (Freedmen's Bureau)
WA-A.........................*Weekly Anglo-African*
WJ..............................*Woman's Journal*
WMQ..........................*William and Mary Quarterly*
WP..............................*Winterthur Portfolio*

Notes

Introduction: "Words Are Easy"

1. "If . . . find": *Liberator*, March 16, 1860; Stephen Kantrowitz, "A Place for 'Colored Patriots': Crispus Attucks Among the Abolitionists, 1842–1863," *MHR* 11 (2009): 190–212; Christopher James Bonner, *Remaking the Republic: Black Politics and the Creation of American Citizenship* (Philadelphia: University of Pennsylvania Press, 2020), 139–40.

2. *Liberator*, March 16, 1860.

3. Ibid.

4. See, for example, James Oliver Horton and Lois E. Horton, *In Hope of Liberty: Culture, Community, and Protest Among Northern Free Blacks, 1700–1860* (New York: Oxford University Press, 1997); Stephen Kantrowitz, *More than Freedom: Fighting for Black Citizenship in a White Republic, 1829–1889* (New York: Penguin, 2013); Leon F. Litwack, *North of Slavery: The Negro in the Free States, 1790–1860* (Chicago: University of Chicago Press, 1961); Patrick Rael, *Black Identity and Black Protest in the Antebellum North* (Chapel Hill: University of North Carolina Press, 2002).

5. Leonard P. Curry, *The Free Black in Urban America, 1800–1850: The Shadow of the Dream* (Chicago: University of Chicago Press, 1981), 15–36; Judith N. Shklar, *American Citizenship: The Quest for Inclusion* (Cambridge, MA: Harvard University Press, 1998).

6. "The pigeon": Gary Collison, "Anti-Slavery, Blacks, and the Boston Elite: Notes on the Reverend Charles Lowell and the West Church," *NEQ* 61 (Sept. 1988): 426; "The laws": Francis and Theresa Pulszky, *White Red Black: Sketches of Society in the United States During the Visit of Their Guest*, vol. 3 (London: Trubner and Company, 1853), 90; James Oliver Horton and Lois E. Horton, *Black Bostonians: Family Life and Community Struggle in the Antebellum North* (New York: Holmes and Meier, 1979); Robert L. Hall,

with Michael M. Harvey, eds., *Making a Living: The Work Experience of African Americans in New England: Selected Readings* (Boston: New England Foundation for the Humanities, 1995). On the implications of fluid definitions of citizenship for Black Americans, see Bonner, *Remaking the Republic*; Erica Armstrong Dunbar, *A Fragile Freedom: African American Women and Emancipation in the Antebellum City* (New Haven, CT: Yale University Press, 2008); Andrew Diemer, *The Politics of Black Citizenship: Free African Americans in the Mid-Atlantic Borderland, 1817–1863* (Athens: University of Georgia Press, 2016).

7. Nancy S. Seasholes, *Gaining Ground: A History of Landmaking in Boston* (Cambridge, MA: MIT Press, 2018); Noel Ignatiev, *How the Irish Became White* (New York: Routledge, 1995), 113, 130.

8. James Russell Lowell, *The Anti-Slavery Papers*, vol. 1 (Bedford, MA: Applewood Books, 1902), 18–21.

9. For a discussion of the radicalism of antebellum abolitionists, see Manisha Sinha, *The Slave's Cause: A History of Abolition* (New Haven, CT: Yale University Press, 2016); on labor, ibid., 347–53, 467, 590–91.

10. John R. Mulkern, *The Know-Nothing Party in Massachusetts: The Rise and Fall of a People's Movement* (Boston: Northeastern University Press, 1990); Kinley J. Brauer, *Cotton Versus Conscience: Massachusetts Whig Politics and Southwestern Expansion, 1843–1848* (Lexington: University of Kentucky Press, 1967); Kantrowitz, *More than Freedom*, 99–109, 158–67, 188, 194, 200–204, 214, 226–34, 262, 278, 285.

11. "Men": Frederick Douglass, "[Free Blacks Must Learn Trades]," in Frederick Douglass, *The Narrative and Selected Writings*, ed. Michael Meyer (New York: Modern Library, 1984), 350.

12. See Isabel Wilkerson, *Caste: The Origins of Our Discontents* (New York: Random House, 2020).

13. Carol Buchalter Stapp, *Afro-Americans in Antebellum Boston: An Analysis of Probate Records* (New York: Routledge, 2018), 92, 96–104, 114, 121; Rael, *Black Identity*, 40.

14. Wendy Warren, *New England Bound: Slavery and Colonization in Early America* (New York: Liveright, 2016); Horton and Horton, *In Hope of Liberty*, 3–54.

15. Catherine Adams and Elizabeth H. Pleck, *Love of Freedom: Black Women in Colonial and Revolutionary New England* (New York: Oxford University Press, 2010), 31, 84, 339, 28; Lorenzo Johnston Greene, *The Negro in Colonial New England, 1620–1776* (New York: Columbia University Press, 1942).

16. Mark Peterson, *The City-State of Boston: The Rise and Fall of an Atlantic Power, 1630–1865* (Princeton, NJ: Princeton University Press, 2019); Greene, *Negro in Colonial New England*, 100–123.

17. "Thus": "Slaves' Appeal to Thomas Gage, Royal Governor of Massachusetts, May 25, 1774," Modern History Sourcebook, Fordham University, https://sourcebooks.fordham.edu/mod/1774slavesappeal.asp; "My": Jeremiah Asher, *An Autobiography, with Details of a Visit to England* (Philadelphia: Published by the author, 1862), 5; Jonathan W. White, ed., *To Address You as My Friend: African Americans' Letters to Abraham Lincoln* (Chapel Hill: University of North Carolina Press, 2021), 185–88; Benjamin Quarles, *The Negro in the American Revolution* (Chapel Hill: University of North Carolina Press, 1996 [1961]).

18. "The real": John Adams to Dr. [Jeremy] Belknap, "Belknap Papers," *Massachusetts Historical Society Collections*, Fifth Series, vol. 3, part 2 (Boston: Published by the Society, 1877), 402; Gloria McCahon Whiting, "Emancipation Without the Courts or Constitution: The Case of Revolutionary Massachusetts," *Slavery and Abolition* 41 (Sept. 2020): 458–78.

19. "My": qu. in John Daniels, *In Freedom's Birthplace: A Study of the Boston Negroes* (Boston: Houghton Mifflin, 1914), 26; James Sidbury, *Becoming African in America: Race and Nation in the Early Black Atlantic, 1760–1830* (New York: Oxford University Press, 2009), 68, 73–77, 89, 91, 210.

20. Joanne Pope Melish, *Disowning Slavery: Gradual Emancipation and "Race" in New England, 1780–1860* (Ithaca, NY: Cornell University Press, 2000), 128, 187–88.

21. "The pursuit": qu. in Bonner, *Remaking the Republic*, 16; Peter P. Hinks, *To Awaken My Afflicted Brethren: David Walker and the Problem of Antebellum Slave Resistance* (University Park: Pennsylvania State University Press, 1997); Rael, *Black Identity*, 27–30, 35–37, 191–93.

22. "Most": *Walker's Appeal, in Four Articles; Together with a Preamble, to the Coloured Citizens of the World, but in Particular, and Very Expressly, to These of the United States of America, Written in Boston, State of Massachusetts, September 28, 1829*, 3rd ed. (Boston: 1830), 2.

23. "My": ibid., 34.

24. For quotations, see Marilyn Richardson, ed., *Maria W. Stewart, America's First Black Woman Political Writer: Essays and Speeches* (Bloomington: Indiana University Press, 1987), 38, 45, 46, 47, 49; ibid., 7. See also Kristin B. Waters, *Maria W. Stewart and the Roots of Black Political Thought* (Jackson: University Press of Mississippi, 2021); Martha S. Jones, *All Bound Up Together: The Woman Question in African American Public Culture, 1830–1900* (Chapel Hill: University of North Carolina Press, 2007), 23–29, 40, 74, 82, 88, 107, 117.

25. "It": Richardson, *Stewart*, 45; "deadens": ibid., 47.

26. "Mrs. Stewart's Farewell Address to Her Friends in the City of Boston," New York, April 14, 1834; Maria W. Stewart, *Meditations from the Pen*

of Mrs. Maria W. Stewart: (Widow of the Late James W. Stewart) now Matron of the Freedman's Hospital, and Presented in 1832 to the First African Baptist Church and Society of Boston, Mass. (Washington, DC: 1879); Richardson, *Stewart*, 67; James Oliver Horton, "Freedom's Yoke: Gender Conventions Among Antebellum Free Blacks," *FS* 12 (Spring 1986): 51–76.

27. "The free": *CA*, Nov. 25, 1837.

28. "From": *Liberator*, Jan. 22, 1831; Henry Mayer, *All on Fire: William Lloyd Garrison and the Abolition of Slavery* (New York: St. Martin's Press, 1998).

29. *Liberator*, Sept. 29, 1832; Kabria Baumgartner, "Gender Politics and the Manual Labor College Initiative at National Colored Conventions in Antebellum America," in *The Colored Conventions Movement: Black Organizing in the Nineteenth Century*, ed. P. Gabrielle Foreman, Jim Casey, and Sarah Lynn Patterson (Chapel Hill: University of North Carolina Press, 2021), 230–45; "a seminary . . . concerns": "Proposal for Establishing a School on the Manual Labor System, for the Education of Colored Youth," broadside, Sept. 26, 1832; "suspicion": Garrison to Samuel Joseph May, Boston, Feb. 14, 1831, Correspondence of William Lloyd Garrison, Boston Public Library Anti-Slavery Collection (hereinafter William Lloyd Garrison, BPL) (available online); Mayer, *All on Fire*, 117–18.

30. *FJ*, Dec. 20, 1828; Kate Masur, *Until Justice Be Done: America's First Civil Rights Movement, from the Revolution to Reconstruction* (New York: W. W. Norton, 2021), 119–51; W. Jeffrey Bolster, *Black Jacks: African American Seamen in the Age of Sail* (Cambridge, MA: Harvard University Press, 1998), 190–214.

Prelude: The Edloe Sixty-Six

1. Edward Rowe Snow, *The Islands of Boston Harbor* (Carlisle, MA: Commonwealth Editions, 2002 [1935]); Christine M. DeLucia, *Memory Lands: King Philip's War and the Place of Violence in the Northeast* (New Haven, CT: Yale University Press, 2019), 29–83.

2. *BC*, Sept. 16, 1847; *BDA*, Sept. 14, 1847.

3. "Thick": *BS-WA*, Sept. 15, 1847; "a hue": *Liberator*, Oct. 15, 1847, 167; ibid., Nov. 5, 1847; Mark Peterson, *The City-State of Boston: The Rise and Fall of an Atlantic Power, 1630–1865* (Princeton, NJ: Princeton University Press, 2019).

4. *BC*, Sept. 16, 1857; "We left": Peter Randolph, *Sketches of Slave Life and From Slave Cabin to the Pulpit*, ed. Katherine Clay Bassard (Morgantown: West Virginia University Press, 2016), 143 (*From Slave Cabin*). References to this work will refer either to Bassard's "Introduction," Randolph's book *Sketches*, or his book *From Slave Cabin*.

5. Randolph, *From Slave Cabin*, 143; Bassard, "Introduction," 1–18. The Robert Morris Papers at the Boston Athenaeum contain some documents related to the Edloe Sixty-Six, including Anthony Randolph's freedom papers (Folder 4).

6. Randolph, *Sketches*, 71–72.

7. The will, court decisions, and subsequent developments are available online under 1855-020-0109: Petersburg, Chancery Cases: Edloe's executor vs Orgain (hereinafter Chancery Case), Virginia Memory, Library of Virginia, www.lva.virginia.gov/chancery/case_detail.asp?CFN=730-1855-020.

8. "This Harriet": Samuel May Jr., Boston, to John Bishop Estlin, Oct. 31, 1847, Correspondence of Samuel May Jr., Rare Books Department, Boston Public Library, Boston (hereinafter May Papers, BPL); Bassard, "Introduction," 2. Monetary conversions are based on calculations by the CPI Inflation Calculator, www.officialdata.org/us/inflation. See, for example, officialdata.org/us/inflation/1847?amount=8000.

9. "Appeared . . . country": John Armistead, May 31, 1847, 12–13, Chancery Case; "Assessment of the Negroes Belonging to the Estate of the Late Carter H. Edloe," ibid., 146; "only": *RE*, Sept. 28, 1847.

10. "We": Randolph, *From Slave Cabin*, 141.

11. "No one": William Still, *Still's Underground Rail Road Records*, rev. ed. (Philadelphia: William Still, 1886), 377; "had . . . *themselves*": Frederick Law Olmsted, *Journey in the Seaboard Slave States* (New York: Dix and Edwards, 1856), 58; Eric Foner, *Gateway to Freedom: The Hidden History of the Underground Railroad* (New York: W. W. Norton, 2016); Cassandra Newby-Alexander, "Hampton Roads and Norfolk, Virginia, as a Waypoint and Gateway for Enslaved Persons Seeking Freedom," and Kathryn Grover, "Seaborne Fugitives from Slavery and the Ports of Eastern Massachusetts," in *Sailing to Freedom: Maritime Dimensions of the Underground Railroad*, ed. Timothy D. Walker (Amherst: University of Massachusetts Press, 2021), 80–98, 160–78.

12. "Purchase . . . benefit": *RE*, Sept. 28, 1847; "Let": *Liberator*, Oct. 15, 1847.

13. "Slaveholders": Randolph, *Sketches*, 44.

14. Bassard, "Introduction"; Randolph, *Sketches*, 55–58, 76–78.

15. "Their . . . trust-worthy": *Emancipator*, Sept. 22, 1847; "they": *CW*, Sept. 24, 1847.

16. Randolph, *Sketches*, 70.

17. Ibid.

18. Peterson, *City-State of Boston*, 574.

19. "Shot": Randolph, *Sketches*, 99; "their . . . years": ibid., 70.

20. David W. Blight, *Frederick Douglass, Prophet of Freedom* (New York: Simon and Schuster, 2020), 87–115.

21. Henry Mayer, *All on Fire: William Lloyd Garrison and the Abolition of Slavery* (New York: St. Martin's Press, 1998), 373–78; Blight, *Frederick Douglass*, 174–83; Christopher James Bonner, *Remaking the Republic: Black Politics and the Creation of American Citizenship* (Philadelphia: University of Pennsylvania Press, 2020), 69.

22. "Unsophisticated . . . race": *CW*, Sept. 24, 1847.

23. "A generous . . . kindness": *ER*, Sept. 22, 1847; "a fine . . . himself": *Liberator*, Sept. 24, 1847.

24. "Boston . . . choice": *RE*, Sept. 28, 1847; *BS*, Oct. 2, 1847.

25. "Now": Randolph, *From Slave Cabin*, 143.

26. "So . . . country": Mary Millburn, qu. in Sydney Nathans, *To Free a Family: The Journey of Mary Walker* (Cambridge, MA: Harvard University Press, 2012), 180; James Oliver Horton and Lois E. Horton, *Black Bostonians: Family Life and Community Struggle in the Antebellum North* (New York: Holmes and Meier, 1979), 106–24; Kathryn Grover and Janine V. Da Silva, "Historic Resource Study: Boston African American National Historic Site," Dec. 31, 2002 (hereinafter Grover and Da Silva, BAANHS).

27. "Thus": Randolph, *From Slave Cabin*, 143.

28. "They . . . itself": Jesse Chickering, *A Statistical View of the Population of Massachusetts, 1765 to 1840* (Boston: Little, Brown, 1846), 156–57.

29. "They . . . all": *NA-SS*, Oct. 7, 1847.

30. "Most": *CR*, June 1, 1867.

31. "Very": Samuel May Jr., Boston, to Samuel Joseph May, Sept. 14, 1847, May Papers, BPL.

32. "Soon": *Emancipator*, Sept. 24, 1847; "and would": *Liberator*, Sept. 24, 1847.

33. "fallen": Samuel May Jr., Boston, to John Bishop Estlin, Oct. 31, 1847, May Papers, BPL.

34. *NA-SS*, Oct. 7, 1847; "the man": Jonathan Walker, *Trial and Imprisonment of Jonathan Walker, at Pensacola, Florida, for Aiding Slaves to Escape from Bondage* (Gainesville: Liberty Press@UF, 2017 [1846]), lxxvi.

35. "Strong": *FDP*, June 13, 1850; "to all": *Liberator*, Oct. 15, 1847.

36. Jean Fagan Yellin, ed., *The Harriet Jacobs Family Papers*, vol. 1 (Chapel Hill: University of North Carolina Press, 2008), 83–88; "On several": *Liberator*, May 26, 1848; ibid., July 14, 1848.

37. "My chief": Randolph, *From Slave Cabin*, 144.

38. "The New England": Rosetta Douglass Sprague, "Anna Murray-Douglass: My Mother as I Recall Her," *JNH* 8 (Jan. 1923): 96.

39. "Gentlemen's": *Liberator*, Jan. 14, 1848; *BET*, Dec. 29, 1847; *CR*, Dec. 25, 1847; Sarah H. Southwick, *Reminiscences of Early Anti-Slavery Days* (Cambridge, MA: Riverside Press, 1893), 36–37.

40. "Green. . . . responsibility": Randolph, *From Slave Cabin*, 147–48; "was worth": ibid., 148; "The Misery . . . preached": ibid., 148.

41. "A plenty . . . slaves": Frederick Douglass, *Narrative of the Life of Frederick Douglass, an American Slave, Written by Himself* (Boston: Anti-Slavery Office, 1845), 119.

42. *NS*, Sept. 29, 1848.

Chapter 1: The Fugitive Economy

1. On southern maroon colonies, see Paul M. Pressly, "The Many Worlds of Titus: Marronage, Freedom, and the Entangled Borders of Lowcountry Georgia and Spanish Florida," *JSH* 84 (Aug. 2018): 545–78.

2. "A most": *FDP*, Feb. 8, 1850.

3. "Once": qu. in Rafia Zafar, "Frederick Douglass and George Teamoh," *Common-Place* 9 (Jan. 2009).

4. "Beyond": Harriet Jacobs, *Incidents in the Life of a Slave Girl* (Boston: Published for the Author, 1861), 274.

5. Stephen E. Maizlish, *A Strife of Tongues: The Compromise of 1850 and the Ideological Foundations of the American Civil War* (Charlottesville: University Press of Virginia, 2018).

6. Friends of Freedom, "Declaration of Sentiments of the Colored Citizens of Boston, on the Fugitive Slave Bill!!!" (Boston: George C. Jenks, 1850); Robert P. Smith, "William Cooper Nell: Crusading Black Abolitionist," *JNH* 55 (July 1970): 182–99.

7. "A vast . . . women": *Liberator*, Oct. 11, 1850; Kellie Carter Jackson, *Force and Freedom: Black Abolitionists and the Politics of Violence* (Philadelphia: University of Pennsylvania Press, 2020), 48–80; Friends of Freedom, "Declaration."

8. See James Oliver Horton and Lois E. Horton, *Black Bostonians : Family Life and Community Struggle in the Antebellum North* (New York: Holmes and Meier, 1979).

9. *Liberator*, Nov. 29, 1850; "to extend": ibid., Dec. 12, 1845; Juliet E.K. Walker, *The History of Black Business in America: Capitalism, Race, Entrepreneurship*, vol. 1, *To 1865*, 2nd ed. (Chapel Hill: University of North Carolina Press, 2009), 135–36, 198, 265, 267, 304–5, 175, 183.

10. "Clothing . . . *garments*": *Liberator*, March 22, 1844; "custom": *Liberator*, Feb. 9, 1855; Carol Buchalter Stapp, *Afro-Americans in Antebellum Boston: An Analysis of Probate Records* (New York: Routledge, 2018).

11. Stanley J. Robboy and Anita W. Robboy, "Lewis Hayden: From Fugitive Slave to Statesman," *NEQ* 46 (Dec. 1973): 591–613.

12. Theda Skocpol and Jennifer Lynn Oser, "Organization Despite Adversity: The Origins and Development of African American Fraternal Associations," *SSH* 28 (Fall 2004): 367–437; *BT*, Aug. 26, 1875. Per the City Charter of 1821, the city council consisted of a board of aldermen (eight members elected at large) and a common council (four representatives from each of twelve wards).

13. Ibid.; *BET*, April 15, 1870; Shirley J. Yee, *Black Women Abolitionists: A Study in Activism, 1828–1860* (Knoxville: University of Tennessee Press, 1992); Jackson, *Force and Freedom*; Horton and Horton, *Black Bostonians*, 21, 32–33, 51, 69–71; Martha S. Jones, *All Bound Up Together: The Woman Question in African American Public Culture, 1830–1900* (Chapel Hill: University of North Carolina Press, 2007), 1–118; Manisha Sinha, *The Slave's Cause: A History of Abolition* (New Haven, CT: Yale University Press, 2016), 266–98.

14. "Principle . . . each": Henry Weeden, Boston, to Watson Freeman, Dec. 4, 1850, Gilder Lehrman Collection, Gilder Lehrman Institute of American History, www.gilderlehrman.org/sites/default/files/inline-pdfs/T-09028-01-final.pdf.

15. William Leonard, "Black and Irish Relations in Nineteenth Century Boston: The Interesting Case of Lawyer Robert Morris," *HJM* 37 (Spring 2009): 65–85; Robert Morris Papers, Folder 03, D37; Folder 07, D22; and Folder 11, D2, BA; Dimmock Charlton, *Narrative of Dimmock Charlton: A British Subject Taken from the Brig "Peacock" by the U.S. Sloop "Hornet," Enslaved While a Prisoner of War, and Retained Forty-Five Years in Bondage*, ed. Mary L. and Susan Cox (Philadelphia: Published by the editors, 1859).

16. Benjamin Drew, *A North-Side View of Slavery: The Refugee; or, the Narratives of Fugitive Slaves in Canada* (Boston: John P. Jewett, 1856), 246.

17. "Firmly": William Still, *Still's Underground Rail Road Records*, rev. ed. (Philadelphia: William Still, 1886), 326.

18. "Posse": ibid., 327; James Oliver Horton, *Free People of Color: Inside the African American Community* (Washington, DC: Smithsonian Institution, 1993), 25–79.

19. "A true-born": Still, *Still's*, 326; George V. Tomashevich, ed., "Some of the Incidents in the Life of Mark DeMortie," *A-ANYLH* 3 (Jan. 1979): 61–72; Still, *Still's*, 167–82.

20. Ibid., 327; Stapp, *Afro-Americans*, 82, 260.

21. Tomashevich, "Incidents," 61–71. Cf. online Encyclopedia Virginia, which claims that DeMortie was born a slave and emancipated shortly before his twenty-first birthday. "Mark DeMortie (1829–1914)," Encyclopedia Virginia, https://encyclopediavirginia.org/entries/demortie-mark-1829-1914.

22. Account Book of Francis Jackson (Boston Vigilance Committee), October 1850–June 1854, Primary Research, www.primaryresearch.org/bh/vcaccountbooks/vcaccountbooks.pdf; Kathryn Grover, *The Fugitive's Gibraltar: Escaping Slaves and Abolitionism in New Bedford, Massachusetts* (Amherst: University of Massachusetts Press, 2009), 250, 326–28.

23. John Hope Franklin and Loren Schweninger, *Runaway Slaves: Rebels on the Plantation* (New York: Oxford University Press, 1999); Andrew Delbanco, *The War Before the War: Fugitive Slaves and the Struggle for America's Soul from the Revolution to the Civil War* (New York: Random House, 2018), 150; Austin Bearse, *Reminiscences of Fugitive-Slave Days in Boston* (Boston: Warren Richardson, 1880), 12.

24. "Miserable": Still, *Still's*, 60–61; *FDP* [*North Star* until 1851], Oct. 24, 1850.

25. "Though": Leonard Black, *The Life and Sufferings of Leonard Black, a Fugitive from Slavery, Written by Himself* (New Bedford, MA: Benjamin Lindsey, 1847), 33.

26. Bearse, *Reminiscences*, 13, 32, 37; "a whaling": *BDB*, March 19, 1851; Sandra Harbert Petrulionis, "Fugitive Slave-Running on the *Moby Dick*: Captain Austin Bearse and the Abolitionist Crusade," *Resources for Literary Study* 28 (2002): 53–81.

27. "I": Drew, *North-Side*, 112.

28. "Breakfasts": *BDB*, Oct. 12, 1850; Charles Dickens, *American Notes for General Circulation and Pictures from Italy* (London: Chapman and Hall, 1913), 21–47.

29. "Came out": Jean Fagan Yellin, ed., *The Harriet Jacobs Family Papers*, vol. 1 (Chapel Hill: University of North Carolina Press, 2008), 178; "hope[d]": ibid., 185, 169–85, 195.

30. Ibid., 186.

31. "All": Sydney Nathans, *To Free a Family: The Journey of Mary Walker* (Cambridge, MA: Harvard University Press, 2012), 59; "Mrs. L.": ibid., 70.

32. Bethany Veney, *The Narrative of Bethany Veney, A Slave Woman* (Worcester, MA: 1889), 38–39.

33. *Liberator*, March 7, 1856.

34. "Dressed up": *BH*, April 10, 1857; *BT*, April 11, 1857.

35. *BDA*, Jan. 16, 1856; "narrating": Oct. 20, 1852; *FDP*, Feb. 8, 1850.

36. "Thinks": Irving H. Bartlett, "Abolitionists, Fugitives, and Imposters in Boston, 1846–1847," *NEQ* 55 (March 1982): 102; "in . . . waist": ibid., 106–7.

37. *BH*, Sept. 14, 1857.

38. "A family": *Liberator*, Jan. 5, 1849; Henry Watson, *Narrative of Henry Watson, a Fugitive Slave* (Boston: Bela Marsh, 1848); Ezra Greenspan,

William Wells Brown: An African American Life (New York: W. W. Norton, 2014), 244–46.

39. "It": Yellin, *Jacobs Family Papers*, 1:147; Stacey M. Robertson, "'A Hard, Cold, Stern Life': Parker Pillsbury and Grassroots Abolitionism, 1840–1865," *NEQ* 70 (June 1997): 179–210.

40. *BDA*, June 25, 1850.

41. Franklin A. Dorman, *Twenty Families of Color in Massachusetts, 1741–1998* (Boston: New England Historic Genealogical Society, 1998), 426; Bassard, "Introduction," 1–36, Chronology, 275–309.

42. George W. Williams, *History of the Twelfth Baptist Church, Boston, Mass., from 1840 to 1874* (Boston: James H. Earle, 1874); George A. Levesque, *Black Boston: African American Life and Culture in Urban America, 1750–1860* (London: Routledge, 1994), 284.

43. Gary Collison, *Shadrach Minkins: From Fugitive Slave to Citizen* (Cambridge, MA: Harvard University Press, 1997).

44. "*The City*": *Savannah Republican*, Feb. 22, 1851.

45. "[They] plump . . . do": Bearse, *Reminiscences*, 19; Boston City Council Minutes, Sept. 16, 1850, 382 (digitized and available online at City of Boston Archives, https://archive.org/details/bostonarchives; "CC Minutes" hereinafter).

46. Leonard W. Levy, "Sims' Case: The Fugitive Slave Law in Boston in 1851," *JNH* 35 (Jan. 1950): 39–74; *Trial of Thomas Sims, on an Issue of Personal Liberty, on the Claim of James Potter, of Georgia, Against Him, as an Alleged Fugitive from Service, Boston, April 7–11, 1851* (Boston: Wm. S. Damrell and Company, 1851); "I": *Liberator*, April 11, 1851.

47. Thomas Wentworth Higginson, *Cheerful Yesterdays* (Boston: Houghton Mifflin, 1898), 142–43.

48. *BWM*, April 9, 1851; *Liberator*, April 11, 1851; R. J. M. Blackett, *The Captive's Quest for Freedom: Fugitive Slaves, the 1850 Fugitive Slave Law, and the Politics of Slavery* (Cambridge: Cambridge University Press, 2018), 68–69.

49. "Some": qu. in Margot Minardi, *Making Slavery History: Abolitionism and the Politics of Memory in Massachusetts* (Oxford: Oxford University Press, 2012), 157–58; James Oliver Horton and Lois E. Horton, *In Hope of Liberty: Culture, Community and Protest Among Northern Free Blacks, 1700–1860* (New York: Oxford University Press, 1997), 237–68; Jackson, *Force and Freedom*, 101.

50. "That as": *Liberator*, Dec. 10, 1852; Horton and Horton, *Black Bostonians*, 94. For the 1855 city tax assessment of Black households, see Primary Research, www.primaryresearch.org/PATH/polltax/20.jpg; David W. Blight, *Frederick Douglass, Prophet of Freedom* (New York: Simon and Schuster, 2020), 353.

51. "Spirit . . . ourselves": *FDP*, Aug. 12, 1853.

52. "We appeal": *FDP*, March 4, 1853; ibid., April 8, 1853; ibid., Aug. 12, 1853; Blight, *Frederick Douglass*, 221–23; Henry Mayer, *All on Fire: William Lloyd Garrison and the Abolition of Slavery* (New York: St. Martin's Press, 1998), 432–33.

53. "Let": Massachusetts Colored Conventions, "[Massachusetts] State Council, in Behalf of Colored Americans," Jan. 2, 1854, Colored Conventions Project, Digital Records, https://omeka.coloredconventions.org/items/show/263; Patrick T.J. Browne, "'To Defend Mr. Garrison': William Cooper Nell and the Personal Politics of Anti-Slavery," *NEQ* 70 (Sept. 1997): 415–42; Patrick Rael, *Black Identity and Black Protest in the Antebellum North* (Chapel Hill: University of North Carolina Press, 2002), 187–88.

Chapter 2: Underground Commons

1. Edward H. Savage, *Police Records and Recollections, Or, Boston by Daylight and Gaslight: For Two Hundred and Forty Years* (Boston: John P. Dale, 1873), 165–66.

2. "Coasting . . . democracy": *BH*, Jan. 4, 1850; Savage, *Police Records*, 160–66; "a line": Sir Charles Lyell, *A Second Visit to the United States of North America*, vol. 1, 2nd ed. (London: John Murray, 1850), 158; Richard Archer, *Jim Crow North: The Struggle for Equal Rights in Antebellum New England* (New York: Oxford University Press, 2017), 252.

3. "Mount": Alan Krieger and David Cobb, eds., with Amy Turner, *Mapping Boston* (Cambridge, MA: MIT Press, 1999), 154; "to have": CC Minutes, March 18, 1850, 92, "there shall": April 6, 1850, ibid., 128.

4. Savage, *Police Records*, 198.

5. "Considerable": *BT*, March 22, 1856.

6. "Col. . . . bill": *BDB*, July 15, 1853; *BH*, July 21, 1853.

7. "Proceedings of the Colored National Convention, held in Franklin Hall . . . Philadelphia" [Oct. 16–18, 1855] (Salem, NJ: National Standard, 1856); "introduced": Henry David Thoreau, *The Writings of Henry David Thoreau: Journal, September 1, 1854–October 30, 1855*, ed. Bradford Torrey (Boston: Houghton Mifflin, 1906), 100; *BH*, Sept. 26, 1855.

8. "Prince": *Liberator*, March 7, 1856; ibid., June 20, 1856; "Still": ibid., Jan. 29, 1858; "the most . . . culture": ibid., April 22, 1859; Ralph M. Watts, *History of the Underground Railroad in Mechanicsburg* (Columbus, OH: F. J. Heer, 1934), 12.

9. "A cross": *Liberator*, April 22, 1859; "a small": ibid., March 7, 1856.

10. *Liberator*, Nov. 6, 1840; *BET*, Aug. 13, 1842; *BDA*, Aug. 15, 1842.

11. "The Trial of Peter York," *Law Reporter*, March 1845, 497–507; *BC*, July 4, 1844; ibid., July 10, 1844; ibid., July 17, 1844.

12. *BH*, Jan. 3, 1849; "Trial and Execution of Washington Goode, Who Was Hung at Boston, May 25, 1849, with Full Particulars of the Horrid Murder of Thomas Harding" (Boston: Skinner's Publications, c. 1849). A copy of Clash's pardon by Governor Everett (dated May 3, 1853) is contained in Folder 6 (D25), Morris Papers, BA.

13. "In no": *FDP*, Aug. 24, 1855; "to get": Nancy Prince, *A Narrative of the Life and Travels of Mrs. Nancy Prince, Born 1799* (Boston: Published by the author, 1853), 16; "nursery . . . away": ibid., 12; "the mother . . . girls": ibid., 14.

14. *BH*, March 21, 1851.

15. "A batch": *BH*, Aug. 6, 1850; "bad": ibid., Aug. 26, 1850.

16. "Made . . . hue": *BR*, April 26, 1851; "of all": *BH*, April 26, 1851; *BET*, April 24, 1851; Savage, *Police Records*, 90–91, 257–58.

17. "Whites . . . father": *BH*, April 24, 1851.

18. Savage, *Police Records*, 258–59.

19. "A very": *BH*, July 1, 1853; "a boy": *BH*, Nov. 7, 1849; "somewhat": *BH*, April 23, 1852.

20. "Fallen": Savage, *Police Records*, 173; Caroline H. Dall, "*Woman's Right to Labor": or, Low Wages and Hard Work, in three Lectures* (Boston: Walker, Wise, and Company, 1860), viii, 12.

21. *Congregationalist*, Aug. 20, 1852.

22. "Seven": *BDA*, July 1, 1853; "some": *BH*, July 1, 1853; "the Grand": *BH*, July 9, 1853.

23. "Mulatto . . . descent": *BDM*, Aug. 26, 1850; "one": *BS-W Advertiser*, Sept. 27, 1851.

24. "The friends": *BH*, March 23, 1854; "noisy": *BDA*, Sept. 7, 1855; "the charge": *BH*, Dec. 11, 1855.

25. "Bloomer . . . daughter": *BH*, Jan. 21, 1857.

26. Ibid., May 25, 1857.

27. Ibid.

Chapter 3: The World of the Streets

1. "An exceedingly": *Documents of the City of Boston for 1853*, Doc. 5, "Annual Report of the Superintendent of Streets," 9; *Documents of the City of Boston for the Year 1855*, vol. 1, Doc. 1 (quotations on pp. 6, 1, 16, and 3–4); Alan Krieger and David Cobb, eds., with Amy Turner, *Mapping Boston* (Cambridge: MIT Press, 1999), 208.

2. Charles Dickens, *American Notes for General Circulation and Pictures from Italy* (London: Chapman and Hall, 1850), 17.

3. Krieger et al., *Mapping Boston*, 4–17, 124–27, 204.

4. Ralph Waldo Emerson, "The Young American" (1844), in *The Complete Works*, vol. 1, *Nature, Addresses, and Lectures* (Boston: Houghton Mifflin, 1904), 452–54.

5. "The mercantile": *BDA*, Aug. 23, 1851; Howard Mumford Jones and Bessie Zaban Jones, *The Many Voices of Boston: A Historical Anthology, 1630–1975* (Boston: Little, Brown, 1975), 267.

6. "Licensed'": CC Minutes, Feb. 4, 1856, 42.

7. "Congregate": ibid., 43; "idle": ibid., Oct. 19, 1854, 686.

8. CC Minutes, Feb. 11, 1856, 47; ibid., Feb. 18, 1856, 57; ibid., Feb. 25, 1856, 75; "the colored": *BH*, March 15, 1851.

9. "Nigger": *BH*, Oct. 27, 1853; *BH*, Jan. 24, 1850; CC Minutes, Feb. 4, 1856, 42.

10. "Driving": *BDB*, Oct. 24, 1853; *BH*, Feb. 27, 1854.

11. *BDA*, March 25, 1852; *BH*, July 21, 1851.

12. *Liberator*, Aug. 17, 1855; "not": *FDP*, Sept. 28, 1855; *BH*, April 12, 1856.

13. *Liberator*, Nov. 27, 1857.

14. "To keep . . . foe": ibid.; *BDB*, Nov. 17, 1857.

15. "The officer": *BDA*, Dec. 7, 1853; CC Minutes, April 22, 1856, 167; ibid., July 7, 1856, 363.

16. "One of the venerable": "The 'Deacon,'" *Ballou's Pictorial* 10 (March 1, 1856): 141; "one of the most": *BDA*, Feb. 28, 1854; "turned out": *BH*, June 14, 1852; *BS-WA*, Nov. 25, 1848.

17. "The celebrated": *BH*, Feb. 16, 1854; "state": *BH*, June 14, 1852; "de Irish": *BET*, March 2, 1854; "His": *BDA*, Feb. 28, 1854; *Ballou's Monthly Magazine* 3–4 (1856): 392; "The 'Deacon,'" *Gleason's Pictorial Drawing-Room Companion*, vol. 10 (March 1, 1856): 141; "both": *BS-WA*, Feb. 20, 1850.

18. "In . . . style": *BH*, March 1, 1854; "brigade . . . file": *BDB*, Nov. 9, 1850; "Deacon": *BET*, Feb. 28, 1854.

19. "What . . . soul": *BET*, March 4, 1854; ibid., March 2, 1854; "hoot": *BH*, March 4, 1854. For the sheet music, see "Deacon Foster and the Coal Dealer: A Local Comic Ballad," Baylor University, Digital Collections, Fine Arts, Francis G. Spencer Collection of American Popular Sheet Music, https://digitalcollections-baylor.quartexcollections.com/Documents/Detail/deacon-foster-and-the-coal-dealer-a-local-comic-ballad/105950.

20. The following discussion is based on Charles Emery Stevens, *Anthony Burns: A History* (Boston: John P. Jewett and Company, 1856); Albert J. von Frank, *The Trials of Anthony Burns: Freedom and Slavery in Emerson's Boston* (Cambridge, MA: Harvard University Press, 1998); and *BWM*, May 31, 1854.

21. "Decidedly": William Still, *Still's Underground Rail Road Records*, rev. ed. (Philadelphia: William Still, 1886), 81; Stevens, *Anthony Burns*, 164–65, 157.

22. *BWM*, May 31, 1854; von Frank, *Trials*, 84–87; *Liberator*, Feb. 24, 1854.

23. "Could . . . handy": *BWM*, May 31, 1854.

24. "He": *BDA*, May 31, 1854.

25. "Respectfully . . . call": *BDT*, Jan. 21, 1843; "a colored . . . behavior": *BP*, April 14, 1843; "towels": "Report of the Cochituate Water Board," City Doc. No. 7 (Boston: Geo. C. Rand and Avery, 1858), 22; Franklin A. Dorman, *Twenty Families of Color in Massachusetts, 1741–1998* (Boston: New England Historic Genealogic Society, 1998), 195, 340–43, 345, 346, 378, 379, 427, 428.

26. "Here": *BWM*, May 31, 1854.

27. Ibid.

28. Ibid.

29. Ibid.

30. Von Frank, *Trials*, 37, 341.

31. "By hard": Austin Bearse, *Reminiscences of Fugitive-Slave Days in Boston* (Boston: Warren Richardson, 1880), 39–40; "to some . . . him": *Liberator*, July 7, 1854.

32. David W. Blight, *Frederick Douglass, Prophet of Freedom* (New York: Simon and Schuster, 2020), 246; *FDP*, June 2, 1854; von Frank, *Trials*, 253–58; "A Boston . . . show": Walt Whitman, "A Boston Ballad," Walt Whitman Archive, https://whitmanarchive.org/published/LG/1891/poems/119.

33. "It . . . livelihood": *BC*, March 5, 1855; "He": Stevens, *Anthony Burns*, 216n.

Chapter 4: Boston in the Shadow of Slavery

1. "Truly . . . environments": Randolph, *From Slave Cabin*, 143.

2. Charles L. Perdue Jr., Thomas E. Barden, and Robert K. Phillips, eds., *Weevils in the Wheat: Interviews with Virginia Ex-Slaves* (Charlottesville: University Press of Virginia, 1991), 246, 267, 278, 263, 310, 189; "under": *African Repository* 27 (Oct. 1, 1851): 324; "*name*": William Wells Brown, *Narrative of William Wells Brown* (Boston: Anti-Slavery Office, 1847), 92.

3. *BET*, March 1, 1851; James Oliver Horton and Lois E. Horton, *Black Bostonians: Family Life and Community Struggle in the Antebellum North* (New York: Holmes and Meier, 1979), 16–18, 23–25, 35, 37, 54, 142.

4. "Excursion": *BDM*, Aug. 2, 1847; Robert Harris, "Early Black Benevolent Societies," *MR* 20 (Autumn 1979): 614; Adelaide M. Cromwell, "The Black Presence in the West End of Boston, 1800–1864," in *Courage and Conscience: Black and White Abolitionists in Boston*, ed. Donald M. Jacobs (Bloomington: Indiana University Press, 1993), 155–67.

5. Peter R. Knights, *The Plain People of Boston: A Study in City Growth* (New York: Oxford University Press, 1973), 120–21.

6. "Working": Randolph, *From Slave Cabin*, 151; "This man": ibid., 153–54.

7. Chancery Case.

8. "A neat . . . toil": *Liberator*, May 18, 1855.

9. "In . . . discharged": Samuel May, *Fugitive Slave Law and Its Victims* (New York: American Anti-Slavery Society, 1861), 64; Eric Foner, *Gateway to Freedom: The Hidden History of the Underground Railroad* (New York: W. W. Norton, 2016), 132, 215.

10. "Honourable": qu. in Foner, *Gateway*, 188, 184.

11. Oscar Handlin, *Boston's Immigrants, 1790–1880: A Study in Acculturation* (Cambridge, MA: Harvard University Press, 1972), 56–59.

12. "By prompt": *Liberator*, Oct. 1, 1852; *Alexandria (VA) Gazette*, June 10, 1852; George V. Tomashevich, ed., "Some of the Incidents in the Life of Mark DeMortie," *A-ANYLH* 3 (Jan. 1979): 61–71; Leigh Fought, *Women in the World of Frederick Douglass* (New York: Oxford, 2017), 359n38; *National Era*, Oct. 14, 1852.

13. "Done": *San Francisco Daily Alta*, Aug. 23, 1854; *Liberator*, Aug. 15, 1854.

14. Ruffin Family Papers, Manuscript Division, Moorland-Spingarn Research Center Library, Howard University, Washington, DC.

15. "This house": Nancy L. Ruffin to George W. Ruffin, Boston, Nov. 12, 1858; Heslip-Ruffin Family Papers, Amistad Research Center, Tulane University, New Orleans, Louisiana.

16. "The Unity": *Liberator*, Oct. 2, 1857; "The Popular": *Philadelphia Public Ledger*, May 17, 1858; "a handsome": review reprinted in *Liberator*, Jan. 26, 1855; Grover and Da Silva, BAANHS, 103; *Philadelphia Public Ledger*, Nov. 26, 1852; *Salem, NJ, National Standard*, Sept. 6, 1850; "If": *BT*, July 1, 1857; *Liberator*, Sept. 5, 1856; George A. Levesque, "Boston's Black Brahmin: Dr. John S. Rock," *CWH* 26 (Dec. 1980): 326–46; "enjoy . . . prejudice": *FDP*, Sept. 28, 1855.

17. Jane Lancaster, "'I Would Have Made Out Very Poorly Had It Not Been for Her': The Life and Work of Christiana Bannister, Hair Doctress and Philanthropist," *Rhode Island History* 59 (Nov. 2001): 103–22.

18. "The crime": *BH*, Oct. 4, 1856; Joseph P. Reidy, "Aaron A. Bradley: Voice of Black Labor in the Georgia Lowcountry," in *Southern Black Leaders of the Reconstruction Era*, ed. Howard N. Rabinowitz (Urbana: University of Illinois Press, 1982); E. Merton Coulter, "Aaron Alpeoria Bradley, Georgia Negro Politician During Reconstruction Times," pt. 1, *GHQ* 51 (March 1967): 15–41; *BH*, June 25, 1856; *BT*, April 24, 1856; *BDA*, April 30, 1856; *BWM*, April 30, 1856; "on charges": *BET*, Oct. 18, 1856; *BP*, Dec. 1, 1856; *Liberator*, June 24, 1859.

19. "Their . . . them": *FDP*, Sept. 7, 1855; "We have": ibid., Sept. 28, 1858.

20. Stephen Kendrick and Paul Kendrick, *Sarah's Long Walk: The Free Blacks of Boston and How Their Struggle for Equality Changed America* (Boston: Beacon Press, 2004); Hilary J. Moss, *Schooling Citizens: The Struggle for African American Education in Antebellum America* (Chicago: University of Chicago Press, 2009), 176–78, 178; Folder 23, D2, Morris Papers, BA.

21. Moss, *Schooling Citizens*, 176–78; Hilary J. Moss, "The Tarring and Feathering of Thomas Paul Smith: Common Schools, Revolutionary Memory, and the Crisis of Black Citizenship in Antebellum Boston," *NEQ* 80 (June 2007): 218–41.

22. "Colorphobia": Scott Hancock, "The Elusive Boundaries of Blackness: Identity Formation in Antebellum Boston," *JNH* 84 (Spring 1999): 119; "as if": *BDB*, Feb. 5, 1850; "characters": *Liberator*, May 2, 1856; Manisha Sinha, *The Slave's Cause: A History of Abolition* (New Haven, CT: Yale University Press, 2016), 328–29; Horton and Horton, *Black Bostonians*, 76–82.

23. "You": *FDP*, Sept. 28, 1855.

24. Jessie Morgan-Owens, *Girl in Black and White: The Story of Mary Mildred Williams and the Abolition Movement* (New York: W. W. Norton, 2019).

25. "Deadly": qu. in ibid., 4; "intense": qu. in ibid., 188.

26. "For . . . blackest child": *FDP*, Sept. 28, 1855; *BH*, Sept. 11, 1855; *AT*, Sept. 13, 1855.

27. "Monstrous . . . curiosity": *Liberator*, May 25, 1855; "public . . . show": *BH*, Sept. 5, 1855; Susan J. Pearson, "'Infantile Specimens': Showing Babies in Nineteenth-Century America," *Journal of Social History* (Winter 2008): 341–70; Robert Wilson, *Barnum: An American Life* (New York: Simon and Schuster, 2019).

28. "But as": *BH*, Sept. 11, 1855; "the public": ibid., Sept. 13, 1855; "opportunity": *BP*, Sept. 12, 1855.

29. "Brutal": *BH*, June 4, 1856; *FDP*, Sept. 28, 1855; "praying": *New York Herald*, Sept. 20, 1856; "col": CC Minutes, Aug. 25, 1856, 442.

30. Van Gosse, *The First Reconstruction: Black Politics in America from the Revolution to the Civil War* (Chapel Hill: University of North Carolina Press, 2021), 283–84.

31. Ibid., 286; "dirty . . . nigger": *Campaign Times*, July 11, 1856.

32. *Campaign Times*, July 12, 1856.

33. "Ceased": "Proceedings of the Colored National Convention held in Franklin Hall, . . . Philadelphia [Oct. 16–18, 1855]" (Salem, NJ: National Standard, 1856), 16; "Working": ibid., 20.

34. "Mechanical": ibid., 12; "Private . . . improvement": ibid., 18.

Chapter 5: Women in Service

1. *CW*, March 20, 1873.

2. James Oliver Horton and Lois E. Horton, "The Affirmation of Manhood: Black Garrisonians in Antebellum Boston," in *Courage and Conscience: Black and White Abolitionists in Boston*, ed. Donald M. Jacobs (Bloomington: Indiana University Press, 1993), 127–54; James Oliver Horton, "Freedom's Yoke: Gender Conventions Among Antebellum Free Blacks," *FS* 12 (Spring 1986): 51–76.

3. Mary Ellen Snodgrass, *The Underground Railroad: An Encyclopedia of People, Places, and Operations* (Armonk, NY: M. E. Sharpe, 2008), 235; Kathryn Grover, *The Fugitive's Gibraltar: Escaping Slaves and Abolitionism in New Bedford, Massachusetts* (Amherst: University of Massachusetts Press, 2009), 318; "piloting": George W. Williams, *History of the Twelfth Baptist Church, Boston, Mass., from 1840 to 1874* (Boston: James H. Earle, 1874), 11; *FDP*, July 20, 1855; George A. Levesque, *Black Boston: African American Life and Culture in Urban America, 1750–1860* (London: Routledge, 1994), 284–331.

4. Albert J. von Frank, *The Trials of Anthony Burns: Freedom and Slavery in Emerson's Boston* (Cambridge, MA: Harvard University Press, 1998), 37–38; *BH*, May 24, 1858; "struck": Williams, *History of Twelfth Baptist*, 20.

5. "The benevolent": *CR*, Oct. 22, 1853; "a truly": *BT*, Oct. 20, 1858.

6. "His": Williams, *History of the Twelfth Baptist*, 12; *Baptist Missionary Magazine* 51–52 (1871–1872): 346.

7. "Whether": *Liberator*, June 24, 1859; "pieces": *Liberator*, Feb. 26, 1858; *Liberator*, Oct. 9, 1857; *BET*, Oct. 12, 1858; Psyche Williams-Forson, "Where Did They Eat? Where Did They Stay? Interpreting Material Culture of Black Women's Domesticity in the Context of the Colored Conventions," in *The Colored Conventions Movement: Black Organizing in the Nineteenth Century*, ed. P. Gabrielle Foreman, Jim Casey, and Sarah Lynn Patterson (Chapel Hill: University of North Carolina Press, 2021), 86–104.

8. "Strange . . . exultations": *BH*, Jan. 2, 1854; Roy E. Finkenbine, "Boston's Black Churches: Institutional Centers of the Antislavery Movement," in Jacobs, *Courage and Conscience*, 171–89; George A. Levesque, "Inherent Reformers-Inherited Orthodoxy: Black Baptists in Boston, 1800–1873," *JNH* 60 (Oct. 1975): 491–525.

9. Finkenbine, "Boston's Black Churches," 184; "A Colored . . . Trigamy": *BH*, Dec. 1, 1853; ibid., Sept. 13, 1853.

10. "A vote": *Liberator*, Aug. 26, 1859; *BET*, Aug. 7, 1858.

11. "Donation . . . family": *CE*, Feb. 28, 1856; "Freedom's": *BT*, March 6, 1858; Grover and Da Silva, BAANHS; Francis Jackson, Boston Vigilance Committee Account Book, 1851, 1854, www.primaryresearch.org/bh/vcaccountbooks/vcaccountbooks.pdf.

12. Stacey M. Robertson, "'A Hard, Cold, Stern Life': Parker Pillsbury and Grassroots Abolitionism, 1840–1865," *NEQ* 70 (June 1997): 184–85; "struggled . . . guest": Rosetta Douglass Sprague, "Anna Murray-Douglass: My Mother as I Recall Her," *JNH* 8 (Jan. 1923): 95–99.

13. "If . . . family": qu. in David W. Blight, *Frederick Douglass, Prophet of Freedom* (New York: Simon and Schuster, 2020), 267.

14. "Stupid": qu. in Maria Diedrich, *Love Across Color Lines: Ottile Assing and Frederick Douglass* (New York: Hill and Wang, 2000), 306; Leigh Fought, *Women in the World of Frederick Douglass* (New York: Oxford University Press, 2017), 112–50.

15. Stephen Kantrowitz, *More than Freedom: Fighting for Black Citizenship in a White Republic* (New York: Penguin, 2013), 246.

16. Julia A.J. Foote, *A Brand Plucked from the Fire: An Autobiographical Sketch* (Cleveland: W. F. Schneider, 1879): "No": ibid., 75; "sneering": ibid., 71; "She can't": ibid., 72; "thresher": ibid., 104–5; "I went": ibid., 80; Martha S. Jones, *All Bound Up Together: The Woman Question in African American Public Culture, 1830–1900* (Chapel Hill: University of North Carolina Press, 2007), 42–44.

17. Manisha Sinha, *The Slave's Cause: A History of Abolition* (New Haven, CT: Yale University Press, 2016), 329, 343, 346, 352; "eloquent": *Liberator*, Sept. 17, 1858; "in the most": *Liberator*, Feb. 18, 1859; Sibyl Ventress Brownlee, "Out of the Abundance of the Heart: Sarah Ann Parker Remond's Quest for Freedom" (PhD diss., University of Massachusetts, Amherst, 1997); *Liberator*, Dec. 5, 1856; Juliet E.K. Walker, *The History of Black Business in America: Capitalism, Race, Entrepreneurship*, vol. 1, *To 1865*, 2nd ed. (Chapel Hill: University of North Carolina Press, 2009), 183.

18. "The battle": Douglass, qu. in Martha S. Jones, *All Bound Up Together: The Woman Question in African American Public Culture, 1830–1900* (Chapel Hill: University of North Carolina Press, 2007), 101.

19. C. W. Bellows, "Commissioner's Report on the Subject of Matrons and Labor in the Common Jails" (Boston: William White, 1854); *BDT*, Oct. 7, 1850; *BH*, Jan. 17, 1853; *BC*, May 17, 1853; *BT*, Aug. 17, 1858; ibid., Feb. 7, 1860; Frances H. Green, *Memoirs of Elleanor Eldridge* (Providence, RI: B. T. Albro, 1838).

20. "Dressed . . . porteress": *BH*, Sept. 13, 1853.

21. Sarah J. Shoenfeld, "Applications and Admissions to the Home for Aged Colored Women in Boston, 1860–1887," pt. 3, *NEHGR* 156 (Jan. 2002): 81; *Liberator*, Oct. 23, 1853; *BH*, Oct. 18, 1853.

22. "Louisa": Jean Fagan Yellin, ed., *The Harriet Jacobs Family Papers*, vol. 1 (Chapel Hill: University of North Carolina Press, 2008), 221; "with busy": ibid., 223.

23. "Housekeeping . . . thin": ibid., 237.

24. "Drop'd": qu. in Sydney Nathans, *To Free a Family: The Journey of Mary Walker* (Cambridge, MA: Harvard University Press, 2012), 126; "so": qu. in ibid., 151, 173.

25. James Oliver Horton, *Free People of Color: Inside the African American Community* (Washington, DC: Smithsonian Institution Press, 1993), 131–34; "Genteel": *Liberator*, Jan. 27, 1843; Walker, *History of Black Business in America*, 1:164–93.

26. Rebecca Lee Crumpler, *A Book of Medical Discourses: In Two Parts* (Boston: Cashman, Keating, 1883); Martha N. Gardner, "Midwife, Doctor, or Doctress? The New England Female Medical College and Women's Place in Nineteenth-Century Medicine" (PhD diss., Brandeis University, 2002); "man-midwifery": Samuel Gregory, "Letter to Ladies: In Favor of Female Physicians for Their Own Sex" (Boston: Female Medical Education Society, 1850); "an outrage": *Chronotype*, Sept. 7, 1847.

27. "Conjurer": *BG*, Jan. 8, 1879; Sharla M. Fett, *Working Cures: Healing, Health, and Power on Southern Slave Plantations* (Chapel Hill: University of North Carolina Press, 2002); David B. Landon and Teresa D. Bulger, "Constructing Community: Experiences of Identity, Economic Opportunity, and Institution Building at Boston's African Meeting House," *IJHA* 17 (March 2013): 130–31.

28. "For Services": Carol Buchalter Stapp, *Afro-Americans in Antebellum Boston: An Analysis of Probate Records* (New York: Routledge, 2018), 94; ibid., 80–81.

29. *BH*, March 23, 1858; ibid., April 13, 1858; Austin Bearse, *Reminiscences of Fugitive Slave Days in Boston* (Boston: Warren Richardson, 1880), 225; *BDA*, Oct. 23, 1851; "very": *BH*, Oct. 22, 1851.

30. "Upper . . . Boston": *BH*, Feb. 25, 1852.

31. "Well known": *BH*, Oct. 22, 1851.

32. "Descent": Edward H. Savage, *Police Records and Recollections, Or, Boston by Daylight and Gaslight: For Two Hundred and Forty Years* (Boston: John P. Dale, 1873), 259–61; "a tip-top . . . attendance": *BH*, June 25, 1860; James Oliver Horton and Lois E. Horton, *Black Bostonians: Family Life and Community Struggle in the Antebellum North* (New York: Holmes and Meier, 1979), 10, 110, 113; *Liberator*, April 26, 1850.

Chapter 6: Making a Living in Unsettled Times

1. *Liberator*, March 12, 1858.

2. "Northern . . . boys": *Liberator*, June 3, 1859; Samuel May, *Fugitive Slave Law and Its Victims* (New York: American Anti-Slavery Society, 1861), 110, 113; *BET*, Sept. 5, 1859.

3. Alan Krieger and David Cobb, eds., with Amy Turner, *Mapping Boston* (Cambridge: MIT Press, 1999), 200; "Colored": *Liberator*, Aug. 15, 1862.

4. Krieger et al., *Mapping Boston*, 127, 204; "Back": "Scene on the Back Bay Lands," *Ballou's Pictorial Drawing Room Companion* 16 (May 21, 1859): 328–29; Walter Muir Whitehill, *Boston: A Topographical History* (Cambridge, MA: Harvard University Press, 1959), 152–55; Nancy S. Seasholes, ed., *The Atlas of Boston History* (Chicago: University of Chicago Press, 2019), 68.

5. "Insolvent": *BDA*, Sept. 29, 1856; James Oliver Horton and Lois E. Horton, *Black Bostonians: Family Life and Community Struggle in the Antebellum North* (New York: Holmes and Meier, 1979), 10.

6. "By . . . largely": George L. Ruffin to George W. Ruffin, Boston, Feb. 28, 1860, Box 87-2, Series E, Folder 75, Family correspondence, Ruffin Family Papers, Moorland-Spingarn Research Center Library, Howard University, Washington, DC.

7. *Liberator*, April 25, 1856; "experts": ibid., Dec. 30, 1853; "These": ibid., April 3, 1857; ibid., Jan. 14, 1859; ibid., June 3, 1859.

8. "Madame . . . Boston": *Liberator*, Jan. 27, 1854; *Documents of the City of Boston for the Year 1858*, vol. 2 (Boston: George C. Rand and Avery, 1859), 99; Lois E. Horton and James Oliver Horton, "Power and Social Responsibility: Entrepreneurs and the Black Community in Antebellum Boston," in *Entrepreneurs: The Boston Business Community, 1700–1850*, ed. Conrad Edick Wright and Katheryn P. Viens (Boston: Northeastern University Press, 1997), 325–41; *Liberator*, April 25, 1856.

9. "The Irish": Charles Mackay, *Life and Labor in America, Or, Sketches of a Tour in the U.S. and Canada (1857–8)* (London: Smith, Elder, and Company, 1859), 45–46; Douglas W. Bristol, Jr., *Knights of the Razor: Black Barbers in Slavery and Freedom* (Baltimore: Johns Hopkins University Press, 2015), 103–4, 109.

10. *BH*, July 13, 1853; W. Jeffrey Bolster, *Black Jacks: African American Seamen in the Age of Sail* (Cambridge, MA: Harvard University Press, 1998), 224.

11. W. Jeffrey Bolster, "'To Feel Like a Man': Black Seamen in the Northern States, 1800–1860," *JAH* 76 (March 1990): 1173–99; *BT*, June 26, 1856; James Oliver Horton and Lois E. Horton, *In Hope of Liberty: Culture, Community and Protest Among Northern Free Blacks, 1700–1860* (New York: Oxford University Press, 1997), 203; *BH*, Oct. 29, 1853; *BWM*, April 9, 1851.

12. Louis Moore, "Fit for Citizenship: Black Sparring Masters, Gymnasium Owners, and the White Body, 1825–1886," *JAAH* 96 (Fall 2011): 448–73; "the renowned": ibid., 452.

13. "One": *BH*, Nov. 30, 1885; *New York Herald*, Feb. 11, 1886; "Panoramic": *BT*, Nov. 8, 1856.

14. David W. Blight, *Frederick Douglass, Prophet of Freedom* (New York: Simon and Schuster, 2020), 253–57, 265; Stephen Kantrowitz, "A Place for 'Colored Patriots': Crispus Attucks Among the Abolitionists, 1842–1863," *MHR* 11 (2009): 190–212.

15. "Brown likes": qu. in Ezra Greenspan, *William Wells Brown: An African American Life* (New York: W. W. Norton, 2014), 189; ibid., 328, 346, 348, 354–56, 360–61; William Wells Brown, *The Narrative of William W. Brown, a Fugitive Slave* (Mineola, NY: Dover Publications, 1969), xii; Samuel May Jr. to John Bishop Estlin, Boston, May 21, 1849, May Papers, Anti-Slavery Collection, BPL.

16. "Dr. Rock": *Philadelphia Bulletin*, qu. in *BT*, July 23, 1859; *Liberator*, Oct. 2, 1857; *BDB*, Nov. 5, 1857; *WA-A*, Dec. 24, 1859.

17. "The distinguished": *BET*, Oct. 7, 1858; "that . . . fire": ibid., Oct. 12, 1858.

18. Henry Mayer, *All on Fire: William Lloyd Garrison and the Abolition of Slavery* (New York: St. Martin's Press, 1998), 453; "Free Soilism": Douglass, qu. in Blight, *Frederick Douglass*, 274.

19. Kate Clifford Larson, *Bound for the Promised Land: Harriet Tubman, Portrait of an American Hero* (New York: Ballantine Books, 2004), 164–66.

20. Grover and Da Silva, BAANHS, 100; Stephen Kantrowitz, *More than Freedom: Fighting for Black Citizenship in a White Republic* (New York: Penguin, 2013), 252; Horton and Horton, *In Hope of Liberty*, 223.

21. "That God . . . race": *BT*, Dec. 2, 1859.

22. "Soiling": Jean Fagan Yellin, ed., *The Harriet Jacobs Family Papers*, vol. 1 (Chapel Hill: University of North Carolina Press, 2008), 343; "aristocrats": ibid., 357; *BET*, April 3, 1861; *Liberator*, April 12, 1861.

23. Robert W. Johannsen, "Stephen A. Douglas' New England Campaign, 1860," *NEQ* 35 (June 1962): 162–86; Thomas H. O'Connor, *Civil War Boston: Home Front and Battlefield* (Boston: Northeastern University Press, 1997), 37.

24. Michael J. Durbin, *United States Presidential Elections, 1788–1860: The Official Results by County and State* (Jefferson, NC: McFarland, 2002), 171.

25. *Liberator*, Oct. 19, 1860; *AT*, Oct. 20, 1860.

26. "Mobcratic": *Liberator*, Dec. 7, 1860; *BDC*, Dec. 5, 1860.

27. William Wells Brown, *The Black Man, His Antecedents, His Genius, and His Achievements* (New York: Thomas Hamilton; Boston: E. F. Wallcut, 1863), 241–45; C. Peter Ripley, ed., *The Black Abolitionist Papers*, vol. 5, *The*

United States, 1859–1865 (Chapel Hill: University of North Carolina Press, 1992), 68–69.

28. *BDC*, Dec. 5, 1860.

29. "A nuisance": *Liberator*, Dec. 7, 1860; Mayer, *All on Fire*, 514–15; Blight, *Frederick Douglass*, 328–30; John W. Blassingame, ed., *The Frederick Douglass Papers*, Series 1, vol. 3, *Speeches, Debates, and Interviews, 1855–1863* (New Haven, CT: Yale University Press, 1986), 387–97; *Harper's Weekly*, Dec. 15, 1860.

30. "That . . . obey" and "You . . . niggers": *Liberator*, Dec. 7, 1860; *BDC*, Dec. 5, 1860; "no more": qu. in Blight, *Frederick Douglass*, 329; "fire-brand": *BT*, Dec. 4, 1860.

31. "Our revered": CC Minutes, Jan. 7, 1861, 5.

32. Franklin A. Dorman, *Twenty Families of Color in Massachusetts, 1741–1998* (Boston: New England Historic Genealogic Society, 1998), 340, 426–29.

33. "A small . . . for": Randolph, *From Slave Cabin*, 156–58.

34. "Received . . . you": ibid., 160; Sarah J. Shoenfeld, "Applications and Admissions to the Home for Aged Colored Women in Boston, 1860–1887," pt. 1, *NEHGR* 155 (July 2001): 253–54. The records of the home are included in the online collections of the Massachusetts Historical Society at Home for Aged Colored Women Records, 1843–1949, www.masshist.org/collection-guides/view/fa0430.

35. Shoenfeld, "Applications and Admissions," pt. 1, 251; George A. Levesque, *Black Boston: African American Life and Culture in Urban America, 1750–1860* (London: Routledge, 1994), 288, 410–13.

Chapter 7: The Politics of Wartime Work and Charitable Assistance

1. "The authority": CC Minutes, April 15, 1861, 226.

2. "Our pilots": *AT*, Nov. 2, 1861; "dull": *BT*, Oct. 29, 1861.

3. "[Had] been . . . invaluable": qu. in Sydney Nathans, *To Free a Family: The Journey of Mary Walker* (Cambridge, MA: Harvard University Press, 2012), 179.

4. "Wanted": *BET*, July 8, 1861.

5. "A diminution": CC Minutes, March 4, 1861, 122.

6. "An audacious": *Official Records of the Union and Confederate Navies in the War of the Rebellion*, Series 1, vol. 1, *The Operation of the Cruisers (January 19, 1861–January 4, 1863)* (Washington, DC: Government Printing Office, 1894), 547; CC Minutes, Sept. 1, 1862, 554.

7. "For days": Jean Fagan Yellin, ed., *The Harriet Jacobs Family Papers*, vol. 1 (Chapel Hill: University of North Carolina Press, 2008), 357.

8. See, for example, Edward Pessen, "How Different from Each Other Were the Antebellum North and South?," *AHR* 85 (Dec. 1980): 1119–49.

9. "Irish": Henry Greenleaf Pearson, *The Life of John A. Andrew, Governor of Massachusetts, 1861–1865*, vol. 1 (Boston: Houghton Mifflin, 1904), 205–6; "the most": *BET*, April 15, 1861.

10. "The embarrassment": *BS-WA*, April 24, 1861; ibid., May 22, 1861; "resources": *BH*, May 21, 1861; "knowing . . . fray": *Liberator*, May 31, 1861.

11. James M. McPherson, *Battle Cry of Freedom: The Civil War Era* (New York: Oxford University Press, 2003), 313–15. Information about Black seamen in the US Navy (place and date of birth, place and date of enlistment, initial rank, and ship assignments) can be found at the National Archives website, www.nps.gov/civilwar/search-sailors.htm.

12. Steven J. Ramold, *Slaves, Sailors, Citizens: African Americans in the Union Navy* (DeKalb: Northern Illinois University Press, 2002).

13. Ronald S. Coddington, *Faces of the Civil War Navies: An Album of Union and Confederate Sailors* (Baltimore: Johns Hopkins University Press, 2016), 46–49; *Massachusetts Soldiers, Sailors, and Marines in the Civil War*, vol. 7 (Boston: The Adjutant General, 1931–1935), 534; Joseph P. Reidy, "Black Men in Navy Blue During the Civil War," pts. 1, 2, and 3, *Prologue* 33 (Fall 2001); Harold D. Langley, "The Negro in the Navy and Merchant Service, 1789–1860," *JNH* 52 (Oct. 1967): 279; McPherson, *Battle Cry*, 382.

14. Langley, "Negro in the Navy," 279.

15. McPherson, *Battle Cry*, 378–79; Ramold, *Slaves, Sailors, Citizens*, 80.

16. *BH*, Dec. 24, 1860; *BET*, March 18, 1854.

17. Ramold, *Slaves, Sailors, Citizens*, 23, 46.

18. Ibid., 133; "monkies . . . heads": qu. in Michael J. Bennett, "'Frictions': Shipboard Relations Between White and Contraband Sailors During the American Civil War," *CWH* 47 (June 2001): 126–27.

19. Reidy, "Black Men in Navy Blue," pt. 2; Ramold, *Slaves, Sailors, Citizens*, 76–78.

20. "To obtain . . . desired": *BET*, Sept. 11, 1861.

21. "Bustle": *BMJ*, Nov. 20, 1861; *Goward's Real Estate Register*, July 12, 1862; "short": *BET*, July 16, 1861; CC Minutes, Nov. 24, 1862, 723–24; Thomas H. O'Connor, *Civil War Boston: Home Front and Battlefield* (Boston: Northeastern University Press, 1997), 161–65.

22. "Labor": CC Minutes, Sept. 9, 1861, 557; "the necessity": ibid., 556; "gladly . . . compensation": ibid., 565; "give": ibid., Sept. 30, 1861, 595; "Far": ibid., Sept. 9, 1861, 556–57.

23. "Begging": ibid., Oct. 28, 1861, 653; "conservative": ibid., May 5, 1862, 271; ibid., Oct. 21, 1861, 636.

24. Roger Lane, *Policing the City: Boston, 1822–1885* (Cambridge, MA: Harvard University Press, 2014), 141; O'Connor, *Civil War Boston*, 169–71;

CC Minutes, Feb. 24, 1862, 125–26; ibid., Dec. 19, 1861, 738; ibid., Sept. 23, 1861, 596; ibid., July 18, 1864.

25. "Waves": ibid., May 13, 1861, 303; "in order": ibid., 307; "wholesome . . . duration": ibid., June 4, 1861, 360; ibid., Sept. 16, 1861, 608.

26. Richard F. Miller, "For His Wife, His Widow, and His Orphan: Massachusetts and Family Aid During the Civil War," *MHR* 6 (2004): 70–106; CC Minutes, Oct. 7, 1861, 608.

27. "The wives": CC Minutes, Oct. 21, 1861, 637; ibid., Dec. 22, 1862, 820; ibid., Jan. 18, 1864, 30, 32.

28. "Whose": ibid., Aug. 11, 1862, 526; ibid., Dec. 1, 1862, 754; ibid., Oct. 17, 1862, 646; "pernicious": ibid., Aug. 18, 1862, 537; "somewhat": Oct. 18, 1862, 647–48; ibid., Sept. 1, 1862, 565; Michael Douma, Anders Bo Rasmussen, and Robert O. Faith, "The Impressment of Foreign-Born Soldiers in the Union Army," *JAEH* 38 (Spring 2019): 76–106.

29. "Tumultuous": CC Minutes, Sept. 8, 1862, 569; "the 'old'": *BH*, Aug. 26, 1862; O'Connor, *Civil War Boston*, 101; CC Minutes, Dec. 26, 1862, 819.

30. "Claim": *BH*, July 28, 1863; "Wanted": *BH*, July 30, 1862; "Madame": *BH*, Oct. 30, 1862; "Union": *BT*, Oct. 25, 1864; "Persian": *BET*, June 22, 1863; "It": *BH*, Sept. 22, 1864; Drew Gilpin Faust, *This Republic of Suffering: Death and the American Civil War* (New York: Vintage, 2008); *BET*, Dec. 23, 1861; ibid., July 29, 1862.

31. *BET*, May 20, 1862; ibid., June 26, 1862; "all": John R. McKivigan, *Forgotten Firebrand: James Redpath and the Making of Nineteenth-Century America* (Ithaca, NY: Cornell University Press, 2008), 70; Ezra Greenspan, *William Wells Brown: An African American Life* (New York: W. W. Norton, 2014), 377; *Congregationalist*, May 17, 1861; *Liberator*, May 17, 1861; *Pine and Palm*, May 18, 1861; David W. Blight, *Frederick Douglass, Prophet of Freedom* (New York: Simon and Schuster, 2020), 337.

32. *BH*, Nov. 30, 1885; "men": *BH*, May 25, 1861; "Colored": *Boston Shipping List*, Jan. 2, 1864.

33. J. Sella Martin to George L. Ruffin, London, Oct. 15, 1861, Box 87-1, Series A, Folder 8, Other Correspondents, Ruffin Family Papers, Moorland-Spingarn Research Center Library, Howard University, Washington, DC.

34. "I write": Jonathan W. White, ed., *To Address You as My Friend: African Americans' Letters to Abraham Lincoln* (Chapel Hill: University of North Carolina Press, 2021), 63; ibid., 201–2.

35. "He": "Opening of Lloyd's Sugar Mill" [reprinted from *Liberia Herald*], *African Repository and Colonization Journal* 40 (Sept. 1864): 269–71; ibid. (1865), 234; William Ezra Allen, "Sugar and Coffee: A History of Settler Agriculture in Nineteenth-Century Liberia" (PhD diss., Florida International University, 2002), 96, 104–6.

36. John H. Nichols "on board the receiving ship Princeton," May 3, 1863, to June 2, 1863, D20-22, Folder 11, Letters, Documents, Etc., 1860–1865, Morris Papers, BA; Peter P. Hinks, *To Awaken my Afflicted Brethren: David Walker and the Problem of Antebellum Slave Resistance* (University Park: Pennsylvania State University Press, 1997), 270–71.

37. "John": *BH*, Oct. 15, 1861; "I": *BET*, Feb. 18, 1862; "can": *BH*, July 21, 1863; *Liberator*, May 2, 1862; *BET*, July 25, 1862; *Camden (NJ) Democrat*, April 20, 1862.

38. "Grand": *BH*, Jan. 31, 1862; "This war . . . breakfast": *Manchester (NH) Weekly Union*, Feb. 25, 1862; "quite": *BJ*, Feb. 1, 1862.

39. CC Minutes, May, 27, 1861, 340–41; ibid., Sept. 22, 1862, 593; "a gentleman . . . fixins": *BMJ*, Feb. 12, 1864; "wants . . . plunder": ibid., Feb. 3, 1862, 74; *BH*, May 13, 1861; Edward H. Savage, *Police Records and Recollections, Or, Boston by Daylight and Gaslight: For Two Hundred and Forty Years* (Boston: John P. Dale, 1873), 193–94; *BH*, Jan. 8, 1861; *BT*, March 11, 1862; "disorderly . . . persons": *BH*, March 18, 1861.

40. *BH*, March 12, 1861; ibid., Feb. 3, 1863; "A woman": "32nd Annual Report of the Managers of the Boston Seamen's Friend" (Boston: T. R. Marvin and Son, 1860), 43; *BH*, March 12, 1861; ibid., Feb. 3, 1863.

41. "Were just": Commonwealth of Massachusetts, House, *Resolve in Favor of Emeline I. Smith*, Resolve Chap. 65, April 24, 1880, https://archives.lib.state.ma.us/handle/2452/814074; "to his": J. B. Smith Petition to the Massachusetts Legislature, Jan. 18, 1879; *BH*, July 30, 1861; *Lowell Daily Citizen*, July 17, 1861; House Bills 0316, 0141, 0347 (1879), Massachusetts House of Representatives.

42. *BET*, March 21, 1861; *BH*, Jan. 2, 1862; ibid., Oct. 30, 1862; ibid., Nov. 3, 1862; "good": *BH*, Feb. 25, 1862; CC Minutes, July 21, 1862, 484–85; *BH*, Jan. 13, 1862; "drop": H. A. Ransom et al to the Senate and House of Representatives, Jan. 1862; J. Henry Hills et al to the Senate and House of Representatives, Jan. 1862, filed in 37A-G20.1, House Committee on Ways and Means, Petitions and Memorials, Series 467, 37th Cong., Record Group 233 [Records of the US House of Representatives], National Archives, Washington, DC [Freedmen and Southern Society Project document D-53].

43. "Grand . . . footing": *BH*, Oct. 27, 1862; "true . . . States": *BP*, Nov. 13, 1862.

44. *Liberator*, Aug. 15, 1862; *Newburyport (MA) Morning Herald*, Aug. 14, 1862; *NYT*, Oct. 7, 1862; *BH*, Aug. 14, 1862; D. W. Gooch to Hon. Simon Cameron, Nov. 16, 1861, enclosing S. E. Sewall to Hon. Simon Cameron, No. 16, 1861, G-211 1861, Letters Received, Record Group 107 [Records of the Office of the Secretary of War], National Archives, Washington, DC [FSSP L-4].

45. *Liberator*, Aug. 15, 1862.

46. "Rough . . . Women": "Annual Report of the City Missionary Society, Boston, for the Year 1862" (Boston: T. R. Marvin and Son, 1863), 18.

47. "Boston": *BH*, Jan. 16, 1862; "whom": "Third Annual Report of the Home for Aged Colored Women" (Boston: John Wilson and Son, 1863), 4; "her": Sarah J. Shoenfeld, "Applications and Admissions to the Home for Aged Colored Women in Boston, 1860–1887," pt. 1, *NEHGR* 155 (July 2001): 266; "would . . . themselves": Esther MacCarthy, "The Home for Aged Colored Women, 1861–1944," *HJM* 21 (Winter 1993): 57.

48. "With bare": *BET*, Sept. 26, 1862; *BT*, Sept. 30, 1862.

49. *BH*, Sept. 26, 1862; *BT*, Sept. 30, 1862; "aged": *BT*, Nov. 17, 1862; *Liberator*, Oct. 10 and 31, 1862; Elizabeth Keckley, *Behind the Scenes, Or, Thirty Years a Slave, and Four Years in the White House* (New York: G. W. Carleton, 1868), 111–16.

50. "The true . . . saw!": *Liberator*, Oct. 24, 1862.

Chapter 8: Boston Diaspora I

1. "The beginning": *BH*, Jan. 1, 1863.

2. "The whole": *Liberator*, Jan. 2, 1863.

3. "As well . . . impetus": *BT*, Jan. 1, 1863.

4. "Thanked . . . about": *BH*, Jan. 3, 1863; David W. Blight, *Frederick Douglass, Prophet of Freedom* (New York: Simon and Schuster, 2020), 382–83.

5. "Gentleman": *BH*, Jan. 2, 1863; *BMJ*, Jan. 2, 1863.

6. "Received": *BH*, Jan. 2, 1863; Thomas Wentworth Higginson, *Army Life in a Black Regiment* (Boston: Fields, Osgood, 1870), 36–42; Elizabeth Ware Pearson, ed., *Letters from Port Royal* (New York: Arno Press and the New York Times, 1969 [1906]), 128–30; Susie King Taylor, *Reminiscences of My Life in Camp: An African American Woman's Civil War Memoir*, ed. Catherine Clinton (Athens: University of Georgia Press, 2006 [1902]), 18–19.

7. Joseph P. Reidy, *Illusions of Emancipation: The Pursuit of Freedom in the Twilight of Slavery* (Chapel Hill: University of North Carolina Press, 2020), 251–52; "simply . . . anarchy": "Memorial of the Emancipation League of Boston, Massachusetts, to the Congress of the United States," Dec. 1862, 37A-H28, Various Subjects, Petitions and Memorials, Series 547, 37th Cong., Record Group 46, Records of the United States Senate, National Archives [FSSP E-83].

8. "They . . . times": Nathaniel Hawthorne, "Chiefly About War Matters," *Atlantic Monthly*, July 1862.

9. "Here": *NA-SS*, Nov. 23, 1861.

10. CC Minutes, Aug. 3, 1863, 440; ibid., Nov. 3, 1863, 623.

11. "As soon": *BH*, April 16, 1863; "their": ibid., April 22, 1863; ibid., Jan. 1, 1864; *Liberator*, April 10, 1863; and these issues of *BH*: Jan. 16, 1863; Jan. 17, 1863; Jan. 18, 1863; April 7, 1863, April 16, 1863; April 22, 1863; and *BET*: April 8, 1863; April 10, 1863; Nov. 11, 1863.

12. Oscar Handlin, *Boston's Immigrants, 1790–1880: A Study in Acculturation* (Cambridge, MA: Harvard University Press, 1972), 162–69; Thomas H. O'Connor, *The Boston Irish: A Political History* (Boston: Back Bay Books, 1995), 91–94; Christian G. Samito, *Becoming American Under Fire: Irish Americans, African Americans, and the Politics of Citizenship During the Civil War* (Ithaca, NY: Cornell University Press, 2009), 39.

13. "Of dear": *BT*, April 24, 1863; Jacqueline Jones, *Saving Savannah: The City and the Civil War* (New York: Knopf, 2008), 174–75; *NYT*, April 25, 1863; ibid., April 26, 1863.

14. "The House": *BH*, May 6, 1863; "possessed . . . livelihood": *BH*, May 7, 1863; *BT*, May 5, 1863; ibid., Feb. 24, 1860; *Liberator*, May 8, 1863; *BMJ*, May 26, 1863.

15. "A general": *BMJ*, Feb. 3, 1863.

16. *BTJ*, Sept. 1, 1862; *BET*, Dec. 3, 1862; *MPNEJA*, Nov. 15, 1862; *Liberator*, Dec. 19, 1862; ibid., Nov. 21, 1862; ibid., Sept. 5, 1862.

17. "The enemy": *BT*, Feb. 1, 1862; Robert F. Engs, *Freedom's First Generation: Black Hampton, Virginia, 1861–1890* (New York: Fordham University Press, 2004), 14.

18. "Employed": Ira Berlin, Barbara J. Fields, Thavolia Glymph, Joseph P. Reidy, and Leslie S. Rowland, eds., *Freedom: A Documentary History of Emancipation, 1861–1867*, Series 1, vol. 1, *The Destruction of Slavery* (Cambridge: Cambridge University Press, 1985), 16; Jaime Amanda Martinez, *Confederate Slave Impressment in the Upper South* (Chapel Hill: University of North Carolina Press, 2013); *BH*, Dec. 18, 1861; "arm[ing]": *Passages from the Life of Henry Warren Howe, Consisting of Diary and Letters Written During the Civil War, 1861–1865* (Lowell, MA: Courier-Citizen Printers, 1899), 125.

19. Henry L. Swint, ed., *Dear Ones at Home: Letters from Contraband Camps* (Nashville, TN: Vanderbilt University Press, 1966); Engs, *Freedom's First Generation*, 55; "On one": Hannah Stevenson, Boston, Nov. 9, 1862, in "Lucy and Sarah Chase as Freedmen's Teachers," American Antiquarian Society Online Resource (AAS hereinafter), www.americanantiquarian.org/Freedmen/Intros/chaseduring.html.

20. "Whipped": *BT*, May 28, 1862; Sing-nan Fen, "Lewis C. Lockwood," *HEQ* 3 (March 1963): 37; *BET*, Jan. 21, 1862; *BH*, Jan. 22, 1862; *Congregationalist*, Jan. 31, 1862; ibid., April 4, 1862; *Liberator*, Oct. 25, 1861; ibid., Jan. 10, 1862; Amy Murrell Taylor, *Embattled Freedom: Journeys Through the*

Civil War's Slave Refugee Camps (Chapel Hill: University of North Carolina Press, 2020), 42–43.

21. "The parties . . . could": *BT*, Feb. 3, 1862; *BH*, Feb. 4, 1862; *BDA*, Jan. 31, 1862; "her rich": *Liberator*, March 27, 1863.

22. "I have": Letter of John Oliver, "Emancipation Proclamation Anniversary, Part V," Amistad Research Center, posted June 4, 2013, https://amistadresearch.wordpress.com/category/john-oliver; *BT*, March 29, 1862.

23. Engs, *Freedom's First Generation*, 34–35.

24. "Every . . . barbarian": *Liberator*, Dec. 26, 1862; Taylor, *Embattled Freedom*, 90.

25. "A perfect": Letter from Lucy Chase, Craney Island, Jan. 29, 1862, in "Lucy and Sarah Chase as Freedmen's Teachers," AAS, www.americanantiquarian.org/Freedmen/Intros/chaseduring.html; "fighting": Engs, *Freedom's First Generation*, 33; Berlin et al., *Destruction of Slavery*, 66; Casandra Lynn Newby-Alexander, "'The World Was All Before Them': A Study of the Black Community in Norfolk, Virginia, 1861–1884" (PhD diss., College of William and Mary, 1992), 21–40; Fen, "Lewis C. Lockwood," 38–42; "all eager": Letter from Lucy Chase, Jan. 29, 1862, AAS.

26. "Life . . . them": *Liberator*, Sept. 5, 1862; "harrowed": Jean Fagan Yellin, ed., *The Harriet Jacobs Family Papers*, vol. 2 (Chapel Hill: University of North Carolina Press, 2008), 421.

27. "My": Yellin, *Jacobs Family Papers*, 2:427.

28. "Such": ibid., 2:461; "many": ibid., 2:486; "O, when": ibid., 2:470; Jean Fagan Yellin, *Harriet Jacobs: A Life* (New York: Basic Books, 2004), 158–63.

29. "The colored": *BET*, Nov. 7, 1862; "Here": *BT*, Jan. 10, 1862.

30. "The party": Pearson, *Letters*, 4; Willie Lee Rose, *Rehearsal for Reconstruction: The Port Royal Experiment* (Athens: University of Georgia Press, 1999); Berlin et al., *Destruction of Slavery*, 103–56; *NYT*, Jan. 19, 1862.

31. "Determined": Pearson, *Letters*, 1; "great": ibid., 2; "materially": John Murray Forbes, *Letters and Recollections of John Murray Forbes*, ed. Sarah Forbes Hughes, vol. 1 (Boston: Houghton Mifflin, 1899), 310.

32. "Jabbering": Pearson, *Letters*, 156; "She": ibid., 213; "it would": ibid., 144.

33. "Dirty": ibid., 18; "I find" ibid., 75.

34. "Black Yankee": ibid., 37–38; "earn": ibid., 77; Rose, *Rehearsal*, 234–35.

35. Pearson, *Letters*, 14; "Red": ibid., 75, 82; "I tell": Ira Berlin, Thavolia Glymph, Steven F. Miller, Joseph P. Reidy, Leslie S. Rowland, and Julie Saville, eds., *Freedom: A Documentary History of Emancipation, 1861–1867*, Series 1, vol. 3, *The Wartime Genesis of Free Labor: The Lower South* (Cambridge: Cambridge University Press, 1990), 183; *NYT*, Jan. 19, 1862.

36. Jonathan A. Glickstein, "Poverty Is Not Slavery: American Abolitionists and the Competitive Labor Market," in *Antislavery Reconsidered: New Perspectives on the Abolitionists*, ed. Lewis Perry and Michael Fellman (Baton Rouge: Louisiana State University Press, 1979), 195–218.

Chapter 9: "A Higher Standard of Courage"

1. "Eight . . . tests": Thomas Wentworth Higginson, *Army Life in a Black Regiment* (Boston: Fields, Osgood, 1870), 4.
2. Ibid., 32.
3. Ibid., 14–15, 38–39.
4. See Office of the American Freedmen's Inquiry Commission, Preliminary Commission Report, June 30, 1863, at Shotgun's Home of the American Civil War, https://civilwarhome.com/prelimcommissionreport.html.
5. "Docility . . . only": ibid.; Joseph P. Reidy, *Illusions of Emancipation: The Pursuit of Freedom in the Twilight of Slavery* (Chapel Hill: University of North Carolina Press, 2020), 251–63; Jeff Strickland, "The American Freedmen's Inquiry Commission, 19th-Century Racial Pseudoscience, and the False Assessment of Black America, 1863–1864," *Federal History 11* (2019): 109–28.
6. "A touching . . . homes": *Liberator*, June 5, 1863.
7. "The entire": ibid.
8. Jean Fagan Yellin, ed., *The Harriet Jacobs Family Papers*, vol. 2 (Chapel Hill: University of North Carolina Press, 2008), 497; "professionals": *BMJ*, May 30, 1863.
9. *BET*, July 14, 1863.
10. Charles Barnard Fox, *Record of Service of the Fifty-Fifth Regiment of Massachusetts Volunteer Infantry* (Cambridge, MA: John Wilson and Son, 1868), 130–32.
11. Iver Bernstein, *The New York City Draft Riots: Their Significance for American Society and Politics in the Age of the Civil War* (New York: Oxford University Press, 1990).
12. "Hurling": Edward H. Savage, *Police Records and Recollections, Or, Boston by Daylight and Gaslight: For Two Hundred and Forty Years* (Boston: John P. Dale, 1873), 350, 355–57; "*there*": ibid., 354; *BET*, July 15, 1863; CC Minutes, July 23, 1863, 413; Brian Kelly, "Ambiguous Loyalties: The Boston Irish, Slavery, and the Civil War," *HJM* 24 (Summer 1996): 165–204; Brett M. Palfreyman, "The Boston Draft Riots," *NYT*, July 16, 2013; Judith Ann Giesberg, "'Lawless and Unprincipled': Women in Boston's Civil War Draft Riot," in *Boston's Histories: Essays in Honor of Thomas H. O'Connor*, ed. James M. O'Toole and David Quigley (Boston: Northeastern University Press, 2003); *BH*, July 17, 1863; *BDA*, July 24, 1863; *BET*, July 15–17, 1863.

13. *BT*, July 16, 1863; "give": Savage, *Police Records*, 362; *BET*, July 23, 1863; CC Minutes, July 23, 1863, 418; ibid., July 27, 1863, 412–13; *BET*, July 15, 1863.

14. Noah Andre Trudeau, ed., *Voices of the 55th: Letters from the 55th Massachusetts Volunteers, 1861–1865* (Dayton, OH: Morningside House, 1996), 37, 43.

15. "With his": Thomas Wentworth Higginson, *Massachusetts in the Army and Navy During the War of 1861–1865*, vol. 1, *Preliminary Narrative* (Boston: Wright and Potter, 1895–1896), 87; Burt G. Wilder, *Practicing Medicine in a Black Regiment: The Civil War Diary of Burt G. Wilder, 55th Massachusetts*, ed. Richard M. Reid (Amherst: University of Massachusetts Press, 2010), 55; Peter Burchard, *One Gallant Rush: Robert Gould Shaw and His Brave Black Regiment* (New York: St. Martin's Press, 1990); "put those": qu. in David W. Blight, *Frederick Douglass, Prophet of Freedom* (New York: Simon and Schuster, 2020), 400.

16. "The only": *BT*, June 22, 1863.

17. "Health": Ira Berlin, Joseph P. Reidy, and Leslie S. Rowland, eds., *Freedom: A Documentary History of Emancipation, 1861–1867*, Series 2, *The Black Military Experience* (Cambridge: Cambridge University Press, 1982), 490; "introduced": James Henry Gooding, *On the Altar of Freedom: A Black Soldier's Civil War Letters from the Front*, ed. Virginia M. Adams (Amherst: University of Massachusetts Press, 1991), 47; "My men": Berlin et al., *Black Military Experience*, 491–92.

18. "The most . . . battle": Trudeau, ed., *Voices*, 56n99; Wilder, *Practicing Medicine*, 23.

19. "Has been . . . water": Berlin et al., *Black Military Experience*, 493; "the interests": ibid., 495.

20. Trudeau, ed., *Voices*, 40n16; ibid., 58–61; Wilder, *Practicing Medicine*, 64.

21. Thomas Selden (Civil War Veterans') Pension File, application #392009; certificate #308727 (hereinafter app. # and cert. #); Widow's App. #332819; cert. #279689, Records of the Department of Veterans Affairs, RG 15, NARA.

22. "I have": Selden Pension; Wilder, *Practicing Medicine*, 64.

23. Selden Pension; Fox, *Record of the Service of the 55th*, 128–32.

24. "Now . . . hirelings": Berlin et al., *Black Military Experience*, 385–86.

25. General Orders no. 98, Head Quarters Dept. of the East, Dec. 1864, P-455 1865, Letters Received, Series 360, Colored Troops Division, RG 94, Records of the Adjutant General's Office, 1780s–1917, NARA [FSSP-282].

26. "For the . . . duties": Isaiah Price to Hon. Edwin M. Stanton, July 14, 1865, ibid.; C. W. Foster to Major H. C. Derandorf, Oct. 26, 1865, ibid.

27. "The most": Trudeau, ed., *Voices*, 156–57.

28. "Minister": Jonathan W. White, ed., *To Address You as My Friend: African Americans' Letters to Abraham Lincoln* (Chapel Hill: University of North Carolina Press, 2021), 184; "of African": ibid., 105; "alike": ibid., 106; "I am": ibid., 106.

29. "The general": Wilder, *Practicing Medicine*, 177.

30. "I kept": William A. Aiken Pension File, app. #1,197,825; cert. #952,130, RG 15, NARA; "The pies . . . whiskey": Trudeau, ed., *Voices*, 177–78; Berlin et al., *Black Military Experience*, 25.

31. "Nearly": Susie King Taylor, *Reminiscences of My Life in Camp: An African American Woman's Civil War Memoir*, ed. Catherine Clinton (Athens: University of Georgia Press, 2006 [1902]), 21.

32. "In his": Trudeau, ed., *Voices*, 63; Wilder, *Practicing Medicine*, 107; Michael A. Halleran, *The Better Angels of Our Nature: Freemasonry in the American Civil War* (Tuscaloosa: University of Alabama Press, 2020), 155–57, 153.

33. Steven J. Ramold, *Slaves, Sailors, Citizens: African Americans in the Union Navy* (DeKalb: Northern Illinois University Press, 2002), 100–101; James M. McPherson, *Battle Cry of Freedom: The Civil War Era* (New York: Oxford University Press, 2003), 378.

34. Ramold, *Slaves, Sailors, Citizens*, 95, 82; William B. Gould IV, ed., *Diary of a Contraband: The Civil War Passage of a Black Sailor* (Stanford, CA: Stanford University Press, 2002), 238; Richard Reid, "Black British North American Sailors in the Civil War," *Northern Mariner / Le marin du nord* 21 (Jan. 2011): 1–26, www.cnrs-scrn.org/northern_mariner/vol21/tnm_21_1-26.pdf.

35. "Sauce": *BH*, June 20, 1861.

36. Berlin et al., *Black Military Experience*, 1–34; Trudeau, ed., *Voices*, 29, 33.

37. Berlin et al., *Black Military Experience*, 402, 502–3; E. N. Hallowell to John A. Andrew, Morris Island, SC, Sept. 19, 1864, ibid., 403, 433–42, 502–3, 20; "sporting . . . doubt": Trudeau, ed., *Voices*, 113.

38. "That it . . . *Color*": ibid., 141.

39. Ramold, *Slaves, Sailors, Citizens*, 121; "look": qu. in Peter C. Luebke, "'Equal to Any Minstrel Concert I Ever Attended at Home': Union Soldiers and Blackface Performance in the Civil War South," *JCWE* 4 (Dec. 2014): 517; Joseph P. Reidy, "Black Men in Navy Blue During the Civil War," pts. 1, 2, and 3, *Prologue* 33 (Fall 2001); "After": "Journal of an Artilleryman," *Salem Register*, Dec. 25, 1861.

40. "I don't": Elizabeth Ware Pearson, ed., *Letters from Port Royal* (New York: Arno Press and the *New York Times*, 1969 [1906]), 124; "only . . . them": qu. in Willie Lee Rose, *Rehearsal for Reconstruction: The Port Royal Experiment* (Athens: University of Georgia Press, 1999), 174.

41. "Astonish[ing]": Pearson, *Letters*, 181; "loafers . . . character": ibid., 175; "enterprise . . . employed": ibid., 220–21; "The fact": ibid., 220–21; Ira

Berlin, Thavolia Glymph, Steven F. Miller, Joseph P. Reidy, Leslie S. Rowland, and Julie Saville, eds., *Freedom: A Documentary History of Emancipation, 1861–1867*, Series 1, vol. 3, *The Wartime Genesis of Free Labor: The Lower South* (Cambridge: Cambridge University Press, 1990), 255–59.

42. "'Any' . . . Admiral": Pearson, *Letters*, 225; Ronald S. Coddington, *Faces of the Civil War Navies: An Album of Union and Confederate Sailors* (Baltimore: Johns Hopkins University Press, 2016), 46–49.

43. "Very": Pearson, *Letters*, 225; ibid.; "utterly": ibid. 214.

44. "The welfare": qu. in Sydney Nathans, *To Free a Family: The Journey of Mary Walker* (Cambridge, MA: Harvard University Press, 2012), 191; "a white": ibid., 199.

45. Ibid., 200.

46. "Be relieved": Pearson, *Letters*, 258.

47. "Wee . . . broken": Berlin et al., *Wartime Genesis of Free Labor*, 297–98.

48. "The eminent . . . customers": ibid., 301–3.

49. "For their . . . will": ibid.; "were": Pearson, *Letters*, 262.

50. "Amusing . . . treat": Pearson, *Letters*, 278; Nathans, *To Free a Family*, 211–15.

51. Office of the American Freedmen's Inquiry Commission, Final Commission Report, May 15, 1864, at Shotgun's Home of the American Civil War, www.civilwarhome.com/commissionreport.html.

52. "Almost": qu. in Nathans, *To Free a Family*, 214; "Fall . . . variety": *BET*, Sept. 17, 1864.

Chapter 10: Hardship on the Homefront

1. "The United": *WA-A*, May 14, 1864; "do not": ibid.; ibid., May 21, 1864; "MANHOOD"; ibid., May 21, 1864 (see Noah Andre Trudeau, ed., *Voices of the 55th: Letters from the 55th Massachusetts Volunteers, 1861–1865* [Dayton, OH: Morningside House, 1996], 85–89); James G. Mendez, *A Great Sacrifice: Northern Black Soldiers, Their Families, and the Experience of Civil War* (New York: Fordham University Press, 2019), 44–87.

2. *WA-A*, May 14, 1864; Trudeau, ed., *Voices*, 81.

3. "Impelled . . . it": Trudeau, ed., *Voices*, 108–9; Stephen R. Fox, "James Monroe Trotter," in *Making a Living: The Work Experience of African Americans in New England*, ed. Robert L. Hall, with Michael M. Harvey (Boston: New England Foundation for the Humanities, 1995), 415–21; "Same . . . Shame": Corporal Thomas D. Freeman to Morris, April 25, 1864, F11 D27, Morris Papers, BA.

4. Jonathan W. White, ed., *To Address You as My Friend: African Americans' Letters to Abraham Lincoln* (Chapel Hill: University of North Carolina Press, 2021), 154–56.

5. David W. Blight, *Frederick Douglass, Prophet of Freedom* (New York: Simon and Schuster, 2020), 409; Ira Berlin, Joseph P. Reidy, and Leslie S. Rowland, eds., *Freedom: A Documentary History of Emancipation, 1861–1867*, Series 2, *The Black Military Experience* (Cambridge: Cambridge University Press, 1982), 19–21; "I want": qu. in Stephen Kantrowitz, *More than Freedom: Fighting for Black Citizenship in a White Republic, 1829–1889* (New York: Penguin, 2013), 292.

6. "We came . . . mesures": Berlin et al., *Black Military Experience*, 401–2; George V. Tomashevich, ed., "Some of the Incidents in the Life of Mark DeMortie," *A-ANYLH* 3 (Jan. 1979): 67–68.

7. "Our . . . country": *WA-A*, May 14, 1864.

8. Noah Andre Trudeau, "Proven Themselves in Every Respect to Be Men: Black Cavalry in the Civil War," *Black Soldiers in Blue: African American Troops in the Civil War Era*, ed. John David Smith (Chapel Hill: University of North Carolina Press, 2002), 276–305; Steven M. LaBarre, *The Fifth Massachusetts Colored Cavalry in the Civil War* (Jefferson, NC: McFarland, 2016).

9. "After": qu. in Trudeau, "Proven," 278; "[took] . . . bearing": ibid., 282.

10. Ibid., 298–99; "A cold": qu. in LaBarre, *Fifth Massachusetts*, 108–9.

11. "Insisted": *BH*, Feb. 14, 1863; "remember": "John S. Rock to the Soldiers of the Fifth United States Colored Heavy Artillery Regiment, 30 May 1864," in *The Black Abolitionist Papers*, vol. 5, *The United States, 1859–1865*, ed. Peter Ripley (Chapel Hill: University of North Carolina Press, 1992), 273, 296; Kantrowitz, *More than Freedom*, 291–92.

12. Robert P. Smith, "William Cooper Nell: Crusading Black Abolitionist," *JNH* 55 (1970): 182–99.

13. *BET*, Aug. 5, 1864; "Here": William B. Gould IV, ed., *Diary of a Contraband: The Civil War Passage of a Black Sailor* (Stanford, CA: Stanford University Press, 2002), 142; "Now . . . clime": ibid., 143.

14. "Constantly": *BMJ*, Feb. 20, 1863.

15. "The celebrated . . . shaver": *BH*, Feb. 3, 1863; ibid., March 13, 1863.

16. *Liberator*, Jan. 8, 1864; "Idleness . . . conduct": *BET*, May 7, 1864.

17. For an account of James Simms's career, see Jacqueline Jones, *Saving Savannah: The City and the Civil War* (New York: Knopf, 2008).

18. "His Conversion": *Christian Watchman*, March 31, 1864; *BR*, Jan. 6, 1865.

19. "How . . . minister": *Christian Recorder*, April 15, 1865; *Liberator*, Dec. 11, 1863; Deborah A. Lee, "Leonard Grimes," in *The Essence of a People*, vol. 2, *African Americans Who Made Their Lives Anew in Loudoun County, Virginia, and Beyond*, ed. Kendra Y. Hamilton (Leesburg, VA: Black History Committee and Friends of the Thomas Balch Library, 2002).

20. "Drunken . . . Dutchman": qu. in Blight, *Frederick Douglass*, 417.

21. CC Minutes, May 4, 1863, 203, 207–8; ibid., June 15, 1863, 298; ibid., June 22, 1863, 323; ibid., July 6, 1863, 362; ibid., July 13, 1863, 376; ibid., Nov. 23, 1863, 672; ibid., Nov. 30, 1863, 685; ibid., March 14, 1864, 96; ibid., June 7, 1864, 287; ibid., July 18, 1864, 365; ibid., July 25, 1864, 374–75; ibid., Nov. 23, 1864, 594.

22. "Is not . . . danger": CC Minutes, May 2, 1864, 202–5; ibid., 199–215; ibid., Nov. 3, 1863, 624; ibid., Dec. 28, 1863, 760; ibid., Jan. 18, 1864, 26; ibid., April 18, 1864, 165; ibid., May 2, 1864.

23. CC Minutes, Feb. 2, 1863, 39–40; Oct. 5, 1863, 548; Nov. 3, 1863, 623; Dec. 7, 1863, 700; Oscar Handlin, *Boston's Immigrants, 1790–1880: A Study in Acculturation* (Cambridge, MA: Harvard University Press, 1972), 240; Richard F. Miller, "For His Wife, His Widow, and His Orphan: Massachusetts and Family Aid During the Civil War," *MHR* 6 (2004): 95; CC Minutes, Nov. 18, 1861, 695; ibid., Dec. 23, 1861; ibid., Oct. 26, 1863, 609–10; ibid., April, 25, 1864, 182; ibid., Jan. 11, 1864, 17.

24. CC Minutes, July 13, 1863, 381–89; *BET*, Jan. 16, 1864; "The plan": *BH*, July 11, 1864; ibid., July 9, 1864; Thomas H. O'Connor, *Civil War Boston: Home Front and Battlefield* (Boston: Northeastern University Press, 1997), 210–11.

25. O'Connor, *Civil War Boston*, 208.

26. Stewart, qu. in Timothy Messer-Kruse, "Eight Hours, Greenbacks, and 'Chinamen': Wendell Phillips, Ira Steward, and the Fate of Labor Reform in Massachusetts," *LH* 42 (2001): 138.

27. "No one . . . market": *AT*, March 11, 1865; *BMJ*, Dec. 6, 1864; O'Connor, *Civil War Boston*, 210–11.

28. "One": *BMJ*, Jan. 14, 1863; "he": *BH*, Nov. 22, 1864; "the friends": *BT*, July 15, 1864; *BH*, July 18, 1864; *BT*, Nov. 24, 1864.

29. "Mitigating": *BET*, Feb. 21, 1865.

30. Howard Mumford Jones, "The Wounds of War: A Tale of Two Cities," *Harvard Library Bulletin* 20, no. 2 (April 1972): 135–57, reprinted in Howard Mumford Jones and Bessie Zaban Jones, eds., *The Many Voices of Boston: A Historical Anthology, 1630–1975* (Boston: Little, Brown, 1975), 275.

31. "I did": Letter to H. C. Russell, Philadelphia, April 4, 1864, "Letters to John A. Andrew, Committee for Syracuse Convention," Box 87-2, Series J, Folder 101, Ruffin Family Papers, Moorland-Spingarn Research Center Library, Howard University, Washington, DC (unless otherwise noted, Rock correspondence cited below is located in this folder); "a set": Rock to Russell, Boston, April 30, 1864; "You": Rock to Russell, Philadelphia, April 4, 1864.

32. Rock to Charles Sumner, Boston, Dec. 17, 1864, MS AM1, Box 21: 5310-5560, Charles Sumner Correspondence, Houghton Library, Harvard University.

33. "To lose": Rock to John A. Andrew, Philadelphia, April 7, 1864; "a more": Rock to L. M. Standish, Philadelphia, April 7, 1864; "I have": Rock to G. E. H. Day, Boston, April 14, 1864.

34. List of exemptions: *BT*, Aug. 7, 1863.

35. "Needy . . . threats": Rock to Mrs. Hester Jane Cooper, Aug. 8, 1864; "prize": Rock to O. C. Hughes, Boston, Nov. 10, 1864; Rock to Stephen J.W. Tabor, Boston, April 22, 1864.

36. "They . . . suffer": Rock to John A. Andrew, April 4, 1864; "but the men": Rock to L. M. Standish, Philadelphia, April 7, 1864.

37. "Unmilitary": "Proceedings of the National Convention of Colored Men, Syracuse," Oct. 4–7, 1864, with the "Bills of Wrongs and Rights and the Address to the American People" (Boston: J. S. Rock and George L. Ruffin, 1864), 34; "and to all": ibid., 35.

38. "A splendid . . . equality": ibid., 23.

39. "Mr. Sumner": Rock to G. E. H. Day, Boston, April 14, 1864; "Letters to John A. Andrew, Committee for Syracuse Convention," Box 87-2, Series J, Folder 101, Ruffin Family Papers, Moorland-Spingarn Research Center Library, Howard University, Washington, DC; George A. Levesque, "Boston's Black Brahmin: Dr. John S. Rock," *CWH* 26 (Dec. 1980): 334. See also Rock to Charles Sumner, Dec. 30, 1863, MS AM1, Box 21: 5310–5560, Charles Sumner Correspondence, Houghton Library, Harvard University.

40. Sumner, qu. in Levesque, "Boston's Black Brahmin," 334.

41. "In the atmosphere": Robert F. Engs, *Freedom's First Generation: Black Hampton, Virginia, 1861–1890* (New York: Fordham University Press, 2004), 38–39.

42. Kantrowitz, *More than Freedom*, 296–97; "Colored": *BET*, Aug. 5, 1864; Engs, *Freedom's First Generation*, 38–40; Sean Kelley, "Scrambling for Slaves: Captive Sales in Colonial South Carolina," *Slavery and Abolition* 34 (2013): 1–21.

43. "Employment . . . riots": John Oliver to C. B. Wilder, Sept. 22, 1863, AAS, www.americanantiquarian.org/Freedmen/Manuscripts/oliver.html; A. A. Taylor, "The Contest for Priority in Reconstruction," *JNH* 11 (July 1926): 459–77.

44. For a history of the commission, see Judith Ann Giesberg, *Civil War Sisterhood: The U.S. Sanitary Commission and Women's Politics in Transition* (Boston: Northeastern University Press, 2000).

45. CC Minutes, Oct. 24, 1864, 542–43; Paul A. Cimbala and Randall M. Miller, *The Northern Home Front During the Civil War* (New York: Praeger, 2017), 73, 75–76; "the display . . . America": *BDA*, Dec. 7, 1863; *BET*, Dec. 7, 1863; *BDA*, Nov. 11, 1864; ibid., Nov. 15, 1864; *BH*, Dec. 9, 1864; "Letter from Boston," *Sacramento Daily Union*, Dec. 15, 1864.

46. "Hundreds . . . raising": *Liberator*, May 20, 1864; "She," qu. in Kantrowitz, *More than Freedom*, 292.

47. "Boys . . . orphans": *Liberator*, Oct. 14, 1864; ibid., Nov. 18, 1864; *BT*, Oct. 13, 1864; *BET*, Oct. 14, 1864.

48. "1st List of Colored Voters After Emancipation, Boston, 1864," Box 87-1, Folder 34, Ruffin Family Papers, Moorland-Spingarn Research Center Library, Howard University, Washington, DC.

Chapter 11: "False and Exaggerated Ideas of Freedom"

1. "The appeal": *BDA*, Jan. 9, 1865; ibid., Jan. 11, 1865; *BET*, Jan. 2, 1865; John P. Dyer, "Northern Relief for Savannah During Sherman's Occupation," *JSH* 19 (Nov. 1953): 457–72; George Winston Smith, "Cotton from Savannah in 1865," *JSH* 21 (Nov. 1955): 495–512; "Account of the Supplies Sent to Savannah: With the Last Appeal of Edward Everett in Faneuil Hall; the Letter to the Mayor of Savannah . . ." (Boston: John Wilson and Son, 1865).

2. "Welcome . . . cities": *BDA*, Jan. 9, 1865; *BET*, Jan. 9, 1865.

3. Richard D. Arnold, *Letters of Richard D. Arnold, M.D., 1808–1876*, ed. Richard H. Shryock, Papers of the Trinity College Historical Society, Double Series, 18–19 (Durham, NC: Seeman Press, 1929), 168; Paul M. Pressly, "The Northern Roots of Savannah's Antebellum Elite, 1780s–1850s," *GHQ* 87 (Summer 2003): 157–99.

4. H. O. Briggs and Henry D. Hyde to Arnold, Boston, March 8, 1865, Richard D. Arnold Papers, Southern Historical Collection, Manuscripts Department, Wilson Library, University of North Carolina at Chapel Hill; "Unless": "Account of the Supplies," 34; "crush[ed] . . . labor": ibid., 25; "never": ibid., 25.

5. William Schouler, *A History of Massachusetts in the Civil War* (Boston: E. P. Dutton, 1868), 585–86.

6. "The American . . . laborers": *Freedmen's Record / Freedmen's Journal*, April 1, 1865.

7. David A. Zonderman, *Uneasy Allies: Working for Labor Reform in Nineteenth-Century Boston* (Amherst: University of Massachusetts Press, 2011), 82–88.

8. "On the": *BDA*, March 11, 1865; "That": Ira Steward, "The Eight Hour Movement: A Reduction of Hours Is an Increase in Wages" (Boston: 221 Washington Street, 1865), 9–10.

9. "Soldiers": *American Missionary*, May 1869.

10. *BET*, Feb. 10, 1865.

11. "Create[d] . . . clothing": Noah Andre Trudeau, ed., *Voices of the 55th: Letters from the 55th Massachusetts Volunteers, 1861–1865* (Dayton, OH: Morningside House, 1996), 180; "Imagine": *New York Tribune* article widely syndicated, including *BET*, March 2, 1865; *Liberator*, March 10, 1865.

12. Selden Pension.

13. "Full": Burt G. Wilder, *Practicing Medicine in a Black Regiment: The Civil War Diary of Burt G. Wilder, 55th Massachusetts*, ed. Richard M. Reid (Amherst: University of Massachusetts Press, 2010), 21; "black . . . blood": ibid., 240.

14. "God bless": Steven M. LaBarre, *The Fifth Massachusetts Colored Cavalry in the Civil War* (Jefferson, NC: McFarland, 2016), 30; "that . . . Army": ibid., 131–32.

15. Eric Foner, *The Fiery Trial: Abraham Lincoln and American Slavery* (New York: W. W. Norton, 2011), 255–56.

16. *BH*, April 20, 1865.

17. "A day": *BDA*, May 30, 1865; *BH*, June 1, 1865.

18. "Growth . . . wretchedness": *NYT*, July 11, 1865, 4.

19. "The Chivalry": Trudeau, ed., *Voices*, 183; "duties . . . freedmen": ibid., 182.

20. *Liberator*, April 22, 1864; Trudeau, ed., *Voices*, 81–82; "already . . . stage": Steven Hahn, Steven F. Miller, Susan E. O'Donovan, John C. Rodrigue, and Leslie Rowland, eds., *Freedom: A Documentary History of Emancipation, 1861–1867*, Series 3, vol. 1, *Land and Labor, 1865* (Chapel Hill: University of North Carolina Press, 2009), 215–22; Wilder, *Practicing*, 124; "of both": ibid., 246.

21. Hahn et al., *Land and Labor, 1865*, 215–22.

22. Ibid.

23. Selden Pension.

24. "Was in": Selden Widow's app. #332819; cert. #279689, Records of the Department of Veterans Affairs, RG 15, NARA.

25. Franklin A. Dorman, *Twenty Families of Color in Massachusetts, 1741–1998* (Boston: New England Historic Genealogic Society, 1998), 342.

26. Selden Pension.

27. "Slavery": qu. in Sydney Nathans, *To Free a Family: The Journey of Mary Walker* (Cambridge, MA: Harvard University Press, 2012), 222, 215–24; Selden Pension.

28. Aiken Pension; Thomas Cannon Pension File, app. #78579; cert. #62799, Records of the Department of Veterans Affairs, RG 15, NARA; Cannon Widow's File, app. #1139727; Contesting Widow's app. #1192282, ibid.; Stephen Kantrowitz, *More than Freedom: Fighting for Black Citizenship in a White Republic* (New York: Penguin, 2013), 324–26.

29. Thomas H. O'Connor, *Civil War Boston: Home Front and Battlefield* (Boston: Northeastern University Press, 1997), 232–47; Christian G. Samito, *Becoming American Under Fire: Irish Americans, African Americans, and the Politics of Citizenship During the Civil War* (Ithaca, NY: Cornell University Press, 2009).

30. *NYT*, June 12, 1865, 5; "Thirtieth Annual Report of the Boston Society for the Prevention of Pauperism, October, 1865" (Boston: John Wilson and Son, 1865), 5, 12; Brian Matthew Jordan, *Marching Home: Union Veterans and Their Unending Civil War* (New York: W. W. Norton, 2014).

31. "The farm": "Thirtieth Annual Report," 17.

32. Charles Barnard Fox, *Record of the Service of the 55th Regiment of Massachusetts Volunteer Infantry* (Cambridge, MA: John Wilson and Son, 1868), 130–32; Burt Green Wilder, *The Fifty-Fifth Regiment of Massachusetts, Volunteer Infantry, Colored, June 1863–September 1865* (Brookline, MA: Riverdale Press, 1919); Steven J. Ramold, William B. Gould IV, and Helen Hannon, "African Americans in the Navy During the Civil War," *JAAH* 89 (Autumn 2004): 359.

33. Kantrowitz, *More than Freedom*, 298–99.

34. "Although . . . few": Lewis Hayden, "Caste Among Masons: Address Before the Prince Hall Grand Lodge of Free and Accepted Masons of the State of Massachusetts . . . Dec. 27, 1865" (Boston: Edward S. Coombs and Company, 1866), 6; "of one": ibid., 11; "Color": ibid., 49.

35. *BDA*, Nov. 22, 1862; "conscience": *Congregationalist*, March 13, 1863; ibid., Sept. 11, 1863; ibid., March 24, 1865; *BR*, Aug. 21, 1863; *BT*, Jan. 4, 1866.

36. C. L. Woodworth, "The Full Enfranchisement of the Negro" [reprinted from the *Congregational Review*, April 1867] (Boston: 1867), 3–5.

Chapter 12: Their Suffering Housekeepers

1. "List of Freedmen Sent North from Petersburg, Virginia: List of Colored Persons Sent North" and "Registers of Freedmen Sent to New England States, 1866–7," Roll 130, Records of the Virginia Office of the United States Bureau of Refugees, Freedmen, and Abandoned Lands, Assistant Subassistant Commissioner, Record Group 105, National Archives and Records Administration (hereinafter VA FB, with category and date of material); "List of Freedmen Sent North," Subassistant Commissioner, Roll 130, VA FB. For Virginia records online, see "Virginia, Freedmen's Bureau Field Office Records, 1865–1872," database with images, FamilySearch, http://FamilySearch.org, January 26, 2022, citing NARA microfilm publication M1913, National Archives and Records Administration, College Park,

Maryland, n.d., www.familysearch.org/search/collection/1596147. Records of the Assistant Commissioner for the District of Columbia, United States Bureau of Refugees, Freedmen, and Abandoned Lands, 1865–1869, Record Group 105, National Archives and Records Administration, are available online via the Smithsonian National Museum of African American History and Culture, https://sova.si.edu/details/NMAAHC.FB.M1055 (hereinafter DC FB).

2. "Not . . . coffee": Lucy Chase to Anna C. Lowell, Richmond, June 1868, in "Northern Visions of Race, Region, and Reform," AAS, www.americanantiquarian.org/Freedmen/Manuscripts/Chase/06-00-1868.html; Robert F. Engs, *Freedom's First Generation: Black Hampton, Virginia, 1861–1890* (New York: Fordham University Press, 2004), 85–97.

3. A. A. Taylor, *The Negro in the Reconstruction of Virginia* (Washington, DC: Association for the Study of Negro Life and History, 1926), 85–104; "very large": Thomas M. Curtis, President of Overseers of the Poor, Aug. 20, 1867, Letters Received, vol. 1, Fortress Monroe Subassistant Commissioner, Roll 121, VA FB; "the cold": C. H. Howard to Miss Lowell, Washington, DC, Dec. 14, 1866, vol. 7, 305–6, Letters Sent, Series 449, DC Assistant Commissioner, FB [FSSP A-9819].

4. "To use . . . success": S. C. Armstrong to Lieutenant M. S. Reed, July 6, 1866, Letters Received, Series 4136, Fort Monroe Virginia Assistant Subassistant Commissioner, RG 105, Records of the FB, NARA [FSSP A-7873]; Robert Francis Engs, *Educating the Disfranchised and the Disinherited: Samuel Chapman Armstrong and Hampton Institute, 1839–1893* (Knoxville: University of Tennessee Press, 1999), 66–72.

5. "We . . . one": Piper and Haskins to General Armstrong, Aug. 3, 1867, Fortress Monroe, Letters Received, Subassistant Commissioner, March 1867–May 1868, Roll 129, VA FB; *Springfield (MA) Republican*, Jan. 18, 1867; Records Relating to Transportation of Freedmen and Bureau Personnel, vol. 2, April 1866–Nov. 1868, DC FB; Robert Harrison, "Welfare and Employment Policies of the Freedmen's Bureau in the District of Columbia," *JSH* 72 (Feb. 2006): 75–110.

6. "Beastly . . . villainous": E. P. Williams to General, Elizabeth, NJ, July 3, 1867, Letters Received, Fort Monroe Subassistant Commissioner, vol. 1, Jan.–June 1866, March–Sept. 1867, Roll 121, VA FB.

7. "Exposing . . . escape": C. H. Armstrong to O. Brown, Fortress Monroe, May 3, 1867, Fortress Monroe Subassistant Commissioner, Unregistered Letters Received, Aug. 1865–June 1867, Roll 122, VA FB.

8. "Leave . . . away": Alfred J.S. Hartwell, Boston, Aug. 19, 1867, Registered Letters Received, vol. 1, Fortress Monroe Subassistant Commissioner, Roll 121, VA FB; Major Clark to General C. H. Howard, Boston, July 25,

1867, Letters Received, April 1866–Aug. 1868, Records of the Field Offices for the District of Columbia, DC FB.

9. The following account is based on correspondence in DC FB, Letters Received, Feb.–April 1867.

10. "Mrs.": *BT*, April 3, 1868.

11. Eliza Casson to C. H. Howard, Boston, April 15, 1867, Letters Received, Register 2, March–July 1867, DC FB.

12. "To appreciate . . . Bureau": Ralph Haskins to C. H. Howard, Boston, April 28, 1867, Letters Received, Register 2, March–July 1867, DC FB.

13. "Peremptorily . . . long": C. C. Jewett to C. H. Howard, Boston, April 15, 1867, Letters Received, Register 2, March–July, 1867, DC FB; "take": Ralph Haskins to C. H. Howard, Boston, April 28, 1867, Letters Received, Register 2, March–July 1867, DC FB; *BET*, May 23, 1866; Records Relating to Transportation of Freedmen and Bureau Personnel, vol. 2, April 1866–Nov. 1868, DC FB.

14. "Rowdies . . . them": Mrs. H. L. Smith to O. O. Howard, Boston, April 28, 1867, Letters Received, Register 2 (March–July 1867), DC FB.

15. "Like": William T. Northrup to C. H. Howard, Providence, RI, April 15, 1867, Letters Received, Register 2, March–July 1867, DC FB: "for which": *BT*, Feb. 16, 1867.

16. *BET*, Feb. 12, 1866; *BT*, Jan. 1, 1867; "relieving": see letters of May 26, June 2, and July 3, 1866, in Subassistant Commissioner, 5th District, 2 (177), Press Copies of Letters Sent, Fortress Monroe, March–July, 1866, Roll 116, VA FB; "young . . . color": *BT*, June 26, 1866.

17. "Intercepting . . . money": Anna Lowell to Captain Clark, Cambridgeport, Dec. 8, 1866, Letters Received, Register 2, Oct. 1866–March 1867, DC FB; Carol Faulkner, "'A New Field of Labor': Antislavery Women, Freedmen's Aid, and Political Power," in *The Great Task Remaining Before Us: Reconstruction as America's Continuing Civil War*, ed. Paul A. Cimbala and Randall M. Miller (New York: Fordham University Press, 2020), 88–100.

18. "Searching for Anna Lowell: The Mystery Behind a Civil War Nurse's Photo Album," National Museum of American History, July 13, 2011, https://americanhistory.si.edu/blog/2011/07/searching-for-anna-lowell-the-mystery-behind-a-civil-war-nurses-photo-album.html.

19. "World . . . neglected": Anna C. Lowell, *Thoughts on the Education of Girls* (Boston: Ticknor, Reed, and Fields, 1853), 4.

20. Anna Lowell to Charles Sumner, Armory Square Hospital, 1863, MS AM1, Box 16, 3918-4257, Charles Sumner Correspondence, Houghton

Library, Harvard University; Jane E. Schultz, *Women at the Front: Hospital Workers in Civil War America* (Chapel Hill: University of North Carolina Press, 2004).

21. "Of obliging": *BET*, Dec. 21, 1866; "the general": Lara Vapnek, "Staking Claims to Independence: Jennie Collins, Aurora Phelps, and the Boston Working Women's League, 1865–1877," in *No Permanent Waves: Recasting Histories of U.S. Feminism*, ed. Nancy Hewitt (New Brunswick, NJ: Rutgers University Press, 2010), 309; Carol S. Lasser, *Mistress, Maid, and Market: The Transformation of Domestic Service in New England* (Cambridge, MA: Harvard University Press, 1981); Danielle Phillips, "Cleaning Race: Irish Immigrant and Southern Black Domestic Workers in the Northeast United States, 1865–1930," in *U.S. Women's History: Untangling the Threads of Sisterhood*, ed. Leslie Brown, Jacqueline Castledine, and Anne Valk (New Brunswick, NJ: Rutgers University Press, 2017), 13–31.

22. "Not only": Jennie Collins, *Nature's Aristocracy; or, Battles and Wounds in Time of Peace: A Plea for the Oppressed* (Boston: Lee and Shepard, 1871), 115, 110; Vapnek, "Staking Claims," 305–28.

23. "Took": Louisa M. Alcott, *Work: A Story of Experience* (Boston: Roberts Brothers, 1873), 25; "I like": ibid., 216–17; "willing": ibid., 148–49.

24. "This undertaking": "Reports of the Soldiers' Memorial Society Presented at Its Third Annual Meeting, June 11, 1867" (Boston: Soldiers' Memorial Society, 1867), 12; "Our female": "Thirty-First Annual Report of the Industrial Aid Society for the Prevention of Pauperism" (Boston: John Wilson and Son, 1866), 15.

25. "While there": "Reports of the Soldiers' Memorial Society," 12; "If the": "Report of the Howard Industrial School for the Relief and Instruction of Colored Women and Children, Cambridge, Mass." (Boston: John M. Whittemore and Company, 1867), 8–9; "tyrannized": qu. in A. A. Taylor, *The Negro in the Reconstruction of Virginia* (Washington, DC: Association for the Study of Negro Life and History, 1926), 89.

26. "Our [Boston's]": *BDA*, March 28, 1867; ibid., 12; "greatest . . . Christian women": *BR*, May 6, 1869.

27. "*Are*": *BDA*, Jan. 5, 1867; "valuable": "Report of the Howard Industrial School," 6.

28. "Free . . . women": Alexandria (superintendent), Press Copies of Letters Sent, vol. 1, March–Nov. 1867, Roll 40, VA FB; Alexandria (superintendent), Roll 55, Miscellaneous Records, 1865–1868, VA FB; "some of": Anna Lowell to General C. H. Howard, Feb. 27, #1053 1867, Letters Received, Series 449, DC FB [FSSP A-9819)]; Anna Lowell, "Report of the Howard Industrial School," Aug. 4, 1867, Monthly Narrative Reports of Industrial

Schools Sponsored by the Bureau, Series 464, DC FB [FSSP A-9910] (hereinafter Lowell, "Report of the Howard Industrial School"); Faulkner, "'A New Field of Labor,'" 95–96.

29. "Well": *Christian Register*, Feb. 1, 1868; "He wore": *BH*, May 22, 1868; ibid., May 25, 1868.

30. Anna Lowell to Major Clark, Cambridgeport, Dec. 15, 1867, Unregistered Letters Received, March 26, 1866–Aug. 26, 1868, DC FB.

31. "Unsafe": Lucretia Cullins to Anna Lowell, Boston, Dec. 4, 1867, Unregistered Letters Received, March 26, 1866–Aug. 26, 1868, DC FB; "as they are": William Cheeseman, Cambridgeport, Dec. 3, 1867, ibid.; "he began": Anna Lowell to Major Clark, Cambridgeport, Dec. 15, 1867, ibid.

32. "List of Freedmen Sent North."

33. Anna Lowell to C. H. Howard, Cambridgeport, Sept. 1, 1867, Series 4, Letters Received, DC FB.

34. *BH*, Nov. 30, 1867; "capable . . . kindness": *BDA*, Jan. 5, 1867; Lowell, "Report of the Howard Industrial School."

35. "Private": *BDA*, Dec. 15, 1868; *BJ*, March 26, 1867; *BT*, April 19, 1867; "he. . . . bill": *BP*, April 24, 1867.

36. *BH*, April 24, 1867; *CW*, Oct. 17, 1867; "the children": *CR*, Jan. 25, 1868; "depot": Lowell, "Report of the Howard Industrial School"; "temporary": *BDA*, March 28, 1867; "a safe . . . person": *CR*, Feb. 1, 1868; Lowell, "Report of the Howard Industrial School," 4.

37. Sarah J. Shoenfeld, "Applications and Admissions to the Home for Aged Colored Women in Boston, 1860–1887," pt. 2, *NEHGR* 155 (Oct. 2001): 400–401.

38. Ibid.; Lowell, "Report of the Howard Industrial School."

39. "Of turning . . . girls": A. E. Buttrick to C. H. Howard, Cambridge, Sept. 29, 1868, Series 4, Register 5, Letters Received, DC FB.

40. Aaron West, "U.S., Colored Troops Military Service Records, 1863–1865," Images NHRH 1462–1465, Compiled Military Service Records of Volunteer Union Soldiers, www.ancestry.com/imageviewer/collections/1107/images/m1817_14-1477?usePUB=true&_phsrc=FHS2103&_phstart=successSource&usePUBJs=true&pId=4794.

41. General Samuel C. Armstrong to Aaron West, July 1, 1867, Roll 117, Press Copies of Letters Sent, vol. 3, July 1866–July 1867, Fortress Monroe Subassistant Commissioner, VA FB; also Roll 116, Miscellaneous Records, Fortress Monroe; "c/o": Letter to West: Fortress Monroe, Press Copies of Letters Sent, vol. 3, July 1866–July 1867, Roll 117, Fortress Monroe Subassistant Commissioner, VA FB.

42. Superintendent, Fredericksburg (superintendent), Oct. 20, 1867, Unregistered Letters Received, Nov. 1865–Dec. 1868, Roll 85, VA FB.

43. *BE*, Aug. 25, 1865. The article gives Anthony a pseudonym, "Benjamin Franklin Mullens."

44. Palo Alto Pierce, *A History of the Town of Freetown, Massachusetts* (Whitefish, MT: Kessinger, 2010 [1902]); Helen Gurney Thomas, compiler, "Vital Records of the Town of Freetown, Massachusetts, 1686 Through 1890," FamilySearch.org, www.familysearch.org/search/catalog/287522?availability=Family%20History%20Library; "Ebenezer Weaver Peirce: An Appreciation," pt. 2, Poor Irish and Pilgrims, August 13, 2017, https://pooririshandpilgrims.com/2017/08/13/ebenezer-w-peirce-an-appreciation-part-2.

45. *The Boston Directory, No. LXVI, for the Year Commencing July 1, 1870* (Boston: Sampson, Davenport, and Company, 1870), 12; "U.S. . . . notice": ibid., 1032; ibid., 673, 302.

Chapter 13: Boston Diaspora II

1. "You": *Savannah Republican*, Dec. 13, 1865; "insurrectionary . . . owners": *BET*, Dec. 21, 1865.

2. "Colored": *BDA*, Sept. 1, 1866; "to resist": *BJ*, Jan. 26, 1867; "all bad": *BH*, April 2, 1868; "Great . . . pettifogger": *Savannah Daily News and Herald*, July 6, 1867; "at an early": *BT*, May 29, 1868. For Bradley's Savannah career, see Jacqueline Jones, *Saving Savannah: The City and the Civil War* (New York: Knopf, 2008).

3. "Boston": *Springfield Republican*, Oct. 12, 1867, and *BDA*, Jan. 4, 1868; Jones, *Saving Savannah*, 273.

4. Jean Fagan Yellin, ed., *The Harriet Jacobs Family Papers*, vol. 2 (Chapel Hill: University of North Carolina Press, 2008), 561; "Slavery": qu. in Jean Fagan Yellin, *Harriet Jacobs: A Life* (New York: Basic Books, 2004), 178.

5. "No": qu. in Yellin, *Harriet Jacobs*, 189.

6. Ibid., 194–99; Ezra Greenspan, *William Wells Brown: An African American Life* (New York: W. W. Norton, 2014), 423; "crowds": Yellin, *Jacobs Family Papers*, 2:655; "The chains": ibid., 668.

7. "We are": Hezekiah Brown to George Whipple, Savannah, Aug. 10, 1869; Brown to E. P. Smith, Savannah, April 30, 1869, American Missionary Association Archives, Amistad Research Center, Tulane University, New Orleans; Lynn Mumma and Marlena Jareaux, "The Tale of Two Hezekiahs," Howard County Lynching Truth & Reconciliation, n.d., www.hocoltr.org/lynchings/rev-hezekiah-brown.

8. Jones, *Saving Savannah*, 226, 298. On the northern teachers who served in Georgia, see Jacqueline Jones, *Soldiers of Light and Love: Northern Teachers and Georgia Blacks, 1865–1873* (Chapel Hill: University of North Carolina Press, 1980).

9. Yellin, *Harriet Jacobs*, 190–209; Yellin, *Jacobs Family Papers*, 2:625–71; "country": Susie King Taylor, *Reminiscences of My Life in Camp: An African American Woman's Civil War Memoir*, ed. Catherine Clinton (Athens: University of Georgia Press, 2006 [1902]), 54. For biographical information about Brown, see his deposits in the US Freedman's Bank in Savannah, Jan. 25, 1868, through April 30, 1874, US Freedman's Bank Records, 1865–1874, *Registers of Signatures of Depositors in Branches of the Freedman's Savings and Trust Co., 1865–1874*, Records of the Office of the Comptroller of the Currency, RG 101, NARA, Washington, DC.

10. Rebecca Lee Crumpler, *A Book of Medical Discourses: In Two Parts* (Boston: Cashman, Keating, 1883), 2, 52–60; "a regular . . . party": *Richmond New Nation*, Jan. 17, 1867; Sara Diaz, "Rebecca Davis Lee Crumpler," March 12, 2007, BlackPast, www.blackpast.org/african-american-history/crumpler-rebecca-davis-lee-1831-1895.

11. "I had . . . last": Randolph, *From Slave Cabin*, 162–63.

12. "His preaching": ibid., 162; "condition": *BET*, Aug. 31, 1865; "shamefully": ibid., 164; *Liberator*, Oct. 20, 1865; ibid., Nov. 10, 1865.

13. "Instigator . . . pass": *New York Tribune*, June 16, 1865; Elsa Barkley Brown, "Negotiating and Transforming the Public Sphere: African American Political Life in the Transition from Slavery to Freedom," *Political Culture* 7 (Fall 1994): 113–15.

14. "Of the voluminous": Monroe A. Majors, *Noted Negro Women: Their Triumphs and Activities* (Chicago: Donohue and Henneberry, 1893), 113; *Liberator*, Feb. 12, 1864; ibid., April 8, 1864; *BT*, April 27, 1865; "a remarkable": William Wells Brown, *The Rising Son, Or, the Antecedents and Advancement of the Colored Race* (Boston: A. G. Brown and Company, 1874), 496–97.

15. "Abusive . . . fist": *New-York Semi-Weekly Tribune*, June 20, 1865.

16. "Made": *Richmond Times*, June 5, 1866; "a man . . . man": *Richmond Examiner*, qu. in *BT*, Dec. 5, 1867; *Richmond Dispatch*, May 4, 1868; A. A. Taylor, *The Negro in the Reconstruction of Virginia* (Washington, DC: Association for the Study of Negro Life and History, 1926), 214, 216, 220, 261, 277; *BET*, Jan. 5, 1866.

17. "The untold": *Richmond Dispatch*, Nov. 12, 1867; ibid., May 5, 1868; ibid., May 4, 1867.

18. "If . . . politics": qu. in Peter J. Rachleff, *Black Labor in Richmond, Virginia, 1865–1890* (Urbana: University of Illinois Press, 1989), 56; Jane Dailey, *Before Jim Crow: The Politics of Race in Postemancipation Virginia* (Chapel Hill: University of North Carolina, 2000), 54.

19. "The war": "Thirty-First Annual Report of the Industrial Aid Society for the Prevention of Pauperism" (Boston: John Wilson and Son, 1866), 8; "a priceless": Harriet Jacobs, "Savannah Freedmen's Orphan Asylum," *Anti-Slavery Reporter*, March 2, 1868.

20. "Influence": *BET*, Oct. 27, 1866; ibid., Feb. 26, 1866; Bassard, "Introduction"; Randolph, *Sketches*, 26.

21. "Brought": Randolph, *From Slave Cabin*, 180.

22. Bassard, "Introduction"; Randolph, *Sketches*, 26.

23. "Sympathetic": Randolph, *From Slave Cabin*, 192.

24. Bassard, "Introduction"; Randolph, *Sketches*, 28; "Much": *BH*, April 10, 1873; *CE*, Nov. 16, 1871; *BT*, Oct. 31, 1871.

25. "Rough . . . benches": Randolph, *From Slave Cabin*, 190; "In the South": ibid., 197; "They were": ibid., 168.

26. *CR*, June 1, 1867.

27. Ibid.

Chapter 14: White Men Demanding Their Own Rights, but Refusing to Concede to Others Theirs

1. George A. Levesque, "Boston's Black Brahmin: Dr. John S. Rock," *CWH* 26 (Dec. 1980): 324–46.

2. "Or some": Massachusetts Wills and Probate Records, 1635–1991, Probate Records, vol. 164–65, 1865–1867, Case #47491, 1 (Nov. 20, 1866).

3. Milton M. James, "The Institute for Colored Youth," *NHB* 21 (Jan. 1958): 83–85.

4. "Never": *BT*, Aug. 2, 1865.

5. Millington W. Bergeson-Lockwood, *Race over Party: Black Politics and Partisanship in Late Nineteenth-Century Boston* (Chapel Hill: University of North Carolina Press, 2018).

6. Nicole Etcheson, "'When Women Do Military Duty': The Civil War's Impact on Woman Suffrage," *JAH* 107 (Dec. 2020): 609–35; Thavolia Glymph, *The Women's Fight: The Civil War's Battles for Home, Freedom, and Nation* (Chapel Hill: University of North Carolina Press, 2020), 127–95.

7. Stephen Kantrowitz, *More than Freedom: Fighting for Black Citizenship in a White Republic* (New York: Penguin, 2013), 312–33, 367.

8. "Fourth . . . feelings": *BDA*, April 15, 1870; *BJ*, April 15, 1870; Christopher James Bonner, *Remaking the Republic: Black Politics and the Creation of American Citizenship* (Philadelphia: University of Pennsylvania Press, 2020), 167.

9. Bergeson-Lockwood, *Race over Party*, 30.

10. Ibid., 6; *New England Postal Record*, Jan. 8, 1870.

11. Bergeson-Lockwood, *Race over Party*, 7; Stanley J. Robboy and Anita W. Robboy, "Lewis Hayden: From Fugitive Slave to Statesman," *NEQ* 46 (Dec. 1973): 609.

12. "The Republican": Morris, qu. in Kantrowitz, *More than Freedom*, 373; Bergeson-Lockwood, *Race over Party*, 46–49; "Letter . . . party": *BET*, Aug. 16, 1872.

13. "A Democratic . . . faith": *BT*, July 25, 1872.

14. Elizabeth Hafkin Pleck, *Black Migration and Poverty in Boston, 1865–1900* (New York: Academic Press, 1979), 7; Bergeson-Lockwood, *Race over Party*, 7–8, 20; *BDA*, April 15, 1870; "signifying . . . whom": *BT*, Sept. 4, 1874.

15. "Since": W. H. Washington of Massachusetts and A. S. Powell of Georgia (Committee of National Colored Convention assembled Oct. 2, 1868), to the Senate and House of Representatives, n. d., 41-A-H21.2, Committee on Public Lands, Petitions and Memorials, 41st Cong., RG 46, Records of the United States Senate, NARA [FSSP E-100]: *BH*, Oct. 3, 1868; "Petition from the National Convention of Colored People . . . Jan. 27, 1870," FSSP; "the heel": "Proceedings of the National Convention of the Colored Men of America held in Washington, D.C." (Washington, DC: 1869), 14.

16. "Believed": John W. Blassingame and John R. McKivigan, eds., *The Frederick Douglass Papers*, Series 1, *Speeches, Debates, and Interviews*, vol. 4, 1864–1880 (New Haven, CT: Yale University Press, 1991), 258; "Right": ibid., 250; "Here": ibid., 245 ("Our Composite Nationality: An Address Delivered in Boston, Massachusetts, on 7 December, 1869").

17. Pleck, *Black Migration*; Henry F. Bedford, ed., *Their Lives and Numbers: The Condition of Working People in Massachusetts, 1870–1900* (Ithaca, NY: Cornell University Press, 1995), 108.

18. "In accordance . . . required": CC Minutes, Feb. 25, 1867, 94; Millington Bergeson-Lockwood, "'We Do Not Care Particularly About the Skating Rinks': African American Challenges to Racial Discrimination in Places of Public Amusement in Nineteenth-Century Boston, Massachusetts," *JCWE* 5 (June 2015): 254–88.

19. Pleck, *Black Migration*, 145, 159.

20. The mayors of Boston in these years were Frederic W. Lincoln (R), Jan. 5, 1863–Jan. 7, 1867; Otis Norcross (R), Jan. 7, 1867–Jan. 6, 1868; Nathaniel B. Shurtleff (D), Jan. 6, 1868–Jan. 2, 1871; William Gaston (D), Jan. 2, 1871–Jan. 6, 1873.

21. "Unfit": CC Minutes, May 8, 1871, 137; ibid., March 8, 1869, 56; ibid., Jan. 16, 1871, 12; Nancy S. Seasholes, ed., *The Atlas of Boston History* (Chicago: University of Chicago Press, 2019), 70–71.

22. "More": CC Minutes, Jan. 2, 1869, 90; ibid., March 1, 1869, 49; ibid., Oct. 28, 1875, 590–93.

23. "If . . . hearted": ibid., Aug. 3, 1874, 477; *BT*, Feb. 20, 1868.

24. "While": CC Minutes, Nov. 30, 1868, 63; "they": ibid., Sept. 15, 1870, 227; ibid., March 23, 1874, 150. Minutes cited for dates after Nov. 1868 are in printed, not handwritten, form.

25. Ibid., Oct. 22, 1868, 42; ibid., Sept. 26, 1872, 272; David Ward, *Poverty, Ethnicity, and the American City, 1840–1925: Changing Conceptions of the Slum and the Ghetto* (Cambridge: Cambridge University Press, 1989), 38.

26. "The capitalists . . . of": CC Minutes, Nov. 2, 1871, 324.

27. "Said . . . pay": CC Minutes, March 11, 1872, 72.

28. Kantrowitz, *More than Freedom*, 338–40; *BET*, April 6, 1868; *BT*, April 7, 1868; George V. Tomashevich, ed., "Some of the Incidents in the Life of Mark DeMortie," *A-ANYLH* 3 (Jan. 1979): 61–72; *BG*, July 27, 1872; ibid., July 22, 1872.

29. "The rights": Philip S. Foner, "A Labor Voice for Black Equality: The *Boston Daily Evening Voice*, 1864–1867," *Science and Society* 38 (Fall 1974): 306.

30. "If the": ibid., 320 (Jan. 13, 1866, issue); "Now" and "he": *Liberator*, Oct. 20, 1865 (reprinted *Boston Daily Voice* article).

31. Foner, "Labor Voice for Black Equality," 320.

32. David A. Zonderman, *Uneasy Allies: Working for Labor Reform in Nineteenth-Century Boston* (Amherst: University of Massachusetts Press, 2011), 99–106.

33. New England Women's Club, "Report of the Committee on Needlewomen" (Boston: John Wilson and Son, 1869), 3, 10–11, 15, 22; "aristocrats": Wendy Gamber, *The Female Economy: The Millinery and Dressmaking Trades, 1860–1930* (Urbana: University of Illinois Press, 1997), 83; Lara Vapnek, "Staking Claims to Independence: Jennie Collins, Aurora Phelps, and the Boston Working Women's League, 1865–1877," in *No Permanent Waves: Recasting Histories of U.S. Feminism*, ed. Nancy A. Hewitt (New Brunswick, NJ: Rutgers University Press, 2010), 320; *BT*, March 5, 1873.

34. Jean Fagan Yellin, *Harriet Jacobs: A Life* (New York: Basic Books, 2004), 202–7; "Mr. Remond": Jean Fagan Yellin, ed., *The Harriet Jacobs Family Papers*, vol. 2 (Chapel Hill: University of North Carolina Press, 2008), 706.

35. Vapnek, "Staking Claims," 311; *Revolution*, Feb. 3, 1870.

36. Yellin, *Jacobs Family Papers*, 2:736; "Something": "Report of the Committee of Needlewomen," 18; "Why Women Avoid Housework," *WJ* 3 (1872): 74.

37. "A poor": Yellin, *Jacobs Family Papers*, 2:727.

38. Dale Baum, "Woman Suffrage and the 'Chinese Question': The Limits of Radical Republicanism in Massachusetts, 1865–1876," *NEQ* 56 (March 1983): 60–77.

39. "SAVE": "Proceedings of the Colored National Labor Convention held in Washington, D.C." (Washington, DC: New Era, 1870), 2; Jacqueline

Jones, *Saving Savannah: The City and the Civil War* (New York: Knopf, 2008), 372; "Proceedings of the Colored National Labor Convention," 18; "we are": ibid., 19; "the white": ibid., 20; "A labor . . . value": ibid., 20; Luke C. D. Stein and Constantine Yannelis, "Financial Inclusion, Human Capital, and Wealth Accumulation: Evidence from the Freedman's Savings Bank," *Review of Financial Studies*, 33 (Nov. 2020):5333-5377.

40. *Revolution*, May 10, 1868; Vapnek, "Staking Claims," 305–6; "we . . . servitude": qu. in Zonderman, *Uneasy Allies*, 120; "How many": "Report of the Committee of Needlewomen," 19.

Chapter 15: Persistent Industry

1. "Machines": *NEF*, April 8, 1871.

2. Selden Pension.

3. Thomas Cannon Pension File, app. #78579; cert. #62799, Records of the Department of Veterans Affairs, RG 15, NARA; Cannon Widow's app. #1139727; Contesting Widow's app. #1192282, ibid.

4. "I worked": Aiken Pension; Franklin A. Dorman, *Twenty Families of Color in Massachusetts, 1741–1998* (Boston: New England Historic Genealogic Society, 1998), 295.

5. *BET*, June 26, 1866; *BH*, Oct. 24, 1866; ibid., Nov. 13, 1866; ibid., Nov. 16, 1866; ibid., March 1, 1869; ibid., Jan. 31, 1871; ibid., Feb. 17, 1871; *Official Records of the Union and Confederate Navies in the War of the Rebellion*, Series 1, vol. 2, *The Operation of the Cruisers (January 1, 1863–March 31, 1864)* (Washington, DC: Government Printing Office, 1895), 215, 461–62, 609; Michael J. Bennett, "'Frictions': Shipboard Relations Between White and Contraband Sailors During the American Civil War," *CWH* 47 (June 2001): 143–45; Grover and Da Silva, BAANHS, 54.

6. "Grand": *BDA*, April 15, 1870.

7. Peter J. Rachleff, "'Members in Good Standing': Richmond's Community of Former Slaves, 1865–1873," *Virginia Cavalcade* (Spring 1990): 157; Theda Skocpol and Jennifer Lynn Oser, "Organization Despite Adversity: The Origins and Development of African American Fraternal Associations," *SSH* 28 (Fall 2004): 367–437; John Daniels, *In Freedom's Birthplace: A Study of the Boston Negroes* (Boston: Houghton Mifflin, 1914), 208–9; *BG*, June 28, 1887; "Non-Masonic Fraternal Orders," BlackOrgs, http://blackorgs.net/non-masonic-fraternal-orders.

8. Henry F. Bedford, ed., *Their Lives and Numbers: The Condition of Working People in Massachusetts, 1870–1900* (Ithaca, NY: Cornell University Press, 1995), 174; "without": *Revolution*, Feb. 3, 1870; New England Women's Club, "Report of the Committee on Needlewomen" (Boston: John Wilson and Son, 1869), 6–7; *BT*, Sept. 1, 1870; *BT*, Aug. 9, 1869.

9. *BDA*, July 22, 1872; "most . . . city": Edward H. Savage, *Police Records and Recollections, Or, Boston by Daylight and Gaslight: For Two Hundred and Forty Years* (Boston: John P. Dale, 1873), 196; "daubed . . . front": *BH*, Aug. 30, 1872; "A West": *BH*, Nov. 21, 1871; *BH*, April 26, 1872.

10. Howard N. Rabinowitz, *Race Relations in the Urban South, 1865–1890* (New York: Oxford University Press, 1978), 249–50; "an unfortunate . . . equality": *Richmond Daily Dispatch*, Sept. 22, 1870.

11. "Mr . . . again": "Fifty-First Annual Report of the City Missionary Society, Boston, for the Year 1867" (Boston: T. R. Marvin and Son, 1868), 15; "a young": "Fifty-Second Annual Report of the City Missionary Society, Boston, for the Year 1868" (Boston: T. R. Marvin and Son, 1869), 27.

12. "Thirty-First Annual Report of the Industrial Aid Society for the Prevention of Pauperism" (Boston: John Wilson and Son, 1866), 6; "asking . . . it": ibid., 9; "continuous . . . work": ibid., 12.

13. "Worn": Sarah J. Shoenfeld, "Applications and Admissions to the Home for Aged Colored Women in Boston, 1860–1887," pt. 2, *NEHGR* 155 (Oct. 2001): 406; "reduced": ibid., 402; "Unreasonably": ibid., 403; "sick": ibid., 397.

14. "His wife": ibid., 407; "but many": ibid., 402.

15. "With great": ibid., 401.

16. "The inmates": "Eighteenth Annual Report of the Directors of the Home for Aged Colored Women for the Year 1877" (Boston: W. L. Deland and Sons, 1878), 6.

17. "Won . . . her": Shoenfeld, "Applications and Admissions," pt. 2, 412–13.

18. Kazuteru Omori, "Race Neutral Individualism and Resurgence of the Color Line: Massachusetts Civil Rights Legislation, 1855–1895," *JAEH* 22 (2002): 58; *NYT*, Dec. 14, 1872; *BJ*, May 19, 1870; "The . . . parlor": *Chicago Tribune*, May 22, 1870; *Chicago Evening Post*, June 3, 1869; John H. Hewitt, "A Black New York Newspaperman's Impressions of Boston, 1883," *MR* 32 (Autumn 1991): 445–63.

19. "Great . . . brightness": Jean Fagan Yellin, ed., *The Harriet Jacobs Family Papers*, vol. 2 (Chapel Hill: University of North Carolina Press, 2008), 744; "dream . . . humble": qu. in Jean Fagan Yellin, *Harriet Jacobs: A Life* (New York: Basic Books, 2004).

20. Yellin, *Harriet Jacobs*, 226; "What": qu. in Sydney Nathans, *To Free a Family: The Journey of Mary Walker* (Cambridge, MA: Harvard University Press, 2012), 247.

21. "All hair": *BT*, Sept. 26, 1870; *Norfolk Virginian*, May 14, 1874.

22. Ezra Greenspan, *William Wells Brown: An African American Life* (New York: W. W. Norton, 2014), 417–97; "a failure": Charles L. Remond to "Chair and Members of the Board of Directors for the Freedmen's Lincoln Monument Association," Albany, July 22, 1867, Box 87-1, Series A, Folder 8, Other Correspondence, Ruffin Papers.

23. "Liquour": *BT*, Aug. 16, 1865; "with a magnificent": ibid., May 26, 1869.

24. "None": *BH*, Oct. 24, 1872; "largely": *BT*, Oct. 28, 1872.

25. *BDA*, Oct. 25, 1875; *BT*, Aug. 1, 1867; *BJ*, Oct. 19, 1869; "vindicate": ibid., Oct. 13, 1870.

26. George A. Levesque, "Inherent Reformers-Inherited Orthodoxy: Black Baptists in Boston, 1800–1873," *JNH* 60 (Oct. 1975): 491–525; Grover and Da Silva, BAANHS, 25–26; *BH*, Aug. 3, 1868; "donation": *BJ*, May 16, 1871; *BT*, Feb. 7, 1873.

27. "Having": *CW*, Sept. 19, 1872.

28. *CE*, March 14, 1867; "the income": *BT*, Oct. 15, 1874.

29. "Unwearied": "Fourteenth Annual Report of the Directors of the Home for Aged Colored Women, for the Year 1873" (Boston: W. L. Deland, 1874), 5–6.

30. *BR*, Jan. 7, 1869; "the daughter": *Buffalo Commercial Advertiser*, Nov. 25, 1869; "a remarkable": *NYT*, Aug. 17, 1876.

31. "Nevertheless": *BG*, July 21, 1873; "a little": *CW*, April 17, 1873.

32. "Showing": *BP*, Oct. 26, 1874; Randolph, *From Slave Cabin*, 194–98.

Chapter 16: "Safely Doing Injustice" to Black Bostonians

1. The following discussion is based on Franklin A. Dorman, *Twenty Families of Color in Massachusetts, 1741–1998* (Boston: New England Historic Genealogic Society, 1998), which features the intertwined Carter Selden (425–36), Stephen Maddox (339–54), Thomas Revaleon (365–402), and Aaron Joseph (193–214) families; city directories; federal manuscript census; and pensions for Thomas Selden and his widow Elizabeth Selden.

2. *BG*, June 28, 1867.

3. Ibid., May 7, 1894.

4. Ronald S. Coddington, *Faces of the Civil War Navies: An Album of Union and Confederate Sailors* (Baltimore: Johns Hopkins University Press, 2016), 46–49.

5. America Barnett Pension File, app. #991315, cert. #758,074; Widow app. # 95152, Records of the Department of Veterans Affairs, RG 15, NARA.

6. Selden Pension; Donald R. Shaffer, "'I Do Not Suppose that Uncle Sam Looks at the Skin': African Americans and the Civil War Pension System, 1865–1914," *CWH* 46 (June 2000): 132–47.

7. Sarah Falck, "Coming Home: Civil War Pensions," *Battlefield Dispatch* 3 (Summer 2019); Theda Skocpol, *Protecting Soldiers and Mothers: The Political Origins of Social Policy in the United States*, rev. ed. (Cambridge, MA: Belknap Press of Harvard University Press, 1995), 102–52.

8. Larry M. Logue and Peter Blanck, "'Benefit of the Doubt': African-American Civil War Veterans and Pensions," *JIH* 38 (Winter 2008): 377–99.

9. Shaffer, "'I Do Not Suppose,'" 132–37.

10. Elias Hall Pension File, app.# 864444, cert. #634126; widow app.# 1087755, Records of the Department of Veterans Affairs, RG 15, NARA.

11. "Outside . . . work": Sarah J. Shoenfeld, "Applications and Admissions to the Home for Aged Colored Women in Boston, 1860–1887," pt. 2, *NEHGR* 155 (Oct. 2001): 73.

12. Sarah Deutsch, *Women and the City: Gender, Space, and Power in Boston, 1870–1940* (New York: Oxford University Press, 2000), 37, 42.

13. "Became": Sarah J. Shoenfeld, "Applications and Admissions to the Home for Aged Colored Women in Boston, 1860–1887," pt. 1, *NEHGR* 155 (July 2001): 70; "[going] out": ibid., 77.

14. "Bad": ibid., 78, 255; Dorman, *Twenty Families*, 2–4; Stephen Kantrowitz, *More than Freedom: Fighting for Black Citizenship in a White Republic* (New York: Penguin, 2013), 415–16. On the Smith case, see the following documents related to committee action: Commonwealth of Massachusetts, House, *Resolve in Relation to the Claim of Joshua B. Smith*, H.R. 316, 100th Gen. Ct., 1st sess., introduced in House March 31, 1879, https://archives.lib.state.ma.us/handle/2452/621544; Commonwealth of Massachusetts, Senate, *Resolve in Relation to the Claim of Joshua B. Smith*, S. 141, 100th Gen. Ct., 1st sess., introduced in Senate March 4, 1879, https://archives.lib.state.ma.us/handle/2452/681608; Commonwealth of Massachusetts, House, *An Act Relative to the Claim of Joshua B. Smith Against the Commonwealth*, H.R. 347, 100th Gen. Ct., 1st sess. (1879), https://archives.lib.state.ma.us/handle/2452/621575; Commonwealth of Massachusetts, House, *Resolve in Favor of Emeline I. Smith*, H.R. 366, 101st Gen. Ct., 1st sess., introduced in House April 19, 1880, https://archives.lib.state.ma.us/handle/2452/687715.

15. "She . . . it": Sarah J. Shoenfeld, "Applications and Admissions to the Home for Aged Colored Women in Boston, 1860–1887," pt. 3, *NEHGR* 156 (Jan. 2002): 81, 81n234; "in the same": ibid., 81n236; "without": *BJ*, June 7, 1897.

16. Charles H. Parkhurst, "The Race Problem in Boston, Massachusetts," *Liberia Bulletin*, no. 9 (Nov. 1896): 7; "The Race": *Manning (South Carolina) Times*, Aug. 26, 1896; "a tendency": Oliver S. Baketel, ed., *The Methodist Yearbook, 1922* (New York: Methodist Book Concern, 1922), 10.

17. "Boston": Parkhurst, "Race Problem," 7.

18. "With . . . artisan": ibid., 11.

19. "The smoothest . . . want": ibid., 11–12.

20. "We . . . Boston": ibid., 13–15; Millington W. Bergeson-Lockwood, "'We Do Not Particularly Care About the Skating Rinks': African American Challenges to Racial Discrimination in Places of Public Amusement in Nineteenth-Century Boston, Massachusetts," *JCWE* 5 (June 2015): 276–77.

21. John Daniels, *In Freedom's Birthplace: A Study of Boston Negroes* (Boston: Houghton Mifflin, 1914), 7, 12, 149, 131–32, 181.

22. Kirk Savage, *Standing Soldiers, Kneeling Slaves: Race, War, and Monument in Nineteenth-Century America* (Princeton, NJ: Princeton University Press, 2018), 162–208; David W. Blight, *Race and Reunion: The Civil War in American Memory* (Cambridge, MA: Belknap Press of Harvard University Press, 2001); Donald R. Shaffer, "Northern Black Civil War Veterans and the GAR," in *Union Soldiers and the Northern Home Front: Wartime Experiences, Postwar Adjustments*, ed. Paul A. Cimbala and Randall M. Miller (New York: Fordham University Press, 2002), 442–62.

23. *BDA*, Aug. 2, 1887; "disaster . . . people": *BH*, Aug. 3, 1887.

24. "They": Millington W. Bergeson-Lockwood, *Race over Party: Black Politics and Partisanship in Late Nineteenth-Century Boston* (Chapel Hill: University of North Carolina Press, 2018), 121; ibid., 89; Adelaide M. Cromwell, *The Other Brahmins: Boston's Black Upper Class, 1750–1950* (Fayetteville: University of Arkansas Press, 1994), 48.

25. Bergeson-Lockwood, *Race over Party*, 111–29; *BDA*, Aug. 12, 1896; *BJ*, Aug. 13, 1896; Kantrowitz, *More than Freedom*, 364–93; Thomas H. O'Connor, *The Boston Irish: A Political History* (Boston: Back Bay Books, 1995).

26. "What . . . her": *BG*, May 27, 1893.

27. Jama Lazerow, "'The Workingman's Hour': The 1886 Labor Uprising in Boston," *LH* 21 (1980): 200–220; Henry F. Bedford, ed., *Their Lives and Numbers: The Condition of Working People in Massachusetts, 1870–1900* (Ithaca, NY: Cornell University Press, 1995), 2, 106–8.

28. Mark Robert Schneider, *Boston Confronts Jim Crow, 1890–1920* (Boston: Northeastern University Press, 1997), 181, 193.

29. Robert A. Woods, "Livelihood," in *Americans in Process: A Settlement Study*, ed. Robert A. Woods (Boston: Houghton Mifflin, 1903), 121; *BG*, May 27, 1893; "inefficient": Charles Phillips Huse, *The Financial History of Boston, from May 1, 1822, to January 31, 1909* (Cambridge: Harvard University Press, 1916), 235; "spoilsmen . . . constituents": ibid., 231.

30. Elizabeth Hafkin Pleck, *Black Migration and Poverty in Boston, 1865–1900* (New York: Academic Press, 1979), 130; "opportunity": Huse, *Financial History*, 236; "an excessive": ibid., 264; "the size": ibid., 264; "to put": ibid., 289.

31. Daniels, *In Freedom's Birthplace*, x.

32. "Industrial . . . traits": ibid., 313–15.

33. "Servility": ibid., 316; "excessive": ibid., 137; "characterized": ibid., 315; "aversion . . . untrustworthiness": ibid., 317; "a lack": ibid., 318.

34. "As a . . . incompetent": ibid., 320; "industrial": 313, 315; Pleck, *Black Migration*, 158, 140.

35. "There is": Daniels, *In Freedom's Birthplace*, 363. On a new era of Black activism in the early twentieth century, see Kerri K. Greenidge, *Black Radical: The Life and Times of William Monroe Trotter* (New York: Liveright, 2019).

36. "Uncle . . . sobs": Randolph, *From Slave Cabin*, 174; "one" ibid., 202.

37. Bassard, "Introduction"; Randolph, *From Slave Cabin*, 6.

38. "The Rev.": *Providence Evening Bulletin*, June 8, 1882; "Proceedings of the One Hundredth Anniversary of the Granting of Warrant 459 to African Lodge at Boston, Massachusetts" [Sept. 29, 1884] (Boston: Franklin Press: Rand, Avery and Company, 1885).

39. Peter Randolph to Samuel J. May Jr., Boston, Sept. 15, 1887, May Correspondence, BPL.

40. Peter Randolph to Samuel May Jr., Boston, Sept. 21, 1887, ibid.

41. "Their . . . hope": *BDA*, June 1, 1892; "represent[ing]": *BH*, Dec. 1, 1893; *BJ*, April 26, 1893; ibid., Oct. 9, 1896; ibid., Jan. 17, 1891; *BH*, April 4, 1891; ibid., April 11, 1897; Randolph, *From Slave Cabin*, 198.

42. "The record": *BJ*, Aug. 9, 1897.

43. Randolph, *From Slave Cabin*, 212.

Index

COURTNEY MEADOR

Jacqueline Jones holds the Ellen C. Temple Chair in Women's History and the Mastin Gentry White Professorship in Southern History at the University of Texas at Austin Emerita. Winner of the Bancroft Prize for *Labor of Love, Labor of Sorrow*, Jones lives in Concord, Massachusetts.